P 5-1A	Net Income, $2,600
P 5-2A	No key figure
P 5-3A	(1) Net Loss, $2,520
P 5-4A	(2) Net Income, $7,440
P 5-1B	Net Income, $2,100
P 5-2B	No key figure
P 5-3B	(1) Net Loss, $6,540
P 5-4B	(2) Net Income, $5,290

P 6-1A	Net Income, $8,600
P 6-2A	Owner, Capital, $27,700
P 6-3A	(2) Owner, Capital, $66,290
P 6-4A	(2) Owner Capital, $97,666
P 6-1B	Net Income, $5,500
P 6-2B	Owner, Capital, $41,800
P 6-3B	(2) Owner, Capital, $18,080
P 6-4B	(2) Owner Capital, $84,600

Accounting Cycle Review Problem   Net Income, $935

P 7-1A	No key figure
P 7-2A	(3) Accounts Receivable, $7,500
P 7-3A	(4) Accounts Receivable, $43,900
P 7-4A	(4) Accounts Receivable, $61,900
P 7-1B	No key figure
P 7-2B	(3) Accounts Receivable, $7,300
P 7-3B	(4) Accounts Receivable, $41,400
P 7-4B	(4) Accounts Receivable, $61,300

P 8-1A	No key figure
P 8-2A	(3) Accounts Payable, $11,100
P 8-3A	(4) Accounts Payable, $13,100
P 8-4A	(4) Accounts Payable, $71,400
P 8-1B	No key figure
P 8-2B	(3) Accounts Payable, $9,500
P 8-3B	(4) Accounts Payable, $31,190
P 8-4B	(4) Accounts Payable, $76,840

(continued on back endpapers)

INTRODUCTION TO
COLLEGE
ACCOUNTING

Chapters
1–14

SECOND EDITION

GREGORY W. BISCHOFF

Houston Community College

THE DRYDEN PRESS
A HARCOURT BRACE JOVANOVICH PUBLISHER

Fort Worth   Philadelphia   San Diego   New York   Orlando   Austin   San Antonio

Toronto   Montreal   London   Sydney   Tokyo

Acquisitions Editor: Bill Teague
Associate Editor: Paul Raymond
Software Editor: Ken Fine
Manuscript Editor: Christopher B. Nelson
Production Editor: David Hill
Designers: Linda Harper and Linda Cable
Art Editor: Karen B. DeLeo
Production Managers: Diane Southworth, Marilyn Williams, and David Hough

ISBN: 0-15-541695-2

Library of Congress Catalog Card Number: 91-70282

Printed in the United States of America

Photo Credits:
Chapter 1: Stock Boston/© Charles Gupton; Chapter 2: © Jim Pickerell/Tony Stone Worldwide; Chapter 3: © Howard Grev/Tony Stone Worldwide; Chapter 4: © J. Turner, FPG International Corp.; Chapter 5: © H. Mark Weidman; Chapter 6: © Peat, Marwick and Mitchell; Chapter 7: © Steve Leonard/Tony Stone Worldwide; Chapter 8: © Todd Powell/ProFiles West; Chapter 9: © H. Mark Weidman; Chapter 10: © Peat, Marwick and Mitchell; Chapter 11: © Charles Gupton/Tony Stone Worldwide; Chapter 12: Reprinted with permission of Compaq Computer Corporation. All Rights Reserved; Chapter 13: Zephyr Pictures/© Melanie Carr; Chapter 14: Photo courtesy of Hewlett-Packard Company.

PREFACE

The Second Edition of *Introduction to College Accounting: Chapters 1–14* provides a straightforward, practical introduction to accounting. The prose is clear and direct, and the examples used throughout the book are both realistic and engaging. This textbook is designed to be "user friendly" to help students:

- Complete an academic degree.
- Complete a technical program.
- Acquire accounting skills for employment or advancement.
- Maintain accounting records if self-employed.
- Prepare for more advanced accounting courses.

Integrated Learning System

The author has prepared or assisted in the preparation of all instructor and student aids. These items are integrated or cross-referenced with the Learning Objectives in each chapter of the textbook. The Second Edition of *Introduction to College Accounting: Chapters 1–14* has as comprehensive a learning system as is available today.

Flexible Organization

Introduction to College Accounting: Chapters 1–14 is suitable for a semester, quarter, or clock-hour program. Since the chapters build in sequence from 1 to 14, coverage can be ended at any point. Chapters 1–6 cover the accounting cycle for a sole proprietorship service-type company. Chapters 7–14 examine a sole proprietorship merchandising-type company. In addition, the following seven appendixes enhance or supplement the text material:

- Appendix A: "Computers and Accounting" (after Chapter 6) examines how business firms use computers to process accounting data.
- Appendix B: "The Electronic Spreadsheet" (after Chapter 12) continues the discussion of computers and accounting by focusing on the electronic spreadsheet.
- Appendix C: "The Combined Journal" (after Chapter 14) explains how to design and use a combined journal.
- Appendix D: "The Voucher System" (after Chapter 14) illustrates how many firms use a voucher system to strengthen their control over cash.
- Appendix E: "Calculating Interest and Discounting a Note" (after Chapter 14) examines simple interest, maturity value, discount and proceeds.
- Appendix F: "Methods for Valuing Inventory and Cost of Goods Sold" (after Chapter 14) explains four valuation methods that include specific identification, average cost, FIFO, and LIFO.
- Appendix G: "Methods for Computing Depreciation" (after Chapter 14) continues the discussion of depreciation introduced in Chapter 4.

Chapter Organization

Each chapter includes these pedagogical aids:

■ Learning Objectives, now with page numbers, are listed at the beginning of each chapter and are noted in the margin where they are discussed in the text; all chapter exercises and problems are also keyed to the objectives. These Learning Objectives serve as an outline for all instructor and student aids, thus contributing to the integrated learning system.

■ Exhibits detail the procedures used in producing important items and forms in accounting practices.

■ Realistic accounting forms are used throughout.

■ The Chapter Review, now with page numbers, summarizes each Learning Objective.

■ The Glossary in each chapter defines the important words and concepts discussed.

■ Five multiple-choice Self-Test Questions for Review give students immediate feedback on their grasp of each chapter. Answers are at the end of each chapter.

■ A Practical Review Problem (with answer) helps students understand significant concepts or processes.

■ Discussion Questions focusing on major concepts and terms can be used to stimulate classroom discussion.

■ Exercises and Problem Sets (A and the alternate B) provide students with a variety of homework assignments. All exercises and problems are new or revised. Each exercise and problem is identified by Learning Objective number(s), and each has a short description. Many chapters have Comprehensive Chapter Review Problems covering all the chapter's Learning Objectives.

■ Problems that can be worked using *The Computer Connection*, Second Edition, are indicated by a computer logo as are problems using Lotus 1-2-3 templates.

Special Review Problems

This textbook includes the following special review problems:

■ The Accounting Cycle Review Problem (after Chapter 6) is a mini-practice set that tests a student's knowledge of the accounting cycle for a service-type company.

■ The Special Journals Review Problem (after Chapter 9), new to this edition, tests a student's knowledge of special journals.

■ The Payroll Review Problem (after Chapter 14), also new to this edition, tests a student's knowledge of payroll.

Special Features

In addition to the special review problems, the book offers a number of special features:

■ A Checklist of Key Figures on the endpapers enables students to check their work.

- Two complete **Reviews of Accounts** follow Chapter 6 and Chapter 10.
- **Diagrams of the Accounting Cycle for a Service Firm** follow Chapter 6.
- **Diagrams of the Accounting Cycle for a Merchandising Firm** follow Chapter 12.

For the Instructor

- **INSTRUCTOR'S MANUAL** This manual has been completely revised and is organized in four sections for each chapter in the textbook: (a) Suggested Teaching or Lecture Outline; (b) Homework Analysis; (c) Demonstration Problem (also available as teaching transparency); and (d) 2 Ten-Minute Quizzes with answers. The manual also includes a list of the Teaching Transparencies and the solutions to Practice Sets A, B, and E.
- **SOLUTIONS MANUAL** This manual contains answers to all discussion questions, exercises, problems, and special review problems in the textbook.
- **SOLUTIONS TRANSPARENCIES** Transparencies of exercises, problems, and special review problems are available to departments adopting the textbook. New to this edition, the Solutions Transparencies have been expanded and are grouped by chapter with a divider.
- **TEACHING TRANSPARENCIES** These one- and two-color teaching transparencies of selected text material and demonstration problems (from the Instructor's Manual) are also available to adopters upon request to the publisher.
- **TEST BOOK** The Test Book has been completely revised with all new questions and exercises by the author. This book offers 22 true/false questions, 22 multiple-choice questions, and 6 exercises for each chapter of the textbook (a total of 50 questions and exercises per chapter). Each question and exercise is organized by learning objective(s) and difficulty level (Easy, Average, or Difficult).
- **COMPUTERIZED TEST BOOK** A computerized version of the Test Book is available to adopters upon request to the publisher. This computerized version of the Test Book enables instructors to vary the order of test items, select items randomly, and modify the tests as needed.
- **ACHIEVEMENT TESTS** This book consists of four series (A, B, C, and D) that are perforated for easy removal and duplication. Series B is an alternate to Series A (in which tests cover two chapters each) and Series D is an alternate to Series C (in which tests cover four to five chapters each).
- **INSTRUCTIONAL VIDEOS** A series of instructional videos is available to adopters upon request to the publisher.
- **LOTUS 1-2-3® TEMPLATES** New to this edition, a user's manual to accompany electronic spreadsheet templates is located at the end of the student Study Guide. Brief instructions for using spreadsheet templates are located at the end of this book. A templates diskette is issued free of charge to adopters; a solutions version of the diskette is available to instructors.

- **MICROSTUDY+**® This computerized study guide is available to adopters upon request to the publisher. Instructions on how to use MicroStudy+ are included in the back of this book.
- **SOLUTIONS MANUAL TO MONOPOLY PRACTICE SET** This manual shows how to grade students' work in the Monopoly Practice Set.

For the Student

- **STUDY GUIDE** The Study Guide provides a review of the learning objectives, a detailed review of the significant concepts and processes, 40 true/false questions, 20 completion questions, two exercises, and answers for self-scoring for each chapter in the textbook. New to this edition is a thorough mathematics review and a user's manual to accompany electronic spreadsheet templates. A templates diskette is issued free of charge to adopters; a solutions version of the diskette is available to instructors.
- **WORKING PAPERS** This revised package is provided for all exercises, problem sets (A or B), and special review problems.
- *THE COMPUTER CONNECTION*, **SECOND EDITION** This "live" general ledger software package, prepared by John W. Wanlass (De Anza College) and Gregory W. Bischoff, adapts selected end-of-chapter problems from the textbook and Practice Sets A and B to a real-world computer system. In this major revision, students can use this powerful software without prior computer training. It is available for use with the IBM® PC and PS/2. (A separate Instructor's Manual and disk contains solutions.)
- **PRACTICE SET A, "THE VILLAGE PRINTER"** This new practice set covers a sole proprietorship service-type company and can be introduced at any point after Chapter 6.
- **COMPUTERIZED PRACTICE SET A, "THE VILLAGE PRINTER"** This version of Practice Set A includes special operating instructions and a 5 1/4-inch disk for use with an IBM PC or PC-compatible microcomputer and an IBM-compatible printer. The software, also available in 3 1/2-inch media, may be installed on a hard disk drive for the user's convenience and requires 256K RAM, PC-DOS, or MS-DOS version 2.1 or higher.
- **PRACTICE SET E WITH BUSINESS PAPERS, "WALT'S WINDOW WASHING"** This new practice set, prepared by Thomas Jackson (Cerritos Community College), covers a sole proprietorship service-type company. It covers the basic steps in the accounting cycle (Chapters 1–6) and provides business documents (invoices, checks, receipts, etc.) for students to work with.
- **PRACTICE SET B, "LAKE PLUMBING SUPPLY"** This practice set covers a sole proprietorship merchandising-type firm and is designed to be used after Chapter 12.
- **MONOPOLY PRACTICE SET** Prepared by W. Robert Knechel (University of Florida), this practice set lets students learn accounting while playing the popular board game.

Acknowledgments

As in the previous edition, many fine educators and professionals have made significant contributions to this book. Once again, I would sincerely like to thank my many students for their participation in the classroom testing of this new edition. My colleagues at Houston Community College have been most helpful, and their valuable input is greatly appreciated.

I am deeply indebted to the many perceptive reviewers and questionnaire respondents throughout the country who helped in the development of the Second Edition:

Terry G. Aime, *Delgado Community College;* **James R. Bryce,** *Del Mar College;* **Donald R. Davis,** *Modesto Junior College;* **Tom Dent,** *St. Louis Community College—Florissant Valley;* **Doris Edwards,** *National Education Centers;* **Jacolin P. Eichelberger,** *Hillsborough Community College;* **Tom Jackson,** *Cerritos Community College;* **Edward A. Klump,** *Knapp Business College;* **Robert J. McCarter,** *Macomb Community College; and* **La Verne Vertrees,** *St. Louis Community College—Meramec.*

Other instructors graciously participated in telephone interviews and surveys, and I am grateful for their comments:

Harold Anderson, *Arizona Western College;* **John Carstens,** *Knapp Business College;* **David Champagne,** *Antelope Valley College;* **John Chestnutt,** *Alan Hancock College;* **Judith Chowen,** *Cerritos Community College;* **Frank Cress,** *Butte College;* **John di Stasio,** *Pikes Peak Community College;* **Karen Durling,** *Beal Business College;* **William M. Evans,** *Cerritos Community College;* **Don Freeman,** *Pikes Peak Community College;* **David Godley,** *Arizona Western College;* **Janet Grant,** *Skyline College;* **Jan Hanson,** *Rancho Santiago College;* **Cynthia Harrison,** *Knapp Business College;* **Jack Heinsius,** *Modesto Junior College;* **Polly Hewes,** *Beal Business College;* **Ed Hinrichs,** *St. Louis Community College—Florissant Valley;* **Gerald Holtke,** *Crafton Hills College;* **Marlene Krause,** *South Puget Sound Community College;* **Carol McCain,** *King's River Community College;* **Pam Melville,** *King's River Community College;* **Albert Motley,** *Arizona Western College;* **Linda Murdock,** *North Harris County Junior College;* **Jose' Ortega,** *Modesto Junior College;* **Kay Pallaviciani,** *North Harris County Junior College;* **Dave Risch,** *St. Louis Community College—Florissant Valley;* **Bonnie Robinson,** *Arizona Western College;* **Francis Sakiey,** *Mercer County Community College;* **Howard Sherman,** *Rancho Santiago College;* **Elaine Simpson,** *St. Louis Community College—Florissant Valley;* **Sharon V. Smith,** *Texas Southmost College;* **Allen Stehle,** *Beal Business College; and* **Penny Westerfield,** *North Harris County Junior College.*

I would also like to acknowledge the fine work and assistance of Thomas Hoar, a CPA in private practice and accounting instructor. His technical and mathematical review of the entire text and Solutions Manual ensured that the material is up-to-date and accurate.

Finally, I would like to thank the members of the book team at Harcourt Brace Jovanovich—Ken Rethmeier, executive editor; Bill Teague, acquisitions editor; Paul Raymond, associate editor; Ken Fine, software editor; Christopher B. Nelson, manuscript editor; David Hill, production editor; Linda Harper and Linda Cable, designers; Karen B. DeLeo, art editor; and Diane Southworth, Marilyn Williams, and David Hough, production managers.

Gregory W. Bischoff

THOMAS HOAR

CERTIFIED PUBLIC ACCOUNTANT
915 OXBOROUGH DRIVE
KATY, TEXAS 77450

Harcourt Brace Jovanovich, Inc.
College Department
1250 Sixth Avenue
San Diego, California 92101-4311

I have examined the text and Solutions Manual of the second
edition of Introduction to College Accounting, by Gregory W.
Bischoff. My examination was directed at this work's technical
and mathematical accuracy as well as its consistency and
appropriateness of references to authoritative literature. I
included such procedures and tests as I considered necessary in
the circumstances.

In my opinion, the material in this book is technically and
mathematically accurate, internally consistent, and references
to professional and other pronouncements are accurate and
appropriate within the framework of introductory accounting
concepts and techniques.

May 1, 1991

CONTENTS

4 CALCULATING ADJUSTMENTS AND COMPLETING THE WORKSHEET 85

5 PREPARING FINANCIAL STATEMENTS; JOURNALIZING AND POSTING ADJUSTMENTS 121

6 CLOSING THE ACCOUNTING RECORDS 155

APPENDIX A: Computers and Accounting 200

7 THE SALES JOURNAL AND ACCOUNTS RECEIVABLE SUBSIDIARY LEDGER 205

8 THE PURCHASES JOURNAL AND ACCOUNTS PAYABLE SUBSIDIARY LEDGER 239

9 THE CASH RECEIPTS AND CASH PAYMENTS JOURNALS 273

10 CASH, PETTY CASH, AND THE CHANGE FUND 311

11 ADJUSTMENTS AND WORKSHEETS FOR A MERCHANDISING FIRM 353

12 FINANCIAL STATEMENTS AND CLOSING ENTRIES FOR A MERCHANDISING FIRM 393

APPENDIX B: The Electronic Spreadsheet 439

13 PAYROLL: EMPLOYEE EARNINGS AND DEDUCTIONS 443

14 PAYROLL: EMPLOYER'S TAXES AND REPORTS 469

1

Accounting and Business Transactions

Money speaks sense in a language all nations understand.

APHRA BEHN

LEARNING OBJECTIVES

After reading this chapter, discussing the questions, and working the exercises and problems, you will be able to do the following:

1. Define accounting and the role of accountants (pp. 4–5).

2. Identify the forms of business organizations (p. 6).

3. Identify the types of business operations (pp. 6–7).

4. Understand the fundamental accounting equation (pp. 7–9).

5. Record business transactions (pp. 9–13).

6. Prepare a balance sheet (pp. 14–15).

Although there are many reasons to study accounting, you will find that the following are among the most important:

1. Accounting is a basic component of business management.
2. Accounting is one means by which managers stay informed of the progress of their companies.
3. Accounting provides a method of recording, evaluating, and interpreting business activities.
4. Government agencies, banks, owners, and investors all require accounting information.

Clearly, accounting is a critical part of any business. In fact, it would be almost impossible for a business to function successfully without accounting information. Consequently, accounting is also an important and dynamic academic discipline. With this in mind, let's begin.

DEFINITION OF ACCOUNTING

Objective 1
Define accounting and the role of accountants.

Accounting is the "language" of business. It translates and communicates the movement of resources throughout economic systems. Accounting also measures the performance and status of business and economic entities—large, multinational corporations; state, local, and federal governments; schools and universities; and individual small businesses. An economic entity is able to analyze, classify, record, report, and interpret each of its transactions using acceptable accounting practices and procedures. These procedures are called **generally accepted accounting principles** (GAAP), which represent an informed agreement on the theory and practice of accounting.

Accountants are the professionals in the business or economic entity who analyze, classify, record, and interpret transactions. Most accountants have at least a four-year college degree.

The American Institute of Certified Public Accountants prepares a comprehensive two and one-half day examination in accounting practice, accounting theory, auditing, and business law. An accountant must pass all four parts of the examination to become a certified public accountant

EXHIBIT 1-1
Career Path(s) of Accounting Students

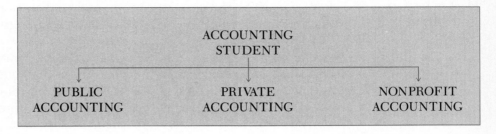

(CPA). Thus, the public is assured of the competency and knowledge of the CPA and can rely upon the CPA's presentations and recommendations. As with many other professions, such as law and medicine, accountants also specialize in various fields and industries. The three broad, professional fields are public accounting, private accounting, and nonprofit accounting. (See Exhibit 1-1 for career paths a student may pursue.)

Public Accounting

Many CPAs work in public accounting, specializing in such areas as tax preparation and consultation, auditing, and management information advisory services. The public relies heavily on auditing, which is an independent analysis of the financial records of an organization. For this reason, the CPA or public accountant must make sure that she has no conflict of interest with a client organization so the public can rely on her review of financial records.

Private Accounting

This field includes such diverse industries as oil and gas businesses, steel manufacturing plants, textile businesses, department stores, and so on. Accountants employed in this area prepare financial statements, internal management reports, tax calculations, and internal audits.

Nonprofit Accounting

Accountants who work in universities, city governments, public hospitals, and other governmental or public organizations help to insure that these nonprofit organizations use their resources wisely and efficiently. Because the nonprofit sector of our economy has grown considerably in recent years, there will be an increasing demand for accountants to perform internal audits, process forms and paperwork, and insure compliance with laws and regulations.

THE FORMS OF BUSINESS ORGANIZATIONS

Objective 2
Identify the forms
of business
organizations.

The three major forms of business organizations in the United States
are **sole proprietorships**, **partnerships**, and **corporations**. All are similar
in that they are started and maintained to make a profit and/or distribute
services to the public. Accountants perceive a business organization as an
economic entity separate from its owners. This separate existence of the
owners from the organization is known as the **entity concept**. For example,
if you owned three businesses, each one would be considered a separate
economic unit, and you would keep separate accounting records for each.
You would also keep your personal, nonbusiness accounting records (for
example, the mortgage papers on your home) separate from each of your
businesses.

Sole Proprietorships

A sole proprietorship is a business formed and owned by one individual. This form of organization represents the largest number of businesses
in the United States. Since there is only one owner, sole proprietorships are
generally the smallest in size and the easiest to create.

Partnerships

A partnership is a business formed and owned by two or more individuals. The partners enter into a contractual agreement, whether written or
oral, whereby they share duties and responsibilities, profits and losses.

Corporations

A corporation, unlike a sole proprietorship or partnership, is a business organization that is legally separate from its owners. Remember that
accountants treat all business organizations as separate from their owners,
but *legally* only the corporation is separate. Corporations represent the
smallest number of business organizations, but they are also the largest.
Ownership is divided into shares of stock.

THE TYPES OF BUSINESS OPERATIONS

Objective 3
Identify the types
of business
operations.

There are three major types of business operations in the United
States: **service**, **merchandising**, and **manufacturing**

Service

Most law firms, accounting firms, consulting firms, and medical practices are service oriented, offering services rather than goods to the public. Chapters 1 through 6 examine the accounting practices of service operations, although much of the same material can be applied to merchandising and manufacturing operations.

Merchandising

Merchandising businesses primarily offer resalable goods (or *merchandise*) for sale to the public. The merchandiser does not produce these goods, but instead usually purchases them from a manufacturer. Grocery stores, department stores, and hardware stores are examples of this type of business operation. Merchandising will be covered after Chapter 6.

Manufacturing

A manufacturing business operation is usually *capital intensive,* meaning the business must purchase expensive machinery and equipment. Working materials are also purchased, in raw or unprocessed form, and are combined with labor to produce a salable product. The manufacturer may either sell directly to the public or to a distributor or merchandising business, who will in turn sell to the public.

ASSETS, LIABILITIES, AND OWNER'S EQUITY

Objective 4
Understand the fundamental accounting equation.

Assets, liabilities, and owner's equity are *broad classes of accounts.* Chapter 2 will introduce you to two other broad classes of accounts — revenues and expenses.

Assets

Assets are anything of value owned by a business. They are usually recorded in the accounting records or books of the acquiring business at *historical cost* (actual cost). Some examples of assets include Cash, Accounts Receivable, Prepaid Expenses (such as Prepaid Insurance and Prepaid Rent), Land, Buildings, Equipment, Furniture, and Supplies.

Liabilities

A **creditor** is one to whom money is owed. **Liabilities** are the creditor's claims against the assets of a business. A common term for liabilities is "debts," the amounts owed by a business. Liabilities are recorded *at the amount to be paid in the future.* Accounts Payable, Wages Payable, Notes Payable, and Bonds Payable are some examples of liabilities.

Owner's Equity

Owner's equity or **Capital** is the owner's claims after the creditor's claims against the assets of a business. This represents the owner's original investment plus any additional investments in the business along with the results of operations. If the owner withdraws any assets from the business, owner's equity (Capital) decreases. Simply defined, owner's equity equals assets minus liabilities.

THE FUNDAMENTAL ACCOUNTING EQUATION

The fundamental accounting equation is stated as follows:

$$\text{Assets} = \text{Liabilities} + \text{Owner's Equity}$$

As with any equation, the left side (assets) must always equal the right side (liabilities plus owner's equity). You'll need this equation to analyze, classify, record, report, and interpret business transactions.

ACCOUNTS   An **account** is a separate record for each asset, liability, and owner's equity. A broad class of accounts would include all the accounts within that particular classification. For example, assets comprise a broad class of accounts, whereas Cash is an *individual asset account*. The broad classes of accounts and individual accounts are illustrated in Exhibit 1-2.

Manipulating the Fundamental Accounting Equation

If you know two parts of the fundamental accounting equation, you can always find the third. We'll look at several examples that follow.

FINDING ASSETS   If liabilities total $10,000 and owner's equity totals $15,000, then total assets can be determined by adding liabilities and owner's equity:

$$\text{Assets} = \text{Liabilities} + \text{Owner's Equity}$$

$?	=	$10,000 +	$15,000
$25,000	=	$10,000 +	$15,000

EXHIBIT 1-2
Broad and Individual Classes of Accounts

	Broad Class of Accounts		
	Assets	**Liabilities**	**Owner's Equity**
Examples of	Cash	Accounts Payable	Kay Loomis, Capital
Individual	Accounts Receivable	Notes Payable	
Accounts	Prepaid Insurance	Bonds Payable	

FINDING LIABILITIES   If assets total $30,500 and owner's equity totals $16,750, then liabilities can be determined as follows:

$$\text{Assets} = \text{Liabilities} + \text{Owner's Equity}$$
$$\$30,500 = \quad \$ \ ? \quad + \quad \$16,750$$

Liabilities are isolated by subtracting owner's equity from each side of the equation:

$$\text{Assets} \ - \ \text{Owner's Equity} = \text{Liabilities}$$
$$\$30,500 - \quad \$16,750 \quad = \$13,750$$

FINDING OWNER'S EQUITY   If assets total $63,190 and liabilities total $27,380, then owner's equity equals:

$$\text{Assets} = \text{Liabilities} + \text{Owner's Equity}$$
$$\$63,190 = \$27,380 + \quad \$ \ ?$$

Owner's equity is isolated by subtracting liabilities from each side of the equation:

$$\text{Assets} \ - \ \text{Liabilities} = \text{Owner's Equity}$$
$$\$63,190 - \quad \$27,380 \quad = \quad \$35,810$$

BUSINESS TRANSACTIONS

Objective 5
Record business
transactions.

An economic event can also be called a *business transaction*. A business transaction occurs when resources move through an organization. These movements can be internal or external in nature. An internal movement is self-contained within the organization, while an external resource movement occurs between two or more separate business organizations. To simplify the terminology, in future discussions an economic event or business transaction will be called a transaction and any type of business organization will be called a firm.

Starting a Sole Proprietorship (Firm)

A firm with a single owner is a sole proprietorship and will commonly have many transactions. Suppose that Kay Loomis is the sole owner of Kay Loomis, CPA, and in starting her firm, she has the following transactions:

a. Investment of cash by owner.

b. Purchase of office equipment for cash.

c. Purchase of office equipment on credit.

d. Purchase of office supplies for cash and on account.

e. Investment of accounting library by owner.

f. Payment of a liability.

Transaction (a).   January 1, 19XX: Investment of cash by owner.

Kay believes that another accounting service is needed in her town. Therefore, she withdraws $10,000 in cash from her personal savings account and deposits it in a bank in the business name Kay Loomis, CPA. (Remember that the entity concept states that the business organization, or firm, must be kept separate from the owners. All accounting records must be maintained separately.)

The fundamental accounting equation looks like this after the investment (for illustration purposes, dollar signs are not presented):

Assets	=	Liabilities +	Owner's Equity
Cash	=		Kay Loomis, Capital
(a) +10,000	=		+10,000

ANALYSIS: The owner invested cash in her newly formed accounting service. Assets increased and owner's equity (Capital) increased. There are no liabilities. Assets = Owner's Equity (10,000 = 10,000).

Transaction (b).   January 3, 19XX: Purchase of office equipment for cash.

Kay purchases a typewriter from Rogers Office Equipment at a total cost of $1,200. She writes a check (which is considered cash) for the purchase.

The fundamental accounting equation now looks like this:

	Assets		=	Liabilities +	Owner's Equity
	Cash +	Office Equip.	=		Kay Loomis, Capital
Prev. Bal.	10,000		=		10,000
(b)	− 1,200 +	1,200	=		
New Bal.	8,800 +	1,200	=		+10,000
		10,000			10,000

ANALYSIS: The firm purchased a typewriter for cash. Assets both increased and decreased. Assets are now 10,000 (8,800 + 1,200). The fundamental accounting equation is still in balance (10,000 = 10,000).

Transaction (c).   January 5, 19XX: Purchase of office equipment on credit.

Kay purchases a computer from Chen Computers at a total cost of $8,000. She decides to buy the computer on account (on credit). The full amount is to be paid within twelve months. A liability account entitled **Accounts Payable** is increased for amounts owed to creditors.

After this transaction the fundamental accounting equation looks like this:

	Assets	=	Liabilities	+	Owner's Equity
	Cash + Office Equip.	=	Accounts Payable	+	Kay Loomis, Capital
Prev. Bal.	8,800 + 1,200	=			10,000
(c)	+ 8,000	=	+8,000		
New Bal.	8,800 + 9,200	=	8,000	+	10,000
	18,000			18,000	

ANALYSIS: The firm purchased a computer on account. Assets increased and liabilities increased. Assets are now 18,000 (8,800 + 9,200). Liabilities and owner's equity are also 18,000 (8,000 + 10,000). The fundamental accounting equation is in balance (18,000 = 18,000).

Transaction (d).   January 8, 19XX: Purchase of office supplies for cash and on account.

Kay purchases $500 of office supplies from Leon's Office Supply. She pays $100 in cash with the remainder on account ($500 − $100 = $400).

The fundamental accounting equation, after this transaction, looks like this:

	Assets			=	Liabilities	+	Owner's Equity
	Cash + Office Equip. + Office Supp.			=	Accounts Payable	+	Kay Loomis, Capital
Prev. Bal.	8,800 +	9,200		=	8,000	+	10,000
(d)	−100	+	500	=	+ 400		
New Bal.	8,700 +	9,200 +	500	=	8,400	+	10,000
	18,400				18,400		

ANALYSIS: The firm purchased office supplies for cash and on account. Assets are both increased and decreased. Liabilities are increased. Assets are now 18,400 (8,700 + 9,200 + 500). Liabilities and owner's equity are 18,400 (8,400 + 10,000). The fundamental accounting equation is in balance (18,400 = 18,400).

Transaction (e).   January 10, 19XX: Investment of accounting library by owner.

Kay invests some personal accounting books worth $75. These books increase the owner's Capital account since the assets of the firm are increased.

The fundamental accounting equation, after this transaction, appears as follows:

	Assets					= Liabilities	+ Owner's Equity
						Accounts	Kay Loomis,
	Cash +	Office Equip. +	Office Supp. +	Library	=	Payable +	Capital
Prev. Bal.	8,700 +	9,200 +	500		=	8,400 +	10,000
(e)				+ 75	=	+	75
New Bal.	8,700 +	9,200 +	500 +	75	=	8,400 +	10,075
		18,475					18,475

ANALYSIS: The owner invested personal assets in the firm. Assets total 18,475 after this transaction. Liabilities and owner's equity also total 18,475. Since these amounts agree (18,475 = 18,475), the fundamental accounting equation is in balance.

Transaction (f).   January 13, 19XX: Payment of a liability.

Kay pays Leon's Office Supply $130 as a partial payment of the $400 owed (see Transaction d).

After this transaction, the fundamental accounting equation appears as follows:

	Assets					= Liabilities	+ Owner's Equity
						Accounts	Kay Loomis,
	Cash +	Office Equip. +	Office Supp. +	Library	=	Payable +	Capital
Prev. Bal.	8,700 +	9,200 +	500 +	75	=	8,400 +	10,075
(f)	−130				=	−130	
New Bal.	8,570 +	9,200 +	500 +	75	=	8,270 +	10,075
		18,345					18,345

ANALYSIS: A partial payment is made on an amount owed. Both assets (Cash) and liabilities (Accounts Payable) are decreased. Assets now total 18,345 (8,570 + 9,200 + 500 + 75). Liabilities and owner's equity are 18,345 (8,270 + 10,075). The fundamental accounting equation is in balance (18,345 = 18,345).

Other Transactions   Any firm will have many more transactions than the ones described above. But there is one common element for all transactions: *the left side of the fundamental accounting equation must always equal the right side.* Assets must always equal liabilities plus owner's equity (Capital).

Summary of Transactions

An accountant is always very careful while recording transactions, but errors do occur. Therefore, the transactions must be summarized and totaled to insure that the total account balances of the left side equal the total account balances of the right side.

Although each transaction is recorded separately, it is interrelated to the other transactions. So far, the firm Kay Loomis, CPA, has used four asset accounts: Cash, Office Equipment, Office Supplies, and Library. One liability account has been used, Accounts Payable, and one owner's equity account, Kay Loomis, Capital. The six previous transactions are summarized as follows:

	Cash	+	Office Equip.	+	Office Supp.	+	Library	=	Accounts Payable	+	Kay Loomis, Capital
					Assets			=	**Liabilities**	+	**Owner's Equity**
(a)	+10,000							=		+	10,000
(b)	−1,200	+	1,200					=			
Bal.	8,800	+	1,200					=			10,000
(c)		+	8,000					=	+8,000		
Bal.	8,800	+	9,200					=	8,000	+	10,000
(d)	−100			+	500			=	+400		
Bal.	8,700	+	9,200	+	500			=	8,400	+	10,000
(e)						+	75	=		+	75
Bal.	8,700	+	9,200	+	500	+	75	=	8,400	+	10,075
(f)	−130							=	−130		
Bal.	8,570	+	9,200	+	500	+	75	=	8,270	+	10,075*

Left Side Equals Right Side

It is imperative that the left side (assets) equals the right side (liabilities plus owner's equity). Therefore, you must add the final balances of all the accounts on the left side and add the final balance of all the accounts on the right side. The right side and the left side must equal.

Left Side		Right Side	
Account	**Final Balance**	**Account**	**Final Balance**
Cash	+8,570	Accounts Payable	+8,270
Office Equipment	+9,200	Kay Loomis, Capital	+10,075
Office Supplies	+500		
Library	+75		
Left Side Totals	18,345	Right Side Totals	18,345

If the account totals are not equal, then the accountant must correct the error(s). Otherwise, the information will be of no use to the firm.

*Remember that Capital is the owner's claims against the assets of the business. At this time, total assets are 18,345 (8,570 + 9,200 + 500 + 75). Creditors have claims of 8,270 with the remaining 10,075 equalling the owner's claim.

THE BALANCE SHEET

Objective 6
Prepare a balance sheet.

The balance sheet is a statement of the financial position of a firm at a point in time (a certain date). The balance sheet is usually prepared at the end of an accounting period—one month, three months, twelve months, and so on. It may, however, be prepared at any time. Most firms use a twelve-month business year, which accountants call a fiscal year. This twelve-month period can start at any time; for example, a firm may start May 1 and end the following year on April 30. Any financial statements prepared for a period of less than one fiscal year are called interim statements.

All asset, liability, and owner's equity accounts that have balances are presented on the balance sheet. The balance sheet, like the fundamental accounting equation, is proof that assets = liabilities + owner's equity (Capital).

Steps in Preparing the Balance Sheet

A balance sheet, in report form, for Kay Loomis, CPA, is prepared in Exhibit 1-3. The point in time (or date) is January 13, 19XX. The following six steps for preparing the balance sheet are keyed ((a), (b), (c), and so on) to Exhibit 1-3:

EXHIBIT 1-3
Preparation of Balance Sheet in Report Form

Kay Loomis, CPA
(a)   Balance Sheet
January 13, 19XX

(b) **Assets**		
Cash	$8 5 7 0 —	
Office Supplies	5 0 0 —	
Office Equipment	9 2 0 0 —	
Library	7 5 —	
Total Assets		$18 3 4 5 —	(c)
(d) **Liabilities**		
Accounts Payable		$ 8 2 7 0 —
(e) **Owner's Equity**		
Kay Loomis, Capital		10 0 7 5 —
Total Liabilities and Owner's Equity		$18 3 4 5 —	(f)

(a) The balance sheet has a three-part heading which is centered and includes, in this order, (1) the name of the firm, (2) the name of the financial statement, and (3) the date for which the financial statement is prepared. Leave one blank line before "Assets."

(b) The most liquid assets (Cash, Receivables, Supplies, and so on) are listed first, followed by the more permanent assets (Equipment, Library, and Building). A dollar sign appears at the beginning of each column. A line is drawn after the column to indicate that there are no more assets. A dash (—) is used in the cents column to indicate that there are no (zero) cents. For example, $8,570 is written as "$8,570 —."

(c) The final total of assets is double underlined. A double underline means "in balance." The single line above the total means that there are no more assets and calculations can be made. In this example the calculation is to sum. A dollar sign appears at the final total. Leave one blank line before "Liabilities."

(d) Liabilities are listed in payment order, with Accounts Payable usually listed first. A dollar sign is given at the beginning of the column. Leave one blank line before "Owner's Equity."

(e) For a sole proprietorship, Owner's Equity is designated by Capital only. A line is drawn after Capital.

(f) Total Liabilities and Owner's Equity are added, and the total is double underlined. This total must equal Total Assets. A dollar sign appears at the final total.

CHAPTER REVIEW

1. **Define accounting and the role of accountants (pp. 4–5).**
   Accounting is the "language" of business. Accountants are the professionals who analyze, classify, record, and interpret transactions.

2. **Identify the forms of business organizations (p. 6).**
   There are three forms of business organizations: sole proprietorships, partnerships, and corporations.

3. **Identify the types of business operations (pp. 6–7).**
   There are three types of business operations: service, merchandising, and manufacturing.

4. **Understand the fundamental accounting equation (pp. 7–9).**
   The fundamental accounting equation is:

$$\text{Assets} = \text{Liabilities} + \text{Owner's Equity}$$

5. **Record business transactions (pp. 9–13).**
   A business transaction occurs when resources move through a business organization. Six transactions were recorded as examples in the chapter.

6. **Prepare a balance sheet (pp. 14–15).**
   A balance sheet is a statement of the financial position of the firm at a given point in time. The six steps for preparing a balance sheet were covered.

GLOSSARY

Account	Individual or single classification within the broad classes of accounts.
Accountant	A professional in an organization who analyzes, classifies, records, and interprets business transactions.
Accounting	The "language" of business. The means of analyzing, classifying, recording, reporting, and interpreting business transactions.
Assets	Anything of value owned by a business.
Auditing	Independent analysis of financial records.
Balance Sheet	Statement of the financial position of a firm at a point in time.
Corporation	Form of business organization that is legally separate from its owner(s). Ownership is divided into shares of stock.
Creditor	One to whom money is owed.
Entity Concept	The owner is perceived as being separate from the business organization.
Firm	Any type of business organization.
Fiscal Year	Twelve-month business period.
Fundamental Accounting Equation	Assets = Liabilities + Owner's Equity
Generally Accepted Accounting Principles	Informed agreement on the theory and practice of accounting. Abbreviated as GAAP.
Interim Statements	Financial statements prepared for a period of less than one fiscal year.
Liabilities	Creditor's claims against the assets of a business.
Owner's Equity	Owner's claims against the assets of the business.
Partnership	Business formed and owned by two or more individuals.
Sole Proprietorship	Business formed and owned by one individual.
Transaction	An economic event.

SELF-TEST QUESTIONS FOR REVIEW

(Answers are on p. 23.)

1. Sole proprietorships are the _____ in size and the _____ to create.
   a. smallest; easiest
   b. largest; most difficult
   c. smallest; most difficult
   d. largest; easiest

2. An example of an asset is
   a. Accounts Payable.
   b. Notes Payable.
   c. Accounts Receivable.
   d. Bonds Payable.

3. Assets are $70,000 and owner's equity is $50,000. Liabilities are
   a. $120,000.
   b. $70,000.
   c. $50,000.
   d. $20,000.

4. An owner invests a library in her accounting firm. Which of the following is increased?
   a. Cash
   b. Owner, Capital
   c. Accounts Payable
   d. Office Supplies

5. Find total assets given these accounts and account balances: Library, $1,000; Accounts Payable, $2,000; Cash, $5,000; Office Supplies, $3,000; and Office Equipment, $10,000.
   a. $19,000
   b. $21,000
   c. $18,000
   d. $20,000

PRACTICAL REVIEW PROBLEM

Objective 6

Preparing a Balance Sheet   Juan Tovar owns Tovar's Consulting Service. Juan lists his accounts in alphabetical order. He had the following accounts and account balances as of September 15, 19XX:

Accounts Payable	$ 2,710
Bonds Payable	21,000
Building	73,440
Cash	9,380
Equipment	7,930
Land	52,070
Notes Payable	12,360
Office Supplies	1,850
Juan Tovar, Capital	107,790
Wages Payable	810

REQUIRED
Prepare a balance sheet.

ANSWER TO PRACTICAL REVIEW PROBLEM

Tovar's Consulting Service
Balance Sheet
September 15, 19XX

Assets			
Cash	$ 9 3 8 0 —		
Office Supplies	1 8 5 0 —		
Equipment	7 9 3 0 —		
Land	52 0 7 0 —		
Building	73 4 4 0 —		
Total Assets		$144 6 7 0 —	
Liabilities			
Accounts Payable	$ 2 7 1 0 —		
Wages Payable	8 1 0 —		
Notes Payable	12 3 6 0 —		
Bonds Payable	21 0 0 0 —		
Total Liabilities		$ 36 8 8 0 —	
Owner's Equity			
Juan Tovar, Capital		107 7 9 0 —	
Total Liabilities and Owner's Equity		$144 6 7 0 —	

DISCUSSION QUESTIONS

Q 1-1   Define accounting. What is GAAP?

Q 1-2   What are the three broad professional accounting fields? Explain the three.

Q 1-3   What are the three forms of business organization? Explain the three.

Q 1-4   What are the three types of business operations? Explain the three.

Q 1-5   State the fundamental accounting equation. Define assets, liabilities, and owner's equity.

Q 1-6   Explain how assets can be determined if you know liabilities and owner's equity. Also, explain how owner's equity can be found if you know assets and liabilities.

Q 1-7   What account is increased and what account is decreased for each of the following transactions: (a) investment of cash by owner; (b) purchase of office equipment on account; and (c) payment of cash to a creditor?

Q 1-8   What accounts are increased and/or decreased for each of the following transactions: (a) purchase of office equipment for cash; (b) purchase of office supplies for cash and on account; and (c) investment of a law library by the owner?

Q 1-9   Define the following: (a) balance sheet; (b) fiscal period; and (c) interim statements.

Q 1-10   Briefly list the six steps in preparing the balance sheet.

EXERCISES

Objective 4

E 1-1   **Identifying Accounts**   Paul Morgan is planning to open and operate a travel agency.
a. Name at least three asset accounts he may use.
b. Name at least three liability accounts he may use.
c. Name at least one owner's equity account he may use.

Objective 5

E 1-2   **Recording Transactions**   Complete the following transactions:
a. Owner invests cash in the firm. The account(s) increased are _____ and _____ .
b. A liability is paid. The account(s) decreased are _____ and _____ .

Objective 4

E 1-3   **Manipulating the Equation**   Fill in the missing amounts:

Assets	Liabilities	Owner's Equity
10,000	6,000	(a)
(b)	4,000	9,000
15,000	(c)	12,000

Objective 6

E 1-4   **Completing a Balance Sheet**   Fill in the missing amounts:

Assets

Cash	$ (a)
Office Supplies	1,000
Equipment	8,000
Land	10,000
Building	80,000
Total Assets	$ (b)

Liabilities

Accounts Payable	$ 3,000
Wages Payable	2,000
Total Liabilities	$ (c)

Owner's Equity

Erin Wade, Capital	(d)
Total Liabilities and Owner's Equity	$110,000

Objective 5   **E 1-5**   **Identifying Transactions**   Determine what happened to cause the following account changes:

a. Cash increased $15,000 and Owner, Capital increased $15,000.
b. Equipment increased $5,000 and Cash decreased $5,000.
c. Accounts Payable decreased $200 and Cash decreased $200.
d. Office Supplies increased $300 and Accounts Payable increased $300.

Objective 6   **E 1-6**   **Using Balance Sheet Amounts**   Thomas Freight has the following accounts and account balances (not including Capital): Cash, $10,000; Accounts Payable, $4,000; Office Supplies, $2,000; Wages Payable, $1,000; Office Equipment, $5,000.

a. What is the amount of total assets?
b. What is the amount of total liabilities?
c. What is the amount of owner's equity?

Objective 5   **E 1-7**   **Finding Missing Amounts**   Fill in the missing amounts:

Cash	Supplies	Equipment	Accounts Payable	Wages Payable	Capital
5,000	2,000	10,000	3,000	1,000	(a)
(b)	1,000	20,000	5,000	2,000	15,000
7,000	3,000	30,000	(c)	4,000	34,000

Objective 6   **E 1-8**   **Preparing a Balance Sheet**   Prepare a balance sheet for Linda Nu, Attorney at Law, in report form, using the following information:

Cash, $26,000; Office Supplies, $3,000; Equipment, $10,000; Library, $4,000; Accounts Payable, $5,000; Linda Nu, Capital, $38,000. The date is April 15, 19XX.

PROBLEM SET A

Objective 5   **P 1-1A**   **Identifying Accounts**   Ray's Market is owned by Ray Sawyer. He had the following transactions:

a. He started Ray's Market by investing $20,000.
b. Paid $3,000 for furniture.
c. Purchased $2,000 of office supplies on account.
d. Purchased $6,000 of furniture on account.
e. Paid $1,000 to apply to the amount owed in (c).

REQUIRED
List the accounts that are increased and/or decreased for each transaction. First, write the account(s) increased, if any, and then write the account(s) decreased, if any.

Objective 5   **P 1-2A**   **Recording Transactions**   Maria Garcia is the sole owner of Garcia's Consulting Service. She had the following transactions:

a. Investment of $30,000 by the owner.
b. Purchased office equipment for cash, $10,000.

c. Purchased $4,000 of office supplies. Paid $1,000 in cash with the remainder on account.
d. Purchased office equipment on account, $8,000.
e. Paid $2,000 to apply to the purchase of office supplies in (c).
f. Owner invested a personal library valued at $3,000.

REQUIRED
1. Write the owner's name in the working papers for Capital.
2. Record the transactions in account columns, using plus and minus
   signs.
3. Prove the equality of Assets = Liabilities + Owner's Equity.

Objective 6   **P 1-3A**   **Preparing a Balance Sheet**   Frank Longia started an accounting service, Frank Longia, CPA. Frank lists his accounts in alphabetical order.
He had the following accounts and account balances as of October 19,
19XX:

Accounts Payable	$ 6,500
Bonds Payable	12,300
Building	70,000
Cash	15,600
Equipment	20,400
Land	43,700
Frank Longia, Capital	124,500
Notes Payable	11,200
Office Supplies	5,900
Wages Payable	1,100

REQUIRED
Prepare a balance sheet.

Objectives 5   **P 1-4A**   **Comprehensive Chapter Review Problem**   Helen Kendall is an attor-
and 6
ney. She started her own firm, Helen Kendall, Attorney at Law. She had
the following transactions:
a. Investment of $50,000 by the owner.
b. Purchased office furniture for cash, $13,670.
c. Purchased $5,790 of office supplies. Paid $2,000 in cash with the remainder on account.
d. Purchased office furniture on account, $9,410.
e. Paid $1,000 to apply to the purchase of office supplies in (c).
f. Owner invested a personal library valued at $6,320.

REQUIRED
1. Write the owner's name in the working papers for Capital.
2. Record the transactions in account columns, using plus and minus
   signs.
3. Prove the equality of Assets = Liabilities + Owner's Equity.
4. Prepare a balance sheet (dated March 31, 19XX).

PROBLEM SET B

Objective 5

P 1-1B   Identifying Accounts   Felipe Nunez is the owner of Felipe Nunez, CPA. He had the following transactions:
a. He started the firm by investing $30,000.
b. Paid $6,000 for equipment.
c. Purchased $4,000 of office supplies on account.
d. Purchased $9,000 of equipment on account.
e. Paid $2,000 to apply to the amount owed in (c).

REQUIRED
List the accounts that are increased and/or decreased for each transaction. First, write the account(s) increased, if any, and then write the account(s) decreased, if any.

Objective 5

P 1-2B   Recording Transactions   Lim Chi is the sole owner of Chi's Consulting Service. He had the following transactions:
a. Investment of $40,000 by the owner.
b. Purchased office equipment for cash, $10,000.
c. Purchased $6,000 of office supplies. Paid $3,000 in cash with the remainder on account.
d. Purchased office equipment on account, $14,000.
e. Paid $1,000 to apply to the purchase of office supplies in (c).
f. Owner invested a personal library valued at $2,000.

REQUIRED
1. Write the owner's name in the working papers for Capital.
2. Record the transactions in account columns, using plus and minus signs.
3. Prove the equality of Assets = Liabilities + Owner's Equity.

Objective 6

P 1-3B   Preparing a Balance Sheet   Floria O'Shea started an accounting service, Floria O'Shea, CPA. Floria lists her accounts in alphabetical order. She had the following accounts and account balances as of September 22, 19XX:

Accounts Payable	$ 8,900
Bonds Payable	18,300
Building	60,000
Cash	23,400
Furniture	15,200
Land	52,600
Notes Payable	14,100
Office Supplies	7,700
Floria O'Shea, Capital	114,800
Wages Payable	2,800

REQUIRED
Prepare a balance sheet.

Objectives 5 and 6   **P 1-4B**

Comprehensive Chapter Review Problem Kyle Peters is an attorney. He started his own firm, Kyle Peters, Attorney at Law. He had the following transactions:

a. Investment of $36,000 by the owner.
b. Purchased office furniture for cash, $11,720.
c. Purchased $7,640 of office supplies. Paid $3,000 in cash with the remainder on account.
d. Purchased office furniture on account, $8,910.
e. Paid $2,000 to apply to the purchase of office supplies in (c).
f. Owner invested a personal library valued at $1,580.

REQUIRED
1. Write the owner's name in the working papers for Capital.
2. Record the transactions in account columns, using plus and minus signs.
3. Prove the equality of Assets = Liabilities + Owner's Equity.
4. Prepare a balance sheet (dated January 31, 19XX).

ANSWERS TO SELF-TEST QUESTIONS

1. a   2. c   3. d   4. b   5. a

2

The Double-Entry System

[Money] is a machine for doing quickly and commodiously what would be done, though less quickly and commodiously, without it.

JOHN STUART MILL

LEARNING OBJECTIVES

After reading this chapter, discussing the questions, and working the exercises and problems, you will be able to do the following:

1. Identify and discuss the broad classes of accounts (pp. 26–27).

2. Utilize the expanded fundamental accounting equation (pp. 27–31).

3. Apply debits and credits to business transactions using the T account format (pp. 31–35).

4. Summarize transactions and prepare a trial balance (pp. 35–37)

5. Prepare financial statements (pp. 37–41).

In Chapter 1 we analyzed transactions and prepared a balance sheet using the fundamental accounting equation:

Assets = Liabilities + Owner's Equity

This equation must, however, be expanded to apply to all possible transactions. In this chapter we will expand the equation and also present a new method for recording transactions that is both easy and efficient.

Because it is crucial that you thoroughly understand *owner's equity* and *Capital,* we will begin this chapter with a discussion of these terms.

THE BROAD CLASSES OF ACCOUNTS

Drawing

Objective 1
Identify and discuss the broad classes of accounts.

A Drawing account is increased whenever the owner of a firm withdraws cash or other assets from the firm for his or her personal use. Drawing may thus be viewed as the opposite of Capital. It would be included in the owner's equity broad class of accounts as a reduction from Capital.

Owner's Equity Versus Capital

Sometimes the terms owner's equity and Capital are used synonymously. But you should remember that owner's equity is a broad class of accounts that includes both Capital and Drawing (see Exhibit 2-1). Capital represents the equity or ownership balance for a single owner of a firm

EXHIBIT 2-1
Owner's Equity Is a Broad Class of Accounts that Includes Capital and Drawing

Broad Class of Accounts	Accounts
Owner's Equity	Kay Loomis, Capital
	Kay Loomis, Drawing

(sole proprietorship). Equity is the owner's claims against the assets of the firm. The balance in the Drawing account would be subtracted from Capital to arrive at a final Capital balance.

Two other broad classes of accounts affect owner's equity and the final Capital balance. These are **revenues** and **expenses**.

Revenues

A firm is established to produce and distribute goods and/or services. These goods and services, when sold to another firm or individual, are called revenues. *Revenues increase Capital.* A firm generates revenues, and thus increases Capital, through selling goods and services. A firm that is operating without a clear set of ideas as to what goods and/or services to sell and deliver will soon go out of business.

Some examples of revenues include legal fees, auditing fees, management advisory services, tax services, interest income, and advertising income. Revenues are earned during a specific period of time—a month, three months, twelve months, and so on; but this period is generally not longer than a year.

Expenses

The final broad class of accounts is expenses. *Expenses reduce Capital.* They are the goods and services that are purchased and consumed to support the revenues. Wages Expense, Advertising Expense, Rent Expense, and Utilities Expense are some examples of expenses. *Do not confuse these expenses with prepaid expenses, such as prepaid rent or prepaid insurance, which are assets.*

A firm cannot generate revenues without expenses. Imagine a business operating without a place to conduct business (Rent Expense) or without employees to do the necessary work (Wages Expense). This, of course, would be impossible.

Like revenues, expenses are also time-related. They too are measured for a month, three months, twelve months, and so on; but usually not longer than twelve months, which is the normal fiscal year.

THE EXPANDED FUNDAMENTAL ACCOUNTING EQUATION

Objective 2
Utilize the
expanded
fundamental
accounting
equation.

In order to include revenues and expenses, the fundamental accounting equation must be expanded as follows:

Assets = Liabilities + Owner's Equity + Revenues − Expenses

As before, the left side of the equation must always equal the right side. You'll use this revised equation to analyze, classify, record, and interpret transactions.

EXHIBIT 2-2
Flow of Assets to Support Revenues

| **ASSET** → | (flow to) → | **EXPENSE** | → (flow to) → | **REVENUES** | |
| Cash → | (payment of cash for) → | Wages Expense for Employees | → (perform work) → | (generate revenues) → | Increase Cash and/or Accounts Receivable (assets) |

Let's examine the fundamental accounting equation in more detail. To begin, on the right side, liabilities represent the creditors' claims against the assets of the firm. Owner's equity is the owner's claims against the assets of the firm. Revenues are generated through selling goods and services. And expenses represent assets that are used to support the revenues. For example, Cash, which is an asset, is used to pay wages to employees (Wages Expense). The employees work for the firm and in turn generate revenues by selling the firm's product or service, billing customers for amounts owed, manufacturing the product, and so on. Exhibit 2-2 illustrates the flow of assets to support revenues.

The Double-Entry System

Every transaction uses two or more accounts for recording purposes. The double-entry system is a method of recording a transaction employing at least two accounts, or a double entry. A transaction that utilizes more than two accounts is called a compound entry. The double-entry system is a system of checks and balances. In accounting, for every resource (asset) that enters the firm, another departs. For example, when the firm purchased office equipment for cash, the equipment received represented the inflow of resources (assets). You can probably guess what the outflow is. You're right—the payment of cash. Thus, the balance of inflows and outflows prevails.

T Accounts

A T account derives its name from its resemblance to a T and is often used to record transactions. It is a tool which will eventually show you how to keep a set of books. A T account should be presented as follows:

The account name is placed at the top of the T:

Account Name

Debit

Debit, in accounting, means *left side only,* and is abbreviated "Dr." In a T account, a debit would always appear on the left side. If you were using the account, Cash, you would place "Cash" at the top of the T:

Cash

Debit
(or Dr.)

Credit

In accounting, **credit** means *right side only,* and is abbreviated "Cr." In a T account, a credit would always be on the right side. If you were using the account, Accounts Payable, you would place "Accounts Payable" at the top of the T, just as you did with Cash before:

Accounts Payable

Credit
(or Cr.)

Applications of Debits and Credits

Debits and credits, along with T accounts, can be used to record transactions. To illustrate, we'll apply debits and credits to the broad classes of accounts in T account form:

RULE: Assets are increased (+) by debits. Credits decrease (−) assets.

Assets

Debit	Credit
+	−

RULE: Liabilities are decreased (−) by debits. Credits increase (+) liabilities.

Liabilities

Debit	Credit
−	+

RULE: Owner's equity is decreased (−) by debits. Credits increase (+) owner's equity.

Owner's Equity

Debit	Credit
−	+

There is, however, an exception to these rules. The Drawing account is increased by debits and decreased by credits. It is a reduction to owner's equity. Drawing is a **contra** account, which means that its normal balance is contrary or "contra" to the normal balance within that broad class of accounts. Owner's equity or Capital normally has a *credit* balance. However, Drawing has a normal *debit* balance (see Exhibit 2-3).

RULE: Revenues are decreased (−) by debits. Credits increase (+) revenues.

Revenues

Debit	Credit
−	+

RULE: Expenses are increased (+) by debits. Credits decrease (−) expenses.

Expenses

Debit	Credit
+	−

Note that expenses decrease the equity of the firm, as they use up or consume assets to support revenues. Thus, we see that expenses are increased by debits and decreased by credits.

EXHIBIT 2-3
Drawing Account Reduces Owner's Equity

Owner's Equity	
Debit	Credit
−	+

Drawing	
Debit	Credit
+	−

Rules for Using T Accounts to Record Transactions

1. Analyze the transaction—mentally review the accounts to be used.
2. Record the transaction's debit(s) first.
3. Record the transaction's credit(s) next.
4. Check to see that the total debit(s) monetary amount equals the total credit(s) monetary amount for the transaction.

Transaction (a).   January 1, 19XX: Investment of cash by owner.[1]

Objective 3
Apply debits and credits to business transactions using the T account format.

Cash			Kay Loomis, Capital	
Dr.	Cr.		Dr.	Cr.
+	−		−	+
(a) 10,000				(a) 10,000

Transaction (b).   January 3, 19XX: Purchase of office equipment for cash.

Office Equipment			Cash	
Dr.	Cr.		Dr.	Cr.
+	−		+	−
(b) 1,200				(b) 1,200

[1]The first six transactions (a–f) are from Chapter 1.

Transaction (c).   January 5, 19XX: Purchase of office equipment on credit.

Office Equipment		Accounts Payable	
Dr.	Cr.	Dr.	Cr.
+	−	−	+
(c) 8,000			(c) 8,000

Transaction (d).   January 8, 19XX: Purchase of office supplies for cash and on account.

Office Supplies		Cash		Accounts Payable	
Dr.	Cr.	Dr.	Cr.	Dr.	Cr.
+	−	+	−	−	+
(d) 500			(d) 100		(d) 400

Transaction (e).   January 10, 19XX: Investment of accounting library by owner.

Library		Kay Loomis, Capital	
Dr.	Cr.	Dr.	Cr.
+	−	−	+
(e) 75			(e) 75

Transaction (f).   January 13, 19XX: Payment of a liability.

Accounts Payable		Cash	
Dr.	Cr.	Dr.	Cr.
−	+	+	−
(f) 130			(f) 130

Transaction (g).   January 14, 19XX: Cash revenues.
Kay Loomis, CPA, bills and collects $1,820 from Andrews Drug Store for tax services. Tax Services is a revenue account and is credited.

Cash		Tax Services	
Dr.	Cr.	Dr.	Cr.
+	−	−	+
(g) 1,820			(g) 1,820

Transaction (h).   January 15, 19XX: Payment of wages.

Kay pays her secretary $600 for two weeks of work. Wages Expense is an expense account and is debited.

Wages Expense		Cash	
Dr.	Cr.	Dr.	Cr.
+	−	+	−
(h) 600			(h) 600

Transaction (i).   January 17, 19XX: Credit revenues.

Kay Loomis, CPA, bills James Kowalski $2,010 for management advisory services. **Accounts Receivable** is used to record the future receipt of the $2,010 and is debited. Management Advisory Services is a revenue account and is credited. Accounts Receivable is an asset account that represents money due to the firm. This money due is usually from the sale of services and goods on credit (on account).

Accounts Receivable		Management Advisory Services	
Dr.	Cr.	Dr.	Cr.
+	−	−	+
(i) 2,010			(i) 2,010

Transaction (j).   January 20, 19XX: Payment of advertising.

Kay advertises the services of her firm in a local newspaper. She pays $85 for the advertising. Advertising Expense is an expense account and is debited.

Advertising Expense		Cash	
Dr.	Cr.	Dr.	Cr.
+	−	+	−
(j) 85			(j) 85

Transaction (k).   January 21, 19XX: Cash revenues.

Kay Loomis, CPA, bills and collects $990 from Feng Li, Attorney at Law, for auditing fees. Auditing Fees is a revenue account and is credited.

Cash		Auditing Fees	
Dr.	Cr.	Dr.	Cr.
+	−	−	+
(k) 990			(k) 990

Transaction (l).   January 23, 19XX: Withdrawal by owner.

Kay withdraws $395 in cash for her personal use. Kay Loomis, Drawing, is a contra account that reduces owner's equity and is debited.

Kay Loomis, Drawing		Cash	
Dr.	Cr.	Dr.	Cr.
+	−	+	−
(l) 395			(l) 395

Transaction (m).   January 26, 19XX: Receipt of utilities bill.

The firm receives but does not pay a utilities bill for $65. Utilities Expense is an expense account and is debited. Accounts Payable is credited to record the liability that will be paid at a future date.

Utilities Expense		Accounts Payable	
Dr.	Cr.	Dr.	Cr.
+	−	−	+
(m) 65			(m) 65

Transaction (n).   January 28, 19XX: Partial collection.

The firm receives $1,005 from James Kowalski as partial payment of the January 17 billing. The revenue has been previously recorded (see Transaction i), so the account, Management Advisory Services, is not used. Cash is debited for the amount received. Accounts Receivable is credited because the firm has received money for an amount previously owed to the firm.

Cash		Accounts Receivable	
Dr.	Cr.	Dr.	Cr.
+	−	+	−
(n) 1,005			(n) 1,005

Transaction (o).   January 31, 19XX: Payment of wages.

Kay pays her secretary $600 for two weeks of work. The Wages Expense account is debited, and Cash is credited.

Wages Expense		Cash	
Dr.	Cr.	Dr.	Cr.
+	−	+	−
(o) 600			(o) 600

Footings and the Final Account Balance

The debit and credit totals of each account are called footings, which are recorded in pencil. The debit footings and the credit footings must be subtracted in order to arrive at the final account balance. The one with the largest balance becomes the new account balance. The final account balance is written in pencil below the footings. By writing the footings and final balance in pencil, any addition or subtraction errors can be easily erased and corrected. For example, assume that Cash had the following transaction amounts:

	Cash		
	Dr.	Cr.	
	1,000	100	
	500	200	
	300	400	
Footing (in pencil)	1,800 `	700	Footing (in pencil)
Final balance (in pencil)	1,100		

Writing Transactions

Transactions should be written in ink and never erased. If an error is made and needs to be corrected, you should draw a line through the incorrect transaction. The correct entry should be written above the incorrect entry in ink. Otherwise it may appear that you are trying to hide something.

SUMMARIZING TRANSACTIONS AND PREPARING THE TRIAL BALANCE

Objective 4
Summarize transactions and prepare a trial balance.

Summarizing Transactions

Let's prepare financial statements for the previous fifteen transactions. First the transactions have to be summarized by account. In Exhibit 2-4, (a) refers to the first transaction, (b) to the second, and so on.

Note that in Exhibit 2-4 whenever a T account has only one amount that amount is the final account balance. A T account that has only one debit and one credit amount does not need footings. The two amounts are subtracted and the difference is the final account balance.

Preparing the Trial Balance

In Chapter 1 we said that it is important that the left side of the accounting equation equals the right side of the accounting equation.

EXHIBIT 2-4
Transactions Summarized in T Account Form

ASSETS	=	LIABILITIES	+	OWNER'S EQUITY	+	REVENUES	−	EXPENSES

Cash

(a)	10,000	(b)	1,200
(g)	1,820	(d)	100
(k)	990	(f)	130
(n)	1,005	(h)	600
		(j)	85
		(l)	395
		(o)	600
	13,815		3,110
	10,705		

Accounts Payable

(f)	130	(c)	8,000
		(d)	400
		(m)	65
	130		8,465
			8,335

Kay Loomis, Capital

		(a)	10,000
		(e)	75
			10,075

Tax Services

		(g)	1,820

Wages Expense

(h)	600		
(o)	600		
1,200			

Accounts Receivable

(i)	2,010	(n)	1,005
	1,005		

Kay Loomis, Drawing

(l)	395		

Management Advisory Services

		(i)	2,010

Advertising Expense

(j)	85		

Office Supplies

(d)	500		

Auditing Fees

		(k)	990

Utilities Expense

(m)	65		

Office Equipment

(b)	1,200		
(c)	8,000		
9,200			

Library

(e)	75		

EXHIBIT 2-5
Preparation of a Trial Balance

Kay Loomis, CPA

Trial Balance

January 31, 19XX

Accounts	Debit	Credit
Cash	10 7 0 5 —	
Accounts Receivable	1 0 0 5 —	
Office Supplies	5 0 0 —	
Office Equipment	9 2 0 0 —	
Library	7 5 —	
Accounts Payable		8 3 3 5 —
Kay Loomis, Capital		10 0 7 5 —
Kay Loomis, Drawing	3 9 5 —	
Tax Services		1 8 2 0 —
Management Advisory Services		2 0 1 0 —
Auditing Fees		9 9 0 —
Wages Expense	1 2 0 0 —	
Advertising Expense	8 5 —	
Utilities Expense	6 5 —	
Totals	23 2 3 0 —	23 2 3 0 —

Exhibit 2-5 lists the accounts and account balances of Kay Loomis, CPA, to make sure that the total debits equal the total credits before preparing financial statements. This procedure, called the **trial balance**, will be examined in more detail in Chapter 3.

PREPARING FINANCIAL STATEMENTS

Objective 5
Prepare financial statements.

When preparing financial statements, the income statement is always prepared first. Next is the statement of owner's equity, followed by the balance sheet.

Income Statements

An **income statement** measures a firm's performance for a stated (or defined) period of time.

Steps in Preparing the Income Statement   An income statement for Kay Loomis, CPA, is prepared in Exhibit 2-6 at January 31, 19XX. The

EXHIBIT 2-6
Preparation of an Income Statement (Net Income)

(a)
Kay Loomis, CPA
Income Statement
For the Month Ended January 31, 19XX

Revenues (b)										
Tax Services		$1	8	2	0	—				
Management Advisory Services		2	0	1	0	—				
Auditing Fees			9	9	0	—				
Total Revenues							$4	8	2	0	—
Expenses (c)										
Wages Expense		$1	2	0	0	—				
Advertising Expense				8	5	—				
Utilities Expense				6	5	—				
Total Expenses							1	3	5	0	—
Net Income (d)							$3	4	7	0	—

following steps in preparing an income statement are keyed ((a), (b), (c), and (d)) to Exhibit 2-6:

(a) The income statement has a three-part heading which is centered and includes, in this order, the name of the firm, the name of the financial statement, and the period of time for which the financial statement is prepared. Leave one blank line before "Revenues."

(b) List the revenues. A dollar sign appears at the beginning of the Revenue column. A line is drawn after the column. Revenues are totaled with a dollar sign. Leave one blank line before "Expenses."

(c) List the expenses. A dollar sign appears at the beginning of the Expense column. Expenses are totaled and underlined. Leave one blank line before "Net Income" or "Net Loss."

(d) Net Income or Net Loss is determined by subtracting Total Expenses from Total Revenues. When Total Revenues exceed Total Expenses there is Net Income. Net Loss occurs when Total Expenses are greater than Total Revenues. The net income or net loss amount is preceded by a dollar sign and double underlined.

EXHIBIT 2-7
Preparation of an Income Statement (Net Loss)

Williams Advisory Service
Income Statement
For the Year Ended December 31, 19XX

Revenue		
Advisory Services		$2 0 0 0 —
Expenses		
Wages Expense	$1 0 0 0 —	
Advertising Expense	9 0 0 —	
Utilities Expense	3 0 0 —	
Total Expenses		2 2 0 0 —
Net Loss		($ 2 0 0 —)

Income Statement with a Net Loss An income statement with a net loss is illustrated in Exhibit 2-7. Assume the accounts and amounts for Williams Advisory Service.

Statement of Owner's Equity

The second financial statement usually prepared is the **statement of owner's equity.** Generally accepted accounting principles (GAAP) do not require that this financial statement be prepared. However, the statement of owner's equity is usually prepared because it summarizes the changes in the owner's Capital account for a stated (or defined) period of time. This financial statement is prepared after the income statement, as net income or net loss must first be determined.

Steps in Preparing the Statement of Owner's Equity In Exhibit 2-8, a statement of owner's equity is prepared for Kay Loomis, CPA, for the month ended January 31, 19XX. The following steps in preparing the statement of owner's equity are keyed (ⓐ, ⓑ, ⓒ, and so on) to Exhibit 2-8:

ⓐ The statement of owner's equity has a three-part heading which is centered and includes, in this order, the name of the firm, the name of the

EXHIBIT 2-8
Preparation of a Statement of Owner's Equity (with Net Income)

Kay Loomis, CPA

(a) Statement of Owner's Equity

For the Month Ended January 31, 19XX

Kay Loomis, Capital, January 1, 19XX	(b)	$10 0 0 0 —
Add: Net Income for January	(c)	3 4 7 0 —
Additional Investment		7 5 —
Subtotal	(d)	$13 5 4 5 —
Deduct: Kay Loomis, Drawing	(e)	3 9 5 —
Kay Loomis, Capital, January 31, 19XX	(f)	$13 1 5 0 —

financial statement, and the period of time for which the statement of owner's equity is prepared. Leave one blank line before "Capital."

(b) List the owner's beginning Capital balance with a dollar sign.

(c) Net Income and Additional Investments, if any, are listed.

(d) Net Income and Additional Investment(s) are added to the beginning Capital for a subtotal, with a dollar sign. A line is drawn· after the amount of the Additional Investment(s).

(e) The owner's Drawing account is listed. A line is drawn after the Drawing account amount.

(f) The final Capital balance is determined by subtracting Drawing from Subtotal. Kay Loomis, Capital, January 31, 19XX, is double underlined with a dollar sign.

Statement of Owner's Equity with a Net Loss A statement of owner's equity with a net loss is illustrated in Exhibit 2-9.

The Balance Sheet

The third financial statement for Kay Loomis, CPA, is the balance sheet (as shown in Exhibit 2-10). This financial statement is usually prepared after the statement of owner's equity, as the owner's Capital account balance must first be determined. Refer to Chapter 1 for the steps in preparing the balance sheet.

EXHIBIT 2-9
Preparation of a Statement of Owner's Equity (with Net Loss)

Sean O'Malley, Computer Consultant

Statement of Owner's Equity

For the Month Ended August 31, 19XX

Sean O'Malley, Capital, August 1, 19XX						$47	6	0	0	—
Add: Additional Investment							4	2	0	0	—
Subtotal						$51	8	0	0	—
Deduct: Net Loss for August	$3	9	0	0	—					
Sean O'Malley, Drawing	1	3	0	0	—					
Total Deductions							5	2	0	0	—
Sean O'Malley, Capital, August 31, 19XX						$46	6	0	0	—

EXHIBIT 2-10
Preparation of a Balance Sheet in Report Form

Kay Loomis, CPA

Balance Sheet

January 31, 19XX

Assets									
Cash	$10	7	0	5	—				
Accounts Receivable	1	0	0	5	—				
Office Supplies		5	0	0	—				
Office Equipment	9	2	0	0	—				
Library			7	5	—				
Total Assets						$21	4	8	5	—
Liabilities									
Accounts Payable						$ 8	3	3	5	—
Owner's Equity									
Kay Loomis, Capital						13	1	5	0	—
Total Liabilities and Owner's Equity						$21	4	8	5	—

CHAPTER REVIEW

1. **Identify and discuss the broad classes of accounts (pp. 26–27).**
   The broad classes of accounts include assets, liabilities, owner's equity, revenues, and expenses.

2. **Utilize the expanded fundamental accounting equation (pp. 27–31).**
   The expanded accounting equation is:

   Assets = Liabilities + Owner's Equity + Revenues − Expenses

3. **Apply debits and credits to business transactions using the T account format (pp. 31–35).**
   Fifteen transactions were examined.

4. **Summarize transactions and prepare a trial balance (pp. 35–37).**
   In order to prepare financial statements, the transactions must be summarized by account and then a trial balance is prepared.

5. **Prepare financial statements (pp. 37–41).**
   The financial statements are prepared in this order: (a) income statement; (b) statement of owner's equity; and (c) balance sheet.

GLOSSARY

Compound Entry	Transaction that utilizes more than two accounts.
Contra Account	Account whose balance is different (contra) than the normal balances within that broad class of accounts.
Credit	Right side only.
Debit	Left side only.
Double-Entry System	Recording of a transaction using two or more accounts.
Drawing	Withdrawals of cash or other assets by the owner for his or her personal use.
Expanded Fundamental Accounting Equation	Assets = Liabilities + Owner's Equity + Revenues − Expenses
Expenses	Goods and/or services purchased and consumed by a firm to support revenues.
Footing	Debit and credit totals of an account.

Income Statement	Financial statement that measures a firm's performance for a stated (or defined) period of time.
Net Income	Revenues are greater than expenses for a stated (or defined) period of time.
Net Loss	Expenses exceed revenues for a stated (or defined) period of time.
Revenues	Sale of goods and/or services.
Statement of Owner's Equity	Financial statement which summarizes changes in the owner's Capital account for a stated (or defined) period of time.
T Account	Resembles a T and is often used to record transactions.
Trial Balance	A listing of accounts and account balances (see Chapter 3 for a more detailed discussion).

SELF-TEST QUESTIONS FOR REVIEW

(Answers are on p. 53.)

1. Revenues _____ Capital and expenses _____ Capital.
   a. decrease; increase
   b. decrease; decrease
   c. increase; decrease
   d. increase; increase

2. Which of the following is subtracted on the right side of the expanded fundamental accounting equation?
   a. Revenues
   b. Liabilities
   c. Owner's Equity
   d. Expenses

3. An owner invests cash in his business. He would
   a. debit Accounts Payable.
   b. debit Cash.
   c. debit Owner, Capital.
   d. debit Accounts Receivable.

4. Tax Services is included under _____ and Auditing Fees is included under _____ on an income statement.
   a. Revenues; Revenues
   b. Revenues; Expenses
   c. Expenses; Expenses
   d. Expenses; Revenues

5. A firm bills for management advisory services and debits
   a. Accounts Receivable.
   b. Cash.
   c. Accounts Payable.
   d. Management Advisory Services.

PRACTICAL REVIEW PROBLEM

Objective 5

Preparing Financial Statements Martha Wheel owns Wheel's Decorating Service. Martha had the following trial balance for the month:

Wheel's Decorating Service
Trial Balance
May 31, 19XX

Accounts	Debit	Credit
Cash	11 2 0 0 —	
Accounts Receivable	1 0 0 0 —	
Store Supplies	1 0 0 0 —	
Accounts Payable		7 5 0 —
Wages Payable		8 0 0 —
Martha Wheel, Capital		13 0 0 0 —
Martha Wheel, Drawing	7 5 0 —	
Decorating Services		1 0 0 0 —
Wages Expense	1 6 0 0 —	
Totals	15 5 5 0 —	15 5 5 0 —

REQUIRED

Prepare an income statement, a statement of owner's equity, and a balance sheet.

ANSWER TO PRACTICAL REVIEW PROBLEM

Wheel's Decorating Service
Income Statement
For the Month Ended May 31, 19XX

Revenue		
Decorator Services		$1 0 0 0 —
Expense		
Wages Expense		1 6 0 0 —
Net Loss		($ 6 0 0 —)

Wheel's Decorating Service
Statement of Owner's Equity
For the Month Ended May 31, 19XX

Martha Wheel, Capital, May 1, 19XX			$13 0 0 0 —
Deduct: Net Loss for May	$ 6 0 0 —		
Martha Wheel, Drawing	7 5 0 —		
Total Deductions		1 3 5 0 —
Martha Wheel, Capital, May 31, 19XX		$11 6 5 0 —

Wheel's Decorating Service
Balance Sheet
May 31, 19XX

Assets		
Cash	$11 2 0 0 —	
Accounts Receivable	1 0 0 0 —	
Store Supplies	1 0 0 0 —	
Total Assets		$13 2 0 0 —
Liabilities		
Accounts Payable	$ 7 5 0 —	
Wages Payable	8 0 0 —	
Total Liabilities		$ 1 5 5 0 —
Owner's Equity		
Martha Wheel, Capital		11 6 5 0 —
Total Liabilities and Owner's Equity		$13 2 0 0 —

DISCUSSION QUESTIONS

Q 2-1   What is the difference between owner's equity and Capital?

Q 2-2   Define revenues and expenses. What effect do revenues have on Capital? What effect do expenses have on Capital?

Q 2-3   State the expanded fundamental accounting equation.

Q 2-4   Describe the double-entry system.

Q 2-5   What is a T account? What does a debit mean in accounting? What does a credit mean?

Q 2-6   Explain how debits and credits increase or decrease each of the following broad classes of accounts: assets, liabilities, owner's equity, drawing, revenues, and expenses.

Q 2-7   Describe the four rules for using T accounts to record transactions.

Q 2-8   Which financial statement is prepared first? Which is usually prepared second? Third? Why are financial statements prepared in this order?

Q 2-9   Briefly list the four steps in preparing the income statement.

Q 2-10   Briefly list the six steps in preparing the statement of owner's equity.

EXERCISES

Objective 3   **E 2-1**   **Identifying Accounts**   Write the account debited and the account credited for each of the following transactions:

a. The owner, Lupe Rodriguez, invested $20,000.

Account debited: _____ *Cash* _____

Account credited: _____ *Owners Eq* _____

b. Paid a secretary $1,000 for two weeks of work.

Account debited: _____ *Wg Ex* _____

Account credited: _____ *Cash* _____

Objective 3   **E 2-2**   **Recording Transactions**   Record the following transactions in T account form:

a. Purchased $2,200 of office equipment with $900 cash and the remainder on account.

b. The owner, Ike Owens, withdrew $400 for his personal use.

c. Billed a customer $700 for advertising services.

d. Owner invested a library valued at $800.

e. Received a utilities bill for $100.

Objective 5

E 2-3   **Completing an Income Statement** Complete the following income statement for Cheng Wu, Attorney at Law, for the month ended April 19XX:

	(a)	
	(b)	
	(c)	

(d)		
Legal Fees	$2,900	
Guardian Fees	1,200	
Total Revenues		(e)

(f)		
Wages Expense	$1,500	
Advertising Expense	600	
Utilities Expense	200	
Total Expenses		(g)

(h)		(i)

Objective 5

E 2-4 **Completing a Statement of Owner's Equity** Complete the following statement of owner's equity for Albert Conner, Medical Doctor, for the month ended November 19XX:

	(a)	
	(b)	
	(c)	

(d) , Capital, November 1, 19XX	$21,400
Add: Net Income for November	5,700
Additional Investment	2,300
Subtotal	(e)
Deduct: (f) , Drawing	1,600
(g) , Capital, November 30, 19XX	(h)

Objective 5

E 2-5 Completing a Balance Sheet   Complete the following balance sheet for Paula Lyski, CPA, for the month ended December 19XX:

_____(a)_____

_____(b)_____

_____(c)_____

_____(d)_____

Cash	$17,300
Accounts Receivable	6,900
Store Supplies	7,500
_____(e)_____	_____(f)_____
_____(g)_____	
Accounts Payable	$ 4,400
Wages Payable	1,200
_____(h)_____	_____(i)_____
_____(j)_____	
_____(k)_____, Capital	_____(l)_____
_____(m)_____	_____(n)_____

Objective 3

E 2-6 Recording Transactions   Record the following transactions in T account form:
a. The owner, Unis Singh, invested $35,000 cash in a new firm named Camino Design Services.
b. Purchased furniture for cash, $11,000.
c. Billed customer $6,000 for design services.
d. Owner invested a library valued at $2,000.
e. Purchased office supplies on account, $4,000.
f. Paid employees for work performed, $3,000.

Objective 4

E 2-7 Summarizing Transactions   Summarize the transactions in E 2-6 using the format presented in Exhibit 2-4.

Objective 5

E 2-8 Preparing Financial Statements   For the month ended August 31, 19XX, prepare (a) an income statement and (b) a statement of owner's equity given the following account balances: Norma Lewis, Capital, August 1, 19XX, $45,000 (credit); Norma Lewis, Drawing, $2,000 (debit); Weather Services, $8,000 (credit); Wages Expense, $4,000 (debit); Advertising Expense, $2,000 (debit); and Utilities Expense, $1,000 (debit). The firm is Lewis Weather Service.

PROBLEM SET A

Objective 3   **P 2-1A   Identifying Accounts**   Grady Kennedy owns Kennedy Door Repair. He had the following transactions for April 19XX:

April 1   He started Kennedy Door Repair by investing $55,000.
April 4   Paid $6,000 for furniture.
April 8   Purchased $2,000 of office supplies on account.
April 14   Paid wages of $3,000.
April 19   Owner invested an additional $5,000 cash.
April 23   Billed a customer $9,000 for repair services.
April 29   Received a utilities bill for $1,000.

REQUIRED
1. Write the date for each transaction.
2. List the account debited and the account credited for each transaction. First, write the account debited, and then write the account credited.

Objective 3   **P 2-2A   Recording Transactions**   Laura McFalls is the sole owner of McFalls Consulting Service. She had the following transactions:
a. Owner invested $60,000 cash.
b. Purchased office furniture for cash, $13,000.
c. Purchased $7,000 of office supplies. Paid $4,000 in cash with the remainder on account.
d. Purchased office equipment on account, $9,000.
e. Paid $2,000 to apply to the purchase of office supplies in (c).
f. Owner invested a personal library valued at $5,000.
g. Paid wages of $6,000.
h. Billed a customer $12,000 for consulting services.
i. Received an advertising bill, $1,000.

REQUIRED
Record the transactions in T account form.

Objective 5

P 2-3A Preparing Financial Statements Howard Potter owns Potter's Catering Service. He had the following trial balance for the month:

Potter's Catering Service
Trial Balance
March 31, 19XX

Accounts	Debit	Credit
Cash	25 9 0 0 —	
Accounts Receivable	3 6 0 0 —	
Office Supplies	1 2 0 0 —	
Accounts Payable		1 8 0 0 —
Wages Payable		9 0 0 —
Howard Potter, Capital		27 4 0 0 —
Howard Potter, Drawing	6 0 0 —	
Catering Services		4 1 0 0 —
Wages Expense	2 9 0 0 —	
Totals	34 2 0 0 —	34 2 0 0 —

REQUIRED
Prepare an income statement, a statement of owner's equity, and a balance sheet (Capital is from March 1 investment).

Objectives 3, 4 and 5

P 2-4A Comprehensive Chapter Review Problem Teresa Galindo owns the firm called Teresa Galindo, CPA. She had the following transactions:
a. Teresa invested $37,520 cash (November 1—beginning capital).
b. Billed and collected $8,290 for auditing fees.
c. Purchased office equipment for cash, $18,610.
d. Purchased $11,340 of office supplies. Paid $6,150 in cash with the remainder on account.
e. Purchased office furniture on account, $23,730.
f. Paid wages, $5,960.
g. Teresa invested a personal library valued at $2,280.
h. Received an advertising bill, $4,840.
i. Billed a customer $7,430 for tax services.
j. Paid $1,160 to apply to the purchase of office supplies in (d).
k. Received $2,620 to apply to the billing in (i).
l. Billed a customer $3,870 for advisory services.
m. Owner withdrew $1,910 in cash for her personal use.

REQUIRED

1. Record the transactions in T account form.
2. Summarize the transactions using the format presented in Exhibit 2-4.
3. Prepare a trial balance (list accounts and account balances) to make sure that total debits equal total credits.
4. Prepare financial statements (income statement, statement of owner's equity, and balance sheet) for the month ended November 30, 19XX.

PROBLEM SET B

Objective 3

P 2-1B   Identifying Accounts   Sharon Kerr owns South City Moving Service. She had the following transactions for February 19XX:

February 2	She started South City Moving Service by investing $62,000.
February 6	Received an advertising bill for $2,000.
February 10	Purchased $6,000 of store supplies on account.
February 13	Purchased $8,000 of equipment on account.
February 16	Owner invested an additional $4,000 cash.
February 20	Paid wages of $3,000.
February 23	Billed a customer $7,000 for moving services.

REQUIRED

1. Write the date for each transaction.
2. List the account debited and the account credited for each transaction. First, write the account debited, and then write the account credited.

Objective 3

P 2-2B   Recording Transactions   Alberto Rocha is the sole owner of Rocha's Furniture Design. He had the following transactions:

a. Owner invested $87,000 cash.
b. Purchased office equipment for cash, $14,000.
c. Purchased $6,000 of store supplies. Paid $2,000 in cash with the remainder on account.
d. Purchased office equipment on account, $23,000.
e. Paid $1,000 to apply to the purchase of store supplies in (c).
f. Owner invested a personal library valued at $4,000.
g. Paid wages of $5,000.
h. Billed a customer $11,000 for design fees.
i. Received an advertising bill, $3,000.

REQUIRED

Record the transactions in T account form.

Objective 5

P 2-3B   Preparing Financial Statements   Pilar Montez owns Pilar's Insurance Service. She had the following trial balance for the month:

Pilar's Insurance Service
Trial Balance
April 30, 19XX

Accounts	Debit	Credit
Cash	16 4 0 0 —	
Accounts Receivable	4 3 0 0 —	
Office Supplies	2 9 0 0 —	
Accounts Payable		5 1 0 0 —
Wages Payable		7 0 0 —
Pilar Montez, Capital		15 9 0 0 —
Pilar Montez, Drawing	2 0 0 —	
Insurance Services		5 6 0 0 —
Wages Expense	3 5 0 0 —	
Totals	27 3 0 0 —	27 3 0 0 —

REQUIRED

Prepare an income statement, a statement of owner's equity, and a balance sheet (Capital is from April 1 investment).

Objectives 3, 4, and 5

P 2-4B   Comprehensive Chapter Review Problem   Tyrone Caruso owns the firm called Tyrone Caruso, CPA. He had the following transactions:

a. Tyrone invested $51,750 cash (August 1—beginning capital).
b. Billed and collected $4,910 for advisory services.
c. Purchased office furniture for cash, $15,470.
d. Purchased $10,100 of office supplies. Paid $5,640 in cash with the remainder on account.
e. Purchased office equipment on account, $32,560.
f. Paid wages, $6,850.
g. Tyrone invested a personal library valued at $1,730.
h. Received an advertising bill, $3,390.
i. Billed a customer $5,120 for auditing fees.
j. Paid $2,580 to apply to the purchase of office supplies in (d).
k. Received $3,160 to apply to the billing in (i).
l. Billed a customer $4,940 for tax services.
m. Owner withdrew $2,790 in cash for his personal use.

REQUIRED
1. Record the transactions in T account form.
2. Summarize the transactions using the format presented in Exhibit 2-4.
3. Prepare a trial balance (list accounts and account balances) to make sure that total debits equal total credits.
4. Prepare financial statements (income statement, statement of owner's equity, and balance sheet) for the month ended August 31, 19XX.

ANSWERS TO SELF-TEST QUESTIONS

1. c   2. d   3. b   4. a   5. a

3

Posting and the Trial Balance

If thou wouldst keep money, save money;
If thou wouldst reap money, sow money.

THOMAS FULLER

LEARNING OBJECTIVES

After reading this chapter, discussing the questions, and working the exercises and problems, you will be able to do the following:

1. Record transactions in the general journal (pp. 56–62).

2. Post from the general journal to the general ledger (pp. 62–70).

3. Prepare a trial balance from the general ledger (pp. 70–71).

Chapters 1 and 2 presented the fundamental accounting equation and the expanded fundamental accounting equation, respectively. The expanded accounting equation is:

$$\text{Assets} = \text{Liabilities} + \text{Owner's equity} + \text{Revenues} - \text{Expenses}$$

Chapter 2 introduced T accounts and illustrated how various transactions are recorded. The double-entry system, where two or more accounts are used to record each transaction, was also examined.

In this chapter, the general journal method of recording transactions, as well as the posting process and preparation of a trial balance, is presented.

THE CHART OF ACCOUNTS

Objective 1
Record
transactions in
the general
journal.

Every business operation—sole proprietorship, partnership, or corporation—must have a **chart of accounts**. A chart of accounts is a detailed listing of all the accounts the firm uses for recording transactions. The chart of accounts for Kevin Young, Attorney at Law, is as follows:

Kevin Young, Attorney at Law
Chart of Accounts

Assets (100–199)

101	Cash
111	Accounts Receivable
121	Office Supplies
131	Prepaid Insurance
141	Furniture

Liabilities (200–299)

201	Accounts Payable

Owner's Equity (300–399)

301	Kevin Young, Capital
311	Kevin Young, Drawing

Revenues (400–499)

401	Legal Fees

Expenses (500–599)

501	Wages Expense
511	Advertising Expense
521	Rent Expense
531	Utilities Expense

The chart-of-accounts numbers precede the account titles and indicate the classification of accounts. Assets usually start with a 1, liabilities with a 2, owner's equity with a 3, revenues with a 4, and expenses with a 5. The second and third digits are used to place the accounts within their particular classification.

The chart of accounts is never static because a firm is always conducting business. The firm should allow for the addition of new accounts as necessary.

THE GENERAL JOURNAL

T Accounts Reviewed

A T account is one of the most useful tools for recording transactions. With T accounts you can easily see if an account is increased or decreased depending on whether there is a debit or credit. The T account method can be extended so that transactions can be *tracked* (audited) more easily and recorded more systematically, using less space.

T Accounts and the General Journal

The general journal is a book of original entry. Making transaction entries in a general journal is called journalizing. The general journal looks somewhat like a T account in that there are debit and credit columns. A T account, you'll remember, looks like this:

Account Name

Debit	Credit

A journal entry looks like this:

GENERAL JOURNAL   Page _____

Date	Description	Post. Ref.	Debit	Credit
Date of Trans-action				
	Account Name		*Amount*	
	Account Name			*Amount*
	Description of Transaction			

Rules for Recording Transactions in the General Journal

There are eight rules for recording transactions (journalizing) in the general journal:

(a) Each page for the period (month, year, and so on) must be in consecutive order.

(b) The date of the transaction must be placed in the Date column. The year and month are only written once on each page.

(c) The transactions are recorded daily or as they occur. There will be some days during the accounting period when transactions may not occur (for example, holidays and weekends).

(d) The debit account(s) and amount(s) are listed first. Once all the debit(s) have been recorded, the credit account(s) and amount(s) are listed. Note that the credit account is commonly indented three spaces to make observation easier. Some accountants may elect to indent using a fraction of an inch. This could be one-quarter inch, one-half inch, and so on. For consistency in presentation, this book will indent three spaces.

(e) The Posting Reference (Post. Ref.) column will be described later in this chapter.

(f) All debit(s) must equal all credit(s) for each transaction.

(g) A brief description of the transaction is made below the last account credited. This description is not indented in this book.

(h) Skip one line between entries.

To illustrate journalizing, assume that Kevin Young, Attorney at Law, started a law practice. He invested $25,000 cash in the firm on April 1, 19XX. The eight rules are keyed ((a), (b), (c), and so on) to this general journal entry as follows:

GENERAL JOURNAL   Page ____1____   (a)

Date		Description	Post. Ref.	Debit	Credit
19XX (b)					
(c) Apr.	1	Cash (d)	(e)	25 0 0 0 —	(f)
		Kevin Young, Capital			25 0 0 0 —
	(g)	Investment by Owner to Start a New Firm,			
		Kevin Young, Attorney at Law			
	(h)				

The general journal is the accounting record into which transactions are first recorded. In future chapters, we will use other journals. But for now, the general journal will be the only one used.

Recording Transactions Using the General Journal

Kevin Young, Attorney at Law, had sixteen transactions during April 19XX. These transactions are recorded in the general journal in Exhibits 3-1 and 3-2. The transactions are as follows (assume that cash is paid or received unless otherwise stated):

April 1   The owner, Kevin Young, started the firm by investing $25,000.

April 1   Paid the rent for the month, $800.

April 1   Paid for a two-year liability insurance policy, $1,200. Prepaid Insurance is debited and Cash is credited. **Prepaid Insurance** is an asset as it benefits future time periods.

April 2   Billed and collected $1,900 in legal fees.

April 3   Purchased furniture, $6,400.

April 4   Purchased $600 of office supplies on account.

April 6   Hired a secretary. No entry is required.

April 7   Received and paid a utilities bill, $100.

April 11 Received a bill for newspaper advertising, $300. Accounts Payable is credited because the bill is not yet paid.

April 14 Owner invested an additional $1,000 in the firm.

April 17 Paid a secretary for wages, $700.

April 19 Billed a customer $1,800 for legal fees.

April 22 Paid $400 to apply to the April 4 purchase.

April 24 Billed a customer $1,500 for legal fees.

April 26 Received $900 from a customer to apply to the April 19 billing.

April 29 Owner withdrew $200 for his personal use.

April 30 Paid a bill received April 11, $300. Accounts Payable is debited because the bill (a liability) is paid.

THE GENERAL LEDGER

The **general ledger** is the book that contains all the accounts of the firm. The accounts are listed numerically with Cash (101) first and Utilities

EXHIBIT 3-1
Transactions (April 1–11, 19XX): Page 1

GENERAL JOURNAL   Page _____1_____

Date		Description	Post. Ref.	Debit	Credit
19XX					
Apr.	1	Cash		25 0 0 0 —	
		Kevin Young, Capital			25 0 0 0 —
		Investment by Owner to Start a New Firm,			
		Kevin Young, Attorney at Law			
	1	Rent Expense		8 0 0 —	
		Cash			8 0 0 —
		For Month Ended April 30			
	1	Prepaid Insurance		1 2 0 0 —	
		Cash			1 2 0 0 —
		Two-year Insurance Policy			
	2	Cash		1 9 0 0 —	
		Legal Fees			1 9 0 0 —
		For Services Provided			
	3	Furniture		6 4 0 0 —	
		Cash			6 4 0 0 —
		Purchased Furniture for Cash			
	4	Office Supplies		6 0 0 —	
		Accounts Payable			6 0 0 —
		Purchased Office Supplies on Account			
	7	Utilities Expense		1 0 0 —	
		Cash			1 0 0 —
		Paid Bill for Utilities			
	11	Advertising Expense		3 0 0 —	
		Accounts Payable			3 0 0 —
		Received Advertising Bill			

EXHIBIT 3-2
Transactions (April 14–30, 19XX): Page 2

GENERAL JOURNAL Page ___2___

Date		Description	Post. Ref.	Debit	Credit
19XX					
Apr.	14	Cash		1 0 0 0 —	
		Kevin Young, Capital			1 0 0 0 —
		Additional Investment by Owner			
	17	Wages Expense		7 0 0 —	
		Cash			7 0 0 —
		Paid Wages April 6–17			
	19	Accounts Receivable		1 8 0 0 —	
		Legal Fees			1 8 0 0 —
		For Services Provided			
	22	Accounts Payable		4 0 0 —	
		Cash			4 0 0 —
		Partial Payment for April 4 Purchase			
	24	Accounts Receivable		1 5 0 0 —	
		Legal Fees			1 5 0 0 —
		For Services Provided			
	26	Cash		9 0 0 —	
		Accounts Receivable			9 0 0 —
		To Apply to April 19 Billing			
	29	Kevin Young, Drawing		2 0 0 —	
		Cash			2 0 0 —
		Withdrawal for Personal Use			
	30	Accounts Payable		3 0 0 —	
		Cash			3 0 0 —
		Paid April 11 Advertising Bill			

Expense (531) last. Of course, other accounts can be added as they are needed or anticipated. These new accounts would also be added to the chart of accounts. A typical general ledger page is presented below:

GENERAL LEDGER ACCOUNT						
Account:						Account No.
Date	Item	Post. Ref.	Debit	Credit	Balance	
					Debit	Credit

An account page in the general ledger usually has four amount columns, one each for the debit or credit transaction entry, and one each for the debit or credit balance. Also included is the Posting Reference (Post Ref.), which is used to reference the general journal to the general ledger. The Post. Ref. column is also used to reference the general ledger to the general journal. The Item column is used to explain or identify unusual transactions. Generally, there is a separate page for each account in the general ledger.

POSTING

Objective 2
Post from the general journal to the general ledger.

Posting is the process of transferring debit and credit amounts from the general journal to the general ledger. The general journal will have at a minimum one debit and one credit for each transaction. The general ledger will have either a debit or a credit for each account used in the general journal. The full transaction will appear in the general ledger but will be on separate account pages depending on the accounts used.

The posting process is illustrated in Exhibit 3-3. The first transaction, Investment of Cash by Owner, is journalized and posted to the general ledger. The rules of posting are keyed (ⓐ, ⓑ, ⓒ, and so on) to Exhibit 3-3.

Rules of Posting

1. The transaction must be properly recorded in the general journal.
2. Post one line at a time from the general journal to the general ledger starting with the first debit. In Exhibit 3-3, the first debit is Cash.

EXHIBIT 3-3
Posting to the General Ledger

GENERAL JOURNAL   ⓓ   ⓓ   Page ___1___

Date		Description	Post. Ref.	Debit	Credit
19XX					
Apr.	1	ⓐ Cash	101	25 0 0 0 — ⓒ	
		Kevin Young, Capital	301		25 0 0 0 —
		Investment by Owner to Start a New Firm,			
		Kevin Young, Attorney at Law			

ⓑ

ⓕ

GENERAL LEDGER ACCOUNTS

Account: *Cash*   Account No.   101

Date		Item	Post. Ref.	Debit	Credit	Balance Debit	Credit
19XX					ⓔ		
Apr.	1		J1	2 5 0 0 0 —		2 5 0 0 0 —	

Account: *Kevin Young, Capital*   Account No.   301

Date		Item	Post. Ref.	Debit	Credit	Balance Debit	Credit
19XX							
Apr.	1		J1		2 5 0 0 0 —		2 5 0 0 0 —

3. You then (a) turn to the proper account in the general ledger. You enter the (b) transaction date, (c) amount, and (d) journal and page number in the Post. Ref. column. "J" is used to signify the general journal. "1" means page 1 of the journal. Thus, J1 would identify page 1 of the general journal.

4. You then (e) calculate the new balance in the account. For now, do not use the Item column.

5. Upon completion of 3 and 4, go back to the general journal and enter the (f) general ledger account number in the Post. Ref. column of the general journal.

6. Then go back to the next line in the general journal and repeat the process for all the additional accounts that are recorded. In Exhibit 3-3, you would repeat the process for Kevin Young, Capital.

Review and Use of the Posting Process

Once the posting is complete, you can determine where amounts and accounts originated. Let's say that you looked at the general ledger account, Kevin Young, Capital, and you wanted to find the complete general journal entry for April 1, 19XX. The J1 in the Post. Ref. column and the Apr. 1 in the Date column would indicate a transaction on page 1 (J1) of the general journal for April 1, 19XX, (Apr. 1). The opposite would also be true. An examination of page 1 of the general journal on April 1 might lead you to inquire about Cash. The 101 in the Post. Ref. Column and Apr. 1 in the Date column would designate that a 25,000 debit was posted to the Cash account on April 1, 19XX, in the general ledger.

The general ledger for Kevin Young, Attorney at Law, is illustrated in Exhibit 3-4. This general ledger shows the account balances after the April 19XX transactions have been posted.

COMMON ERRORS

The accountant should not be misled by debits and credits alone. Account balances should also be *normal*. Assets normally have debit balances; liabilities and Capital, credit balances; Drawing, debit balance; revenues, credit balances; and expenses, debit balances. If the final balance of an account has other than a normal balance, a variety of errors could have taken place. Some of these errors include:

1. *Reversal of the original entry.* For example, a transaction that should have been recorded as a debit of 100 to Cash and a credit of 100 to

EXHIBIT 3-4
General Ledger Accounts

GENERAL LEDGER ACCOUNTS

Account: *Cash* — Account No. 101

Date		Item	Post. Ref.	Debit	Credit	Balance Debit	Balance Credit
19XX							
Apr.	1		J1	25000—		25000—	
	1		J1		800—	24200—	
	1		J1		1200—	23000—	
	2		J1	1900—		24900—	
	3		J1		6400—	18500—	
	7		J1		100—	18400—	
	14		J2	1000—		19400—	
	17		J2		700—	18700—	
	22		J2		400—	18300—	
	26		J2	900—		19200—	
	29		J2		200—	19000—	
	30		J2		300—	18700—	

Account: *Accounts Receivable* — Account No. 111

Date		Item	Post. Ref.	Debit	Credit	Balance Debit	Balance Credit
19XX							
Apr.	19		J2	1800—		1800—	
	24		J2	1500—		3300—	
	26		J2		900—	2400—	

Account: *Office Supplies* — Account No. 121

Date		Item	Post. Ref.	Debit	Credit	Balance Debit	Balance Credit
19XX							
Apr.	4		J1	600—		600—	

(continued)

(Ex. 3-4 continued)

Account: Prepaid Insurance									Account No. 131	
		Post.						Balance		
Date	Item	Ref.	Debit		Credit		Debit		Credit	
19XX										
Apr. 1		J1	1200 —				1200 —			

Account: Furniture									Account No. 141	
		Post.						Balance		
Date	Item	Ref.	Debit		Credit		Debit		Credit	
19XX										
Apr. 3		J1	6400 —				6400 —			

Account: Accounts Payable									Account No. 201	
		Post.						Balance		
Date	Item	Ref.	Debit		Credit		Debit		Credit	
19XX										
Apr. 4		J1			600 —				600 —	
11		J1			300 —				900 —	
22		J2	400 —						500 —	
30		J2	300 —						200 —	

Account: Kevin Young, Capital									Account No. 301	
		Post.						Balance		
Date	Item	Ref.	Debit		Credit		Debit		Credit	
19XX										
Apr. 1		J1			25000 —				25000 —	
14		J2			1000 —				26000 —	

(continued)

(Ex. 3-4 continued)

Account: *Kevin Young, Drawing*   **Account No.**   *311*

Date	Item	Post. Ref.	Debit	Credit	Balance Debit	Balance Credit
19XX						
Apr. 29		J2	2 0 0 —		2 0 0 —	

Account: *Legal Fees*   **Account No.**   *401*

Date	Item	Post. Ref.	Debit	Credit	Balance Debit	Balance Credit
19XX						
Apr. 2		J1		1 9 0 0 —		1 9 0 0 —
19		J2		1 8 0 0 —		3 7 0 0 —
24		J2		1 5 0 0 —		5 2 0 0 —

Account: *Wages Expense*   **Account No.**   *501*

Date	Item	Post. Ref.	Debit	Credit	Balance Debit	Balance Credit
19XX						
Apr. 17		J2	7 0 0 —		7 0 0 —	

Account: *Advertising Expense*   **Account No.**   *511*

Date	Item	Post. Ref.	Debit	Credit	Balance Debit	Balance Credit
19XX						
Apr. 11		J1	3 0 0 —		3 0 0 —	

(continued)

(Ex. 3-4 concluded)

Account: *Rent Expense*								Account No. 521	
		Post.						**Balance**	
Date	**Item**	**Ref.**	**Debit**		**Credit**		**Debit**		**Credit**
19XX									
Apr. 1		J1	8 0 0 —				8 0 0 —		

Account: *Utilities Expense*								Account No. 531	
		Post.						**Balance**	
Date	**Item**	**Ref.**	**Debit**		**Credit**		**Debit**		**Credit**
19XX									
Apr. 7		J1	1 0 0 —				1 0 0 —		

Service Fees may have been reversed. This, of course, is incorrect; but debits do equal credits.

Correction of this error. The entry was journalized incorrectly as follows:

	Debit	Credit
Service Fees	100	
Cash		100

The correct entry was the opposite. Therefore, you would correct this by the following entry:

	Debit	Credit
Cash	200	
Service Fees		200

The resulting account balances would be a debit of 100 for Cash (100 credit and 200 debit equals a 100 debit) and a credit of 100 for Service Fees (100 debit and 200 credit equals a 100 credit).

2. *Transposition or slide error.* A transposition error occurs whenever the order of digits is reversed. A transposition always results in an error divisable by 9. For example, 85 is written as 58. 85 minus 58 equals 27. 27 is divisable by 9. 27 divided by 9 equals 3. Any error divisable by 9 is a transposition error. A slide is when a decimal is incorrectly moved (for example, 9.08 is written as 90.80). *Correction of this error.* Whenever a transposition or slide error occurs, the erroneous entry should be reversed and the correct entry then entered. For example, assume that Supplies should have been debited for 7.65 and Cash should have been credited for 7.65. Instead, the following incorrect entry was made:

	Debit	Credit
Supplies	76.50	
Cash		76.50

To correct this error, the original incorrect entry is reversed as follows:

	Debit	Credit
Cash	76.50	
Supplies		76.50

And then correctly entered as follows:

	Debit	Credit
Supplies	7.65	
Cash		7.65

3. *The proper account is not used.* Suppose an entry should have been made as follows: debit Accounts Payable 200 and credit Cash 200. However, the entry was actually recorded as debit Telephone Expense 200 and credit Cash 200. This is not correct, but debits do equal credits. *Correction of this error.* The entry was journalized incorrectly as follows:

	Debit	Credit
Telephone Expense	200	
Cash		200

The correct entry was a debit to Accounts Payable for 200 and a credit to Cash for 200. Since Cash is correct, only Accounts Payable is corrected, as follows:

	Debit	Credit
Accounts Payable	200	
Telephone Expense		200

The resulting account balances would be a credit of 200 for Cash, a 200 debit to Accounts Payable, and Telephone Expense would be eliminated (200 debit and 200 credit equals 0).

There are many ways to make errors when recording and posting transactions. But the best way to avoid such errors is to be careful while you work.

THE TRIAL BALANCE

Objective 3
Prepare a trial balance from the general ledger.

We briefly examined the **trial balance** in Chapter 2. Let's now examine this topic in more detail. The trial balance is prepared from the final account balances in the general ledger at a certain date. A trial balance can be prepared at any time, but most often it is done at the end of the accounting period.

The purpose of the trial balance is two-fold: first, to make sure that total debits equal total credits. Financial statements cannot be prepared unless total debits equal total credits. If debits do not equal credits, then any error(s) must be found and corrected. Second, we use the trial balance to insure that account balances are "normal." Sometimes an entry or entries are made to incorrect accounts but are in balance (debits equal credits). If this happens, the accounts must be analyzed to see if an error or errors were made. Then the error(s) must be corrected.
The normal balances are as follows:

Account	Normal Balance
Assets	Debits
Liabilities	Credits
Capital	Credit
Drawing	Debit
Revenues	Credits
Expenses	Debits

Preparing the Trial Balance

The trial balance is prepared by listing the accounts in chart-of-accounts number order, the same sequence we used in the general ledger. Any account that has a zero balance is not listed. The trial balance is prepared after all transactions are posted to the general ledger. The trial balance for Kevin Young, Attorney at Law, is illustrated in Exhibit 3-5.

EXHIBIT 3-5
Preparation of a Trial Balance

Kevin Young, Attorney at Law
Trial Balance
April 30, 19XX

Accounts	Debit	Credit
Cash	18 7 0 0 —	
Accounts Receivable	2 4 0 0 —	
Office Supplies	6 0 0 —	
Prepaid Insurance	1 2 0 0 —	
Furniture	6 4 0 0 —	
Accounts Payable		2 0 0 —
Kevin Young, Capital		26 0 0 0 —
Kevin Young, Drawing	2 0 0 —	
Legal Fees		5 2 0 0 —
Wages Expense	7 0 0 —	
Advertising Expense	3 0 0 —	
Rent Expense	8 0 0 —	
Utilities Expense	1 0 0 —	
Totals	31 4 0 0 —	31 4 0 0 —

CHAPTER REVIEW

1. **Record transactions in the general journal (pp. 56–62).**
   The general journal is a book of original entry. Making transaction entries in a general journal is called journalizing. There are eight rules for recording transactions in the general journal.

2. **Post from the general journal to the general ledger (pp. 62–70).**
   Posting is the process of transferring debit and credit amounts from the general journal to the general ledger. There are six rules of posting.

3. **Prepare a trial balance from the general ledger (pp. 70–71).**
   The trial balance is prepared from the final account balances in the general ledger at a certain date. Although a trial balance can be prepared at any time during the accounting period, this is usually done at the end of the accounting period.

GLOSSARY

Chart of Accounts	Detailed listing of all the accounts a firm uses for recording transactions.
General Journal	Book of original entry.
General Ledger	Book that contains all the accounts of the firm.
Journalizing	Process of recording transactions in a journal.
Posting	Process of transferring amounts from a journal to the general ledger.
Prepaid Expense	Prepayment of an expense that is classified as an asset. Benefits future time periods.
Slide	When a decimal is incorrectly moved.
Transposition	The order of the digits is reversed in a number. This error is divisible by 9.
Trial Balance	Listing of the final balances of the general ledger accounts in chart-of-accounts number order (first introduced in Chapter 2).

SELF-TEST QUESTIONS FOR REVIEW

(Answers are on p. 83.)

1. In a chart of accounts, number 521 would most likely refer to
   a. Accounts Payable.
   b. Homer Smith, Drawing.
   c. Legal Fees.
   d. Rent Expense.

2. A description for a transaction reads: For Services Provided. Which of the following accounts could be debited?
   a. Accounts Receivable
   b. Legal Fees
   c. Accounts Payable
   d. Advertising Expense

3. Which of the following accounts could be listed in the debit column of a trial balance?
   a. Accounts Payable
   b. Bill O'Malley, Capital
   c. Yolanda Vega, Drawing
   d. Legal Fees

4. A. K. Lim invests a library in his law firm. Which of the following is correct?
   a. Credit Library
   b. Credit A. K. Lim, Capital
   c. Credit A. K. Lim, Drawing
   d. Credit Accounts Payable

5. A firm debits Accounts Payable. Which of the following transactions could be correct?
   a. Paid wages.
   b. Received utilities bill.
   c. Withdrawal by owner.
   d. Paid previous advertising bill.

PRACTICAL REVIEW PROBLEM

Objective 3

Preparing a Trial Balance   Doris Newly, CPA, lists her general ledger accounts in alphabetical order. The accounts and account balances (all balances are normal) for October 31, 19XX, are as follows:

Accounts Payable	$ 1,020
Accounts Receivable	2,310
Advertising Expense	630
Auditing Fees	5,480
Cash	18,690
Equipment	5,430
Furniture	3,900
Doris Newly, Capital	29,260
Doris Newly, Drawing	380
Office Supplies	540
Prepaid Insurance	1,500
Rent Expense	930
Utilities Expense	140
Wages Expense	1,310

REQUIRED

Prepare a trial balance in proper account order (assets listed first, followed by liabilities, and so on).

ANSWER TO PRACTICAL REVIEW PROBLEM

Doris Newly, CPA

Trial Balance

October 31, 19XX

Accounts	Debit	Credit
Cash	18 6 9 0 —	
Accounts Receivable	2 3 1 0 —	
Office Supplies	5 4 0 —	
Prepaid Insurance	1 5 0 0 —	
Furniture	3 9 0 0 —	
Equipment	5 4 3 0 —	
Accounts Payable		1 0 2 0 —
Doris Newly, Capital		29 2 6 0 —
Doris Newly, Drawing	3 8 0 —	
Auditing Fees		5 4 8 0 —
Wages Expense	1 3 1 0 —	
Advertising Expense	6 3 0 —	
Rent Expense	9 3 0 —	
Utilities Expense	1 4 0 —	
Totals	35 7 6 0 —	35 7 6 0 —

DISCUSSION QUESTIONS

Q 3-1   How is a general journal somewhat like a T account? Define general journal and journalizing.

Q 3-2   Name the eight rules for recording transactions in the general journal.

Q 3-3   Give the debit(s) and credit(s) for each of the following transactions: (a) owner started firm by investing cash; (b) paid rent for the month; (c) paid for a three-year insurance policy; and (d) purchased office supplies for cash and on account.

Q 3-4   Give the debit(s) and credit(s) for each of the following transactions: (a) received a utilities bill; (b) paid for a previously received advertising bill; (c) owner invested additional cash in the firm; and (d) purchased office equipment for cash and on account.

Q 3-5   What is a chart of accounts? What do the account numbers indicate? Why is the chart of accounts never static?

Q 3-6   What is the general ledger? How are accounts listed in the general ledger?

Q 3-7   Name the seven columns for a general ledger account page.

Q 3-8   What is posting? Name the six rules for posting.

Q 3-9   Briefly explain how the following errors could have taken place and explain how the errors are corrected: (a) reversal of the original entry; (b) transposition or slide error; and (c) use of wrong account.

Q 3-10   Name the two purposes of the trial balance. How is the trial balance prepared?

EXERCISES

Objective 1   E 3-1   **Completing Transactions**   Complete the following transactions:

	Debit	Credit
a. Cash	10,000	
_____(a)_____		10,000

Investment by Owner to Start a New Firm, Eddie Greer, Attorney at Law

b. _____(b)_____	4,000	
Accounts Payable		4,000

Received Advertising Bill

c. Cash	6,000	
Legal Fees		6,000
_____(c)_____		

Objective 1

E 3-2   Designing Chart of Accounts   J. G. Patel is starting a law firm. She is in the process of designing a chart of accounts.
a. Name at least five asset accounts that she could use.
b. Name at least one liability account that she could use.
c. Name two owner's equity accounts that she could use.
d. Name at least one revenue account that she could use.
e. Name at least four expense accounts that she could use.

Objective 1

E 3-3   Reviewing T Accounts   Record the following transactions in T account form (see Chapter 2 if you need help):
a. The owner, John Tipton, invested $17,000.
b. Purchased office supplies on account, $4,000.
c. Paid creditor, $3,000.
d. Paid a secretary $1,000 for two weeks of work.

Objective 1

E 3-4   Recording Transactions   Record the following transactions in the general journal for 19XX, page 1:

March 1   The owner Gene Roark, invested $15,000 to start his new business called Gene Roark, Graphics Designer.

March 5   Purchased office funiture for $9,000 on account.

March 7   Hired a secretary.

March 11   Owner withdrew $1,000 for his personal use.

March 15   Billed customer $6,000 for design fees.

March 20   Paid for a four-year insurance policy, $3,000.

March 26   Paid rent for the month, $4,000.

March 31   Owner invested an additional $5,000.

Objective 2

E 3-5   Posting Transactions   Post the transactions in E 3-4 to the general ledger using the following chart-of-accounts numbers:

Cash 101; Accounts Receivable 111; Prepaid Insurance 121; Office Furniture 131; Accounts Payable 201; Gene Roark, Capital 301; Gene Roark, Drawing 311; Design Fees 401; Rent Expense 501.

Objective 3

E 3-6   Completing a Trial Balance   Complete the following trial balance for Kimberly Green, Computer Consultant (June 30, 19XX):

	(a)	
	(b)	
	(c)	
(d)	Debit	(e)
Cash	34,000	
Accounts Receivable	4,000	
Office Supplies	2,000	
Accounts Payable		5,000
(f) , Capital		(g)
(h) , Drawing	1,000	
Consulting Fees		12,000
Wages Expense	8,000	
(i)	(j)	(k)

Objective 2

E 3-7 **Correcting Errors** Use a general journal to correct the following errors:

a. A transaction that should have been recorded as a debit of 569 to Cash and a credit of 569 to Service Fees was reversed.

b. Office Supplies should have been debited for 9.63. Cash should have been credited for 9.63. Instead, the following incorrect entry was made:

	Debit	Credit
Office Supplies	96.30	
Cash		96.30

c. This entry was incorrectly journalized as:

	Debit	Credit
Advertising Expense	783	
Cash		783

The correct entry was a debit to Accounts Payable for 783 and a credit to Cash for 783.

Objective 3

E 3-8 **Preparing a Trial Balance** Prepare a trial balance for Ralph Polinski, Tennis Instructor. He had the following general ledger account balances at October 31, 19XX. All account balances are normal (assets are debits, liabilities are credits, and so on):

Cash, $71,000; Accounts Receivable, $16,000; Store Supplies, $11,000; Office Furniture, $21,000; Library, $3,000; Accounts Payable, $18,000; Ralph Polinski, Capital, $100,000; Ralph Polinski, Drawing, $2,000; Tennis Fees, $26,000; Wages Expense, $12,000; Advertising Expense, $7,000; Rent Expense, $1,000.

PROBLEM SET A

Objective 1

P 3-1A **Recording Transactions**   Cheng Lui owns Lui Advertising Service. She had the following transactions for March 19XX:

March 1	The owner started the firm by investing $98,000.
March 1	Paid the rent for the month, $10,000.
March 1	Paid for a two-year liability insurance policy, $6,000.
March 3	Billed and collected $12,000 in advertising fees.
March 4	Purchased furniture, $31,000.
March 5	Purchased $9,000 of office supplies on account.
March 7	Hired a secretary.
March 8	Received and paid a utilities bill, $2,000.
March 12	Received a bill for newspaper advertising, $13,000.
March 15	Owner invested an additional $5,000 in the firm.
March 20	Billed a customer $8,000 for advertising fees.
March 23	Paid $3,000 to apply to the March 5 purchase.
March 24	Paid a secretary for wages, $1,000 (March 7–24).
March 25	Received $4,000 from a customer to apply to the March 20 billing.
March 28	Owner withdrew $10,000 for her personal use.
March 31	Paid a bill received March 12.

REQUIRED
Record the March transactions in a general journal, pages 1 and 2.

Objective 2

P 3-2A **Posting Transactions**   You are hired as the accountant for Foteh Investment Advisors. The accountant you replaced recorded transactions in the general journal and included the proper general ledger account numbers in the Post. Ref. column of the general journal. However, he did not post to the general ledger. These transactions are:

GENERAL JOURNAL

Page ___1___

Date		Description	Post. Ref.	Debit	Credit
19XX					
Nov.	1	Cash	101	18 6 0 0 —	
		A.J. Foteh, Capital	301		18 6 0 0 —
		Investment by Owner to Start a New Firm,			
		Foteh Investment Advisors			
	1	Rent Expense	521	2 4 0 0 —	
		Cash	101		2 4 0 0 —
		For Month Ended November 30			
	2	Prepaid Insurance	131	1 2 0 0 —	
		Cash	101		1 2 0 0 —
		Four-year Insurance Policy			
	4	Accounts Receivable	111	6 8 0 0 —	
		Advisement Fees	401		6 8 0 0 —
		For Services Provided			
	7	Advertising Expense	511	3 7 0 0 —	
		Accounts Payable	201		3 7 0 0 —
		Received Advertising Bill			

REQUIRED

1. Using the general ledger account numbers in the Post. Ref. column, write the account names and account numbers in the general ledger. List Cash (101) first, followed by Accounts Receivable (111), and so on.
2. Post the week's transactions to the general ledger. Include all posting references in the general ledger.

Objective 3

P 3-3A **Preparing a Trial Balance** Alvin Teng, Graphics Consultant, lists his general ledger accounts in alphabetical order. The accounts and account balances (all balances are normal) for December 31, 19XX are as follows:

Accounts Payable	$ 23,890	Office Supplies	$ 3,900
Accounts Receivable	78,090	Prepaid Insurance	2,640
Advertising Expense	10,560	Rent Expense	1,560
Cash	54,120	Alvin Teng, Capital	166,180
Equipment	34,890	Alvin Teng, Drawing	4,560
Furniture	11,780	Utilities Expense	980
Graphics Fees	18,900	Wages Expense	5,890

REQUIRED

Prepare a trial balance in proper account order (assets listed first, followed by liabilities, and so on).

Objectives 1, 2 and 3

P 3-4A   Comprehensive Chapter Review Problem   Powers Syms owns Syms Advertising Service. The firm's chart of accounts is as follows:

Syms Advertising Service
Chart of Accounts

Assets (10–19)		**Owner's Equity (30–39)**	
11	Cash	31	Powers Syms, Capital
12	Accounts Receivable	32	Powers Syms, Drawing
13	Office Supplies		
14	Prepaid Insurance		**Revenues (40–49)**
15	Equipment	41	Advertising Fees
Liabilities (20–29)		**Expenses (50–59)**	
21	Accounts Payable	51	Wages Expense
		52	Advertising Expense
		53	Rent Expense
		54	Utilities Expense

Powers had the following transactions for March 19XX:

March 1   Powers started Syms Advertising Service by investing $74,920.

March 1   Paid for a two-year insurance policy, $960.

March 1   Paid rent for the month, $1,230.

March 2   Received a utilities bill, $630.

March 3   Hired an advertising assistant.

March 4   Billed and collected $2,980 in advertising fees.

March 6   Purchased equipment on account, $6,900.

March 11   Purchased $850 of office supplies. Paid $340 in cash with the remainder on account.

March 12   Paid the March 2 utilities bill.

March 12   Billed a customer $2,780 for advertising fees.

March 13   Received a bill for advertising, $780.

March 16   Owner invested an additional $1,090 in the firm.

March 19   Paid $200 to apply to the March 11 purchase.

March 23   Received $2,000 to apply to the March 12 billing.

March 26   Received an advertising bill, $510.

March 28   Paid wages, $820 (March 3–28).

March 30   Paid $250 to apply to the March 26 advertising bill.

March 31   Owner withdrew $1,900 for his personal use.

REQUIRED

1. Record the March transactions in a general journal, pages 1 and 2.
2. Post the March transactions to the general ledger (use the chart of accounts to first write the accounts and account numbers in the general ledger).
3. Prepare a trial balance.

PROBLEM SET B

Objective 1   P 3-1B   **Recording Transactions**   Bill Ray owns Ray Advertising Service. He had the following transactions for October 19XX:

October 1   The owner started the firm by investing $106,000.

October 1   Paid the rent for the month, $8,000.

October 1   Paid for a two-year liability insurance policy, $5,000.

October 2   Billed and collected $7,000 in advertising fees.

October 5   Purchased equipment, $19,000.

October 7   Purchased $4,000 of office supplies on account.

October 8   Hired a secretary.

October 10   Received and paid a utilities bill, $1,000.

October 13   Received a bill for newspaper advertising, $17,000.

October 17   Owner invested an additional $12,000 in the firm.

October 23   Billed a customer $11,000 for advertising fees.

October 25   Paid $2,000 to apply to the October 7 purchase.

October 26   Paid a secretary for wages, $1,000 (October 8–26).

October 27   Received $6,000 from a customer to apply to the October 23 billing.

October 29   Owner withdrew $3,000 for his personal use.

October 31   Paid a bill received October 13.

REQUIRED

Record the October transactions in a general journal, pages 1 and 2.

Objective 2   P 3-2B   **Posting Transactions**   You are hired as the accountant for Brannigan Chimney Sweepers. The accountant you replaced recorded transactions in the general journal and included the proper general ledger account numbers in the Post. Ref. column of the general journal. However, she did not post to the general ledger. These transactions are:

GENERAL JOURNAL   Page _____1_____

Date		Description	Post. Ref.	Debit	Credit
19XX					
Sep.	1	Cash	101	21 8 0 0 —	
		Mary Brannigan, Capital	301		21 8 0 0 —
		Investment by Owner to Start a New Firm,			
		Brannigan Chimney Sweepers			
	1	Rent Expense	521	3 1 0 0 —	
		Cash	101		3 1 0 0 —
		For Month Ended September 30			
	3	Prepaid Insurance	131	1 6 0 0 —	
		Cash	101		1 6 0 0 —
		Five-year Insurance Policy			
	5	Accounts Receivable	111	7 3 0 0 —	
		Sweeping Fees	401		7 3 0 0 —
		For Services Provided			
	7	Advertising Expense	511	4 9 0 0 —	
		Accounts Payable	201		4 9 0 0 —
		Received Advertising Bill			

REQUIRED

1. Using the general ledger account numbers in the Post. Ref. column, write the account names and account numbers in the general ledger. List Cash (101) first, followed by Accounts Receivable (111), and so on.
2. Post the week's transactions to the general ledger. Include all posting references in the general ledger.

Objective 3

P 3-3B **Preparing a Trial Balance** T. J. Wright, Attorney at Law, lists her general ledger accounts in alphabetical order. The accounts and account balances (all balances are normal) for November 30, 19XX, are as follows:

Accounts Payable	$ 87,450	Office Supplies	$ 11,890
Accounts Receivable	97,670	Prepaid Insurance	5,900
Advertising Expense	14,370	Rent Expense	2,550
Attorney Fees	29,780	Utilities Expense	870
Cash	89,450	Wages Expense	7,900
Equipment	70,670	T. J. Wright, Capital	232,260
Furniture	37,380	T. J. Wright, Drawing	10,840

REQUIRED
Prepare a trial balance in proper account order (assets listed first, followed by liabilities, and so on).

Objectives 1, 2, and 3

P 3-4B   Comprehensive Chapter Review Problem   Billie Ayers owns Ayers Advertising Service. The firm's chart of accounts is as follows:

Ayers Advertising Service
Chart of Accounts

Assets (10–19)

11	Cash
12	Accounts Receivable
13	Office Supplies
14	Prepaid Insurance
15	Furniture

Liabilities (20–29)

21	Accounts Payable

Owner's Equity (30–39)

31	Billie Ayers, Capital
32	Billie Ayers, Drawing

Revenues (40–49)

41	Advertising Fees

Expenses (50–59)

51	Wages Expense
52	Advertising Expense
53	Rent Expense
54	Utilities Expense

Billie had the following transactions for April 19XX:

April 1	Billie started Ayers Advertising Service by investing $59,670.
April 1	Paid rent for the month, $1,370.
April 1	Paid for a two-year insurance policy, $870.
April 2	Hired an advertising assistant.
April 3	Received an advertising bill, $570.
April 5	Billed and collected $3,890 in advertising fees.
April 5	Purchased furniture on account, $7,900.
April 10	Purchased $910 of office supplies. Paid $520 in cash with the remainder on account.
April 11	Paid the April 3 advertising bill.
April 12	Billed a customer $3,940 for advertising fees.
April 13	Received a bill for utilities, $90.
April 16	Owner invested an additional $1,230 in the firm.
April 20	Paid $150 to apply to the April 10 purchase.
April 24	Received $2,670 to apply to the April 12 billing.
April 27	Received a utilities bill, $120.

April 28   Paid wages, $1,130 (April 2–28).

April 29   Paid $70 to apply to the April 27 utilities bill.

April 30   Owner withdrew $2,190 for her personal use.

REQUIRED

1. Record the April transactions in a general journal, pages 1 and 2.
2. Post the April transactions to the general ledger (use the chart of accounts to first write the accounts and account numbers in the general ledger).
3. Prepare a trial balance.

ANSWERS TO SELF-TEST QUESTIONS

1. d   2. a   3. c   4. b   5. d

4

Calculating Adjustments and Completing the Worksheet

His brow is wet with honest sweat,
And he looks the whole world in the face,
For he owes not any man.

HENRY WADSWORTH LONGFELLOW

LEARNING OBJECTIVES

After reading this chapter, discussing the questions, and working the exercises and problems, you will be able to do the following:

1. Explain the matching concept (pp. 86–87).

2. Calculate adjustments (pp. 87–92).

3. Complete the worksheet (pp. 92–104).

■n Chapter 3 we recorded the April 19XX transactions for Kevin Young, Attorney at Law, in a general journal. We then posted the transactions from the general journal to the general ledger and prepared a trial balance. In this chapter we will examine the matching concept, calculate adjustments, and complete a worksheet. Let's begin with a discussion of the accounting cycle.

The **accounting cycle** contains the basic steps that must be followed in specific order for each accounting period. The following steps (in order) represent the accounting cycle:

1. Analyze transactions from source documents (Chapters 1, 2, and 3).
2. Record the transactions in a journal (Chapter 3).
3. Post to the general ledger accounts (Chapter 3).
4. Prepare a trial balance (Chapters 2 and 3).
5. Adjust the general ledger accounts (Chapter 4).
6. Complete the worksheet (Chapter 4).
7. Prepare financial statements (Chapter 5).
8. Journalize and post adjusting entries (Chapter 5).
9. Journalize and post closing entries (Chapter 6).
10. Prepare a post-closing trial balance (Chapter 6).

We will concentrate on steps 5 and 6 in this chapter—adjusting the general ledger accounts and completing the worksheet.

THE MATCHING CONCEPT

Objective 1
Explain the
matching concept.

Many individuals and small businesses operate on a **cash basis** of accounting, where revenues are recorded only when cash is received and expenses are recorded only when cash is paid. Tax laws require that many individuals and some small businesses function on the cash basis. However, the cash basis is not GAAP. Generally accepted accounting principles *and* the **matching concept** require a proper matching of revenues and expenses in a given time period (accounting period). Therefore, GAAP dictates that revenues must be recognized when earned and expenses must be recognized when incurred. This recognition of revenues and expenses is the basis for the matching concept.

Cash Basis

Not all revenues and expenses are realized into cash for an accounting period. How many times have you heard, "The check is in the mail"? Even though you have earned the money, you haven't received it.

When using the cash basis, revenues earned but not yet received in cash would not be recorded. Expenses incurred but not yet paid would also not be recorded. For example, suppose that employees are always paid on Fridays. If the end of the accounting period falls on Thursday, then the next accounting period will receive a portion of this period's expense. The expense will only be acknowledged if cash is paid.

Accrual Basis

The accrual basis of accounting solves the problems caused by the cash basis and is GAAP. Revenues are recorded when earned. A revenue can be recorded without the actual receipt of cash, which may be received in future periods. One example would be the billing of a customer for services performed.

Expenses are also recorded when incurred. Whenever an asset is consumed or used up to support a revenue, an expense exists. Like a revenue, the expense does not have to be paid in that particular period to be considered an expense. One example would be the receipt of a utilities bill which will be paid later.

The accrual basis of accounting is used throughout this book, unless stated otherwise. Accrual accounting requires that general ledger accounts be brought to their proper balances at the end of an accounting period. This process is known as *calculating adjustments* or *adjusting entries.*

ADJUSTING ENTRIES

Objective 2
Calculate
adjustments.

Adjusting entries are necessary to insure that there is a proper matching of revenues and expenses for an accounting period. Sometimes a revenue or expense is not known or may not be determinable in the normal course of business for an accounting period. That is, the transaction has not been journalized and posted with the other transactions of the accounting period. Adjustments provide a means of placing assets, liabilities, owner's equity, revenue, and expense accounts at their proper balances for the accounting period.

Certain correcting entries (see Chapter 3) are sometimes made during the adjustment process. Correcting entries are transactions that rectify or correct errors that have been made. In the case of adjusting entries, no errors were made. The necessary information was not available to prepare a journal entry until after the accounting period was closed. An accounting period is opened on a particular day and closed on a particular day. For example, if you prepared the accounting records for the month of May, then the accounting records would be opened May 1 and closed May 31. Any transactions that were not entered in the accounting records during this period, but that apply to the month of May, would be entered as adjusting entries.

TYPES OF ADJUSTING ENTRIES

Remember that the accrual basis of accounting requires that revenues be recorded when earned and expenses be recorded when incurred. Adjusting entries allow you to apply the accrual basis of accounting to transactions that cover two or more accounting periods.

There are two types of adjusting entries, deferrals and accruals. The deferral type of adjusting entry is used to postpone the recognition of a revenue already received or an expense already paid. An accrual type of adjusting entry is used to recognize an *unrecorded* revenue that has been earned or an *unrecorded* expense that has been incurred.

Adjustments for Kevin Young, Attorney at Law

Four adjusting entries are necessary to place the general ledger accounts at their proper balances for the accounting period April 1–30, 19XX. The adjustments and types of adjustments are as follows (the adjustments are keyed a, b, c, and d):

Adjustment	Type of Adjustment
a. Adjust Office Supplies	Deferral–Expense
b. Adjust Prepaid Insurance	Deferral–Expense
c. Adjust Furniture	Deferral–Expense
d. Adjust Wages Expense	Accrual–Expense

Adjust Office Supplies (a)   On April 4, 19XX, Kevin Young purchased $600 of office supplies, but not all were to be used in the month of April. Kevin wanted a certain amount of supplies on hand so no one would have to spend productive time buying supplies one item at a time as they were needed. On April 30, 19XX, a physical count was made. The actual office supplies on hand totaled $390. But, because this balance was not available until after the accounting records were closed, an adjustment was necessary. A brief illustration to show the accounting treatment follows:

April 1, 19XX, Beginning Balance	$ 0
Add: April 4, 19XX, Purchase	600
Office Supplies Available to be Used	$600
Less: April 30, 19XX, Ending Balance	390
Office Supplies Used or Expensed	$210

Remember, these office supplies were used or consumed to support revenues. Without pencils, pens, paper, staples, and so on, the firm would not be able to provide services (revenues) to its customers. Adjustments are not journalized and posted until the worksheet is complete so the accounts can be reviewed, so preparing T accounts is a good method for organizing this adjusting entry. Let's examine the adjustment using T accounts:

Office Supplies Expense		Office Supplies	
(a) adjusting 210		bal. 600	(a) adjusting 210
		new bal. 390	

Office Supplies Expense is an expense account that represents the office supplies used during April. The $390 debit balance in Office Supplies is the amount of supplies on hand and ready to be used.

Adjust Prepaid Insurance (b)   On April 1, 19XX, Kevin paid $1,200 for a two-year liability insurance policy. The payment of the insurance policy was originally recorded as a debit to Prepaid Insurance and a credit to Cash. Prepaid Insurance is classified as an asset account because it benefits future accounting periods. The benefits are allocated to the future accounting periods by adjusting entries. At the end of the month (or accounting period) the Prepaid Insurance adjustment is calculated by dividing the cost of the asset by the total number of accounting periods:

$1,200 ÷ 24 months (2 years) = $50 per month

Let's organize the adjusting entry with T accounts:

Insurance Expense		Prepaid Insurance	
(b) adjusting 50		bal. 1,200	(b) adjusting 50
		new bal. 1,150	

Insurance Expense is an expense account that represents the amount of prepaid insurance that was used during April 19XX. The $1,150 debit balance in Prepaid Insurance is the amount of prepaid insurance that remains to be used (expensed).

Adjust Furniture (c)   Fixed material assets, such as furniture, automobiles, computers, and so on, that benefit more than one accounting period are usually depreciated. **Depreciation** is the systematic and rational allocation of the cost of certain tangible assets over their useful lives. A *fixed material asset* is an asset that is tangible (can be seen or felt). In order to be classified as a fixed asset, the asset will have benefitted more than one accounting period and will meet certain cost levels set by the firm. For example, a small firm may set a cost level of $100. That small firm will classify all assets benefitting more than one accounting period and costing more than $100 as fixed assets. A larger firm may decide that $1,000 is the minimum for classifying assets benefitting more than one period as fixed. These two criteria, cost and time-benefitted, must both be met in order to classify an asset as fixed. The firm Kevin Young, Attorney at Law, depreciates all fixed material assets that cost more than $200. Thus, any fixed material assets that cost less than $200 will be expensed in the accounting period in which the asset is purchased.

There are many methods of depreciating assets. The one used in this chapter is called the **straight-line method.** The straight-line method allocates the same amount of depreciation to each accounting period. The formula is as follows:

$$\text{Depreciation per Accounting Period} = \frac{\text{Cost} - \text{Salvage Value}}{\text{Useful Life}}$$

Cost is the total amount paid to acquire and prepare an asset for use. **Salvage value** is an estimate of the amount an asset can be sold for after a firm is done using it. **Useful life** is an estimate of the time the asset can be productively and economically utilized.

On April 3, 19XX, Kevin Young purchased furniture at a cost of $6,400. He estimates that the furniture will have a salvage value of $1,000 after three years (36 months) of useful life. The calculation for one month of depreciation expense is as follows:

$$\text{Depreciation Expense for One Month} = \frac{\$6,400 - \$1,000}{36 \text{ months}} = \frac{\$5,400}{36}$$

$$= \$150 \text{ per Month}$$

Using T accounts, the adjusting entry is organized as follows:

Depreciation Expense, Furniture		Accumulated Depreciation, Furniture	
(c) adjusting 150			(c) adjusting 150

Depreciation Expense, Furniture is an expense account that represents the decline in the useful life of the furniture. Accumulated Depreciation, Furniture is a contra asset account—an account whose normal balance is contrary or "contra" to the debit balance of furniture. **Accumulated depreciation** is the total depreciation that the firm has taken (expensed) since the purchase of the asset. Accumulated depreciation is subtracted from the cost of the asset to arrive at its **book value**. Book value is what the asset is worth *on the books,* which is not necessarily what it can be sold for. In Exhibit 4-1, Furniture and Accumulated Depreciation, Furniture are shown on a partial balance sheet for Kevin Young, Attorney at Law. Book value is $6,250 ($6,400 − $150 = $6,250).

Adjust Wages Expense (d)   Kevin Young pays his secretary every two weeks on Friday. The secretary was hired April 6, 19XX, and was paid April 17, 19XX. A calendar for the month of April is as follows:

April 19XX

(S)	(M)	(T)	(W)	(T)	(F)	(S)
			1	2	3	4
5	(6)	7	8	9	10	11
12	13	14	15	16	(17)	18
19	20	21	22	23	24	25
26	27	28	29	30	(May 1)	

Hired Secretary → (6)

Paydays

The next payday is Friday, May 1, 19XX. Wages Expense of $630 has not been recorded for the second pay period in April (April 18–30). This expense has been incurred in April 19XX so it must be recorded in April

EXHIBIT 4-1
Book Value of Assets

Kevin Young, Attorney at Law
Balance Sheet (partial)
April 30, 19XX

Assets			
Furniture	$6 4 0 0 —		
Less: Accumulated Depreciation	1 5 0 —	$6 2 5 0 —	

19XX using adjusting entries. Let's organize this adjusting entry with T accounts:

Wages Expense			Wages Payable	
bal.	700			
(d) adjusting	630		(d) adjusting	630
new bal.	1,330			

Wages Expense is debited $630 to record wages expense incurred in April 19XX. A liability account, Wages Payable, is credited $630 to record the obligation to pay wages expense in the future (Friday, May 1, 19XX, is the next payday).

THE TEN-COLUMN WORKSHEET

Objective 3
Complete the worksheet.

The worksheet is a tool used by accountants to compile the information needed for the preparation of financial statements. It is not part of the firm's formal accounting records, but instead is an internal document. A ten-column worksheet has ten columns. There are debit and credit columns for the Trial Balance (unadjusted), Adjustments, Adjusted Trial Balance, Income Statement, and Balance Sheet.

Steps in Completing the Worksheet

Step 1: Heading   In Exhibit 4-2 the worksheet has a three-part heading which includes (in this order) the name of the firm, the term, "Worksheet," and the period of time for which the worksheet is prepared.

Step 2: Trial Balance (Unadjusted)   In Exhibit 4-3 the unadjusted trial balance is entered in the Trial Balance columns. The trial balance accounts and amounts are taken from the trial balance prepared in Chapter 3. This is step four of the accounting cycle. The columns are underlined and added. If they are equal, the columns are double underlined. Once you are sure that total debits equal total credits you can go on to the next step.

Step 3: Adjustments   The adjusting entries (as calculated earlier in this chapter) are entered in the Adjustments columns as shown in Exhibit 4-4. The adjustments are keyed (a), (b), (c), and (d) to make it easier to identify all amounts relating to a particular adjustment. If any accounts not appearing in the unadjusted Trial Balance columns require adjustment, their titles are listed as needed below the accounts already recorded. The debit and credit columns are underlined and added. The totals are calculated and double underlined, if equal. Once you have verified that total debits equal total credits you can go on to the next step.

Step 4: Adjusted Trial Balance   The Trial Balance amounts, plus or minus the Adjustment amounts, are extended to the Adjusted Trial Balance in Exhibit 4-5. The amounts in the Adjusted Trial Balance columns are the account balances reflecting the combination of the Trial Balance and the Adjustments. These amounts are determined by combining horizontally, line by line, the amounts in the first four amount (debit and credit) columns.

 To illustrate this process, let's review the first three lines of Exhibit 4-5. The first line shows Cash with a debit of $18,700 in the Trial Balance. There is no adjustment for Cash, so the $18,700 debit is extended to the debit column of the Adjusted Trial Balance. The same is true for the second line, Accounts Receivable. Office Supplies (line 3) begins with a debit of $600 in the Trial Balance. A $210 adjustment appears in the credit column of the Adjustments. The $210 credit is subtracted from the $600 debit. The $390 debit difference ($600 debit − $210 credit = $390 debit) is extended to the debit column in the Adjusted Trial Balance.

EXHIBIT
Heading of a

Kevin Young,
Work
For the Month Ended

		Trial Balance			Adjustments	
Account		Debit	Credit		Debit	Credit

EXHIBIT
Trial Balance Columns

Kevin Young,
Work
For the Month Ended

Account	Trial Balance Debit	Trial Balance Credit	Adjustments Debit	Adjustments Credit
Cash	18 7 0 0 —			
Accounts Receivable	2 4 0 0 —			
Office Supplies	6 0 0 —			
Prepaid Insurance	1 2 0 0 —			
Furniture	6 4 0 0 —			
Accounts Payable		2 0 0 —		
Kevin Young, Capital		26 0 0 0 —		
Kevin Young, Drawing	2 0 0 —			
Legal Fees		5 2 0 0 —		
Wages Expense	7 0 0 —			
Advertising Expense	3 0 0 —			
Rent Expense	8 0 0 —			
Utilities Expense	1 0 0 —			
Totals	31 4 0 0 —	31 4 0 0 —		

4-2
Ten-column Worksheet

Attorney at Law

sheet

April 30, 19XX

Adjusted Trial Balance		Income Statement		Balance Sheet	
Debit	Credit	Debit	Credit	Debit	Credit

4-3
of a Worksheet

Attorney at Law

sheet

April 30, 19XX

Adjusted Trial Balance		Income Statement		Balance Sheet	
Debit	Credit	Debit	Credit	Debit	Credit

EXHIBIT
Adjustments Columns

Kevin Young,
Work
For the Month Ended

Account	Trial Balance		Adjustments	
	Debit	Credit	Debit	Credit
Cash	18 7 0 0 —			
Accounts Receivable	2 4 0 0 —			
Office Supplies	6 0 0 —			(a) 2 1 0 —
Prepaid Insurance	1 2 0 0 —			(b) 5 0 —
Furniture	6 4 0 0 —			
Accounts Payable		2 0 0 —		
Kevin Young, Capital		26 0 0 0 —		
Kevin Young, Drawing	2 0 0 —			
Legal Fees		5 2 0 0 —		
Wages Expense	7 0 0 —		(d) 6 3 0 —	
Advertising Expense	3 0 0 —			
Rent Expense	8 0 0 —			
Utilities Expense	1 0 0 —			
Totals	31 4 0 0 —	31 4 0 0 —		
Office Supplies Expense			(a) 2 1 0 —	
Insurance Expense			(b) 5 0 —	
Depreciation Expense, Furniture			(c) 1 5 0 —	
Accumulated Depreciation, Furniture				(c) 1 5 0 —
Wages Payable				(d) 6 3 0 —
			1 0 4 0 —	1 0 4 0 —

After all amounts are extended to the Adjusted Trial Balance, the debit and credit columns are underlined and added. The totals are double underlined. Total debits must equal total credits before you can go on to the next step.

Step 5: Extensions to Income Statement and Balance Sheet Columns The amounts in the Adjusted Trial Balance columns are "extended" as follows:

4-4
of the Worksheet

Attorney at Law
sheet
April 30, 19XX

Adjusted Trial Balance		Income Statement		Balance Sheet	
Debit	Credit	Debit	Credit	Debit	Credit

Assets with Debit Balances ⟶ Debit Column of Balance Sheet
Assets with Credit Balances ⟶ Credit Column of Balance Sheet
(Accumulated Depreciation)
Liabilities ⟶ Credit Column of Balance Sheet
Owner's Capital ⟶ Credit Column of Balance Sheet
Owner's Drawing ⟶ Debit Column of Balance Sheet
Revenues ⟶ Credit Column of Income Statement
Expenses ⟶ Debit Column of Income Statement

EXHIBIT
Adjusted Trial

Kevin Young,
Work
For the Month Ended

Account	Trial Balance				Adjustments				
	Debit			Credit		Debit			Credit
Cash	18 7 0 0 —								
Accounts Receivable	2 4 0 0 —								
Office Supplies	6 0 0 —							(a) 2 1 0 —
Prepaid Insurance	1 2 0 0 —							(b) 5 0 —
Furniture	6 4 0 0 —							
Accounts Payable			2 0 0 —					
Kevin Young, Capital			26 0 0 0 —					
Kevin Young, Drawing	2 0 0 —							
Legal Fees			5 2 0 0 —					
Wages Expense	7 0 0 —			(d) 6 3 0 —				
Advertising Expense	3 0 0 —							
Rent Expense	8 0 0 —							
Utilities Expense	1 0 0 —							
Totals	31 4 0 0 —		31 4 0 0 —					
Office Supplies Expense				(a) 2 1 0 —				
Insurance Expense				(b) 5 0 —				
Depreciation Expense, Furniture				(c) 1 5 0 —				
Accumulated Depreciation, Furniture							(c) 1 5 0 —
Wages Payable							(d) 6 3 0 —
				1 0 4 0 —			1 0 4 0 —

In Exhibit 4-6 the account balances in the Adjusted Trial Balance are extended to the proper Income Statement and Balance Sheet columns.

Step 6: Balancing the Worksheet In Exhibit 4-7 the Income Statement and Balance Sheet columns are underlined and added. The column totals are recorded on the same line as the totals of the Adjusted Trial Balance columns. In the Income Statement columns, the difference between the total debits and the total credits is the net income (or net loss) for the accounting period. The Balance Sheet columns should also differ by the same

4-5
Balance Columns

Attorney at Law

sheet

April 30, 19XX

Adjusted Trial Balance		Income Statement		Balance Sheet	
Debit	Credit	Debit	Credit	Debit	Credit
18 7 0 0 —					
2 4 0 0 —					
3 9 0 —					
1 1 5 0 —					
6 4 0 0 —					
	2 0 0 —				
	26 0 0 0 —				
2 0 0 —					
	5 2 0 0 —				
1 3 3 0 —					
3 0 0 —					
8 0 0 —					
1 0 0 —					
2 1 0 —					
5 0 —					
1 5 0 —					
	1 5 0 —				
	6 3 0 —				
32 1 8 0 —	32 1 8 0 —				

amount of net income (or net loss). After the net income (or net loss) is added to the proper columns, the columns are totaled and double underlined. "Net Income" (or "Net Loss") is placed in the Account column on the same line as the net income (or net loss) amount. The rules for the placement of net income (or net loss) amounts are as follows:

1. Place Net Income on the worksheet when the Credit column is greater than the Debit column of the Income Statement and the Debit column of the Balance Sheet is greater than the Credit column. This

EXHIBIT
Extensions to Income Statement and

Kevin Young,
Work
For the Month Ended

Account	Trial Balance		Adjustments	
	Debit	Credit	Debit	Credit
Cash	18 7 0 0 —			
Accounts Receivable	2 4 0 0 —			
Office Supplies	6 0 0 —			(a) 2 1 0 —
Prepaid Insurance	1 2 0 0 —			(b) 5 0 —
Furniture	6 4 0 0 —			
Accounts Payable		2 0 0 —		
Kevin Young, Capital		26 0 0 0 —		
Kevin Young, Drawing	2 0 0 —			
Legal Fees		5 2 0 0 —		
Wages Expense	7 0 0 —		(d) 6 3 0 —	
Advertising Expense	3 0 0 —			
Rent Expense	8 0 0 —			
Utilities Expense	1 0 0 —			
Totals	31 4 0 0 —	31 4 0 0 —		
Office Supplies Expense			(a) 2 1 0 —	
Insurance Expense			(b) 5 0 —	
Depreciation Expense, Furniture			(c) 1 5 0 —	
Accumulated Depreciation, Furniture				(c) 1 5 0 —
Wages Payable				(d) 6 3 0 —
			1 0 4 0 —	1 0 4 0 —

indicates that the net income amount has not been transferred to the owner's Capital account, which has a credit balance.

2. Place Net Loss on the worksheet when the Debit column is greater than the Credit column of the Income Statement and the Credit column of the Balance Sheet is greater than the Debit column. This indicates that the net loss amount has not been transferred to the owner's Capital account, which will reduce the normal credit balance.

4-6
Balance Sheet Columns of the Worksheet

Attorney at Law

sheet

April 30, 19XX

Adjusted Trial Balance		Income Statement		Balance Sheet	
Debit	Credit	Debit	Credit	Debit	Credit
18 7 0 0 —				18 7 0 0 —	
2 4 0 0 —				2 4 0 0 —	
3 9 0 —				3 9 0 —	
1 1 5 0 —				1 1 5 0 —	
6 4 0 0 —				6 4 0 0 —	
	2 0 0 —				2 0 0 —
	26 0 0 0 —				26 0 0 0 —
2 0 0 —				2 0 0 —	
	5 2 0 0 —		5 2 0 0 —		
1 3 3 0 —		1 3 3 0 —			
3 0 0 —		3 0 0 —			
8 0 0 —		8 0 0 —			
1 0 0 —		1 0 0 —			
2 1 0 —		2 1 0 —			
5 0 —		5 0 —			
1 5 0 —		1 5 0 —			
	1 5 0 —				1 5 0 —
	6 3 0 —				6 3 0 —
32 1 8 0 —	32 1 8 0 —				

(A worksheet with a net loss is completed in the Practical Review Problem at the end of this chapter.)

The worksheet is now complete. Financial statements can be prepared by using the account data on the worksheet. We will prepare the financial statements and journalize and post the adjusting entries in Chapter 5. But, before we leave this section on completing the worksheet, let's look at how to correct worksheet errors.

Account	Trial Balance		Adjustments	
	Debit	**Credit**	**Debit**	**Credit**
Cash	18 7 0 0 —			
Accounts Receivable	2 4 0 0 —			
Office Supplies	6 0 0 —			(a) 2 1 0 —
Prepaid Insurance	1 2 0 0 —			(b) 5 0 —
Furniture	6 4 0 0 —			
Accounts Payable		2 0 0 —		
Kevin Young, Capital		26 0 0 0 —		
Kevin Young, Drawing	2 0 0 —			
Legal Fees		5 2 0 0 —		
Wages Expense	7 0 0 —		(d) 6 3 0 —	
Advertising Expense	3 0 0 —			
Rent Expense	8 0 0 —			
Utilities Expense	1 0 0 —			
Totals	31 4 0 0 —	31 4 0 0 —		
Office Supplies Expense			(a) 2 1 0 —	
Insurance Expense			(b) 5 0 —	
Depreciation Expense, Furniture			(c) 1 5 0 —	
Accumulated Depreciation, Furniture				(c) 1 5 0 —
Wages Payable				(d) 6 3 0 —
			1 0 4 0 —	1 0 4 0 —
Net Income				

CORRECTING WORKSHEET ERRORS

Procedures

Follow these quick and simple procedures if your worksheet does not balance:

1. Read and total all columns vertically.

4-7
Worksheet

Attorney at Law
sheet
April 30, 19XX

Adjusted Trial Balance		Income Statement		Balance Sheet	
Debit	Credit	Debit	Credit	Debit	Credit
18 7 0 0 —				18 7 0 0 —	
2 4 0 0 —				2 4 0 0 —	
3 9 0 —				3 9 0 —	
1 1 5 0 —				1 1 5 0 —	
6 4 0 0 —				6 4 0 0 —	
	2 0 0 —				2 0 0 —
	26 0 0 0 —				26 0 0 0 —
2 0 0 —				2 0 0 —	
	5 2 0 0 —		5 2 0 0 —		
1 3 3 0 —		1 3 3 0 —			
3 0 0 —		3 0 0 —			
8 0 0 —		8 0 0 —			
1 0 0 —		1 0 0 —			
2 1 0 —		2 1 0 —			
5 0 —		5 0 —			
1 5 0 —		1 5 0 —			
	1 5 0 —				1 5 0 —
	6 3 0 —				6 3 0 —
32 1 8 0 —	32 1 8 0 —	2 9 4 0 —	5 2 0 0 —	29 2 4 0 —	26 9 8 0 —
		2 2 6 0 —			2 2 6 0 —
		5 2 0 0 —	5 2 0 0 —	29 2 4 0 —	29 2 4 0 —

2. If the worksheet still does not balance, then verify that the net income (or net loss) amounts are correct.

3. Visually examine all accounts and amounts to make sure that the account balances are in the correct columns.

4. If you still have not discovered the error, then read or subtract all accounts horizontally.

Usually, one of these procedures will detect the error.

Common Worksheet Errors

As you follow the four previous procedures you will see that there are a variety of errors that can occur when you are completing a worksheet. Let's examine two common errors. Remember that with a little practice you will soon be proficient at completing a worksheet.

1. *An amount is placed in the wrong income statement or balance sheet column.* For example, assume that the Furniture amount of $6,400 is placed in the Debit column of the Income Statement rather than the Debit column of the Balance Sheet. If this occurred, the worksheet would have totals of:

	Income Statement		Balance Sheet	
	Debit	Credit	Debit	Credit
	9,340	5,200	22,840	26,980
Net Loss		4,140	4,140	
	9,340	9,340	26,980	26,980

As we saw earlier in this chapter, the difference between the two sets of columns should agree, which they do. This indicates that a net loss has occurred, which of course is incorrect. Since most firms are in business to generate a profit (net income) you should be very cautious whenever a net loss occurs. In this case, a second glance would quickly point out that the Furniture amount is in the wrong column.

2. *An amount is placed in the wrong debit or credit column.* Let's use the Furniture example again and assume that the $6,400 is placed in the Credit column of the Balance Sheet rather than the Debit column. If this occurred, the worksheet would have totals of:

	Income Statement		Balance Sheet	
	Debit	Credit	Debit	Credit
	2,940	5,200	22,840	33,380
	2,260	←(CANNOT OCCUR)→	10,540	
	5,200	5,200	33,380	33,380

This error is easier to see because the differences do not agree. The best way to avoid errors is to take your time and be careful. When an error does occur, follow the procedures above to correct the worksheet error.

CHAPTER REVIEW

1. **Explain the matching concept (pp. 86–87).**
   Many individuals and small businesses operate on a cash basis of accounting, where revenues are recorded only when cash is received and expenses are recorded only when cash is paid. But the cash basis is not GAAP. Generally accepted accounting principles and the matching concept require a proper matching of revenues and expenses in a specific time period (accounting period). Therefore, revenues must be recognized when earned and expenses must be recognized when incurred.

2. **Calculate adjustments (pp. 87–92).**
   Adjusting entries are necessary to insure that there is a proper matching of revenues and expenses for an accounting period. Adjustments provide a means for placing assets, liabilities, owner's equity, revenue, and expense accounts at their proper balances for the accounting period.

3. **Complete the worksheet (pp. 92–104).**
   The worksheet is a tool used by accountants to compile the information necessary for the preparation of financial statements. It is not part of the firm's formal accounting records; the worksheet is an internal document. A ten-column worksheet has Debit and Credit columns for Trial Balance (Unadjusted), Adjustments, Adjusted Trial Balance, Income Statement, and Balance Sheet.

GLOSSARY

Accounting Cycle	Basic steps that are followed in a specific order for each accounting period.
Accrual	Type of adjusting entry that is used to recognize an unrecorded revenue that has already been earned or an unrecorded expense that has already been incurred.
Accrual Basis	Revenues are recorded when earned. Expenses are recorded when incurred.
Accumulated Depreciation	Total depreciation expense since the purchase (acquisition) of the asset.
Adjustments (Adjusting Entries)	Necessary to insure that there is a proper matching of revenues and expenses for an accounting period.
Book Value	Cost of an asset less accumulated depreciation.
Cash Basis	Revenues are recognized when cash is received. Expenses are recognized when cash is paid.

Cost	Total amount paid to acquire an asset.
Deferral	Type of adjusting entry that is used to postpone the recognition of a revenue already received or an expense already paid.
Depreciation	Systematic and rational allocation of the cost of certain tangible assets over their useful lives.
Matching Concept	Proper matching of revenues and expenses in an accounting period.
Salvage Value	Estimate of the amount an asset can be sold for after a firm is done using it.
Straight-line Method	Depreciation method that allocates the same amount of depreciation to each accounting period.
Useful Life	Estimate of the time the asset can be productively and economically utilized.
Worksheet	Tool used by accountants to compile the information necessary for the preparation of financial statements.

SELF-TEST QUESTIONS FOR REVIEW

(Answers are on p. 119.)

1. Using the accrual basis of accounting, expenses are recorded when _____ and revenues are recorded when _____ .
   a. earned; incurred
   b. incurred; incurred
   c. incurred; earned
   d. earned; earned

2. You would adjust Wages Expense by crediting
   a. Wages Payable.
   b. Wages Expense.
   c. Accounts Payable.
   d. Prepaid Insurance.

3. Which of the following accounts could be listed in the debit column of the balance sheet on a completed worksheet?
   a. Accounts Payable
   b. Owen Davis, Capital
   c. Wages Expense
   d. Vera Howard, Drawing

4. Calculate monthly depreciation given this data: Furniture costs $30,000 and has a useful life of five years; the salvage value is $6,000.
   a. $500
   b. $400
   c. $600
   d. $100

5. A firm paid $3,000 for a two-year insurance policy. In the monthly adjusting entry _____ is credited for _____ .
   a. Prepaid Insurance; $125
   b. Insurance Expense; $125
   c. Accounts Payable; $1,500
   d. Depreciation Expense, Insurance; $1,500

PRACTICAL REVIEW PROBLEM

Objectives 2
and 3

Calculating Adjustments and Completing the Worksheet   Louis Moyer is the owner of Northside Advertising Service. He had the following trial balance and adjustments at the end of August 19XX:

Northside Advertising Service
Trial Balance
August 31, 19XX

Accounts	Debit	Credit
Cash	18 3 7 0 —	
Accounts Receivable	9 8 4 0 —	
Office Supplies	11 7 2 0 —	
Prepaid Insurance	5 4 0 0 —	
Automobile	15 4 4 0 —	
Accounts Payable		12 7 3 0 —
Louis Moyer, Capital		51 7 6 0 —
Louis Moyer, Drawing	5 5 8 0 —	
Advertising Fees		11 8 9 0 —
Consulting Fees		6 2 7 0 —
Wages Expense	8 4 5 0 —	
Advertising Expense	4 7 2 0 —	
Rent Expense	2 6 0 0 —	
Utilities Expense	5 3 0 —	
Totals	82 6 5 0 —	82 6 5 0 —

Adjustments:
  a. Office Supplies had a beginning balance of $860. During the month, $10,860 of office supplies were purchased. A count was made at the end of the month and $9,560 of office supplies were on hand.
  b. On August 1, 19XX, the firm paid $5,400 for a three-year liability insurance policy.
  c. An automobile was purchased August 5, 19XX at a cost of $15,440. Louis estimates that the automobile will have a $2,000 salvage value after seven years of useful life.
  d. At August 31, 19XX, $6,340 of wages expense is incurred but unrecorded.

REQUIRED
1. Calculate the adjusting entries in T account form.
2. Complete the worksheet.

ANSWER TO PRACTICAL REVIEW PROBLEM

1. Calculate Adjusting Entries
   a. Office Supplies:

August 1, 19XX, Beginning Balance	$ 860
Add: August Purchases	10,860
Office Supplies Available to be Used	$11,720
Less: August 31, 19XX, Ending Balance	9,560
Office Supplies Used or Expensed	$ 2,160

Office Supplies Expense		Office Supplies	
(a) adjusting 2,160		bal. 11,720	(a) adjusting 2,160
		new bal. 9,560	

   b. Prepaid Insurance:

   $5,400 ÷ 36 months (3 years) = $150 per month

Insurance Expense		Prepaid Insurance	
(b) adjusting 150		bal. 5,400	(b) adjusting 150
		new bal. 5,250	

   c. Depreciation:

   $$\text{Depreciation Expense} = \frac{\$15,440 - \$2,000}{84 \text{ months}} = \frac{\$13,440}{84} = \$160$$

Depreciation Expense, Automobile		Accumulated Depreciation, Automobile	
(c) adjusting 160			(c) adjusting 160

   d. Wages Expense:

Wages Expense		Wages Payable	
bal. 8,450			(d) adjusting 6,340
(d) adjusting 6,340			
new bal. 14,790			

2. Complete the Worksheet (pp. 110–111)

DISCUSSION QUESTIONS

Q 4-1   What is the accounting cycle?

Q 4-2   Name the ten steps that represent the accounting cycle.

Q 4-3   Briefly explain the matching concept.

Q 4-4   Briefly describe the cash basis and the accrual basis of accounting.

Q 4-5   Name the two types of adjusting entries. When are adjusting entries prepared? Why are adjusting entries prepared?

Q 4-6   Name the accounts that are debited and credited for each of the following adjusting entries: (a) adjust Office Supplies; (b) adjust Prepaid Insurance; (c) adjust Furniture; and (d) adjust Wages Expense.

Q 4-7   Define depreciation. Describe and give the formula for the straight-line method of depreciation.

Q 4-8   What is a worksheet? What columns would you find on a ten-column worksheet?

Q 4-9   List the six steps in preparing a worksheet in their proper order.

Q 4-10 What are the four procedures that should be followed if your worksheet does not balance? Identify two common worksheet errors.

EXERCISES

Objective 2   **E 4-1   Calculating and Organizing Adjustments**   Calculate and organize the following adjustments for Office Supplies in T account form:

Firm	Month	Beginning Balance	Purchases During the Month	Ending Count
Logan Service	June, 19XX	$ 0	$ 1,000	$ 500
A. Wong, CPA	July, 19XX	2,890	3,860	2,230

Objective 2   **E 4-2   Calculating and Organizing Adjustments**   Calculate and organize the following adjusting entries in T account form for Prepaid Insurance per accounting period:

Firm	Cost	Total Number of Months	Month Ended
Ruiz Service	$1,920	24	October, 19XX
Smith Consulting	3,360	48	August, 19XX

Northside

Work

For the Month Ended

Account	Trial Balance Debit	Trial Balance Credit	Adjustments Debit	Adjustments Credit
Cash	18 3 7 0 —			
Accounts Receivable	9 8 4 0 —			
Office Supplies	11 7 2 0 —			(a) 2 1 6 0 —
Prepaid Insurance	5 4 0 0 —			(b) 1 5 0 —
Automobile	15 4 4 0 —			
Accounts Payable		12 7 3 0 —		
Louis Moyer, Capital		51 7 6 0 —		
Louis Moyer, Drawing	5 5 8 0 —			
Advertising Fees		11 8 9 0 —		
Consulting Fees		6 2 7 0 —		
Wages Expense	8 4 5 0 —		(d) 6 3 4 0 —	
Advertising Expense	4 7 2 0 —			
Rent Expense	2 6 0 0 —			
Utilities Expense	5 3 0 —			
Totals	82 6 5 0 —	82 6 5 0 —		
Office Supplies Expense			(a) 2 1 6 0 —	
Insurance Expense			(b) 1 5 0 —	
Depreciation Expense, Automobile			(c) 1 6 0 —	
Accumulated Depreciation, Automobile				(c) 1 6 0 —
Wages Payable				(d) 6 3 4 0 —
			8 8 1 0 —	8 8 1 0 —
Net Loss				

Objective 2   **E 4-3 Calculating and Organizing Adjustments** Calculate and organize the
following adjustments for Depreciation Expense in T account form using
the straight-line method (hint: convert the useful life into months):

Asset	Month Ended	Cost	Useful Life	Salvage Value
Furniture	July, 19XX	$10,000	3 years	$1,000
Computer	June, 19XX	12,200	5 years	2,000

Advertising Service

sheet

August 31, 19XX

Adjusted Trial Balance		Income Statement		Balance Sheet	
Debit	Credit	Debit	Credit	Debit	Credit
18 3 7 0 —				18 3 7 0 —	
9 8 4 0 —				9 8 4 0 —	
9 5 6 0 —				9 5 6 0 —	
5 2 5 0 —				5 2 5 0 —	
15 4 4 0 —				15 4 4 0 —	
	12 7 3 0 —				12 7 3 0 —
	51 7 6 0 —				51 7 6 0 —
5 5 8 0 —				5 5 8 0 —	
	11 8 9 0 —		11 8 9 0 —		
	6 2 7 0 —		6 2 7 0 —		
14 7 9 0 —		14 7 9 0 —			
4 7 2 0 —		4 7 2 0 —			
2 6 0 0 —		2 6 0 0 —			
5 3 0 —		5 3 0 —			
2 1 6 0 —		2 1 6 0 —			
1 5 0 —		1 5 0 —			
1 6 0 —		1 6 0 —			
	1 6 0 —				1 6 0 —
	6 3 4 0 —				6 3 4 0 —
89 1 5 0 —	89 1 5 0 —	25 1 1 0 —	18 1 6 0 —	64 0 4 0 —	70 9 9 0 —
			6 9 5 0 —	6 9 5 0 —	
		25 1 1 0 —	25 1 1 0 —	70 9 9 0 —	70 9 9 0 —

Objective 2   **E 4-4   Finding Book Values**   Find the book value of each of the following assets:

Asset	Cost	Accumulated Depreciation
a. Automobile	$19,000	$ 200
b. Equipment	26,500	1,300
c. Machinery	79,430	8,850

Objective 2

E 4-5 Organizing Adjustments   Organize the following adjusting entries in T accounts for wages expense incurred but not paid:

Firm	End of Accounting Period	Amount of Wages Expense Incurred
Lopez Consulting	December 31, 19XX	$ 600
Molsky Service	February 28, 19XX	920
Li & Wu Consulting	August 31, 19XX	2,540

Objective 2

E 4-6 Organizing Adjustments   Organize the following adjustments in T accounts for the month ended October 31, 19XX:

Adjusting Entry for	Adjustment Amount
(a) Office Supplies	$2
(b) Prepaid Insurance	3
(c) Furniture	4
(d) Wages Expense	1

Objective 3

E 4-7 Completing a Worksheet   Use the adjustments from E 4-6 for the following partial worksheet and then complete the worksheet:

Cornerstone Services

Worksheet (partial)

For the Month Ended October 31, 19XX

Account	Trial Balance Debit	Trial Balance Credit
Cash	1 0 —	
Office Supplies	8 —	
Prepaid Insurance	6 —	
Furniture	2 4 —	
Lois Emery, Capital		3 7 —
Lois Emery, Drawing	2 —	
Consulting Fees		1 8 —
Wages Expense	5 —	
Totals	5 5 —	5 5 —

Objective 3   **E 4-8   Completing a Worksheet**   Complete the following partial worksheet (Hint: this worksheet has a net loss):

Florida Services

Worksheet (partial)

For the Month Ended January 31, 19XX

Account	Trial Balance		Adjustments	
	Debit	**Credit**	**Debit**	**Credit**
Cash	6 9 3 0 —			
Office Supplies	1 2 0 0 —			(a) 3 6 0 —
Prepaid Insurance	1 5 6 0 —			(b) 6 0 —
Equipment	3 8 7 0 —			
Cheng Lu, Capital		13 5 0 0 —		
Cheng Lu, Drawing	2 1 0 —			
Service Fees		2 9 0 0 —		
Wages Expense	2 6 3 0 —		(d) 6 5 0 —	
Totals	16 4 0 0 —	16 4 0 0 —		
Office Supplies Expense			(a) 3 6 0 —	
Insurance Expense			(b) 6 0 —	
Depreciation Expense, Equipment			(c) 1 0 0 —	
Accumulated Depreciation, Equipment				(c) 1 0 0 —
Wages Payable				(d) 6 5 0 —

PROBLEM SET A

Objective 2   **P 4-1A   Calculating Adjustments**   Dora Jaynes is the accountant for Peterson Computer Repair. Dora accumulated the following information concerning adjustments at the end of November 19XX:

a. A count of office supplies was made at the end of the month, and $7,200 of office supplies were on hand. Office supplies had a beginning balance of $4,600 and on November 6, 19XX, $3,300 of office supplies were purchased.

b. On November 1, 19XX, the firm paid $5,400 for a five-year (60 months) liability insurance policy.

c. The firm uses the straight-line method to depreciate assets. A copier was purchased November 3, 19XX, and will have a useful life of four years. The cost was $29,400. The salvage value is $3,000.

d. On November 30, 19XX, $2,400 of wages expense is incurred but unrecorded.

REQUIRED
1. Calculate the adjusting entries in T account form.
2. Find the book value of the copier.

Objectives 2 and 3

P 4-2A   **Calculating Adjustments and Completing the Worksheet** Elvira Dixon, CPA, had the following adjustments and trial balance at the end of January 19XX:

Adjustments:
a. Furniture was purchased January 2, 19XX at a cost of $10,000. Elvira estimates that the furniture will have a $1,000 salvage value after three years of useful life. Use the straight-line method.
b. At January 31, 19XX, $800 of wages expense is incurred but unrecorded.

Elvira Dixon, CPA
Trial Balance
January 31, 19XX

Accounts	Debit	Credit
Cash	16 9 0 0 —	
Accounts Receivable	2 8 0 0 —	
Furniture	10 0 0 0 —	
Accounts Payable		3 4 0 0 —
Elvira Dixon, Capital		25 3 0 0 —
Elvira Dixon, Drawing	4 5 0 0 —	
Auditing Fees		2 8 0 0 —
Tax Services		1 7 0 0 —
Management Advisory Services		3 8 0 0 —
Wages Expense	9 0 0 —	
Advertising Expense	1 0 0 0 —	
Rent Expense	8 0 0 —	
Utilities Expense	1 0 0 —	
Totals	37 0 0 0 —	37 0 0 0 —

REQUIRED
1. Calculate the adjusting entries in T account form.
2. Complete the worksheet.

Objectives 2 and 3

P 4-3A   **Calculating Adjustments and Completing a Worksheet** Lawanda Knapp is the owner of Kansas Design Service. She had the following adjustments and trial balance at the end of March 19XX:

Adjustments:

a. Office Supplies had a beginning balance of $0. During the month, $3,900 of office supplies were purchased. A count was made at the end of the month and $3,000 of office supplies were on hand.

b. On March 1, 19XX, the firm paid $16,200 for a three-year liability insurance policy.

c. An automobile was purchased March 4, 19XX, at a cost of $19,600. Lawanda estimates that the automobile will have a $4,000 salvage value after five years of useful life. Use the straight-line method.

d. On March 31, 19XX, $800 of wages expense is incurred but unrecorded.

Kansas Design Service
Trial Balance
March 31, 19XX

Accounts	Debit	Credit
Cash	31 6 0 0 —	
Accounts Receivable	8 9 0 0 —	
Office Supplies	3 9 0 0 —	
Prepaid Insurance	16 2 0 0 —	
Automobile	19 6 0 0 —	
Accounts Payable		11 6 0 0 —
Lawanda Knapp, Capital		64 8 0 0 —
Lawanda Knapp, Drawing	1 5 0 0 —	
Design Fees		9 7 0 0 —
Wages Expense	1 2 0 0 —	
Advertising Expense	1 9 0 0 —	
Rent Expense	1 1 0 0 —	
Utilities Expense	2 0 0 —	
Totals	86 1 0 0 —	86 1 0 0 —

REQUIRED

1. Calculate the adjusting entries in T account form.
2. Complete the worksheet.

Objectives 2 and 3

P 4-4A   **Comprehensive Chapter Review Problem**   Anthony Cruz is the owner of Cruz Advertising Agency. He had the following adjustments and trial balance at the end of January 19XX:

Adjustments:

a. Office Supplies had a beginning balance of $430. During the month, $12,300 of office supplies were purchased. A count was made at the end of the month, and $9,560 of office supplies were on hand.

   b. On January 1, 19XX, the firm paid $5,760 for a four-year liability insurance policy.

   c. A computer was purchased January 5, 19XX, at a cost of $16,680. Anthony estimates that the computer will have a $3,000 salvage value after six years of useful life. Use the straight-line method.

   d. On January 31, 19XX, $3,880 of wages expense is incurred but unrecorded.

Cruz Advertising Agency
Trial Balance
January 31, 19XX

Accounts	Debit	Credit
Cash	21 4 1 0 —	
Accounts Receivable	19 3 4 0 —	
Office Supplies	12 7 3 0 —	
Prepaid Insurance	5 7 6 0 —	
Computer	16 6 8 0 —	
Accounts Payable		15 7 8 0 —
Anthony Cruz, Capital		67 2 8 0 —
Anthony Cruz, Drawing	5 9 6 0 —	
Advertising Fees		9 9 5 0 —
Consulting Fees		6 9 6 0 —
Wages Expense	8 7 8 0 —	
Advertising Expense	6 8 2 0 —	
Rent Expense	2 1 0 0 —	
Utilities Expense	3 9 0 —	
Totals	99 9 7 0 —	99 9 7 0 —

REQUIRED

1. Calculate the adjusting entries in T account form.
2. Complete the worksheet (see the Practical Review Problem if you need help).

PROBLEM SET B

Objective 2   **P 4-1B**   **Calculating Adjustments**   Ty Tran is the accountant for Gibson Park Television Repair. Ty accumulated the following information concerning adjustments at the end of October 19XX:

   a. A count of office supplies was made at the end of the month, and $4,700 of office supplies were on hand. Office supplies had a beginning balance of $2,100 and on October 9, 19XX, $3,800 of office supplies were purchased.

b. On October 1, 19XX, the firm paid $7,200 for a six-year (72 months) liability insurance policy.

c. The firm uses the straight-line method to depreciate assets. A computer was purchased October 2, 19XX, and will have a useful life of four years. The cost was $20,800. The salvage value is $4,000.

d. On October 31, 19XX, $3,900 of wages expense is incurred but unrecorded.

REQUIRED
1. Calculate the adjusting entries in T account form.
2. Find the book value of the computer.

Objectives 2 and 3

P 4-2B **Calculating Adjustments and Completing the Worksheet** Gene Clark, CPA, had the following adjustments and trial balance at the end of February 19XX:

Adjustments:

a. Equipment was purchased February 3, 19XX, at a cost of $9,200. Gene estimates that the equipment will have a $2,000 salvage value after four years of useful life. Use the straight-line method.

b. On February 28, 19XX, $1,200 of wages expense is incurred but unrecorded.

Gene Clark, CPA
Trial Balance
February 28, 19XX

Accounts	Debit	Credit
Cash	39 7 0 0 —	
Accounts Receivable	4 9 0 0 —	
Equipment	9 2 0 0 —	
Accounts Payable		6 9 0 0 —
Gene Clark, Capital		49 2 0 0 —
Gene Clark, Drawing	6 9 0 0 —	
Auditing Fees		4 7 0 0 —
Tax Services		2 6 0 0 —
Management Advisory Services		1 2 0 0 —
Wages Expense	1 4 0 0 —	
Advertising Expense	1 2 0 0 —	
Rent Expense	1 1 0 0 —	
Utilities Expense	2 0 0 —	
Totals	64 6 0 0 —	64 6 0 0 —

REQUIRED
1. Calculate the adjusting entries in T account form.
2. Complete the worksheet.

Objectives 2
and 3

P 4-3B   **Calculating Adjustments and Completing a Worksheet**   Mary LaFluer

is the owner of LaFluer Consulting Service. She had the following
adjustments and trial balance at the end of April 19XX:

Adjustments:
a. Office Supplies had a beginning balance of $0. During the month,
   $6,900 of office supplies were purchased. A count was made at the
   end of the month and $4,800 of office supplies were on hand.
b. On April 1, 19XX, the firm paid $12,600 for a three-year liability
   insurance policy.
c. A truck was purchased April 6, 19XX, at a cost of $15,800. Mary
   estimates that the truck will have a $5,000 salvage value after six
   years of useful life. Use the straight-line method.
d. On April 30, 19XX, $1,900 of wages expense is incurred but
   unrecorded.

LaFluer Consulting Service
Trial Balance
April 30, 19XX

Accounts	Debit	Credit
Cash	21 4 0 0 —	
Accounts Receivable	9 3 0 0 —	
Office Supplies	6 9 0 0 —	
Prepaid Insurance	12 6 0 0 —	
Truck	15 8 0 0 —	
Accounts Payable		13 6 0 0 —
Mary LaFluer, Capital		51 7 0 0 —
Mary LaFluer, Drawing	7 8 0 0 —	
Consulting Fees		16 7 0 0 —
Wages Expense	3 7 0 0 —	
Advertising Expense	1 7 0 0 —	
Rent Expense	2 5 0 0 —	
Utilities Expense	3 0 0 —	
Totals	82 0 0 0 —	82 0 0 0 —

REQUIRED
1. Calculate the adjusting entries in T account form.
2. Complete the worksheet.

Objectives 2
and 3

P 4-4B **Comprehensive Chapter Review Problem** Pierre Baxter is the owner of Eastern City Advertising Service. He had the following adjustments and trial balance at the end of September 19XX:

Adjustments:

a. Office Supplies had a beginning balance of $810. During the month, $16,160 of office supplies were purchased. A count was made at the end of the month, and $14,760 of supplies were on hand.

b. On September 1, 19XX, the firm paid $6,720 for a four-year liability insurance policy.

c. A delivery van was purchased September 4, 19XX, at a cost of $21,960. Pierre estimates that the delivery van will have a $6,000 salvage value after seven years of useful life. Use the straight-line method.

d. On September 30, 19XX, $5,180 of wages expense is incurred but unrecorded.

Eastern City Advertising Service
Trial Balance
September 30, 19XX

Accounts	Debit	Credit
Cash	35 2 8 0 —	
Accounts Receivable	10 3 8 0 —	
Office Supplies	16 9 7 0 —	
Prepaid Insurance	6 7 2 0 —	
Delivery Van	21 9 6 0 —	
Accounts Payable		20 7 7 0 —
Pierre Baxter, Capital		73 3 9 0 —
Pierre Baxter, Drawing	6 0 8 0 —	
Advertising Fees		10 7 5 0 —
Consulting Fees		8 5 4 0 —
Wages Expense	7 0 7 0 —	
Advertising Expense	5 2 9 0 —	
Rent Expense	3 2 6 0 —	
Utilities Expense	4 4 0 —	
Totals	113 4 5 0 —	113 4 5 0 —

REQUIRED
1. Calculate the adjusting entries in T account form.
2. Complete the worksheet (see the Practical Review Problem if you need help).

ANSWERS TO SELF-TEST QUESTIONS

1. c 2. a 3. d 4. b 5. a

5

Preparing Financial Statements; Journalizing and Posting Adjustments

He that wants money, means, and content, is without three good friends.

WILLIAM SHAKESPEARE

LEARNING OBJECTIVES

After reading this chapter, discussing the questions, and working the exercises and problems, you will be able to do the following:

1. Prepare financial statements (pp. 122–31).
2. Journalize and post adjustments (pp. 131–34).

In Chapter 4 the matching concept was explained along with the accrual basis of accounting. Steps 5 and 6 of the accounting cycle—adjusting the general ledger accounts and completing a worksheet—were also introduced. In this chapter we will concentrate on steps 7 and 8—preparing financial statements, and journalizing and posting adjusting entries.

FINANCIAL STATEMENTS

Objective 1
Prepare financial statements.

Financial statements are usually prepared from the worksheet. Remember that the worksheet is a tool used by accountants to compile the information necessary for the preparation of financial statements. It is not part of a firm's formal accounting records, but is, instead, an internal document.

Kevin Young, Attorney at Law, had the following four adjustments in April 19XX:

    a.   Adjust Office Supplies.
    b.   Adjust Prepaid Insurance.
    c.   Adjust Furniture.
    d.   Adjust Wages Expense.

These four adjustments were entered on the worksheet along with the Unadjusted Trial Balance. A worksheet for the month ended April 30, 19XX, was completed as shown in Exhibit 5-1.

The Chart of Accounts

Remember that a chart of accounts is a detailed listing of all the accounts the firm uses for recording transactions. Kevin expanded his chart of accounts to include the accounts necessary to record the adjusting entries as follows (Income Summary is discussed in Chapter 6):

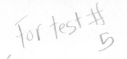

Kevin Young, Attorney at Law
Chart of Accounts

Assets (100–199)

101 Cash
111 Accounts Receivable
121 Office Supplies
131 Prepaid Insurance
141 Furniture
142 *Accumulated Depreciation,
      Furniture

Liabilities (200–299)

201 Accounts Payable
211 *Wages Payable

Owner's Equity (300–399)

301 Kevin Young, Capital
311 Kevin Young, Drawing
321 *Income Summary

Revenues (400–499)

401 Legal Fees

Expenses (500–599)

501 Wages Expense
511 Advertising Expense
521 Rent Expense
531 Utilities Expense
541 *Office Supplies Expense
551 *Insurance Expense
561 *Depreciation Expense,
      Furniture

Financial statements are prepared from the completed worksheet in this order: the income statement, the statement of owner's equity, and the balance sheet.

The Income Statement

The income statement measures the performance of a firm over a period of time. This financial statement is prepared from the account data on the worksheet in a series of steps. These steps are keyed (①, ②, ③, and so on) in Exhibit 5-2. We will only use the Income Statement columns of the worksheet to prepare the income statement.

*Added accounts.

EXHIBIT
Completed

Kevin Young,
Work
For the Month Ended

Account	Trial Balance Debit	Trial Balance Credit	Adjustments Debit	Adjustments Credit
Cash	18 7 0 0 —			
Accounts Receivable	2 4 0 0 —			
Office Supplies	6 0 0 —			(a) 2 1 0 —
Prepaid Insurance	1 2 0 0 —			(b) 5 0 —
Furniture	6 4 0 0 —			
Accounts Payable		2 0 0 —		
Kevin Young, Capital		26 0 0 0 —		
Kevin Young, Drawing	2 0 0 —			
Legal Fees		5 2 0 0 —		
Wages Expense	7 0 0 —		(d) 6 3 0 —	
Advertising Expense	3 0 0 —			
Rent Expense	8 0 0 —			
Utilities Expense	1 0 0 —			
Totals	31 4 0 0 —	31 4 0 0 —		
Office Supplies Expense			(a) 2 1 0 —	
Insurance Expense			(b) 5 0 —	
Depreciation Expense, Furniture			(c) 1 5 0 —	
Accumulated Depreciation, Furniture				(c) 1 5 0 —
Wages Payable				(d) 6 3 0 —
			1 0 4 0 —	1 0 4 0 —
Net Income				

5-1
Worksheet

Attorney at Law
sheet
April 30, 19XX

Adjusted Trial Balance		Income Statement		Balance Sheet	
Debit	Credit	Debit	Credit	Debit	Credit
18 7 0 0 —				18 7 0 0 —	
2 4 0 0 —				2 4 0 0 —	
3 9 0 —				3 9 0 —	
1 1 5 0 —				1 1 5 0 —	
6 4 0 0 —				6 4 0 0 —	
	2 0 0 —				2 0 0 —
	26 0 0 0 —				26 0 0 0 —
2 0 0 —				2 0 0 —	
	5 2 0 0 —		5 2 0 0 —		
1 3 3 0 —		1 3 3 0 —			
3 0 0 —		3 0 0 —			
8 0 0 —		8 0 0 —			
1 0 0 —		1 0 0 —			
2 1 0 —		2 1 0 —			
5 0 —		5 0 —			
1 5 0 —		1 5 0 —			
	1 5 0 —				1 5 0 —
	6 3 0 —				6 3 0 —
32 1 8 0 —	32 1 8 0 —	2 9 4 0 —	5 2 0 0 —	29 2 4 0 —	26 9 8 0 —
		2 2 6 0 —			2 2 6 0 —
		5 2 0 0 —	5 2 0 0 —	29 2 4 0 —	29 2 4 0 —

EXHIBIT 5-2
Preparation of an Income Statement from the Worksheet

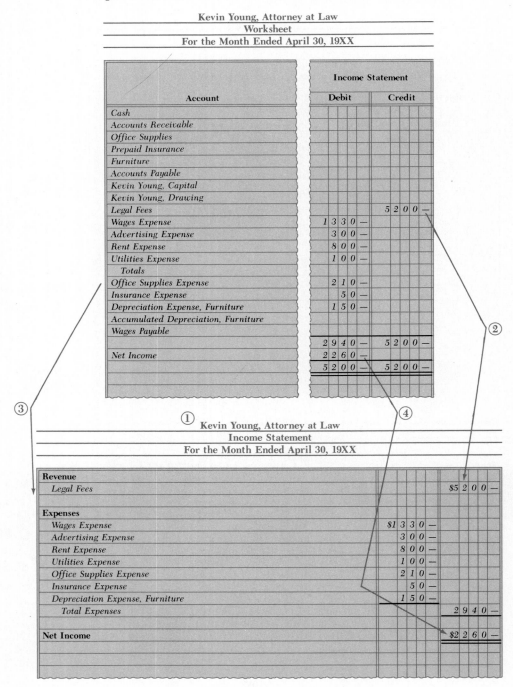

Kevin Young, Attorney at Law
Worksheet
For the Month Ended April 30, 19XX

Account	Income Statement Debit	Income Statement Credit
Cash		
Accounts Receivable		
Office Supplies		
Prepaid Insurance		
Furniture		
Accounts Payable		
Kevin Young, Capital		
Kevin Young, Drawing		
Legal Fees		5 2 0 0 —
Wages Expense	1 3 3 0 —	
Advertising Expense	3 0 0 —	
Rent Expense	8 0 0 —	
Utilities Expense	1 0 0 —	
Totals		
Office Supplies Expense	2 1 0 —	
Insurance Expense	5 0 —	
Depreciation Expense, Furniture	1 5 0 —	
Accumulated Depreciation, Furniture		
Wages Payable		
	2 9 4 0 —	5 2 0 0 —
Net Income	2 2 6 0 —	
	5 2 0 0 —	5 2 0 0 —

② ③ ① ④

Kevin Young, Attorney at Law
Income Statement
For the Month Ended April 30, 19XX

Revenue			
Legal Fees			$5 2 0 0 —
Expenses			
Wages Expense	$1 3 3 0 —		
Advertising Expense	3 0 0 —		
Rent Expense	8 0 0 —		
Utilities Expense	1 0 0 —		
Office Supplies Expense	2 1 0 —		
Insurance Expense	5 0 —		
Depreciation Expense, Furniture	1 5 0 —		
Total Expenses			2 9 4 0 —
Net Income			$2 2 6 0 —

The steps to preparing an income statement are as follows:

① The heading for the income statement includes the name of the firm, "Income Statement," and the period of time. Leave one blank line before "Revenue."

② Revenues are taken from the income statement Credit column of the worksheet and are listed in chart-of-accounts number order. Kevin Young, Attorney at Law, has only one revenue account, Legal Fees. Since there is only one revenue account it is not necessary to total revenues. The Legal Fees amount carries a dollar sign. Leave one blank line before "Expenses."

③ Expenses are taken from the income statement Debit column of the worksheet and are listed in chart-of-accounts number order. A dollar sign appears at the beginning of the expense column. Expenses are totaled and underlined. Leave one blank line before "Net Income" or "Net Loss."

④ The amount of net income is taken from the Income Statement Debit column of the worksheet. A debit indicates that revenues are greater than expenses. A net loss would appear on the Credit column of the worksheet. A credit indicates that expenses exceed revenues. You should subtract the total expenses from the total revenues to check that the net income or net loss amount is correct. The net income or net loss amount is double underlined and includes a dollar sign.

The Statement of Owner's Equity

The statement of owner's equity is prepared after the income statement. This financial statement summarizes the changes in the owner's Capital account for a definite period of time. The statement of owner's equity serves as a "bridge." It covers the space between the income statement and balance sheet. This space is the ending balance of owner's equity (Capital). The steps in preparing the statement of owner's equity are keyed (①, ②, ③, and so on) in Exhibit 5-3. We will use the Balance Sheet columns of the worksheet and the owner's Capital account in the general ledger to prepare the statement of owner's equity. The steps in preparing the statement of owner's equity from the worksheet and Capital account are as follows:

① The heading for the statement of owner's equity includes the name of the firm, "Statement of Owner's Equity," and the period of time. Leave one blank line before "Capital."

EXHIBIT 5-3
Preparation of the Statement of Owner's Equity from the Worksheet

Kevin Young, Attorney at Law
Worksheet
For the Month Ended April 30, 19XX

Account	Balance Sheet Debit	Balance Sheet Credit
Cash	18 7 0 0 —	
Accounts Receivable	2 4 0 0 —	
Office Supplies	3 9 0 —	
Prepaid Insurance	1 1 5 0 —	
Furniture	6 4 0 0 —	
Accounts Payable		2 0 0 —
Kevin Young, Capital		26 0 0 0 —
Kevin Young, Drawing	2 0 0 —	
Legal Fees		
Wages Expense		
Advertising Expense		
Rent Expense		
Utilities Expense		
Totals		
Office Supplies Expense		
Insurance Expense		
Depreciation Expense, Furniture		
Accumulated Depreciation, Furniture		1 5 0 —
Wages Payable		6 3 0 —
	29 2 4 0 —	26 9 8 0 —
Net Income		2 2 6 0 —
	29 2 4 0 —	29 2 4 0 —

③

⑤

GENERAL LEDGER ACCOUNT

Account: Kevin Young, Capital   Account No.   301

Date	Item	Post. Ref.	Debit	Credit	Balance Debit	Balance Credit
19XX						
Apr. 1		J1		2 5 0 0 0 —		2 5 0 0 0 —
14		J2		1 0 0 0 —		2 6 0 0 0 —

②

① Kevin Young, Attorney at Law
Statement of Owner's Equity
For the Month Ended April 30, 19XX

Kevin Young, Capital, April 1, 19XX		$25 0 0 0 —
Add: Net Income for April		2 2 6 0 —
④ Additional Investment		1 0 0 0 —
Subtotal		$28 2 6 0 —
Deduct: Kevin Young, Drawing		2 0 0 —
Kevin Young, Capital, April 30, 19XX		$28 0 6 0 —

② The owner's Capital balance is taken from the beginning balance in the owner's Capital account in the general ledger. Additional Investments are also found in the Capital account in the general ledger.

③ Net Income is transferred from the Credit column of the Balance Sheet on the worksheet. You should verify this balance to the net income (or net loss) amount on the income statement. A credit balance indicates an increase in the owner's Capital account (net income). A net loss would be taken from the Debit column of the Balance Sheet on the worksheet. A debit balance indicates a decrease in the owner's Capital account (net loss).

④ Net Income and Additional Investment(s) are added to beginning Capital for a subtotal (include a dollar sign). A line is drawn after the amount of Additional Investment(s).

⑤ Owner's Drawing is taken from the Debit column of the Balance Sheet on the worksheet. This amount is subtracted from the subtotal for the final Capital balance. Kevin Young, Capital, April 30, 19XX, is double underlined with a dollar sign.

The Balance Sheet

The balance sheet is prepared after the income statement and statement of owner's equity. Remember that the balance sheet is a statement of the financial position of the firm at a point in time. The steps in preparing the balance sheet are keyed (①, ②, ③, and so on) in Exhibit 5-4. We will use the Balance Sheet columns of the worksheet and the statement of owner's equity to prepare the balance sheet. The steps for preparing the balance sheet from the worksheet and statement of owner's equity are as follows:

① The heading for the balance sheet includes the name of the firm, "Balance Sheet," and the date. The date is April 30, 19XX. Leave one blank line before "Assets."

② Assets are taken from the Debit and Credit Balance Sheet columns of the worksheet. Most assets will have debit balances but contra assets; for example, Accumulated Depreciation will have credit balances. Assets are listed in chart-of-accounts number order. A dollar sign appears at the beginning of each column. A line is drawn after the column. The final total of Assets is double underlined with a dollar sign. Leave one blank line before "Liabilities."

EXHIBIT 5-4
Preparation of a Balance Sheet from the Worksheet

Kevin Young, Attorney at Law
Worksheet
For the Month Ended April 30, 19XX

	Balance Sheet	
Account	Debit	Credit
Cash	18 7 0 0 —	
Accounts Receivable	2 4 0 0 —	
Office Supplies	3 9 0 —	
Prepaid Insurance	1 1 5 0 —	
Furniture	6 4 0 0 —	
Accounts Payable		2 0 0 —
Kevin Young, Capital		26 0 0 0 —
Kevin Young, Drawing	2 0 0 —	
Legal Fees		
Wages Expense		
Advertising Expense		
Rent Expense		
Utilities Expense		
Totals		
Office Supplies Expense		
Insurance Expense		
Depreciation Expense, Furniture		
Accumulated Depreciation, Furniture		1 5 0 —
Wages Payable		6 3 0 —
	29 2 4 0 —	26 9 8 0 —
Net Income		2 2 6 0 —
	29 2 4 0 —	29 2 4 0 —

Kevin Young, Attorney at Law
Statement of Owner's Equity (partial)
For the Month Ended April 30, 19XX

Kevin Young, Capital, April 30, 19XX	-	$28 0 6 0 —

① Kevin Young, Attorney at Law
Balance Sheet
April 30, 19XX

Assets			
Cash		$18 7 0 0 —	
Accounts Receivable		2 4 0 0 —	
Office Supplies		3 9 0 —	
Prepaid Insurance		1 1 5 0 —	
Furniture	$6 4 0 0 —		
Less: Accumulated Depreciation	1 5 0 —	6 2 5 0 —	
Total Assets			$28 8 9 0 —
Liabilities			
Accounts Payable		$ 2 0 0 —	
Wages Payable		6 3 0 —	
Total Liabilities			$ 8 3 0 —
Owner's Equity			
Kevin Young, Capital			28 0 6 0 —
Total Liabilities and Owner's Equity			$28 8 9 0 —

② ③ ④ ⑤

③ Liabilities are transferred from the Balance Sheet Credit column of the worksheet. They are listed in chart-of-accounts number order. A dollar sign is placed at the beginning of the column. Since there is more than one liability, Liabilities are totaled. The first column is underlined, and the total carries a dollar sign. Leave one blank line before "Owner's Equity."

④ Kevin Young, Capital, is taken from the statement of owner's equity. A line is drawn after Capital.

⑤ Total Liabilities and Owner's Equity are added and the total is double underlined. This amount must equal Total Assets. A dollar sign appears at the final total.

JOURNALIZING AND POSTING ADJUSTMENTS

Objective 2
Journalize and
post adjustments.

Adjustments provide a means of placing assets, liabilities, owner's equity, revenue, and expense accounts at their proper balances for the accounting period. Adjusting entries are not journalized and posted until the worksheet is complete. This way you can see the "full picture" of how the financial statements will look. By examining the completed worksheet, you can determine if any additional accounts are to be adjusted. Once you are satisfied with the account balances on the worksheet, you can journalize and post adjusting entries. The adjusting entries are taken directly from the Adjustments columns of the worksheet.

The adjusting entries as calculated in Chapter 4 are as follows:

a. Adjust Office Supplies.
b. Adjust Prepaid Insurance.
c. Adjust Furniture.
d. Adjust Wages Expense.

These four adjusting entries are journalized in the general journal in Exhibit 5-5 and posted to the general ledger in Exhibit 5-6. You should indicate in the general journal and general ledger that these entries and postings are from adjusting entries. In the general journal you would write "Adjusting Entries" in the Description column before the first adjustment is entered. You would not need to write a description for each adjusting entry since you have indicated that they are adjusting entries. When you post the adjusting entry to the general ledger you would write "Adjusting" in the Item column. You would then be able to distinguish adjusting entries from other entries.

EXHIBIT 5-5
Journalizing Adjusting Entries

GENERAL JOURNAL   Page ___3___

Date		Description	Post. Ref.	Debit	Credit
		Adjusting Entries			
19XX					
Apr.	30	Office Supplies Expense	541	2 1 0 —	
		Office Supplies	121		2 1 0 —
	30	Insurance Expense	551	5 0 —	
		Prepaid Insurance	131		5 0 —
	30	Depreciation Expense, Furniture	561	1 5 0 —	
		Accumulated Depreciation, Furniture	142		1 5 0 —
	30	Wages Expense	501	6 3 0 —	
		Wages Payable	211		6 3 0 —

These adjusting entries are posted to the general ledger in Exhibit 5-6, which shows a partial general ledger for Kevin Young, Attorney at Law. Only those general ledger accounts that are used for this posting process are listed.

EXHIBIT 5-6
General Ledger Accounts Used to Post Adjusting Entries

GENERAL LEDGER ACCOUNTS

Account: *Office Supplies*   Account No. *121*

Date	Item	Post. Ref.	Debit	Credit	Balance Debit	Balance Credit
19XX						
Apr. 4		J1	600—		600—	
30	Adjusting	J3		210—	390—	

Account: *Prepaid Insurance*   Account No. *131*

Date	Item	Post. Ref.	Debit	Credit	Balance Debit	Balance Credit
19XX						
Apr. 1		J1	1200—		1200—	
30	Adjusting	J3		50—	1150—	

Account: *Accumulated Depreciation, Furniture*   Account No. *142*

Date	Item	Post. Ref.	Debit	Credit	Balance Debit	Balance Credit
19XX						
Apr. 30	Adjusting	J3		150—		150—

Account: *Wages Payable*   Account No. *211*

Date	Item	Post. Ref.	Debit	Credit	Balance Debit	Balance Credit
19XX						
Apr. 30	Adjusting	J3		630—		630—

(continued)

(Ex. 5-6 concluded)

Account: *Wages Expense*   **Account No.** *501*

Date		Item	Post. Ref.	Debit	Credit	Balance Debit	Balance Credit
19XX							
Apr.	*17*		*J2*	7 0 0 —		7 0 0 —	
	30	*Adjusting*	*J3*	6 3 0 —		1 3 3 0 —	

Account: *Office Supplies Expense*   **Account No.** *541*

Date		Item	Post. Ref.	Debit	Credit	Balance Debit	Balance Credit
19XX							
Apr.	*30*	*Adjusting*	*J3*	2 1 0 —		2 1 0 —	

Account: *Insurance Expense*   **Account No.** *551*

Date		Item	Post. Ref.	Debit	Credit	Balance Debit	Balance Credit
19XX							
Apr.	*30*	*Adjusting*	*J3*	5 0 —		5 0 —	

Account: *Depreciation Expense, Furniture*   **Account No.** *561*

Date		Item	Post. Ref.	Debit	Credit	Balance Debit	Balance Credit
19XX							
Apr.	*30*	*Adjusting*	*J3*	1 5 0 —		1 5 0 —	

CHAPTER REVIEW

1. **Prepare financial statements (pp. 122–31).**
   The worksheet is a tool used by accountants to compile the information necessary for the preparation of financial statements. Financial statements are prepared from the completed worksheet in this order: the income statement, the statement of owner's equity, and the balance sheet.

2. **Journalize and post adjustments (pp. 131–34).**
   Adjusting entries are not journalized and posted until the worksheet is complete. This way you can see the "full picture" of how the financial statements will look. By examining the completed worksheet, you can determine if any additional accounts are to be adjusted. Once you are satisfied with the account balances on the worksheet, you can then journalize and post adjusting entries. The adjusting entries are taken directly from the Adjustments columns of the worksheet.

SELF-TEST QUESTIONS FOR REVIEW

(Answers are on p. 153.)

1. In a chart of accounts for a legal firm, account number 321 would probably be
   a. Income Summary.   b. Legal Fees.
   c. Wages Expense.   d. Wages Payable.

2. To prepare an income statement, the revenues are taken from the _____ column of the worksheet.
   a. balance sheet Debit   b. income statement Credit
   c. balance sheet Credit   d. income statement Debit

3. To adjust Office Supplies, the account _____ is credited.
   a. Office Supplies Expense   b. Accounts Payable
   c. Prepaid Insurance   d. Office Supplies

4. Which of the following accounts will probably have a credit balance after adjustments have been posted (assume adjustments for office supplies, insurance, and wages)?
   a. Prepaid Insurance   b. Office Supplies
   c. Wages Payable   d. Insurance Expense

5. To complete a balance sheet, liabilities are transferred from the _____ column of the worksheet.
   a. balance sheet Debit   b. income statement Debit
   c. balance sheet Credit   d. income statement Credit

PRACTICAL REVIEW PROBLEM

Objectives 1
and 2

Preparing an Income Statement and Journalizing and Posting Adjustments
Pedro Ramos is the owner of Ramos Truck Service. Pedro had the following partial worksheet at the end of June 19XX:

Ramos Truck Service
Worksheet (partial)
For the Month Ended June 30, 19XX

	Adjustments		Income Statement	
Account	**Debit**	**Credit**	**Debit**	**Credit**
Cash				
Accounts Receivable				
Truck Supplies		(a) 1 2 9 0 —		
Prepaid Insurance		(b) 5 4 0 —		
Equipment				
Accounts Payable				
Pedro Ramos, Capital				
Pedro Ramos, Drawing				
Truck Service Fees				7 8 9 0 —
Wages Expense	(d) 1 5 8 0 —		4 0 7 0 —	
Advertising Expense			5 6 0 —	
Rent Expense			2 1 7 0 —	
Utilities Expense			2 6 0 —	
Totals				
Truck Supplies Expense	(a) 1 2 9 0 —		1 2 9 0 —	
Insurance Expense	(b) 5 4 0 —		5 4 0 —	
Depreciation Expense, Equipment	(c) 1 5 0 —		1 5 0 —	
Accumulated Depreciation, Equipment		(c) 1 5 0 —		
Wages Payable		(d) 1 5 8 0 —		
	3 5 6 0 —	3 5 6 0 —	9 0 4 0 —	7 8 9 0 —
Net Loss				1 1 5 0 —
			9 0 4 0 —	9 0 4 0 —

The chart-of-accounts numbers that apply to the adjusting entries are as follows:

Truck Supplies, 131; Prepaid Insurance, 141; Accumulated Depreciation, Equipment, 152; Wages Payable, 221; Wages Expense, 511; Truck Supplies Expense, 551; Insurance Expense, 561; Depreciation Expense, Equipment, 571.

REQUIRED
1. Prepare an income statement.
2. Record adjusting entries in a general journal, page 4.
3. Post only the adjusting entries to the general ledger.

ANSWER TO PRACTICAL REVIEW PROBLEM

1. Prepare an income statement.

Ramos Truck Service
Income Statement
For the Month Ended June 30, 19XX

Revenue		
Truck Service Fees		$7 8 9 0 —
Expenses		
Wages Expense	$4 0 7 0 —	
Advertising Expense	5 6 0 —	
Rent Expense	2 1 7 0 —	
Utilities Expense	2 6 0 —	
Truck Supplies Expense	1 2 9 0 —	
Insurance Expense	5 4 0 —	
Depreciation Expense, Equipment	1 5 0 —	
Total Expenses		9 0 4 0 —
Net Loss		($1 1 5 0 —)

2. Record adjusting entries.

GENERAL JOURNAL   Page ___4___

Date		Description	Post. Ref.	Debit	Credit
		Adjusting Entries			
19XX					
June	*30*	Truck Supplies Expense	*551*	1 2 9 0 —	
		Truck Supplies	*131*		1 2 9 0 —
	30	Insurance Expense	*561*	5 4 0 —	
		Prepaid Insurance	*141*		5 4 0 —
	30	Depreciation Expense, Equipment	*571*	1 5 0 —	
		Accumulated Depreciation, Equipment	*152*		1 5 0 —
	30	Wages Expense	*511*	1 5 8 0 —	
		Wages Payable	*221*		1 5 8 0 —

3. Post to the general ledger.

GENERAL LEDGER ACCOUNTS

Account: *Truck Supplies*   Account No.   *131*

Date		Item	Post. Ref.	Debit	Credit	Balance Debit	Balance Credit
19XX							
June	*30*	Adjusting	*J4*		1 2 9 0 —		

Account: *Prepaid Insurance*   Account No.   *141*

Date		Item	Post. Ref.	Debit	Credit	Balance Debit	Balance Credit
19XX							
June	*30*	Adjusting	*J4*		5 4 0 —		

Account: Accumulated Depreciation, Equipment							Account No. 152		
		Post.					Balance		
Date	Item	Ref.	Debit		Credit		Debit	Credit	
19XX									
June 30	Adjusting	J4			1 5 0 —				

Account: Wages Payable							Account No. 221		
		Post.					Balance		
Date	Item	Ref.	Debit		Credit		Debit	Credit	
19XX									
June 30	Adjusting	J4			1 5 8 0 —				

Account: Wages Expense							Account No. 511		
		Post.					Balance		
Date	Item	Ref.	Debit		Credit		Debit	Credit	
19XX									
June 30	Adjusting	J4	1 5 8 0 —						

Account: Truck Supplies Expense							Account No. 551		
		Post.					Balance		
Date	Item	Ref.	Debit		Credit		Debit	Credit	
19XX									
June 30	Adjusting	J4	1 2 9 0 —						

Account: *Insurance Expense*							Account No. 561	
		Post.				Balance		
Date	Item	Ref.	Debit	Credit		Debit	Credit	
19XX								
June 30	Adjusting	J4	5 4 0 —					

Account: *Depreciation Expense, Equipment*							Account No. 571	
		Post.				Balance		
Date	Item	Ref.	Debit	Credit		Debit	Credit	
19XX								
June 30	Adjusting	J4	1 5 0 —					

DISCUSSION QUESTIONS

Q 5-1   Which of the ten steps of the accounting cycle were covered in this chapter?

Q 5-2   Name the ten steps that represent the accounting cycle.

Q 5-3   Name at least four accounts that were added to the chart of accounts for journalizing and posting adjusting entries in this chapter.

Q 5-4   In what order are financial statements prepared from the worksheet?

Q 5-5   Name and describe the four steps to prepare an income statement from the worksheet.

Q 5-6   When is the statement of owner's equity prepared? What items (columns, financial statements, and so on) are used to prepare the statement of owner's equity?

Q 5-7   Name and describe the five steps to prepare a statement of owner's equity from the worksheet.

Q 5-8   Name and describe the five steps to prepare a balance sheet from the worksheet.

Q 5-9   What do adjustments provide? When are adjusting entries journalized and posted and why?

Q 5-10   Where and what do you write in the general journal to indicate that the entries are from adjusting entries? Where and what do you write in the general ledger to indicate that the postings are from adjusting entries?

EXERCISES

Objective 1   **E 5-1   Selecting a Chart of Accounts**   Melanie Conyers is starting a law firm.
a. Name at least six asset accounts that she could use.
b. Name two liability accounts that she could use.
c. Name three owner's equity accounts that she could use.
d. Name one revenue account that she could use.
e. Name at least six expense accounts that she could use.

Objective 1   **E 5-2   Completing an Income Statement**   Complete the following income statement for Ramon Herrera, Attorney at Law, for the month ended May 19XX:

(a)		
(b)		
(c)		
(d)		
Legal Fees		$5,000
(e)		
Wages Expense	$2,000	
Rent Expense	1,000	
Utilities Expense	200	
Insurance Expense	100	
(f)		(g)
(h)		$ (i)

Objective 1   **E 5-3   Completing a Statement of Owner's Equity**   Complete the following statement of owner's equity for Laura McKinnon, Medical Doctor, for the month ended October 19XX:

(a)		
(b)		
(c)		
(d)		$12,000
Add: (e)		2,000
(f)		3,000
Subtotal		$ (g)
Deduct: (h)		4,000
(i)		$ (j)

Objective 2

E 5-4   Completing Adjusting Entries   Complete the following adjusting entries:

	Debit	Credit
Office Supplies Expense	300	
_____(a)_____		300
_____(b)_____	200	
Prepaid Insurance		200
Depreciation Expense, Equipment	100	
_____(c)_____		100
_____(d)_____	600	
Wages Payable		600

Objective 1

E 5-5   Completing a Balance Sheet   Complete the following balance sheet for Stuart Nelson, Computer Consultant (the accounting period ends April 30, 19XX):

_____(a)_____
_____(b)_____
_____(c)_____

_____(d)_____

Cash		$3,000
Accounts Receivable		2,000
Office Supplies		1,000
Equipment	$8,000	
Less: Accumulated Depreciation	(e)	3,000
_____(f)_____		$ (g)
_____(h)_____		
Accounts Payable		$2,000
Wages Payable		1,000
_____(i)_____		$ (j)
_____(k)_____		
Stuart Nelson, Capital		(l)
_____(m)_____		$ (n)

Use the following partial worksheet for E 5-6:

Norman Tool Design

Worksheet (partial)

For the Month Ended September 30, 19XX

Account	Adjustments Debit	Adjustments Credit
Cash		
Accounts Receivable		
Tool Supplies		(a) 3 6 0 0 —
Prepaid Insurance		(b) 7 0 0 —
Design Equipment		
Accounts Payable		
L. T. Quan, Capital		
L. T. Quan, Drawing		
Tool Design Fees		
Wages Expense	(d) 4 9 0 0 —	
Advertising Expense		
Rent Expense		
Utilities Expense		
Totals		
Tool Supplies Expense	(a) 3 6 0 0 —	
Insurance Expense	(b) 7 0 0 —	
Depreciation Expense, Design Equipment	(c) 8 0 0 —	
Accumulated Depreciation, Design Equipment		(c) 8 0 0 —
Wages Payable		(d) 4 9 0 0 —
	10 0 0 0 —	10 0 0 0 —

Objective 2 **E 5-6 Journalizing Adjusting Entries**   Journalize (page 3) the adjusting entries for Norman Tool Design from the partial worksheet.

Objective 1 **E 5-7 Preparing an Income Statement**   Prepare an income statement for D. H. Yothers (use the Income Statement columns of the following partial worksheet):

D. H. Yothers Landscaping Services
Worksheet (partial)
For the Month Ended December 31, 19XX

Account	Income Statement Debit	Income Statement Credit
Cash		
Accounts Receivable		
Store Supplies		
Prepaid Insurance		
Office Furniture		
Accounts Payable		
D. H. Yothers, Capital		
D. H. Yothers, Drawing		
Landscaping Services		12 8 0 0 —
Wages Expense	5 1 0 0 —	
Advertising Expense	2 7 0 0 —	
Rent Expense	1 5 0 0 —	
Utilities Expense	3 0 0 —	
Totals		
Store Supplies Expense	4 0 0 —	
Insurance Expense	1 0 0 —	
Depreciation Expense, Office Furniture	2 0 0 —	
Accumulated Depreciation, Office Furniture		
Wages Payable		

Objective 2   **E 5-8**   **Journalizing and Posting Adjusting Entries**   The following data was taken from the worksheet of Mills Auto Service.

1. The adjustments are as follows:

(a) adjust Store Supplies, $190; (b) adjust Prepaid Insurance, $50; (c) adjust Depreciation Expense, Computer, $100; and (d) adjust Wages Expense, $970.

2. The chart-of-accounts numbers are as follows:

Store Supplies, 131; Prepaid Insurance, 141; Accumulated Depreciation, Computer, 152; Wages Payable, 221; Wages Expense, 511; Store Supplies Expense, 551; Insurance Expense, 561; Depreciation Expense, Computer, 571.

Journalize the adjusting entries in a general journal, page 5. The date is October 31, 19XX. Also, post the adjusting entries to the general ledger.

PROBLEM SET A

Objective 1

P 5-1A **Preparing Financial Statements** The accountant for Poston Consulting Service completed a worksheet for the month ended August 31, 19XX. The Income Statement and Balance Sheet columns and Capital account are as follows:

Poston Consulting Service

Worksheet (partial)

For the Month Ended August 31, 19XX

Account	Income Statement Debit	Income Statement Credit	Balance Sheet Debit	Balance Sheet Credit
Cash			28 6 0 0 —	
Accounts Receivable			13 7 0 0 —	
Office Supplies			10 4 0 0 —	
Prepaid Insurance			6 9 0 0 —	
Machinery			19 0 0 0 —	
Accounts Payable				12 4 0 0 —
Oliver Poston, Capital				64 5 0 0 —
Oliver Poston, Drawing			2 6 0 0 —	
Consulting Fees		8 6 0 0 —		
Wages Expense	2 7 0 0 —			
Advertising Expense	3 0 0 —			
Rent Expense	2 1 0 0 —			
Utilities Expense	1 0 0 —			
Totals				
Office Supplies Expense	3 0 0 —			
Insurance Expense	1 0 0 —			
Depreciation Expense, Machinery	4 0 0 —			
Accumulated Depreciation, Machinery				4 0 0 —
Wages Payable				1 3 0 0 —
	6 0 0 0 —	8 6 0 0 —	81 2 0 0 —	78 6 0 0 —
Net Income	2 6 0 0 —			2 6 0 0 —
	8 6 0 0 —	8 6 0 0 —	81 2 0 0 —	81 2 0 0 —

GENERAL LEDGER ACCOUNT

Account: *Oliver Poston, Capital*   Account No. *301*

Date	Item	Post. Ref.	Debit	Credit	Balance Debit	Balance Credit
19XX						
Aug. 1		J1		63 6 0 0 —		63 6 0 0 —
9		J3		9 0 0 —		64 5 0 0 —

REQUIRED

Prepare financial statements from the worksheet and Capital account.

Objective 2

P 5-2A **Recording and Posting Adjusting Entries** Delagarza Kitchen Designers has the following chart-of-account numbers:

Store Supplies, 141; Prepaid Insurance, 151; Accumulated Depreciation, Copier, 162; Wages Payable, 231; Wages Expense, 521; Store Supplies Expense, 561; Insurance Expense, 571; Depreciation Expense, Copier, 581.

The firm's accountant finds the adjusting entries from the Adjustments columns of a completed worksheet (month ended April 30, 19XX):
a. Adjust Store Supplies, $340.
b. Adjust Prepaid Insurance, $120.
c. Adjust Copier, $260.
d. Adjust Wages Expense, $1,370.

REQUIRED
1. Enter the accounts and account numbers in the general ledger in chart of-accounts number order.
2. Record the adjusting entries in a general journal, page 9.
3. Post the adjusting entries to the general ledger.

Objectives 1 and 2

P 5-3A **Preparing an Income Statement and Journalizing and Posting Adjustments** Cecil Hargis is the owner of Hargis Hat Repair. Cecil had the following partial worksheet at the end of April 19XX:

Hargis Hat Repair

Worksheet (partial)

For the Month Ended April 30, 19XX

Account	Adjustments Debit	Adjustments Credit	Income Statement Debit	Income Statement Credit
Cash				
Accounts Receivable				
Hat Supplies		(a) 3 7 8 0 —		
Prepaid Insurance		(b) 6 2 0 —		
Repair Equipment				
Accounts Payable				
Cecil Hargis, Capital				
Cecil Hargis, Drawing				
Hat Repair Fees				12 7 8 0 —
Wages Expense	(d) 5 8 9 0 —		7 8 9 0 —	
Advertising Expense			1 0 3 0 —	
Rent Expense			1 2 9 0 —	
Utilities Expense			1 5 0 —	
Totals				
Hat Supplies Expense	(a) 3 7 8 0 —		3 7 8 0 —	
Insurance Expense	(b) 6 2 0 —		6 2 0 —	
Depreciation Expense, Repair Equipment	(c) 5 4 0 —		5 4 0 —	
Accumulated Depreciation, Repair Equipment		(c) 5 4 0 —		
Wages Payable		(d) 5 8 9 0 —		
	10 8 3 0 —	10 8 3 0 —	15 3 0 0 —	12 7 8 0 —
Net Loss				2 5 2 0 —
			15 3 0 0 —	15 3 0 0 —

The chart-of-accounts numbers that apply to the adjusting entries are as follows:

Hat Supplies, 13; Prepaid Insurance, 14; Accumulated Depreciation, Repair Equipment, 16; Wages Payable, 22; Wages Expense, 51; Hat Supplies Expense, 55; Insurance Expense, 56; Depreciation Expense, Repair Equipment, 57.

REQUIRED

1. Prepare an income statement.
2. Enter the accounts and account numbers in the general ledger in chart-of-accounts number order.
3. Record adjusting entries in a general journal, page 3.
4. Post only the adjusting entries to the general ledger.

**Objectives 1
and 2**

P 5-4A   Comprehensive Review Problem—Chapters 4 and 5   Yong Suh is the owner of Southwest Insurance Agency. Yong had the following trial balance, Capital account, and adjustments at the end of July 19XX:

Southwest Insurance Agency

Trial Balance

July 31, 19XX

Accounts	Debit	Credit
Cash	25 2 4 0 —	
Accounts Receivable	14 7 3 0 —	
Office Supplies	22 8 9 0 —	
Prepaid Insurance	8 1 6 0 —	
Automobile	15 8 0 0 —	
Accounts Payable		12 7 8 0 —
Yong Suh, Capital		66 5 3 0 —
Yong Suh, Drawing	5 6 5 0 —	
Auto Insurance Fees		9 7 9 0 —
Life Insurance Fees		11 6 4 0 —
Wages Expense	4 3 2 0 —	
Advertising Expense	1 7 8 0 —	
Rent Expense	2 0 0 0 —	
Utilities Expense	1 7 0 —	
Totals	100 7 4 0 —	100 7 4 0 —

GENERAL LEDGER ACCOUNT							
Account: Yong Suh, Capital						Account No. 308	
		Post.				Balance	
Date	Item	Ref.	Debit	Credit	Debit	Credit	
19XX							
July 1		J1		6 2 6 4 0 —		6 2 6 4 0 —	
22		J3		3 8 9 0 —		6 6 5 3 0 —	

Adjustments:

    a. Office Supplies had a beginning balance of $15,450. During the month, $7,440 of office supplies were purchased. A count was made at the end of the month and $19,560 of supplies were on hand.

    b. On July 1, 19XX, the firm paid $8,160 for a four-year liability insurance policy.

    c. An automobile was purchased July 3, 19XX, at a cost of $15,800. Yong estimates that the automobile will have a $2,000 salvage value after five years of useful life.

    d. On July 31, 19XX, $1,990 of wages expense is incurred but unrecorded.

The chart-of-accounts numbers that apply to the adjusting entries are as follows:

    Office Supplies, 131; Prepaid Insurance, 141; Accumulated Depreciation, Automobile, 152; Wages Payable, 221; Wages Expense, 511; Office Supplies Expense, 551; Insurance Expense, 561; Depreciation Expense, Automobile, 571.

REQUIRED

1. Calculate and organize adjustments using T accounts.
2. Complete the worksheet (refer to Chapter 4).
3. Prepare financial statements from the worksheet and Capital account.
4. Record adjusting entries in a general journal, page 5.
5. Post only the adjusting entries to the general ledger (include accounts, account numbers, and previous balances).

PROBLEM SET B

Objective 1   P 5-1B   **Preparing Financial Statements**   The accountant for Goodman Consulting Service completed a worksheet for the month ended November 30, 19XX. The Income Statement and Balance Sheet columns and Capital account are as follows:

Goodman Consulting Service
Worksheet (partial)
For the Month Ended November 30, 19XX

Account	Income Statement Debit	Income Statement Credit	Balance Sheet Debit	Balance Sheet Credit
Cash			32 3 0 0 —	
Accounts Receivable			17 4 0 0 —	
Office Supplies			9 2 0 0 —	
Prepaid Insurance			4 8 0 0 —	
Equipment			11 8 0 0 —	
Accounts Payable				9 5 0 0 —
Dee Goodman, Capital				65 7 0 0 —
Dee Goodman, Drawing			3 3 0 0 —	
Consulting Fees		9 4 0 0 —		
Wages Expense	3 0 0 0 —			
Advertising Expense	4 0 0 —			
Rent Expense	2 6 0 0 —			
Utilities Expense	3 0 0 —			
Totals				
Office Supplies Expense	7 0 0 —			
Insurance Expense	1 0 0 —			
Depreciation Expense, Equipment	2 0 0 —			
Accumulated Depreciation, Equipment				2 0 0 —
Wages Payable				1 3 0 0 —
	7 3 0 0 —	9 4 0 0 —	78 8 0 0 —	76 7 0 0 —
Net Income	2 1 0 0 —			2 1 0 0 —
	9 4 0 0 —	9 4 0 0 —	78 8 0 0 —	78 8 0 0 —

GENERAL LEDGER ACCOUNT								
Account: Dee Goodman, Capital							Account No. 302	
		Post.					Balance	
Date	Item	Ref.	Debit		Credit		Debit	Credit
19XX								
Nov. 1		J1			63 9 0 0 —			63 9 0 0 —
16		J3			1 8 0 0 —			65 7 0 0 —

REQUIRED

Prepare financial statements from the worksheet and Capital account.

Objective 2

P 5-2B Recording and Posting Adjusting Entries Edward Jackson, Sports Psychologist, has the following selected chart of accounts:

Office Supplies, 13; Prepaid Insurance, 14; Accumulated Depreciation, Computer, 16; Wages Payable, 23; Wages Expense, 53; Office Supplies Expense, 56; Insurance Expense, 58; Depreciation Expense, Computer, 59.

The firm's accountant finds the adjusting entries from the Adjustments columns of a completed worksheet (month ended February 28, 19XX):

a. Adjust Office Supplies, $520.
b. Adjust Prepaid Insurance, $80.
c. Adjust Computer, $310.
d. Adjust Wages Expense, $2,090.

REQUIRED

1. Enter the accounts and account numbers in the general ledger in chart-of-accounts number order.
2. Record the adjusting entries in a general journal, page 7.
3. Post the adjusting entries to the general ledger.

Objectives 1 and 2

P 5-3B   **Preparing an Income Statement and Journalizing and Posting Adjustments**   Alan Blumberg is the owner of Blumberg Tire Service. Alan had the following partial worksheet at the end of May 19XX:

Blumberg Tire Service

Worksheet (partial)

For the Month Ended May 31, 19XX

Account	Adjustments Debit	Adjustments Credit	Income Statement Debit	Income Statement Credit
Cash				
Accounts Receivable				
Tire Supplies		(a) 5 9 8 0 —		
Prepaid Insurance		(b) 1 4 5 0 —		
Tire Repair Equipment				
Accounts Payable				
Alan Blumberg, Capital				
Alan Blumberg, Drawing				
Tire Repair Fees				15 8 9 0 —
Wages Expense	(d) 7 2 9 0 —		10 6 7 0 —	
Advertising Expense			1 3 7 0 —	
Rent Expense			2 1 0 0 —	
Utilities Expense			2 6 0 —	
Totals				
Tire Supplies Expense	(a) 5 9 8 0 —		5 9 8 0 —	
Insurance Expense	(b) 1 4 5 0 —		1 4 5 0 —	
Depreciation Expense, Tire Repair Equipment	(c) 6 0 0 —		6 0 0 —	
Accumulated Depreciation, Tire Repair Equipment		(c) 6 0 0 —		
Wages Payable		(d) 7 2 9 0 —		
	15 3 2 0 —	15 3 2 0 —	22 4 3 0 —	15 8 9 0 —
Net Loss				6 5 4 0 —
			22 4 3 0 —	22 4 3 0 —

The chart-of-accounts numbers that apply to the adjusting entries are as follows:

Tire Supplies, 15; Prepaid Insurance, 16; Accumulated Depreciation, Tire Repair Equipment, 18; Wages Payable, 23; Wages Expense, 50; Tire Supplies Expense, 56; Insurance Expense, 57; Depreciation Expense, Tire Repair Equipment, 58.

REQUIRED
1. Prepare an income statement.
2. Enter the accounts and account numbers in the general ledger in chart-of-accounts number order.
3. Record adjusting entries in a general journal, page 9.
4. Post only the adjusting entries to the general ledger.

Objectives 1 and 2

P 5-4B

Comprehensive Review Problem—Chapters 4 and 5 Maxine Wyatt is the owner of Wyatt Fitness Consultants. Maxine had the following trial balance, Capital account, and adjustments at the end of December 19XX:

Accounts	Debit	Credit
Wyatt Fitness Consultants		
Trial Balance		
December 31, 19XX		
Cash	75 8 8 0 —	
Accounts Receivable	24 8 1 0 —	
Store Supplies	31 7 8 0 —	
Prepaid Insurance	9 3 6 0 —	
Truck	19 2 8 0 —	
Accounts Payable		15 8 9 0 —
Maxine Wyatt, Capital		141 4 1 0 —
Maxine Wyatt, Drawing	7 1 5 0 —	
Training Fees		12 6 7 0 —
Consulting Fees		8 3 4 0 —
Wages Expense	5 3 5 0 —	
Advertising Expense	1 8 9 0 —	
Rent Expense	2 5 8 0 —	
Utilities Expense	2 3 0 —	
Totals	178 3 1 0 —	178 3 1 0 —

GENERAL LEDGER ACCOUNT

Account: *Maxine Wyatt, Capital*   Account No.   *304*

Date	Item	Post. Ref.	Debit	Credit	Balance Debit	Balance Credit
19XX						
Dec. 1		J1		1 3 3 4 9 0 —		1 3 3 4 9 0 —
9		J4		7 9 2 0 —		1 4 1 4 1 0 —

Adjustments:

    a. Store Supplies had a beginning balance of $18,490. During the month, $13,290 of store supplies were purchased. A count was made at the end of the month and $29,380 of supplies were on hand.

    b. On December 1, 19XX, the firm paid $9,360 for a six-year liability insurance policy. 130 month

    c. A truck was purchased December 6, 19XX, at a cost of $19,280. Maxine estimates that the truck will have a $2,000 salvage value after four years of useful life.

    d. On December 31, 19XX, $2,780 of wages expense is incurred but unrecorded.

The chart-of-accounts numbers that apply to the adjusting entries are as follows:

Store Supplies, 135; Prepaid Insurance, 143; Accumulated Depreciation, Truck, 155; Wages Payable, 231; Wages Expense, 522; Store Supplies Expense, 555; Insurance Expense, 565; Depreciation Expense, Truck, 575.

REQUIRED

1. Calculate and organize adjustments using T accounts.
2. Complete the worksheet (refer to Chapter 4).
3. Prepare financial statements from the worksheet and Capital account.
4. Record adjusting entries in a general journal, page 8.
5. Post only the adjusting entries to the general ledger (include accounts, account numbers, and previous balances).

ANSWERS TO SELF-TEST QUESTIONS

1. a 2. b 3. d 4. c 5. c

6

Closing the Accounting Records

Money begets money.

JOHN RAY

LEARNING OBJECTIVES

After reading this chapter, discussing the questions, and working the exercises and problems, you will be able to do the following:

1. Journalize and post closing entries (pp. 156–71).
2. Prepare a post-closing trial balance (pp. 172–73).

■n Chapter 4 you completed the worksheet for a service-type organization or firm. The worksheet is a tool that is used to help prepare financial statements. Since adjustments (as calculated in Chapter 4) are prepared as they are needed without regard to chart-of-accounts numbers, you needed a tool, like the worksheet, to account for the haphazard account listings. Then we saw that net income or net loss placed the worksheet in debits-equal-credits balance.

The balance sheet represents the financial position of the firm for a *point* in time. The statement of owner's equity and the income statement measured performance for a definite *period* of time. Once the measured period of time is over, you must set those applicable accounts to zero to begin the new accounting period. In this chapter we will prepare **closing entries** that will clear the appropriate accounts. By the end of this chapter we will have completed the accounting cycle for a service-type firm.

JOURNALIZING AND POSTING CLOSING ENTRIES

Objective 1
Journalize and post closing entries.

Those accounts that measure performance and affect capital (that is, revenues, expenses, and Drawing) must be closed or cleared at the end of one accounting period for the start of the next accounting period. Remember that revenues increase Capital while expenses decrease Capital. Drawing is included here because the use of this account indicates that the owner has taken valuable assets, such as Cash, Office Supplies, and so on out of the firm, thus reducing owner's equity or Capital.

Revenues, expenses, and Drawing are called **nominal** or **temporary** accounts. These accounts start at zero at the beginning of the accounting period, accumulate a balance, and then are reduced to zero again for the start of the next accounting period. Thus, their balances are temporary or nominal. To illustrate the nominal accounts used for Kevin Young, Attorney at Law, the income statement, statement of owner's equity, and balance sheet are listed in Exhibit 6-1. The nominal or temporary accounts are noted by the term, "Nominal," at the left side.

All balance sheet accounts, with the exception of drawing, are **real** or **permanent** accounts. These accounts may start with a balance other than

EXHIBIT 6-1
Real and Nominal Accounts Identified

Kevin Young, Attorney at Law
Income Statement
For the Month Ended April 30, 19XX

Revenue

Nominal   Legal Fees $ 5,200

Expenses

Wages Expense	$ 1,330	
Advertising Expense	300	
Rent Expense	800	
Nominal Utilities Expense	100	
Office Supplies Expense	210	
Insurance Expense	50	
Depreciation Expense, Furniture	150	
Total Expenses		2,940

Net Income $ 2,260

Kevin Young, Attorney at Law
Statement of Owner's Equity
For the Month Ended April 30, 19XX

Real	Kevin Young, Capital, April 1, 19XX	$25,000
	Add: Net Income for April	2,260
Real	Additional Investment	1,000
	Subtotal	$28,260
Nominal	Deduct: Kevin Young, Drawing	200
	Kevin Young, Capital, April 30, 19XX	$28,060

(continued)

(Ex. 6-1 continued)

Kevin Young, Attorney at Law
Balance Sheet
April 30, 19XX

Assets

Cash		$18,700
Accounts Receivable		2,400
Office Supplies		390
Prepaid Insurance		1,150
Furniture	$6,400	
Less: Accumulated Depreciation	150	6,250
Total Assets		$28,890

Real *(bracketing Cash through Less: Accumulated Depreciation)*

Liabilities

Accounts Payable	$ 200	
Wages Payable	630	
Total Liabilities		$ 830

Real *(bracketing Accounts Payable and Wages Payable)*

Owner's Equity

Kevin Young, Capital	28,060
Total Liabilities and Owner's Equity	$28,890

Real *(Kevin Young, Capital)*

zero, and accumulate more or less during the accounting period, but their balances are not closed or cleared at the end of the period. Thus, the ending balances of real or permanent accounts for one accounting period will be the beginning balances for the next period. In Exhibit 6-1 the real or permanent accounts used by Kevin Young, Attorney at Law, so far are noted by "Real" at the left side.

In Exhibit 6-1, Net Income is not an account. Remember that net income is the difference between the revenue and expense accounts for an accounting period. Beginning Capital and Additional Investments are part of the ending balance of Capital.

At this time, before closing entries are made, the balance of the account Kevin Young, Capital, is a $26,000 credit. However, both the statement of owner's equity and balance sheet show $28,060. We will bring this account balance up to date by using closing entries.

Let's use a T account to review the activity in the owner's Capital account in April 19XX which corresponds to the statement of owner's equity in Exhibit 6-1. Remember that net income increases Capital.

Kevin Young, Capital

		−	+		
(4/29) Owner withdrew cash		200	25,000	(4/1)	Initial investment by owner
			1,000	(4/14)	Additional investment by owner
			2,260	(4/1–4/30)	Net income for April 19XX
			28,060		Ending Capital balance

We can see that closing entries have the following purposes:

1. To set the nominal or temporary accounts to zero at the end of an accounting period.
2. To bring the owner's Capital account balance up to date to reflect the balance as shown on the statement of owner's equity and balance sheet.

Income Summary

To facilitate the closing process, a new account—**Income Summary**—must be introduced. The chart-of-accounts number will be 321. Income Summary is a nominal account that will only be used during the closing process. It has a zero balance before and after the closing process.

CLOSING ENTRIES

There are four closing entries to clear the nominal accounts, which consist of revenues, expenses, Income Summary, and Drawing. The closing entries occur in this order: (1) close revenues to Income Summary; (2) close expenses to Income Summary; (3) close Income Summary to Capital; and (4) close Drawing to Capital.

Closing Revenues

To clear the revenue accounts of Kevin Young, Attorney at Law, a general journal entry would be made. This entry would then be posted to the general ledger. The term "Closing Entries" is written after the end of the adjusting entries in the general journal. A description is not needed after each general journal entry as the term "Closing Entries" signifies that the nominal accounts are being cleared. In the general ledger, the term "Closing" is written in the Item column to indicate that the posting is from a closing entry.

Since the revenue accounts have credit balances they must be debited to have a resulting zero balance. The first closing entry is journalized and posted as follows:

GENERAL JOURNAL   Page ____3____

Date		Description	Post. Ref.	Debit	Credit
		(after the last adjusting entry)			
		Closing Entries			
Apr.	30	Legal Fees	401	5 2 0 0 —	
		Income Summary	321		5 2 0 0 —

GENERAL LEDGER ACCOUNTS

Account: *Income Summary*   Account No.   321

Date		Item	Post. Ref.	Debit	Credit	Balance Debit	Balance Credit
19XX							
Apr.	30	Closing	J3		5 2 0 0 —		5 2 0 0 —

Account: *Legal Fees*   Account No.   401

Date		Item	Post. Ref.	Debit	Credit	Balance Debit	Balance Credit
19XX							
Apr.	2		J1		1 9 0 0 —		1 9 0 0 —
	19		J2		1 8 0 0 —		3 7 0 0 —
	24		J2		1 5 0 0 —		5 2 0 0 —
	30	Closing	J3	5 2 0 0 —			— 0 —

At this time, the revenue account is closed to Income Summary. Now let's clear the expense accounts.

Closing Expenses

Expenses normally have a debit balance. Thus, to clear expenses, a credit is applied to each expense account. The total of the expenses is debited to Income Summary. The second closing entry is journalized and posted as follows:

GENERAL JOURNAL   Page ___3___

Date	Description	Post. Ref.	Debit	Credit
30	Income Summary	321	2 9 4 0 —	
	Wages Expense	501		1 3 3 0 —
	Advertising Expense	511		3 0 0 —
	Rent Expense	521		8 0 0 —
	Utilities Expense	531		1 0 0 —
	Office Supplies Expense	541		2 1 0 —
	Insurance Expense	551		5 0 —
	Depreciation Expense, Furniture	561		1 5 0 —

GENERAL LEDGER ACCOUNTS

Account: *Income Summary*   Account No.   321

Date	Item	Post. Ref.	Debit	Credit	Balance Debit	Balance Credit
19XX						
Apr. 30	Closing	J3		5 2 0 0 —		5 2 0 0 —
30	Closing	J3	2 9 4 0 —			2 2 6 0 —

Account: *Wages Expense*   Account No.   501

Date	Item	Post. Ref.	Debit	Credit	Balance Debit	Balance Credit
19XX						
Apr. 17		J2	7 0 0 —		7 0 0 —	
30	Adjusting	J3	6 3 0 —		1 3 3 0 —	
30	Closing	J3		1 3 3 0 —	— 0 —	

(continued)

Account: Advertising Expense								Account No.		511
		Post.						Balance		
Date	Item	Ref.	Debit		Credit		Debit		Credit	
19XX										
Apr. 11		J1	3 0 0 —				3 0 0 —			
30	Closing	J3			3 0 0 —		— 0 —			

Account: Rent Expense								Account No.		521
		Post.						Balance		
Date	Item	Ref.	Debit		Credit		Debit		Credit	
19XX										
Apr. 1		J1	8 0 0 —				8 0 0 —			
30	Closing	J3			8 0 0 —		— 0 —			

Account: Utilities Expense								Account No.		531
		Post.						Balance		
Date	Item	Ref.	Debit		Credit		Debit		Credit	
19XX										
Apr. 7		J1	1 0 0 —				1 0 0 —			
30	Closing	J3			1 0 0 —		— 0 —			

Account: Office Supplies Expense								Account No.		541
		Post.						Balance		
Date	Item	Ref.	Debit		Credit		Debit		Credit	
19XX										
Apr. 30	Adjusting	J3	2 1 0 —				2 1 0 —			
30	Closing	J3			2 1 0 —		— 0 —			

(continued)

Account: *Insurance Expense*						Account No. *551*	
		Post.				**Balance**	
Date	**Item**	**Ref.**	**Debit**	**Credit**		**Debit**	**Credit**
19XX							
Apr. 30	*Adjusting*	*J3*	5 0 —			5 0 —	
30	*Closing*	*J3*		5 0 —		— 0 —	

Account: *Depreciation Expense, Furniture*						Account No. *561*	
		Post.				**Balance**	
Date	**Item**	**Ref.**	**Debit**	**Credit**		**Debit**	**Credit**
19XX							
Apr. 30	*Adjusting*	*J3*	1 5 0 —			1 5 0 —	
30	*Closing*	*J3*		1 5 0 —		— 0 —	

Now all the expense accounts have been cleared to Income Summary. The next step is to close Income Summary to Capital.

Closing Income Summary

Income Summary is a nominal or temporary account. It must have a zero balance at the start of the next accounting period. The balance of Income Summary after all revenues and expenses have been cleared is equal to net income or net loss. Remember that Kevin Young, Attorney at Law, had a net income of $2,260 for April 19XX (see Exhibit 6-1). This corresponds to the Income Summary balance after total revenues and total expenses have been posted. Let's use a T account to illustrate the Income Summary balance:

Income Summary

Beginning balance (4/1) —0—	—0—	
	5,200	Credit balance after revenues are posted
Posting of total expenses 2,940		
	2,260	*Credit balance after revenues and expenses are posted (Net Income)

*If there is a credit balance, then revenues (5,200) are greater than expenses (2,940) and the difference is net income (5,200 credit − 2,940 debit = 2,260 credit).

The third closing entry clears the Income Summary balance to the owner's Capital account as follows:

GENERAL JOURNAL Page ___3___

Date		Description	Post. Ref.	Debit	Credit
	30	Income Summary	321	2 2 6 0 —	
		Kevin Young, Capital	301		2 2 6 0 —

GENERAL LEDGER ACCOUNTS

Account: *Kevin Young, Capital* Account No. 301

Date		Item	Post. Ref.	Debit	Credit	Balance Debit	Balance Credit
19XX							
Apr.	1		J1		2 5 0 0 0 —		2 5 0 0 0 —
	14		J2		1 0 0 0 —		2 6 0 0 0 —
	30	Closing	J3		2 2 6 0 —		2 8 2 6 0 —

Account: *Income Summary* Account No. 321

Date		Item	Post. Ref.	Debit	Credit	Balance Debit	Balance Credit
19XX							
Apr.	30	Closing	J3		5 2 0 0 —		5 2 0 0 —
	30	Closing	J3	2 9 4 0 —			2 2 6 0 —
	30	Closing	J3	2 2 6 0 —			— 0 —

Let's use a T account again to illustrate the Income Summary balance after the third closing entry is made:

Income Summary

Beginning balance (4/1) —0—	—0—	
	5,200	Credit balance after revenues are posted
Posting of total expenses 2,940		
	2,260	Credit balance after revenues and expenses are posted (Net Income)
Third closing entry to clear Income Summary 2,260		
—0—	—0—	(4/30) Ending balance

Closing Drawing

Drawing is the only nominal account that appears in a Balance Sheet column on the worksheet. As we have previously seen, whenever the owner removes an asset from the firm (Cash, Furniture, and so on) the asset is credited and Drawing is debited. To reflect this decrease in the owner's equity of the firm, the fourth closing entry is made to reduce owner's equity and clear Drawing.

The closing process for the Drawing account is as follows:

GENERAL JOURNAL   Page ___3___

Date	Description	Post. Ref.	Debit	Credit
30	Kevin Young, Capital	301	2 0 0 —	
	Kevin Young, Drawing	311		2 0 0 —

GENERAL LEDGER ACCOUNTS

Account: *Kevin Young, Capital*   Account No.   301

Date	Item	Post. Ref.	Debit	Credit	Balance Debit	Balance Credit
19XX						
Apr. 1		J1		2 5 0 0 0 —		2 5 0 0 0 —
14		J2		1 0 0 0 —		2 6 0 0 0 —
30	Closing	J3		2 2 6 0 —		2 8 2 6 0 —
30	Closing	J3	2 0 0 —			* 2 8 0 6 0 —

*This 28,060 balance in Capital is the ending balance of Kevin Young, Capital, on the statement of owner's equity and the balance sheet (see Exhibit 6-1).

Account: *Kevin Young, Drawing*					Account No. 311	
Date	Item	Post. Ref.	Debit	Credit	Balance Debit	Balance Credit
19XX						
Apr. 29		*J2*	2 0 0 —		2 0 0 —	
30	*Closing*	*J3*		2 0 0 —	— 0 —	

Upon completion of these postings, Drawing has a zero balance.

Journalizing Closing Entries

So far we have journalized the closing entries separately. However, they would be journalized in the general journal in order, with revenues first, expenses second, and so on. The four closing entries are illustrated in Exhibit 6-2.

EXHIBIT 6-2
Four Closing Entries Journalized in the General Journal

GENERAL JOURNAL   Page ___3___

Date	Description	Post. Ref.	Debit	Credit
	(after the last adjusting entry)			
	Closing Entries			
Apr. 30	Legal Fees	401	5 2 0 0 —	
	Income Summary	321		5 2 0 0 —
30	Income Summary	321	2 9 4 0 —	
	Wages Expense	501		1 3 3 0 —
	Advertising Expense	511		3 0 0 —
	Rent Expense	521		8 0 0 —
	Utilities Expense	531		1 0 0 —
	Office Supplies Expense	541		2 1 0 —
	Insurance Expense	551		5 0 —
	Depreciation Expense, Furniture	561		1 5 0 —
30	Income Summary	321	2 2 6 0 —	
	Kevin Young, Capital	301		2 2 6 0 —
30	Kevin Young, Capital	301	2 0 0 —	
	Kevin Young, Drawing	311		2 0 0 —

The General Ledger (after Closing Entries)

Let's bring ourselves up to date on the account balances in the general ledger at the close of the accounting period. The general ledger accounts for Kevin Young, Attorney at Law, are illustrated in Exhibit 6-3. (Notice that Income Summary, account number 321, is included.)

EXHIBIT 6-3
General Ledger Accounts at Close of Accounting Period

GENERAL LEDGER ACCOUNTS

Account: *Cash*   Account No.   *101*

Date	Item	Post. Ref.	Debit	Credit	Balance Debit	Balance Credit
19XX						
Apr. 1		J1	25000—		25000—	
1		J1		800—	24200—	
1		J1		1200—	23000—	
2		J1	1900—		24900—	
3		J1		6400—	18500—	
7		J1		100—	18400—	
14		J2	1000—		19400—	
17		J2		700—	18700—	
22		J2		400—	18300—	
26		J2	900—		19200—	
29		J2		200—	19000—	
30		J2		300—	18700—	

Account: *Accounts Receivable*   Account No.   *111*

Date	Item	Post. Ref.	Debit	Credit	Balance Debit	Balance Credit
19XX						
Apr. 19		J2	1800—		1800—	
24		J2	1500—		3300—	
26		J2		900—	2400—	

(continued)

(Ex. 6-3 continued)

Account: *Office Supplies*						Account No. 121	
Date	Item	Post. Ref.	Debit	Credit	Balance Debit		Credit
19XX							
Apr. 4		J1	600—		600—		
30	Adjusting	J3		210—	390—		

Account: *Prepaid Insurance*						Account No. 131	
Date	Item	Post. Ref.	Debit	Credit	Balance Debit		Credit
19XX							
Apr. 1		J1	1200—		1200—		
30	Adjusting	J3		50—	1150—		

Account: *Furniture*						Account No. 141	
Date	Item	Post. Ref.	Debit	Credit	Balance Debit		Credit
19XX							
Apr. 3		J1	6400—		6400—		

Account: *Accumulated Depreciation, Furniture*						Account No. 142	
Date	Item	Post. Ref.	Debit	Credit	Balance Debit		Credit
19XX							
Apr. 30	Adjusting	J3		150—			150—

(continued)

(Ex. 6-3 continued)

Account: *Accounts Payable* — **Account No.** 201

Date		Item	Post. Ref.	Debit	Credit	Balance Debit	Balance Credit
19XX							
Apr.	4		J1		6 0 0 —		6 0 0 —
	11		J1		3 0 0 —		9 0 0 —
	22		J2	4 0 0 —			5 0 0 —
	30		J2	3 0 0 —			2 0 0 —

Account: *Wages Payable* — **Account No.** 211

Date		Item	Post. Ref.	Debit	Credit	Balance Debit	Balance Credit
19XX							
Apr.	30	Adjusting	J3		6 3 0 —		6 3 0 —

Account: *Kevin Young, Capital* — **Account No.** 301

Date		Item	Post. Ref.	Debit	Credit	Balance Debit	Balance Credit
19XX							
Apr.	1		J1		2 5 0 0 0 —		2 5 0 0 0 —
	14		J2		1 0 0 0 —		2 6 0 0 0 —
	30	Closing	J3		2 2 6 0 —		2 8 2 6 0 —
	30	Closing	J3	2 0 0 —			2 8 0 6 0 —

Account: *Kevin Young, Drawing* — **Account No.** 311

Date		Item	Post. Ref.	Debit	Credit	Balance Debit	Balance Credit
19XX							
Apr.	29		J2	2 0 0 —		2 0 0 —	
	30	Closing	J3		2 0 0 —	— 0 —	

(continued)

(Ex. 6-3 continued)

Account: *Income Summary*							Account No.	321	
		Post.					Balance		
Date	Item	Ref.	Debit		Credit		Debit	Credit	
19XX									
Apr. 30	Closing	J3			5 2 0 0 —			5 2 0 0 —	
30	Closing	J3	2 9 4 0 —					2 2 6 0 —	
30	Closing	J3	2 2 6 0 —					— 0 —	

Account: *Legal Fees*							Account No.	401	
		Post.					Balance		
Date	Item	Ref.	Debit		Credit		Debit	Credit	
19XX									
Apr. 2		J1			1 9 0 0 —			1 9 0 0 —	
19		J2			1 8 0 0 —			3 7 0 0 —	
24		J2			1 5 0 0 —			5 2 0 0 —	
30	Closing	J3	5 2 0 0 —					— 0 —	

Account: *Wages Expense*							Account No.	501	
		Post.					Balance		
Date	Item	Ref.	Debit		Credit		Debit	Credit	
19XX									
Apr. 17		J2	7 0 0 —				7 0 0 —		
30	Adjusting	J3	6 3 0 —				1 3 3 0 —		
30	Closing	J3			1 3 3 0 —		— 0 —		

Account: *Advertising Expense*							Account No.	511	
		Post.					Balance		
Date	Item	Ref.	Debit		Credit		Debit	Credit	
19XX									
Apr. 11		J1	3 0 0 —				3 0 0 —		
30	Closing	J3			3 0 0 —		— 0 —		

(continued)

(Ex. 6-3 concluded)

Account: *Rent Expense* — **Account No.** *521*

Date		Item	Post. Ref.	Debit	Credit	Balance Debit	Balance Credit
19XX							
Apr.	1		J1	800 —		800 —	
	30	Closing	J3		800 —	— 0 —	

Account: *Utilities Expense* — **Account No.** *531*

Date		Item	Post. Ref.	Debit	Credit	Balance Debit	Balance Credit
19XX							
Apr.	7		J1	100 —		100 —	
	30	Closing	J3		100 —	— 0 —	

Account: *Office Supplies Expense* — **Account No.** *541*

Date		Item	Post. Ref.	Debit	Credit	Balance Debit	Balance Credit
19XX							
Apr.	30	Adjusting	J3	210 —		210 —	
	30	Closing	J3		210 —	— 0 —	

Account: *Insurance Expense* — **Account No.** *551*

Date		Item	Post. Ref.	Debit	Credit	Balance Debit	Balance Credit
19XX							
Apr.	30	Adjusting	J3	50 —		50 —	
	30	Closing	J3		50 —	— 0 —	

Account: *Depreciation Expense, Furniture* — **Account No.** *561*

Date		Item	Post. Ref.	Debit	Credit	Balance Debit	Balance Credit
19XX							
Apr.	30	Adjusting	J3	150 —		150 —	
	30	Closing	J3		150 —	— 0 —	

PREPARING A POST-CLOSING TRIAL BALANCE

Objective 2
Prepare a
post-closing
trial balance.

An accountant may be very confident that all appropriate closing entries have been properly journalized and posted. However, if by chance an error is made, the accountant may not find it until the next accounting period is under way. Thus, valuable time could be spent correcting error(s) that occurred in a previous accounting period. To insure that the accounting records, in particular the general ledger, are ready for the start of the next accounting period a **post-closing trial balance** is prepared. The post-closing trial balance has the following purposes:

1. To assure that all nominal accounts are closed.
2. To assure that total debits equal total credits.
3. To assure that all account balances are normal.

The post-closing trial balance is very similar to the beginning trial balance prepared in Chapter 3. The general ledger accounts are listed in chart-of-accounts order. Any account that has a zero balance is not listed. The post-closing trial balance for Kevin Young, Attorney at Law at the end of the accounting period, April 19XX is as follows:

Kevin Young, Attorney at Law
Post-Closing Trial Balance
April 30, 19XX

Accounts	Debit	Credit
Cash	18 7 0 0 —	
Accounts Receivable	2 4 0 0 —	
Office Supplies	3 9 0 —	
Prepaid Insurance	1 1 5 0 —	
Furniture	6 4 0 0 —	
Accumulated Depreciation, Furniture		1 5 0 —
Accounts Payable		2 0 0 —
Wages Payable		6 3 0 —
Kevin Young, Capital		28 0 6 0 —
Totals	29 0 4 0 —	29 0 4 0 —

Now that the post-closing trial balance is prepared, let's see if the three purposes are met. First we can see that no nominal accounts are listed. This indicates that all nominal accounts have zero balances. Next, we see that total debits equal total credits. Then, looking at the accounts and account balances, we see that all account balances are normal; that is, Cash has a debit balance, Accounts Payable a credit balance, and so on. Therefore the accounting records are properly set for the next accounting period. You should always thoroughly examine the accounting records to make sure that all journal entries, postings, descriptions, and so on, are correct before you go on to the next accounting period.

Review of the Accounting Cycle

We have now completed the accounting cycle for a service-type firm. The steps to the accounting cycle are as follows:

1. Analyze transactions from source documents.
2. Record the transactions in a journal.
3. Post to the general ledger accounts.
4. Prepare a trial balance.
5. Adjust the general ledger accounts.
6. Complete the worksheet.
7. Prepare financial statements.
8. Journalize and post adjusting entries.
9. Journalize and post closing entries.
10. Prepare a post-closing trial balance. *What left Equal*

CHAPTER REVIEW

1. **Journalize and post closing entries (pp. 156–71).**
   Those accounts that measure performance and affect capital (revenues, expenses, and Drawing) must be closed or cleared at the end of one accounting period for the start of the next accounting period. There are four closing entries to clear the nominal accounts—revenues, expenses, Income Summary, and Drawing. The closing entries occur in this order: (a) close revenues to Income Summary; (b) close expenses to Income Summary; (c) close Income Summary to Capital; and (d) close Drawing to Capital.

2. **Prepare a post-closing trial balance (pp. 172–73).**
   To insure that the accounting records, in particular the general ledger, are ready for the start of the next accounting period, a post-closing trial balance is prepared. The post-closing trial balance has the

following purposes: (a) to assure that all nominal accounts are closed; (b) to assure that total debits equal total credits; and (c) to assure that all account balances are normal.

GLOSSARY

Closing Entry	Entry made to clear the balance of a nominal account.
Income Summary	Nominal account used during the closing process.
Nominal Account	Account that is cleared at the end of an accounting period.
Permanent Account	Another term for real account.
Post-Closing Trial Balance	Trial balance prepared after closing entries have been journalized and posted.
Real Account	Account that is not cleared at the end of an accounting period. The account balance remains open from one accounting period to the next.
Temporary Account	Another term for nominal account.

SELF-TEST QUESTIONS FOR REVIEW

(Answers are on p. 185.)

1. Legal Fees is a _____ account and H. L. Jones, Drawing is a _____ account.
   a. nominal; real
   b. real; nominal
   c. real; real
   d. nominal; nominal

2. Closing expenses is the _____ closing entry and closing drawing is the _____ closing entry.
   a. first; second
   b. third; fourth
   c. second; fourth
   d. first; third

3. Which of the following accounts would probably have a credit balance after all closing entries are posted?
   a. Income Summary
   b. Mary Conners, Drawing
   c. Accounts Receivable
   d. Fred Moore, Capital

4. The account _____ could be listed in the debit column of a post-closing trial balance.
   a. Prepaid Insurance
   b. Accounts Payable
   c. Wages Payable
   d. J. Nguyen, Drawing

5. Preparing a post-closing trial balance is step _____ of the accounting cycle.
   a. 8
   b. 7
   c. 10
   d. 9

PRACTICAL REVIEW PROBLEM

Objectives 1 and 2

Journalizing Closing Entries and Preparing a Post-Closing Trial Balance
Lydia Flores owns and operates The Flores Repair Shop. She had the following accounts, chart-of-accounts numbers, and account balances as of March 31, 19XX. All account balances are normal. The firm had a net loss for the month.

Account	Account Number	Account Balance
Cash	103	9,620
Accounts Receivable	108	7,810
Store Supplies	131	1,630
Prepaid Insurance	141	2,900
Office Equipment	151	72,270
Accumulated Depreciation, Office Equipment	152	2,050
Accounts Payable	211	41,890
Wages Payable	221	3,600
Lydia Flores, Capital	301	54,620
Lydia Flores, Drawing	311	2,770
Income Summary	321	0
Service Fees	401	1,910
Consulting Fees	411	2,500
Wages Expense	501	3,600
Advertising Expense	511	1,490
Rent Expense	521	1,670
Utilities Expense	531	100
Store Supplies Expense	541	540
Insurance Expense	551	120
Depreciation Expense, Office Equipment	561	2,050

REQUIRED
1. Journalize the four closing entries in the general journal, page 6. DO NOT post to the general ledger.
2. Prepare a post-closing trial balance.

ANSWER TO THE PRACTICAL REVIEW PROBLEM

1.   **GENERAL JOURNAL**   Page ____6____

Date		Description	Post. Ref.	Debit	Credit
		Closing Entries			
Mar.	31	Service Fees		1 9 1 0 —	
		Consulting Fees		2 5 0 0 —	
		Income Summary			4 4 1 0 —
	31	Income Summary		9 5 7 0 —	
		Wages Expense			3 6 0 0 —
		Advertising Expense			1 4 9 0 —
		Rent Expense			1 6 7 0 —
		Utilities Expense			1 0 0 —
		Store Supplies Expense			5 4 0 —
		Insurance Expense			1 2 0 —
		Depreciation Expense, Office Equipment			2 0 5 0 —
	31	Lydia Flores, Capital		5 1 6 0 —	
		Income Summary			5 1 6 0 —
	31	Lydia Flores, Capital		2 7 7 0 —	
		Lydia Flores, Drawing			2 7 7 0 —

2.   The Flores Repair Shop
                                 Post-Closing Trial Balance
                                 March 31, 19XX

Accounts	Debit	Credit
Cash	9 6 2 0 —	
Accounts Receivable	7 8 1 0 —	
Store Supplies	1 6 3 0 —	
Prepaid Insurance	2 9 0 0 —	
Office Equipment	72 2 7 0 —	
Accumulated Depreciation, Office Equipment		2 0 5 0 —
Accounts Payable		41 8 9 0 —
Wages Payable		3 6 0 0 —
Lydia Flores, Capital		*46 6 9 0 —
Totals	94 2 3 0 —	94 2 3 0 —

*54,620 beginning balance − 5,160 net loss − 2,770 drawing = 46,690 ending Capital balance.

DISCUSSION QUESTIONS

Q 6-1 What are the two purposes of closing entries?

Q 6-2 Define and describe nominal accounts. Name the financial statement(s) where you would find nominal accounts.

Q 6-3 Define and describe real accounts. Name the financial statement(s) where you would find real accounts.

Q 6-4 What is the purpose of the Income Summary account? How and when is it used?

Q 6-5 List the four closing entries in their proper sequence.

Q 6-6 Record the following activity for owner's Capital in a T account: May 1, initial investment by owner, $19,341; May 11, additional investment by owner, $3,987; May 31, net income for May 19XX, $7,099. Determine the balance.

Q 6-7 Record the following activity for Income Summary in a T account: June 1, beginning balance, $0; closing of revenues, $3,076; closing of expenses, $2,012. Determine the balance.

Q 6-8 Why must a post-closing trial balance be prepared?

Q 6-9 What are the three purposes of a post-closing trial balance?

Q 6-10 Name the ten steps in the accounting cycle. Which of the steps were covered in this chapter?

EXERCISES

Objective 1

E 6-1 **Listing Accounts**   List at least ten nominal accounts. List at least ten real accounts.

Objective 2

E 6-2 **Listing Accounts**   You are the accountant for the firm Greta Weiss, Attorney at Law. List at least nine accounts that could possibly appear on a post-closing trial balance.

Objective 1

E 6-3 **Identifying Accounts**   Indicate whether the following accounts are nominal or real:

a. Cash
b. Ed Gold, Capital
c. Accounts Receivable
d. Prepaid Insurance
e. Rent Expense
f. Ed Gold, Drawing
g. Income Summary
h. Wages Expense
i. Furniture
j. Store Supplies
k. Legal Fees
l. Rent Expense
m. Depreciation Expense, Truck
n. Accumulated Depreciation, Truck

Objective 1   E 6-4   **Finding Revenues, Expenses, and Net Income**   A firm had the following T account after the second closing entry:

Income Summary	
12,800	13,900

From the T account find: (a) total revenues; (b) total expenses; and (c) net income.

Objective 1   E 6-5   **Finding Net Income, Drawing, and Ending Capital**   Ruben Mata is the owner of a CPA firm. His capital account appears as follows after all closing entries have been journalized and posted:

GENERAL LEDGER ACCOUNTS							
Account: *Ruben Mata, Capital*						Account No. *301*	
		Post.				Balance	
Date	Item	Ref.	Debit	Credit		Debit	Credit
19XX	*Aug. 31 Balance*						*1 2 0 9 0 0 —*
Aug. 31	*Closing*	*J13*		*6 4 0 0 —*			
31	*Closing*	*J13*	*1 8 0 0 —*				

From the capital account find: (a) net income; (b) drawing; and (c) the ending capital balance.

Objective 1   E 6-6   **Determining Net Income and Journalizing Closing Entries**   After the first two closing entries have been journalized and posted, the Income Summary account of a dental firm (Randi Martin, owner) is as follows:

Income Summary	
35,890	38,120

From the T account: (a) determine net income and (b) journalize the entry necessary to close the Income Summary account (October 31, 19XX).

Objective 1   E 6-7   **Journalizing Closing Entries**   A firm has the following selected accounts and account balances (all account balances are normal) at March 31, 19XX:

Jay Puhlman, Drawing	$ 1,100	Rent Expense	$2,500
Income Summary	–0–	Utilities Expense	700
Medical Fees	10,500	Medical Supplies Expense	200
Wages Expense	3,600	Insurance Expense	300
Advertising Expense	1,300		

Journalize the four closing entries in the general journal, page 6.

Objective 2

E 6-8 Preparing a Post-Closing Trial Balance Keystone Consulting Service has the following accounts and account balances at August 31, 19XX after all closing entries are journalized and posted:

Cash	$27,190	Accounts Receivable	$13,460
Office Supplies	8,950	Prepaid Insurance	2,770
Computer	19,840	Accumulated Depreciation, Computer	4,850
Accounts Payable	10,620	Wages Payable	360
Enid Garrison, Capital	56,380		

Prepare a post-closing trial balance. (Note: All account balances are normal.)

PROBLEM SET A

Objective 1

P 6-1A Journalizing Closing Entries Deng Recording Service is owned by Kim Deng. The firm had the following accounts and account balances as of September 30, 19XX. All account balances are normal.

Account	Account Balance
Cash	9,700
Accounts Receivable	3,200
Office Supplies	1,600
Prepaid Insurance	2,800
Truck	17,300
Accumulated Depreciation, Truck	600
Accounts Payable	4,100
Wages Payable	1,200
Kim Deng, Capital	22,300
Kim Deng, Drawing	2,200
Income Summary	0
Recording Fees	6,700
Consulting Fees	8,500
Wages Expense	4,400
Rent Expense	1,100
Office Supplies Expense	300
Insurance Expense	200
Depreciation Expense, Truck	600

REQUIRED

Journalize the four closing entries in the general journal, page 3.

Objective 1   **P 6-2A   Posting Closing Entries**   You are hired as the accountant for Callahan Design Studio. You find the following closing entries:

GENERAL JOURNAL   Page ___5___

Date		Description	Post. Ref.	Debit	Credit
		Closing Entries			
19XX					
Dec.	31	Design Fees	401	13 4 0 0 —	
		Income Summary	321		13 4 0 0 —
	31	Income Summary	321	11 8 0 0 —	
		Wages Expense	501		6 2 0 0 —
		Advertising Expense	511		2 3 0 0 —
		Rent Expense	521		1 9 0 0 —
		Utilities Expense	531		2 0 0 —
		Design Supplies Expense	541		8 0 0 —
		Insurance Expense	551		1 0 0 —
		Depreciation Expense, Furniture	561		3 0 0 —
	31	Income Summary	321	1 6 0 0 —	
		Tom Callahan, Capital	301		1 6 0 0 —
	31	Tom Callahan, Capital	301	7 0 0 —	
		Tom Callahan, Drawing	311		7 0 0 —

The accountant you replaced recorded the closing entries in the general journal and included the proper general ledger account numbers in the Post. Ref. column of the general journal. However, he did not post to the general ledger.

REQUIRED

1. Using the general ledger account numbers in the Post. Ref. column, write the account names, account numbers, and previous balances (the owner's Capital account has a $26,800 credit balance before closing entries; Income Summary has a zero balance before closing entries; all other account balances from closing entries) in the general ledger. List Owner, Capital (301) first, followed by Owner, Drawing (311), and so on.

2. Post the closing entries to the general ledger. Include all posting references in the general ledger.

Objectives
1 and 2

P 6-3A   Journalizing Closing Entries and Preparing a Post-Closing Trial Balance   Lemke Wrecker Service is owned by Nancy Lemke. She had the following accounts, chart-of-accounts numbers, and account balances as of January 31, 19XX. All account balances are normal. The firm had a net loss for the month.

Account	Account Number	Account Balance
Cash	101	36,140
Accounts Receivable	110	11,230
Wrecker Supplies	121	4,890
Prepaid Insurance	135	3,780
Wrecker	141	17,900
Accumulated Depreciation, Wrecker	142	300
Accounts Payable	201	5,900
Wages Payable	211	1,450
Nancy Lemke, Capital	301	70,310
Nancy Lemke, Drawing	311	2,650
Income Summary	321	0
Wrecker Fees	401	6,890
Storage Fees	411	5,820
Wages Expense	501	9,910
Rent Expense	511	2,990
Wrecker Supplies Expense	531	320
Insurance Expense	541	560
Depreciation Expense, Wrecker	561	300

REQUIRED
1. Journalize the four closing entries in the general journal, page 8. DO NOT post to the general ledger.
2. Prepare a post-closing trial balance (see Practical Review Problem).

Objectives
1 and 2

P 6-4A   Comprehensive Chapter Review Problem   P. K. Lam owns Lam's Financial Services. P. K. had the following accounts, chart-of-accounts numbers, and account balances as of August 31, 19XX. All account balances are normal.

Account	Account Number	Account Balance
Cash	101	45,902
Accounts Receivable	110	27,912
Office Supplies	121	12,673
Prepaid Insurance	132	8,674

Automobile	151	15,892
Accumulated Depreciation,		
Automobile	152	356
Computer	161	11,878
Accumulated Depreciation,		
Computer	162	234
Accounts Payable	201	19,784
Wages Payable	211	4,891
P. K. Lam, Capital	301	108,218
P. K. Lam, Drawing	311	12,346
Income Summary	321	0
Financial Services	401	17,564
Consulting Fees	411	7,899
Wages Expense	501	12,655
Rent Expense	511	4,892
Advertising Expense	521	1,909
Utilities Expense	531	347
Office Supplies Expense	535	2,734
Insurance Expense	541	542
Depreciation Expense,		
Automobile	552	356
Depreciation Expense,		
Computer	553	234

REQUIRED

1. Journalize the four closing entries in the general journal, page 13.
2. Post the closing entries to the general ledger (include accounts, account numbers, and previous balances).
3. Prepare a post-closing trial balance.

PROBLEM SET B

Objective 1

P 6-1B   Journalizing Closing Entries   Heinz Service Co. is owned by A. E. Heinz. The firm had the following accounts and account balances as of June 30, 19XX. All account balances are normal.

Account	Account Balance
Cash	12,600
Accounts Receivable	8,900
Service Supplies	6,300
Prepaid Insurance	3,700
Furniture	15,800
Accumulated Depreciation,	
Furniture	900

Accounts Payable	11,200
Wages Payable	1,400
A. E. Heinz, Capital	30,900
A. E. Heinz, Drawing	2,600
Income Summary	0
Service Fees	6,500
Consulting Fees	7,300
Wages Expense	4,100
Rent Expense	2,200
Service Supplies Expense	600
Insurance Expense	500
Depreciation Expense, Furniture	900

REQUIRED

Journalize the four closing entries in the general journal, page 4.

Objective 1   **P 6-2B   Posting Closing Entries**   You are hired as the accountant for Thompson Flower Decorators. You find the following closing entries:

GENERAL JOURNAL   Page ___6___

Date		Description	Post. Ref.	Debit	Credit
		Closing Entries			
19XX					
Feb.	*28*	*Decorating Fees*	401	25 1 0 0 —	
		Income Summary	321		25 1 0 0 —
	28	*Income Summary*	321	21 8 0 0 —	
		Wages Expense	501		8 9 0 0 —
		Advertising Expense	511		4 8 0 0 —
		Rent Expense	521		2 5 0 0 —
		Utilities Expense	531		6 0 0 —
		Decorating Supplies Expense	541		3 9 0 0 —
		Insurance Expense	551		4 0 0 —
		Depreciation Expense, Truck	561		7 0 0 —
	28	*Income Summary*	321	3 3 0 0 —	
		Alice Thompson, Capital	301		3 3 0 0 —
	28	*Alice Thompson, Capital*	301	9 0 0 —	
		Alice Thompson, Drawing	311		9 0 0 —

The accountant you replaced recorded the closing entries in the general journal and included the proper general ledger account numbers in the Post. Ref. column of the general journal. However, she did not post to the general ledger.

REQUIRED
1. Using the general ledger account numbers in the Post. Ref. column, write the account names, account numbers, and previous balances (the owner's Capital account has a $39,400 credit balance before closing entries; Income Summary has a zero balance before closing entries; all other account balances from closing entries) in the general ledger. List Owner, Capital (301) first, followed by Owner, Drawing (311), and so on.
2. Post the closing entries to the general ledger. Include all posting references in the general ledger.

Objectives 1 and 2

P 6-3B **Journalizing Closing Entries and Preparing a Post-closing Trial Balance**   Denning's Coffee Service is owned by Rich Denning. He had the following accounts, chart-of-accounts numbers, and account balances as of March 31, 19XX. All account balances are normal. The firm had a net loss for the month.

Account	Account Number	Account Balance
Cash	101	19,630
Accounts Receivable	110	3,410
Coffee Supplies	121	6,890
Prepaid Insurance	135	3,890
Coffee Equipment	141	5,750
Accumulated Depreciation, Coffee Equipment	142	210
Accounts Payable	201	17,560
Wages Payable	211	3,720
Rich Denning, Capital	301	23,240
Rich Denning, Drawing	311	4,150
Income Summary	321	0
Coffee Fees	401	4,030
Consulting Fees	411	3,910
Wages Expense	501	6,090
Rent Expense	511	1,670
Coffee Supplies Expense	531	470
Insurance Expense	541	510
Depreciation Expense, Coffee Equipment	561	210

REQUIRED
1. Journalize the four closing entries in the general journal, page 9. DO NOT post to the general ledger.
2. Prepare a post-closing trial balance (see Practical Review Problem).

Objectives
1 and 2

P 6-4B Comprehensive Chapter Review Problem Diane Starks owns Starks Consulting Services. She had the following accounts, chart-of-accounts numbers, and account balances as of January 31, 19XX. All account balances are normal.

Account	Account Number	Account Balance
Cash	101	42,892
Accounts Receivable	110	13,267
Office Supplies	121	11,909
Prepaid Insurance	132	2,092
Furniture	141	35,347
Accumulated Depreciation, Furniture	142	1,203
Delivery Truck	151	16,241
Accumulated Depreciation, Delivery Truck	152	587
Accounts Payable	201	32,212
Wages Payable	211	3,146
Diane Starks, Capital	301	88,300
Diane Starks, Drawing	311	9,621
Income Summary	321	0
Consulting Fees	401	12,896
Service Fees	411	9,674
Wages Expense	501	6,392
Rent Expense	511	2,981
Advertising Expense	521	948
Utilities Expense	528	209
Office Supplies Expense	531	3,876
Insurance Expense	541	453
Depreciation Expense, Furniture	551	1,203
Depreciation Expense, Delivery Truck	552	587

REQUIRED
1. Journalize the four closing entries in the general journal, page 14.
2. Post the closing entries to the general ledger (include accounts, account numbers, and previous balances).
3. Prepare a post-closing trial balance.

ANSWERS TO SELF-TEST QUESTIONS

1. d 2. c 3. d 4. a 5. c

ACCOUNTING CYCLE REVIEW, CHAPTERS 1–6 (SERVICE FIRM)

Chapter 6 completed the accounting cycle for a service-type firm. This review section contains a series of diagrams of the accounting cycle for a service-type firm:

(A.) An overview of the accounting cycle

(B.) Accounting equation: applying debits and credits

(C.) Journalizing and posting

(D.) Worksheet

(E.) Financial statements

(F.) Adjusting entries (placed after Diagram G on pp. 194–95)

(G.) Closing entries

Follow the arrows, where indicated, for the proper sequence.

DIAGRAM A
Accounting Cycle—Overview (see Chapter 4)

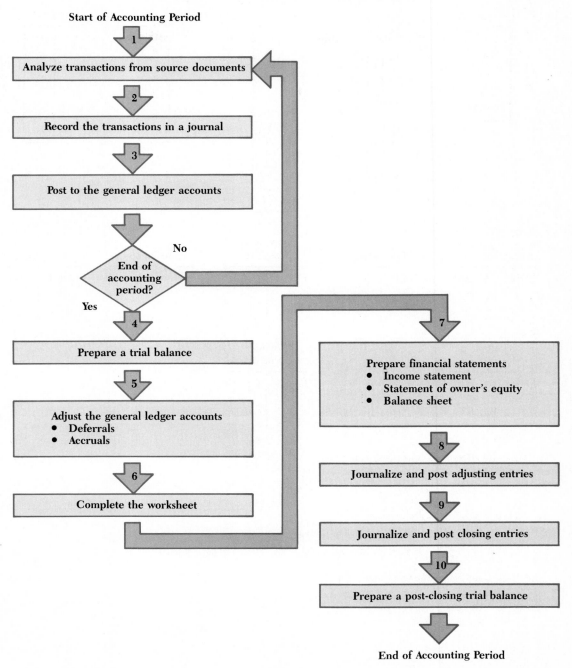

Start of Accounting Period

1 Analyze transactions from source documents

2 Record the transactions in a journal

3 Post to the general ledger accounts

End of accounting period?   No

Yes

4 Prepare a trial balance

5 Adjust the general ledger accounts
- Deferrals
- Accruals

6 Complete the worksheet

7 Prepare financial statements
- Income statement
- Statement of owner's equity
- Balance sheet

8 Journalize and post adjusting entries

9 Journalize and post closing entries

10 Prepare a post-closing trial balance

End of Accounting Period

DIAGRAM B
Accounting Equation: Applying Debits and Credits (see Chapter 2)

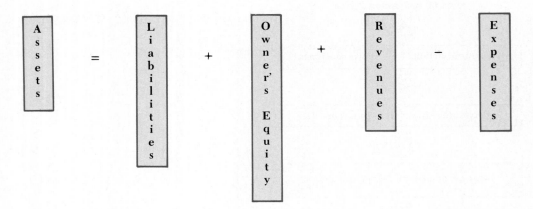

	Assets			Liabilities			Owner's Capital			Revenues			Expenses	
	Debit	Credit		Debit	Credit		Debit	Credit		Debit	Credit		Debit	Credit
	+	−		−	+		−	+		−	+		+	−

	Contra Assets			Owner's Drawing	
	Debit	Credit		Debit	Credit
	−	+		+	−

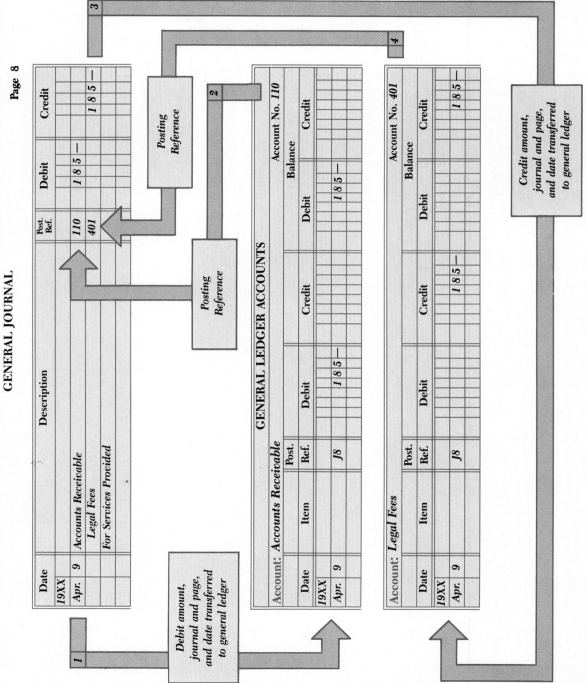

DIAGRAM C
Journalizing and Posting (see Chapter 3)

DIAGRAM D
Completing the Worksheet (see Chapter 4)

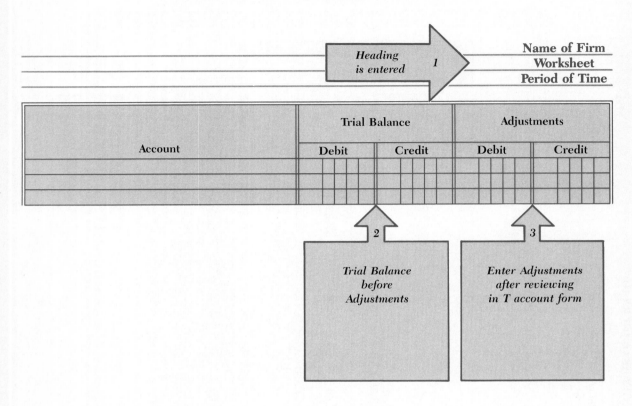

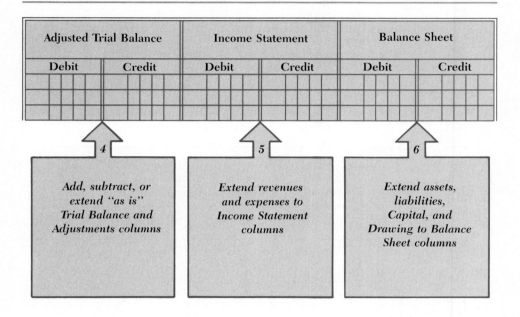

DIAGRAM E
Financial Statements (see Chapters 1, 2, and 5)

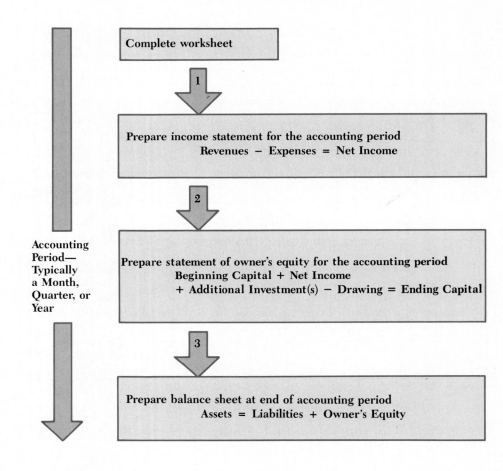

DIAGRAM G
Closing Entry Sequence (See Chapter 6)

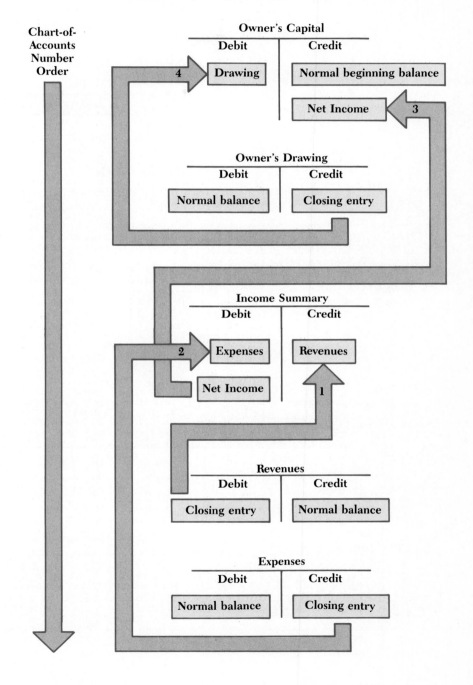

DIAGRAM F
Journalizing and Posting Adjusting Entries—Expenses *Only*—
(see Chapter 5)

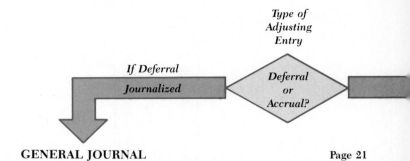

Type of Adjusting Entry

If Deferral

Journalized

Deferral or Accrual?

GENERAL JOURNAL   Page 21

Date		Description	Post. Ref.	Debit	Credit
		Adjusting Entries			
19XX					
Nov.	*30*	Insurance Expense	*561*	*1 0 0* —	
		Prepaid Insurance	*131*		*1 0 0* —

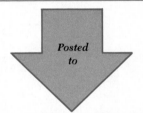

Posted to

GENERAL LEDGER ACCOUNTS

Account: *Prepaid Insurance*   Account No. *131*

Date		Item	Post. Ref.	Debit	Credit	Balance Debit	Credit
19XX		Previous Balance				*1 0 0 0* —	
Nov.	*30*	Adjusting	*J21*		*1 0 0* —	*9 0 0* —	

Account: *Insurance Expense*   Account No. *561*

Date		Item	Post. Ref.	Debit	Credit	Balance Debit	Credit
19XX							
Nov.	*30*	Adjusting	*J21*	*1 0 0* —		*1 0 0* —	

If Accrual

Journalized

GENERAL JOURNAL   Page 9

Date		Description	Post. Ref.	Debit	Credit
		Adjusting Entries			
19XX					
Jan.	*31*	Wages Expense	*501*	8 0 0 —	
		Wages Payable	*211*		8 0 0 —

Posted to

GENERAL LEDGER ACCOUNTS

Account: *Wages Payable*   Account No. *211*

Date		Item	Post. Ref.	Debit	Credit	Balance Debit	Balance Credit
19XX							
Jan.	*31*	Adjusting	*J9*		8 0 0 —		8 0 0 —

Account: *Wages Expense*   Account No. *501*

Date		Item	Post. Ref.	Debit	Credit	Balance Debit	Balance Credit
19XX							
Jan.	*31*	Adjusting	*J9*	8 0 0 —		8 0 0 —	

REVIEW OF ACCOUNTS

Account	Normal Balance	Increased by A	Decreased by A	Classification	Financial Statement	Nominal or Real
Cash	Debit	Debit	Credit	Asset	Balance Sheet	Real
Accounts Receivable	Debit	Debit	Credit	Asset	Balance Sheet	Real
Office Supplies	Debit	Debit	Credit	Asset	Balance Sheet	Real
Prepaid Insurance	Debit	Debit	Credit	Asset	Balance Sheet	Real
Furniture	Debit	Debit	Credit	Asset	Balance Sheet	Real
Equipment	Debit	Debit	Credit	Asset	Balance Sheet	Real
Automobile	Debit	Debit	Credit	Asset	Balance Sheet	Real
Truck	Debit	Debit	Credit	Asset	Balance Sheet	Real
Accumulated Depreciation, Asset	Credit	Credit	Debit	Asset (Contra)	Balance Sheet	Real
Accounts Payable	Credit	Credit	Debit	Liability	Balance Sheet	Real
Wages Payable	Credit	Credit	Debit	Liability	Balance Sheet	Real
Owner, Capital	Credit	Credit	Debit	Owner's Equity	Statement of Owner's Equity and Balance Sheet	Real
Owner, Drawing	Debit	Debit	Credit	Owner's Equity	Statement of Owner's Equity	Nominal
Income Summary	(used only during closing)			Owner's Equity	(used only during closing)	Nominal
Auditing Fees	Credit	Credit	Debit	Revenue	Income Statement	Nominal
Tax Services	Credit	Credit	Debit	Revenue	Income Statement	Nominal
Service Fees	Credit	Credit	Debit	Revenue	Income Statement	Nominal
Legal Fees	Credit	Credit	Debit	Revenue	Income Statement	Nominal
Wages Expense	Debit	Debit	Credit	Expense	Income Statement	Nominal
Advertising Expense	Debit	Debit	Credit	Expense	Income Statement	Nominal
Rent Expense	Debit	Debit	Credit	Expense	Income Statement	Nominal
Utilities Expense	Debit	Debit	Credit	Expense	Income Statement	Nominal
Office Supplies Expense	Debit	Debit	Credit	Expense	Income Statement	Nominal

Insurance Expense	Debit	Debit	Credit	Expense	Income Statement	Nominal
Depreciation Expense, Asset	Debit	Debit	Credit	Expense	Income Statement	Nominal

ACCOUNTING CYCLE REVIEW PROBLEM (CHAPTERS 1–6)

To test your knowledge of the accounting cycle, complete the following review problem. The working papers are in your Working Papers manual. The answer to this review problem will be provided by your instructor.

Paula Stone is the sole owner of Northwest Insurance Agency. She established the following chart of accounts:

Northwest Insurance Agency
Chart of Accounts

Assets (100–199)

101	Cash
111	Accounts Receivable
121	Office Supplies
131	Prepaid Insurance
141	Office Equipment
142	Accumulated Depreciation, Office Equipment
151	Office Furniture
152	Accumulated Depreciation, Office Furniture

Liabilities (200–299)

201	Accounts Payable
211	Wages Payable

Owner's Equity (300–399)

301	Paula Stone, Capital
311	Paula Stone, Drawing
321	Income Summary

Revenues (400–499)

401	Automobile Insurance Fees
411	Life Insurance Fees
421	Health Insurance Fees

Expenses (500–599)

501	Wages Expense
511	Advertising Expense
521	Rent Expense
531	Utilities Expense
541	Office Supplies Expense
551	Insurance Expense
561	Depreciation Expense, Office Equipment
571	Depreciation Expense, Office Furniture

Northwest Insurance Agency had thirty transactions during April 19XX. These transactions are to be recorded in the general journal. The transactions are as follows (assume that cash is paid or received unless otherwise stated):

April 1   The owner, Paula Stone, started the firm by investing $54,075.

April 1   Paid the rent for the month, $2,866.

April 1   Paid for a three-year liability insurance policy, $7,272.

April 2   Billed and collected $3,459 in automobile insurance fees.

April 2   Purchased office equipment, $6,907, paying $2,000 cash with the remainder due within 30 days.

April 3   Purchased $984 of office supplies on account.

April 3   Hired a receptionist.

April 3   Received and paid a utilities bill, $103.

April 4   Billed a customer for health insurance fees, $1,378.

April 4   Received a bill for newspaper advertising, $672.

April 4   Purchased office furniture, $6,899, paying $1,595 cash with the remainder due within 30 days.

April 5   Owner invested an additional $4,000 in the firm.

April 5   Billed a customer for life insurance fees, $3,846.

April 7   Paid the receptionist for wages, $495.

April 10 Received a utilities bill, $238.

April 11 Paid $458 to apply to the April 3 purchase of office supplies.

April 12 Billed a customer $5,878 for life insurance fees.

April 12 Received $1,378 from a customer to apply to the April 4 billing.

April 13 Owner withdrew $975 for her personal use.

April 14 Paid the April 4 advertising bill.

April 14 Paid the receptionist for wages, $495.

April 17 Paid $1,054 to apply to the April 2 purchase of office equipment.

April 18 Paid $2,895 to apply to the April 4 purchase of office furniture.

April 20   Owner withdrew $1,023 for her personal use.

April 21   Paid the receptionist for wages, $495.

April 24   Received $2,038 from a customer to apply to the April 5 billing.

April 25   Received an advertising bill, $5,789.

April 26   Billed a customer $1,673 for automobile insurance fees.

April 28   Paid the receptionist for wages, $495.

April 28   Received and paid an advertising bill, $2,192.

April 30   Paid $3,045 to apply to the April 25 advertising bill.

REQUIRED

1. Journalize the transactions in a general journal, starting on page 1.
2. Post the transactions to the general ledger.
3. Prepare a trial balance, using the first two columns of the worksheet.
4. Adjustments are calculated as follows:
   a. Office Supplies Expense, $670.
   b. Insurance Expense, $202.
   c. Depreciation of Office Equipment, $150.
   d. Depreciation of Office Furniture, $140.
   e. Wages incurred but unrecorded at April 30, $297.
5. Complete the worksheet.
6. Prepare financial statements.
7. Journalize and post adjusting entries.
8. Journalize and post closing entries.
9. Prepare a post-closing trial balance.

APPENDIX A
Computers and Accounting

More and more business firms are using computers to process accounting data. This is mainly due to advancing technology which has lowered the cost of computer systems and reduced the physical size of computers. In this appendix we will focus on three questions:

1. What is a computer?
2. How does a computer work?
3. How are computers used by accountants?

WHAT IS A COMPUTER?

Definition

A computer is a high-speed electronic tool that rapidly collects, processes, and reports large amounts of information.

Types of Computers

There are three general categories of computers: (1) mainframes; (2) minicomputers; and (3) microcomputers.

Mainframes Mainframes are the largest, fastest, and most expensive computers.

Minicomputers Minicomputers are medium-sized, scaled-down versions of mainframes. Minicomputers have less memory and less speed than mainframes.

Microcomputers Microcomputers are the smallest and least expensive computers. The microcomputer has become the fastest growing segment of the computer industry.

HOW DOES A COMPUTER WORK?

The basic elements that make a computer work are hardware and software.

EXHIBIT A-1
Hardware Components of a Computer System

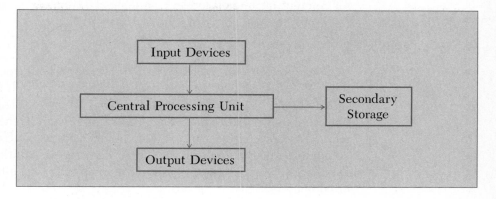

Hardware

The equipment (or hardware) of a computer consists of three main components (as shown in Exhibit A-1): (1) **input devices**; (2) a **central processing unit**; and (3) **output devices.**

Input Devices   Input devices are necessary for transferring information and instructions to the computer. The major input devices are terminals, disks, punched cards, and magnetic tape.

Central Processing Unit   The central processing unit (CPU) is the heart of a computer. This is where the "computing" actually takes place. The central processing unit *controls*, *computes* (that is, adds, subtracts, multiplies, divides, and performs other computations), and *stores* (primary storage) the data. A computer system should also have secondary storage, because a computer normally processes more information than can be held in the primary storage. The most common forms of secondary storage are magnetic tape and magnetic disk.

Output Devices   Output devices are necessary for transferring information out of a computer. Output devices include printers, disk drives, diskettes, and magnetic tape. Printers are used to print accounting documents, such as the general journal, general ledger, and financial statements.

Software

Software is necessary to make use of the computer hardware. Software contains the procedures and specific instructions used to operate the computer. In a sense, software tells the computer hardware what to do (or what to process). In accounting, software packages have been developed for completing general ledgers, worksheets, financial statements, and so on.

HOW ARE COMPUTERS USED BY ACCOUNTANTS?

Accountants are faced with two choices when processing accounting data. The first choice is to use a manual system, which we have described in this book. The second choice is to use a computerized accounting system. Computers are now cheaper and smaller than in the past, so many accountants are choosing to use a computerized accounting system. Since a computer processes information very fast, the accountant has been freed from many tedious tasks. Let's look at some of the specific accounting uses of computers.

Uses of Computers

General Ledger   The general ledger is the foundation of all accounting systems. In a computerized accounting system, the general ledger is maintained in the memory of the computer as a large data base. And, since a computer processes information faster than human beings, accounts can be quickly updated.

Electronic Spreadsheet   The electronic spreadsheet is a computerized version of the worksheet. A spreadsheet is laid out just as a manual worksheet. The spreadsheet performs all the mathematical calculations (adding and subtracting account balances) that are normally done by hand. As with the general ledger, the computer processes this information faster than people.

Graphics   Accountants have found that graphs can be very useful. A computer can be directed by the appropriate software program to present financial information in graphic form. Two- or three-dimensional graphs can be prepared using a variety of colors.

Other Uses   Computerized accounting systems can also be used to eliminate most of the limitations of manual accounting systems. Accountants use computers to record, classify, summarize, and categorize accounting data. This accounting data can be retrieved from the computer, where it is stored, and used in any number of shapes and forms. The various computerized accounting systems can be quite detailed and complex. A detailed discussion of these systems is beyond the scope of this book. The author hopes this brief discussion has nevertheless helped you appreciate the usefulness of computers.

Students who want to learn more about computerized accounting are referred to *The Computer Connection,* Second Edition, by Gregory W. Bischoff and John W. Wanlass. This microcomputer software package supplies a general ledger entry system that classifies, summarizes, and categorizes accounting data in a number of report formats. The Student Manual provides operating instructions, problems, two practice sets, and a thorough discussion of the differences between manual and computerized approaches to accounting.

7

The Sales Journal and Accounts Receivable Subsidiary Ledger

If you would know the value of money, go and try to borrow some.

BENJAMIN FRANKLIN

LEARNING OBJECTIVES

After reading this chapter, discussing the questions, and working the exercises and problems, you will be able to do the following:

1. Understand and use the sales journal (pp. 208–12).

2. Understand and use the accounts receivable subsidiary ledger (pp. 212–17).

3. Account for sales returns and allowances (pp. 217–20).

4. Record the sale of assets other than merchandise on account (pp. 220–22).

In the first six chapters of this book, we discussed service firms wherein revenues are received for services provided. Both of the firms examined up to now, Kay Loomis, CPA, and Kevin Young, Attorney at Law, were service-type firms. The CPA firm provided accounting services, and the law firm provided legal services. At the end of Chapter 6, we completed the accounting cycle for the service-type firm, Kevin Young, Attorney at Law.

MERCHANDISING FIRMS

Let's look now at United Auto Supply for an example of a *merchandising* firm. United Auto Supply sells discount auto parts (which we call merchandise). **Merchandise inventory** represents goods (in this case, auto parts) that a firm buys to resell to its customers *in the same form.* The accounting cycle of a merchandising firm is the same as the accounting cycle of a service firm. Let's begin with steps one and two of the accounting cycle—analyzing transactions and recording the transactions in a journal.

Sales and Sales Invoice

On October 4, 19XX, United Auto Supply sold nine automobile transmissions to one of its customers, Emma's Auto Repair, on account. The transmissions are considered merchandise inventory. United Auto Supply filled out a sales ticket as shown in Exhibit 7-1.

If United Auto Supply recorded the credit sale in a general journal, the sale would be journalized as follows:

GENERAL JOURNAL   Page ____19____

Date		Description	Post. Ref.	Debit	Credit
19XX					
Oct.	4	Accounts Receivable		1 8 0 0 —	
		Sales			1 8 0 0 —
		Invoice Number 831, Emma's Auto Repair			

EXHIBIT 7-1
Sales Ticket

Customer Sales Ticket   **Invoice No.** _831_

Charge Sale ___X___   **Cash Sale** _____

United Auto Supply
100 Main Street, Houston, Texas 77001

Account Nos.: *111/401*   **Sold by:** *Frank Rylski*
Sale Date: *10/4/XX*   **Terms:** *2/10, n30*
Invoice (billing) Date: *10/4/XX*

Sold to: *Emma's Auto Repair*
Address: *101 Pinemont Houston, TX 77006*
Ship to: *same*

Quantity	Merchandise	Amount (each)	Total Amount
9	*Transmissions*	*200*	*1,800*
Total			*1,800*

Accounts Receivable is debited for the credit sale, and the corresponding credit is to **Sales**. Sales is a revenue account used to record the sale of merchandise inventory. United Auto Supply does not use a general journal for the following reasons:

1. For each credit sale, the terms "Accounts Receivable" and "Sales" must be written.
2. For each credit sale, both Accounts Receivable and Sales must be posted to the general ledger.

Thus, to save time and effort, and to increase efficiency, the firm uses special journals.

INTRODUCTION TO SPECIAL JOURNALS

Objective 1
Understand and use the sales journal.

Many merchandising firms use special journals to record transactions. A special journal is a book of original entry that groups similar transactions together. The special journals that we will use are as follows:

Type of Special Journal	Posting Reference Designation	Used To:
Sales Journal	S	Record all sales of merchandise on account only.
Purchases Journal	P	Record all purchases of merchandise on account only.
Cash Receipts Journal	CR	Record cash received from any source.
Cash Payments Journal	CP	Record cash paid for any purpose.

Where "J" was used as the posting reference for the general journal, "S" is used as the posting reference for sales journal, "P" is used for the purchases journal, and so on. Any transaction that cannot be recorded in a special journal is recorded using a general journal. In this chapter we will examine the sales journal.

Purposes of the Sales Journal

A sales journal has the following purposes:

1. To record all credit sales of merchandise in one journal, thus saving space.
2. To save journalizing time by recording each sale amount only once on one line.
3. Customer names, invoice numbers, and terms can be easily identified.
4. Individual credit sales are added and posted as one total to the general ledger at the end of the accounting period. This total is posted as a debit to Accounts Receivable and a credit to Sales.

Structure of the Sales Journal

The sales journal is used to record the sale of merchandise on account (credit) only. The October 4, 19XX, credit sale to Emma's Auto Repair is recorded in a single-column sales journal as illustrated in Exhibit 7-2:

EXHIBIT 7-2
Single-Column Sales Journal

SALES JOURNAL   Page ____10____

Date		Customer	Invoice Number	Terms	Post. Ref.	Amount A/R (Dr.) Sales (Cr.)
19XX						
Oct.	4	Emma's Auto Repair	831	2/10, n30		1 8 0 0 —

In the Amount column of the sales journal, "A/R" is an abbreviation for Accounts Receivable. (The Post. Ref. column will be used later.)

Credit Terms

Many firms offer a discount to encourage their customers to pay their bills (amounts owed) early. Referring to Exhibits 7-1 and 7-2, the term **2/10, n30** indicates that if the invoice or bill is paid within ten days there is a 2 percent discount. If not, the total amount is due within thirty days. The term **1/10, n20** says that the total amount is due within twenty days but a 1 percent discount will be given if paid within ten days. The term **n30** by itself means that no discount is offered and the total is due within thirty days. We will assume that United Auto Supply calculates the discount from the invoice date, which is counted as the first day. (Some firms start the discount period the day after the invoice date. In this book we will start with the invoice date.) Therefore the ten-day discount period for Emma's Auto Repair would start on October 4 and end on October 13 as follows:

Month of October

Days: Oct. 4   5   6   7   8   9   10   11   12   13

Counted: 1 + 1 + 1 + 1 + 1 + 1 + 1 + 1 + 1 + 1 = 10 days

Any payment received October 14 or later would not be subject to a discount.

Posting from the Sales Journal

The sales of merchandise on account for the month of October for United Auto Supply are recorded and posted in Exhibit 7-3.

EXHIBIT 7-3
Recording and Posting Credit Merchandise Sales

SALES JOURNAL Page __10__

Date		Customer	Invoice Number	Terms	Post. Ref.	Amount A/R (Dr.) Sales (Cr.)	
19XX							
Oct.	4	Emma's Auto Repair	831	2/10, n30		1 8 0 0 —	
	6	Montana Company	832	2/10, n30		2 8 0 0 —	
	8	Jane's Fine Cars	833	2/10, n30		3 1 0 0 —	
	11	Lucky's Auto Repair	834	2/10, n30		9 0 0 —	
	15	Atlanta Company	835	2/10, n30		2 2 0 0 —	
	22	Montana Company	836	2/10, n30		1 9 0 0 —	
	25	Zumwalt Company	837	2/10, n30		1 5 0 0 —	
	28	Lai Auto Repair	838	2/10, n30		7 0 0 —	
	30	Jane's Fine Cars	839	2/10, n30		2 1 0 0 —	
	31	Tamborello Motors	840	2/10, n30	③	2 4 0 0 —	
						19 4 0 0 —	①
						(111) (401)	

GENERAL LEDGER ACCOUNTS

Account: *Accounts Receivable*   Account No. 111

Date		Item	Post. Ref.	Debit		Credit		Balance Debit		Credit	
19XX						②					
Oct.	31		S10	1 9 4 0 0 —				1 9 4 0 0 —			

Account: *Sales*   Account No. 401

Date		Item	Post. Ref.	Debit		Credit		Balance Debit		Credit ④	
19XX											
Oct.	31		S10			1 9 4 0 0 —				1 9 4 0 0 —	

There are four steps for posting from the sales journal to the general ledger. These steps are keyed ①, ②, ③, and ④ in Exhibit 7-3. The steps are as follows:

① The Amount column in the sales journal is underlined after the final sale is entered. The sales are totaled and double underlined.

② The total is posted as a debit to Accounts Receivable in the general ledger. "S10" is written in the Post. Ref. column of the general ledger to indicate that the posting is from page 10 of the sales journal.

③ After posting the debit to Accounts Receivable, you would go back to the amount column in the sales journal and write "111" in parenthesis below the total. This shows that a posting was made to the accounts receivable general ledger account.

④ Repeat steps 2 and 3 for the credit posting to sales.

Recording Sales Tax Payable

Many merchandising firms collect sales taxes from their customers. Usually the *final user* pays the sales tax. By final user we mean the person or firm who will use the goods; these same goods or merchandise will not be sold to another person or firm. Once collected, the sales tax (or taxes) is later paid to the taxing authority, such as the state, county, city, and so on.

For example, on January 9, 19XX, a firm sells merchandise on account to Parr, Inc. for $200. The sales tax is 5 percent. This transaction may be illustrated using T accounts as follows:

Accounts Receivable		Sales		Sales Tax Payable	
+	−	−	+	−	+
210			200		10

The sales tax is calculated as follows:

$$\$200 \times 5 \text{ percent} = \$200 \times .05 = \$10$$

Parr, Inc. owes the firm the sale amount plus the sales tax ($200 + $10 = $210). The firm uses a three-column sales journal to record this transaction (see Exhibit 7-4).

The accountant debits Sales Tax Payable and credits Cash when the tax is paid to the taxing authority. For our purposes, we'll assume that United Auto Supply is not required to collect sales tax from its customers.

EXHIBIT 7-4
Three-Column Sales Journal

SALES JOURNAL   Page ___1___

Date	Customer	Invoice Number	Terms	Post. Ref.	Debit Accounts Receivable	Credits Sales Tax Payable	Sales
19XX							
Jan. 9	Parr, Inc.	A342	n30		2 1 0 —	1 0 —	2 0 0 —

THE ACCOUNTS RECEIVABLE SUBSIDIARY LEDGER

Objective 2
Understand and use the accounts receivable subsidiary ledger.

An accounts receivable subsidiary ledger is used in conjunction with the sales journal to identify and accumulate amounts owed by individual customers (as shown in Exhibit 7-5). Most firms need to maintain individual customer information. Imagine asking a large department store how much you owed them today. If the store did not have an accounts receivable subsidiary ledger, you would have to wait while they searched through all the sales journal entries until your name was found.

There is usually a separate page in this ledger for each customer. The customers' names in the accounts receivable subsidiary ledger are often arranged alphabetically, and most accountants use a loose-leaf binder so they can add new customers or remove ex-customers as needed. Exhibit 7-5 shows the accounts receivable subsidiary ledger card for Montana Company.

EXHIBIT 7-5
Customer's Card in Accounts Receivable Subsidiary Ledger

ACCOUNTS RECEIVABLE SUBSIDIARY LEDGER

Customer: *Montana Company*

Date	Inv. No.	Item	Post. Ref.	Debit	Credit	Balance
19XX						
Oct. 6	832		S10	2 8 0 0 —		2 8 0 0 —
22	836		S10	1 9 0 0 —		4 7 0 0 —

The Control Account

The Accounts Receivable account in the general ledger is called a **control** account because the Accounts Receivable balance in the general ledger provides a check or "control" over the accounts receivable subsidiary ledger. The total of all the customer's balances which are kept in the accounts receivable subsidiary ledger must equal the Accounts Receivable account balance in the general ledger when all postings are up to date.

Posting to the Accounts Receivable Subsidiary Ledger

There are three steps to follow when posting from the sales journal to the accounts receivable subsidiary ledger, keyed ①, ②, and ③ in Exhibit 7-6. The posting process is shown for Atlanta Company. The credit sales for the other customers are posted in the same manner. The steps for posting are as follows:

① As sales of merchandise on account are entered in the sales journal, they are posted daily or as they occur to the accounts receivable subsidiary ledger. When a customer buys merchandise on account, the total sale amount, including any tax, is entered into the debit column of the accounts receivable subsidiary ledger. A credit is made whenever the customer pays on his or her account. The Balance column has either a debit or zero balance. (A credit balance would indicate that the customer has paid too much.)

② "S10" for sales journal (S), page 10, is entered in the Post. Ref. column of the customer's accounts receivable subsidiary ledger page after the amount owed has been posted from the sales journal.

③ Once the posting has been entered into the customer's accounts receivable subsidiary ledger page, a check mark (√) is placed in the Post. Ref. column of the sales journal. This signifies that the credit sale amount, including any sales tax, has been posted to the accounts receivable subsidiary ledger for that customer.

In Exhibit 7-6, we see the postings to the general ledger and the accounts receivable subsidiary ledger. The accounts receivable subsidiary ledger is not posted to the general ledger. A subsidiary ledger (such as the accounts receivable subsidiary ledger) *supports* a book of original entry or journal, which in this case is the sales journal. By utilizing an accounts receivable subsidiary ledger, a firm is able to keep track of the account balances (amounts owed) of its customers. When a customer inquires about his or her balance, you can quickly reference that customer's page in the

EXHIBIT 7-6
Posting to the Accounts Receivable Subsidiary Ledger

②

Date	Customer	Invoice Number	Terms	Post. Ref.	Amount A/R (Dr.) Sales (Cr.)
19XX					
Oct. 4	Emma's Auto Repair	831	2/10, n30	√	1 8 0 0 —
6	Montana Company	832	2/10, n30	√	2 8 0 0 —
8	Jane's Fine Cars	833	2/10, n30	√	3 1 0 0 —
11	Lucky's Auto Repair	834	2/10, n30	√	9 0 0 —
15	Atlanta Company	835	2/10, n30	√ ③	2 2 0 0 —
22	Montana Company	836	2/10, n30	√	1 9 0 0 —
25	Zumwalt Company	837	2/10, n30	√	1 5 0 0 —
28	Lai Auto Repair	838	2/10, n30	√	7 0 0 —
30	Jane's Fine Cars	839	2/10, n30	√	2 1 0 0 —
31	Tamborello Motors	840	2/10, n30	√	2 4 0 0 —
					19 4 0 0 —
					(111) (401)

①

GENERAL LEDGER ACCOUNTS

Account: Accounts Receivable — **Account No. 111**

Date	Item	Post. Ref.	Debit	Credit	Balance Debit	Balance Credit
19XX						
Oct. 31		S10	1 9 4 0 0 —		1 9 4 0 0 —	

Account: Sales — **Account No. 401**

Date	Item	Post. Ref.	Debit	Credit	Balance Debit	Balance Credit
19XX						
Oct. 31		S10		1 9 4 0 0 —		1 9 4 0 0 —

ACCOUNTS RECEIVABLE SUBSIDIARY LEDGER

Customer: Atlanta Company

Date	Inv. No.	Item	Post. Ref.	Debit	Credit	Balance
19XX						
Oct. 15	835	②	S10	2 2 0 0 —		2 2 0 0 —

(continued)

(Ex. 7-6 continued)

Customer: *Emma's Auto Repair*

Date	Inv. No.	Item	Post. Ref.	Debit	Credit	Balance
19XX						
Oct. 4	831		S10	1800 —		1800 —

Customer: *Jane's Fine Cars*

Date	Inv. No.	Item	Post. Ref.	Debit	Credit	Balance
19XX						
Oct. 8	833		S10	3100 —		3100 —
30	839		S10	2100 —		5200 —

Customer: *Lai Auto Repair*

Date	Inv. No.	Item	Post. Ref.	Debit	Credit	Balance
19XX						
Oct. 28	838		S10	700 —		700 —

Customer: *Lucky's Auto Repair*

Date	Inv. No.	Item	Post. Ref.	Debit	Credit	Balance
19XX						
Oct. 11	834		S10	900 —		900 —

(continued)

(Ex. 7-6 concluded)

Customer: *Montana Company*

Date		Inv. No.	Item	Post. Ref.	Debit	Credit	Balance
19XX							
Oct.	6	832		S10	2 8 0 0 —		2 8 0 0 —
	22	836		S10	1 9 0 0 —		4 7 0 0 —

Customer: *Tamborello Motors*

Date		Inv. No.	Item	Post. Ref.	Debit	Credit	Balance
19XX							
Oct.	31	840		S10	2 4 0 0 —		2 4 0 0 —

Customer: *Zumwalt Company*

Date		Inv. No.	Item	Post. Ref.	Debit	Credit	Balance
19XX							
Oct.	25	837		S10	1 5 0 0 —		1 5 0 0 —

accounts receivable subsidiary ledger and supply the customer with the requested information.

The Schedule of Accounts Receivable

A **schedule of accounts receivable** is normally prepared directly from the accounts receivable subsidiary ledger at the end of the accounting period. As we see in Exhibit 7-7, each customer and the balance owed is listed on the schedule of accounts receivable. The control account, Accounts Receivable, in the general ledger is also shown. The total of the schedule of accounts receivable must equal the control account, Accounts Receivable, in the general ledger. If the two totals do not agree, then a mistake has been made and must be corrected.

EXHIBIT 7-7
Schedule of Accounts Receivable

United Auto Supply
Schedule of Accounts Receivable
October 31, 19XX

Customer	Amount Owed
Atlanta Company	$ 2 2 0 0 —
Emma's Auto Repair	1 8 0 0 —
Jane's Fine Cars	5 2 0 0 —
Lai Auto Repair	7 0 0 —
Lucky's Auto Repair	9 0 0 —
Montana Company	4 7 0 0 —
Tamborello Motors	2 4 0 0 —
Zumwalt Company	1 5 0 0 —
	$19 4 0 0 —

GENERAL LEDGER ACCOUNT

Account: *Accounts Receivable*　　　　　　Account No.　111

Date	Item	Post. Ref.	Debit	Credit	Balance Debit	Balance Credit
19XX						
Oct. 31		S10	1 9 4 0 0 —		1 9 4 0 0 —	

SALES RETURNS AND ALLOWANCES

Objective 3
Account for sales returns and allowances.

The Sales Returns and Allowances account is used to record two types of transactions that apply to merchandise that has been previously sold. A return is the physical return of merchandise by the customer to the seller. An allowance is granted by the seller to the customer for inferior, defective, or damaged merchandise. A prenumbered credit memorandum is given to the customer by the seller whenever such returns and allowances occur (called a credit memorandum because the customer's account is credited for the return or allowance). A general journal is used to record the return or allowance of merchandise previously purchased on account. Remember that the sales journal is only used to record merchandise sold on account.

The Sales Returns and Allowances account is a contra revenues account; that is, it reduces sales and has a normal debit balance. Sales Returns and Allowances is included in the revenues' broad class of accounts, along with Sales, on the chart of accounts.

Assume that on October 27, 19XX, a customer of United Auto Supply—Montana Company—returns $78 of defective merchandise previously purchased on account. Credit memorandum number CM29 is issued to Montana Company as shown in Exhibit 7-8. (The sale transaction was originally recorded in the sales journal, as shown in Exhibit 7-3.)

Journalizing and Posting Sales Returns and Allowances

To record a return of merchandise previously sold on credit, Sales Returns and Allowances is debited and Accounts Receivable is credited. In

EXHIBIT 7-8
Prenumbered Credit Memorandum

Credit Memorandum No. *CM 29*

Charge Return ___ X ___ Cash Return _____

United Auto Supply
100 Main Street, Houston, Texas 77001

Account Nos.: *111/402*　　　　　　　　　　　　Sold by: *Frank Rylski*
Sale Date: *10/6/XX*　　　　　　　　　　　　　Terms: *2/10, n30*
Invoice (billing) Date: *10/6/XX*　　　　　　　Return Date: *10/27/XX*

Sold to: *Montana Company*
Address: *P.O. Box 87641 Houston, TX 77001*

Return Information

Quantity	Merchandise	Amount (each)	Total Amount
6	*Water Pump*	*$13*	*$78*

Total Amount To Be Credited　　　　　　　　　　　　　　　　*$78*

Exhibit 7-9 the return is journalized and posted to the general ledger and accounts receivable subsidiary ledger. The journalizing and posting steps are keyed ①, ②, and ③. These steps are as follows:

① The return or allowance of a previous credit sale of merchandise must be recorded in the general journal.

EXHIBIT 7-9

Recording and Posting Sales Returns and Allowances

①   **GENERAL JOURNAL**   Page ___26___

Date		Description	Post. Ref.	Debit	Credit
19XX					
Oct.	27	Sales Returns and Allowances	402	7 8 — ②	
		Accounts Receivable—Montana Company	111/✓ ③		7 8 —
		Return of Defective Merchandise, Credit Memorandum CM29			

GENERAL LEDGER ACCOUNTS

Account: Accounts Receivable						Account No. 111	
		Post.				Balance	
Date	Item	Ref.	Debit	Credit	Debit	Credit	
Oct.	27	③	J26		7 8 —		

Account: Sales Returns and Allowances						Account No. 402	
		Post.				Balance	
Date	Item	Ref.	Debit	Credit	Debit	Credit	
19XX							
Oct.	27		J26	7 8 — ②			

(continued)

(Ex. 7-9 concluded)

ACCOUNTS RECEIVABLE SUBSIDIARY LEDGER

Customer: *Montana Company*

Date		Inv. No.	Item	Post. Ref.	Debit	Credit	Balance
19XX							
Oct.	6	832		S10	2 8 0 0 —		2 8 0 0 —
	22	836		S10	1 9 0 0 —		4 7 0 0 —
	27			J26		③ 7 8 —	4 6 2 2 —

② The debit is posted to Sales Returns and Allowances in the general ledger. "J26" is entered in the Post. Ref. column of the general ledger and then "402" is entered in the Post. Ref. column of the general journal.

③ A $78 credit is posted to both the Accounts Receivable account in the general ledger and the customer's account in the accounts receivable subsidiary ledger. "J26" is entered in the Post. Ref. columns. Once the posting is complete, "111/√" is entered in the Post. Ref. column of the general journal. The term "111" indicates a posting to Accounts Receivable in the general ledger. The "√" indicates a posting to the customer's account in the accounts receivable subsidiary ledger. The slash "/" is used to keep the two references separate.

RECORDING OTHER TRANSACTIONS

Objective 4
Record the sale of assets other than merchandise on account.

There are other transactions that cannot be recorded in a special journal. Any asset (other than merchandise inventory sold on account) must be recorded using a general journal. For example, let's assume that on October 20, 19XX, United Auto Supply sold $2,000 of office equipment (beginning balance $15,000), which is not merchandise inventory, to Paul Henley on account. The terms are 2/10, EOM, n30. We will also assume that this transaction is not taxable. The terms 2/10, EOM, n30 mean that a 2 percent discount will be given if paid within ten days after the end of the month. Otherwise the full amount is due within thirty days of the invoice date. This transaction would be recorded in the general journal as follows:

GENERAL JOURNAL   Page ___26___

Date		Description	Post. Ref.	Debit	Credit
19XX					
Oct.	20	Accounts Receivable—Paul Henley	111/√	2 0 0 0 —	
		Office Equipment	141		2 0 0 0 —
		Terms 2/10, EOM, n30			

For illustration purposes, let's also record this transaction using T accounts:

Accounts Receivable		Office Equipment	
(10/20) 2,000			2,000 (10/20)

This general journal entry would be posted to the general ledger and accounts receivable subsidiary ledger as follows:

GENERAL LEDGER ACCOUNTS

Account: *Accounts Receivable*   Account No.   *111*

Date		Item	Post. Ref.	Debit	Credit	Balance Debit	Balance Credit
19XX							
Oct.	20		J26	2 0 0 0 —		2 0 0 0 —	
	27		J26		7 8 —	1 9 2 2 —	
	31		S10	1 9 4 0 0 —		2 1 3 2 2 —	

Account: *Office Equipment*   Account No.   *141*

Date		Item	Post. Ref.	Debit	Credit	Balance Debit	Balance Credit
19XX		Previous Balance				1 5 0 0 0 —	
Oct.	20		J26		2 0 0 0 —	1 3 0 0 0 —	

(continued)

ACCOUNTS RECEIVABLE SUBSIDIARY LEDGER

Customer: *Paul Henley*

Date	Inv. No.	Item	Post. Ref.	Debit	Credit	Balance
19XX						
Oct.. 20			J26	2 0 0 0 —		2 0 0 0 —

CHAPTER REVIEW

1. **Understand and use the sales journal (pp. 208–12).**
   Many merchandising firms use special journals to record transactions. A special journal is a book of original entry that groups similar transactions together. The sales journal is used to record the sale of merchandise on account (credit) only.

2. **Understand and use the accounts receivable subsidiary ledger (pp. 212–17).**
   An accounts receivable subsidiary ledger is used in conjunction with the sales journal to identify and accumulate amounts owed by individual customers. There is usually a separate page in this ledger for each customer. The customers' names are often arranged alphabetically.

3. **Account for sales returns and allowances (pp. 217–20).**
   The Sales Returns and Allowances account is used to record two types of transactions that apply to merchandise that has been previously sold. A return is the physical return of merchandise by the customer to the seller. An allowance is granted by the seller to the customer for inferior, defective, or damaged merchandise. A general journal is used to record the return or allowance of merchandise previously purchased on account.

4. **Record the sale of assets other than merchandise on account (pp. 220–22).**
   When using special journals, any asset (other than merchandise inventory) sold on account must be recorded using a general journal.

GLOSSARY

Accounts Receivable Subsidiary Ledger	Used in conjunction with the sales journal to identify and accumulate amounts owed by individual customers. Supports a book of original entry.
Allowance	Granted by the seller to the customer for inferior, defective, or damaged merchandise.
Cash Payments Journal	Special journal used to record cash paid for any purpose.
Cash Receipts Journal	Special journal used to record cash received from any source.
Control Account	Account that provides a check or control over a subsidiary ledger.
Credit Memorandum	Prenumbered document given to the customer by the seller whenever returns and allowances occur.
Merchandise (Merchandise Inventory)	Goods that a firm buys to resell to its customers in identical form.
Purchases Journal	Special journal used to record all purchases of merchandise on account only.
Return	Physical return of merchandise by the customer to the seller.
Sales	Revenue account that is used to record the sale of merchandise inventory.
Sales Journal	Special journal used to record all sales of merchandise on account only.
Sales Returns and Allowances	Contra revenues account used to record transactions that apply to merchandise that has been previously sold.
Schedule of Accounts Receivable	Listing of each customer and the balance the customer owes.
Special Journal	Book of original entry that groups similar transactions together.

SELF-TEST QUESTIONS FOR REVIEW

(Answers are on p. 237.)

1. Sales is a _____ account used to record the sale of _____.
   a. revenue; services
   b. asset; services
   c. liability; merchandise inventory
   d. revenue; merchandise inventory

2. The discount period for "2/10, n30" is
   a. thirty days.
   b. exactly one month.
   c. ten days.
   d. two days.

3. The debit column in a three-column sales journal is posted to
   a. Sales Tax Payable.
   b. Accounts Receivable
   c. Sales.
   d. Cash.

4. Credit memorandum CM781 is listed in the description of a transaction in a general journal. The account debited in this transaction is
   a. Cash.
   b. Sales.
   c. Sales Returns and Allowances.
   d. Accounts Receivable.

5. Office Equipment (not merchandise inventory) is sold on account. The account credited is
   a. Office Equipment.
   b. Sales.
   c. Accounts Receivable.
   d. Sales Returns and Allowances.

PRACTICAL REVIEW PROBLEM

**Objectives
1 through 4**

Recording and Posting Sales   Alice Copier Supply had the following credit transactions during the month of October 19XX:

October   3   Sold $1,500 of merchandise on credit to Tellez Company, invoice number T204. Terms are n30.

October   5   Sold to McCree Company $1,300 of office supplies, account number 135, on credit; terms are 1/10, EOM, n30.

October   8   Tellez Company returned $200 of damaged merchandise previously purchased October 3. Credit memorandum CM17 is issued.

October 16   Sold $2,300 of merchandise on credit to Edwards Company, invoice number T205. Terms are n30.

October 27   Sold $1,900 of merchandise on account to Tellez Company, invoice number T206. Terms are 1/10, n30.

October 31   Edwards Company returned $400 of inferior merchandise previously purchased October 16. Credit memorandum CM18 is issued.

REQUIRED

1. Open the previous balance in the Office Supplies account, $1,800. Record the sale of merchandise in a sales journal, page 1.

2. Record the return of merchandise and the sale of assets other than merchandise in a general journal, page 22. Sales Returns and Allowances is account number 432.

3. Post to the accounts receivable subsidiary ledger. List the customers alphabetically.

4. Post to the general ledger. Accounts Receivable is account number 118, and sales is 431.

5. Prepare a schedule of accounts receivable.

ANSWER TO PRACTICAL REVIEW PROBLEM

1.   **SALES JOURNAL**   Page ___1___

Date	Customer	Invoice Number	Terms	Post. Ref.	Amount A/R (Dr.) Sales (Cr.)
19XX					
Oct. 3	Tellez Company	T204	n30	√	1 5 0 0 —
16	Edwards Company	T205	n30	√	2 3 0 0 —
27	Tellez Company	T206	1/10, n30	√	1 9 0 0 —
					5 7 0 0 —
					(118) (431)

2.   **GENERAL JOURNAL**   Page ___22___

Date	Description	Post. Ref.	Debit	Credit
19XX				
Oct. 5	Accounts Receivable — McCree Company	118/√	1 3 0 0 —	
	Office Supplies	135		1 3 0 0 —
	Terms 1/10, EOM, n30			
8	Sales Returns and Allowances	432	2 0 0 —	
	Accounts Receivable — Tellez Company	118/√		2 0 0 —
	Return of Damaged Merchandise, Credit Memorandum CM17			
31	Sales Returns and Allowances	432	4 0 0 —	
	Accounts Receivable — Edwards Company	118/√		4 0 0 —
	Return of Inferior Merchandise, Credit Memorandum CM18			

3. ACCOUNTS RECEIVABLE SUBSIDIARY LEDGER

Customer: *Edwards Company*

Date		Inv. No.	Item	Post. Ref.	Debit	Credit	Balance
19XX							
Oct.	16	T205		S1	2 3 0 0 —		2 3 0 0 —
	31			J22		4 0 0 —	1 9 0 0 —

Customer: *McCree Company*

Date		Inv. No.	Item	Post. Ref.	Debit	Credit	Balance
19XX							
Oct.	5			J22	1 3 0 0 —		1 3 0 0 —

Customer: *Tellez Company*

Date		Inv. No.	Item	Post. Ref.	Debit	Credit	Balance
19XX							
Oct.	3	T204		S1	1 5 0 0 —		1 5 0 0 —
	8			J22		2 0 0 —	1 3 0 0 —
	27	T206		S1	1 9 0 0 —		3 2 0 0 —

4.

GENERAL LEDGER ACCOUNTS

Account: *Accounts Receivable*　　　　　　　　　　　　　　　　**Account No.**　118

Date	Item	Post. Ref.	Debit	Credit	Balance Debit	Balance Credit
19XX						
Oct. 5		J22	1 3 0 0 —		1 3 0 0 —	
8		J22		2 0 0 —	1 1 0 0 —	
31		J22		4 0 0 —	7 0 0 —	
31		S1	5 7 0 0 —		6 4 0 0 —	

Account: *Office Supplies*　　　　　　　　　　　　　　　　**Account No.**　135

Date	Item	Post. Ref.	Debit	Credit	Balance Debit	Balance Credit
19XX	Previous Balance				1 8 0 0 —	
Oct. 5		J22		1 3 0 0 —	5 0 0 —	

Account: *Sales*　　　　　　　　　　　　　　　　**Account No.**　431

Date	Item	Post. Ref.	Debit	Credit	Balance Debit	Balance Credit
19XX						
Oct. 31		S1		5 7 0 0 —		5 7 0 0 —

Account: *Sales Returns and Allowances*　　　　　　　　　　　　　　　　**Account No.**　432

Date	Item	Post. Ref.	Debit	Credit	Balance Debit	Balance Credit
19XX						
Oct. 8		J22	2 0 0 —		2 0 0 —	
31		J22	4 0 0 —		6 0 0 —	

5.

Alice Copier Supply
Schedule of Accounts Receivable
October 31, 19XX

Customer	Amount Owed
Edwards Company	$1 9 0 0 —
McCree Company	1 3 0 0 —
Tellez Company	3 2 0 0 —
	$6 4 0 0 —

DISCUSSION QUESTIONS

Q 7-1   Briefly explain the difference between a service-type firm and a merchandising-type firm.

Q 7-2   Briefly describe the following credit terms: (a) n30; (b) 2/10, n30; (c) 1/10, n20; and (d) 2/10, EOM, n30.

Q 7-3   Name the two reasons why a merchandising firm would not use a general journal if a special journal could be used.

Q 7-4   Name the four special journals. State the Posting Reference symbol for each. Also, briefly describe what each special journal is used for.

Q 7-5   Name the four purposes of a sales journal.

Q 7-6   Name the four steps for posting from the sales journal to the general ledger.

Q 7-7   What is the accounts receivable subsidiary ledger used for? Name the three steps to follow when posting to the accounts receivable subsidiary ledger.

Q 7-8   Briefly describe the Sales Returns and Allowances account. What is a return? An allowance? A credit memorandum?

Q 7-9   Name the three steps in journalizing and posting the return of merchandise previously sold on account.

Q 7-10   Which journal and ledgers would the following transaction be recorded in: sold equipment, which is not merchandise inventory, on account, for $165 to Quinn Company? Also, give the appropriate accounts that would be debited and credited.

EXERCISES

Objective 1	E 7-1	**Recording Sales** Record this transaction in (a) a general journal, page 7, and then (b) a sales journal, page 7:

June 9   Sold $1,200 of merchandise on account to Robin Haws, terms 2/10, n30. Invoice number 765. The year is 19XX.

Objective 2	E 7-2	**Completing Customer's Card** Complete a customer's card in the accounts receivable subsidiary ledger given the following information for 19XX:

May 14   Sold to Hawthorne Service, $400 of merchandise on account, invoice number 098. The entry was made in page 5 of the sales journal.

May 20   Sold to Hawthorne Service, $300 of merchandise on account, invoice number 103 (page 5 of the sales journal).

Objective 3	E 7-3	**Recording Sales Returns and Allowances** Record this transaction in a general journal, page 13: On August 19, 19XX, Logan Company returned $800 of inferior merchandise previously sold on account. Credit memorandum CM15 is issued.

Objective 4	E 7-4	**Recording Other Transactions** On April 19, 19XX, Smith Grocery Supply sold $2,800 of office equipment (not merchandise inventory) to Pham Company on account. Record this transaction using T accounts.

Objectives 1, 3, and 4	E 7-5	**Describing Transactions** Describe the three transactions recorded in the following T accounts:

Accounts Receivable	Machinery
(a) 1,280	(b) 860		(c) 2,540
(c) 2,540			

Sales	Sales Returns and Allowances
	(a) 1,280	(b) 860	

Objective 1	E 7-6	**Recording Sales** Record this transaction (a) using T accounts and then (b) using a three-column sales journal, page 2: On April 12, 19XX, a firm sold $500 of merchandise on account to Jay Brown, terms n30. The invoice number is C390. The sales tax is 6 percent.

Objective 2   **E 7-7**   **Completing a Schedule of Accounts Receivable**   Complete the following schedule of accounts receivable for Oklahoma Gasket Supply (June 30, 19XX):

	(a)	
	(b)	
	(c)	

(d)	(e)
Benson Company	$3,000
Gantley Repair	4,000
Petrovich Enterprises	2,000
Smallwood Manufacturing	6,000
	$ (f)

Objective 4   **E 7-8**   **Recording and Posting Other Transactions**   On December 19, 19XX, a firm sold a $5,000 computer (not merchandise inventory) to Alvin Computer Service, terms 2/10, EOM, n30. The balance in the computer account (151) was $10,000 before this transaction. In your answer, open the previous balance in the computer account. Also, record this transaction in a general journal, page 8, and post to the accounts receivable subsidiary ledger and the general ledger. Accounts Receivable is account number 111.

PROBLEM SET A

Objectives 1 and 2   **P 7-1A**   **Recording and Posting Sales**   Jones Plumbing Supply is owned by Lisa Jones. The firm had the following credit sales of merchandise during the first half of October 19XX:

Date	Amount	Terms	Invoice Number	Customer
October 1	$300	2/10, n30	M452	Alvaro Rojas
October 5	$600	2/10, n30	M453	Terri Gray
October 8	$800	2/10, n30	M454	Alvaro Rojas
October 12	$100	2/10, n30	M455	John Satori
October 13	$500	2/10, n30	M456	Terri Gray
October 15	$900	2/10, n30	M457	John Satori

REQUIRED
1. Record the sale of merchandise in a sales journal, page 8.
2. Post to the accounts receivable subsidiary ledger. List the customers alphabetically.

Objectives
1 and 2

P 7-2A   Posting Sales Transactions   You are hired as the accountant for Green Office Supply. You find the following sales journal:

SALES JOURNAL   Page ___11___

Date		Customer	Invoice Number	Terms	Post. Ref.	Amount A/R (Dr.) Sales (Cr.)
19XX						
Aug.	2	Bronson Company	V071	1/10, n30	√	9 0 0 —
	6	Mathisen Company	V072	1/10, n30	√	5 0 0 —
	9	Ellison Company	V073	1/10, n30	√	4 0 0 —
	12	Bronson Company	V074	1/10, n30	√	1 9 0 0 —
	16	Ellison Company	V075	1/10, n30	√	1 2 0 0 —
	18	Mathisen Company	V076	1/10, n30	√	2 0 0 —
	24	Ellison Company	V077	1/10, n30	√	7 0 0 —
	31	Bronson Company	V078	1/10, n30	√	1 7 0 0 —
						7 5 0 0 —
						(110) (411)

The accountant you replaced recorded the sales transactions in the sales journal and included the proper posting references. However, she did not post to the accounts receivable subsidiary ledger and the general ledger.

REQUIRED
1. Using the general ledger account numbers below the Amount column, write the account names and account numbers in the general ledger. List Accounts Receivable first, followed by Sales.
2. Post to the accounts receivable subsidiary ledger. List the customers alphabetically.
3. Post to the general ledger.
4. Prepare a schedule of accounts receivable.

Objectives
1, 2, 3, and 4

P 7-3A   Comprehensive Chapter Review Problem   Huan Paper Supply had the following credit transactions during the month of March 19XX:

March   1   Sold $1,800 of merchandise on account to Elroy Company, invoice number S563. Terms are n30.

March   4   Sold $3,700 of merchandise on credit to Kossman Company, invoice number S564. Terms are n30.

March 6   Sold to Steen Company $4,000 of machinery, account number 171, on account. Terms are n30. Machinery had an $8,500 balance before this sale.

March 8   Elroy Company returned $1,000 of inferior merchandise previously purchased March 1. Credit memorandum CM13 is issued.

March 11   Sold $5,400 of merchandise on account to Pruski Company, invoice number S565. Terms are n30.

March 17   Sold $6,900 of merchandise on account to Kossman Company, invoice number S566. Terms are n30.

March 20   Sold $7,100 of merchandise on credit to Lerma Company, invoice number S567. Terms are n30.

March 24   Pruski Company returned $1,500 of damaged merchandise previously purchased March 11. Credit memorandum CM14 is issued.

March 27   Sold $2,800 of merchandise on account to Elroy Company, invoice number S568. Terms are n30.

March 29   Sold to Philip Company $9,700 of equipment, account number 181, on account. Terms are n30. Equipment had a $29,400 balance before this sale.

March 31   Sold $5,000 of merchandise to Evans, Inc. Terms are n30. Invoice number is S569.

REQUIRED

1. Open the previous balances in the Machinery and Equipment accounts. Record the sale of merchandise in a sales journal, page 10.
2. Record the return of merchandise and the sale of assets other than merchandise in a general journal, page 19. Sales Returns and Allowances is account number 421.
3. Post to the accounts receivable subsidiary ledger. List the customers alphabetically.
4. Post to the general ledger. Accounts Receivable is account number 112, and Sales is 420.
5. Prepare a schedule of accounts receivable.

**Objectives
1 through 4**

P 7-4A   **Comprehensive Chapter Review Problem**   Lomas Medical Supply had the following credit transactions during the month of August 19XX:

August 1   Sold $3,700 of merchandise on credit to Slatten Company, invoice number P786. Terms are 1/10, n30.

August 3   Sold $8,400 of merchandise on account to Waller Company, invoice number P787. Terms are 1/10, n30.

August 6   Sold to Johns Company $3,800 of merchandise on credit. Terms are 1/10, n30. The invoice number is P788.

August 8	Sold to Diman Company $8,900 of furniture, account number 151, on credit. Terms are n30. Furniture had a $23,700 balance before this sale.
August 10	Slatten Company returned $2,900 of damaged merchandise previously purchased August 1. Credit memorandum CM96 is issued.
August 13	Sold $1,800 of merchandise on credit to Bonner Company, invoice number P789. Terms are 1/10, n30.
August 16	Sold $5,800 of merchandise on account to Johns Company, invoice number P790. Terms are 1/10, n30.
August 19	Sold $2,700 of merchandise on credit to Slatten Company, invoice number P791. Terms are 1/10, n30.
August 21	Sold to Franklin Company $2,700 of equipment, account number 161, on account. Terms are n30. Equipment had a $4,700 balance before this sale.
August 24	Bonner Company returned $600 of inferior merchandise previously purchased August 13. Credit memorandum CM97 is issued.
August 25	Sold $4,800 of merchandise on account to Waller Company, invoice number P792. Terms are 1/10, n30.
August 27	Sold to Rogers Company a $10,600 automobile, account number 171, on account. Terms are n30. The automobile had a $10,600 balance before this sale.
August 28	Sold $3,600 of merchandise to Abbot, Inc. Terms are 1/10, n30. Invoice number is P793.
August 30	Waller Company was allowed a $1,100 credit for defective merchandise previously purchased August 3. Credit memorandum CM98 is issued.
August 31	Sold $9,700 of merchandise on credit to Xeno Company. Terms are 1/10, n30. The invoice number is P794.

REQUIRED

1. Open the previous balances in the Furniture, Equipment, and Automobile accounts. Record the sale of merchandise in a sales journal, page 12.
2. Record the return of merchandise and the sale of assets, other than merchandise, in a general journal, page 18. Sales Returns and Allowances is account number 432.
3. Post to the accounts receivable subsidiary ledger. List the customers alphabetically.
4. Post to the general ledger. Accounts Receivable is account number 109, and Sales is 431.
5. Prepare a schedule of accounts receivable.

PROBLEM SET B

Objectives
1 and 2

P 7-1B   **Recording and Posting Sales**   Nuñez Sports Supply is owned by Maria Nuñez. The firm had the following credit sales of merchandise during the first half of December 19XX:

Date	Amount	Terms	Invoice Number	Customer
December 2	$100	1/10, n30	R145	Jeff Grand
December 6	$400	1/10, n30	R146	Serat Komar
December 9	$200	1/10, n30	R147	Jeff Grand
December 11	$500	1/10, n30	R148	Wiley Herren
December 13	$2,000	1/10, n30	R149	Serat Komar
December 15	$300	1/10, n30	R150	Wiley Herren

REQUIRED
1. Record the sale of merchandise in a sales journal, page 6.
2. Post to the accounts receivable subsidiary ledger. List the customers alphabetically.

Objectives
1 and 2

P 7-2B   **Posting Sales Transactions**   You are hired as the accountant for Zorn Cable Supply. You find the following sales journal:

SALES JOURNAL   Page _____9_____

Date		Customer	Invoice Number	Terms	Post. Ref.	Amount A/R (Dr.) Sales (Cr.)
19XX						
Feb.	1	Charles Company	S29A	2/10, n30	√	5 0 0 —
	5	Ralph Company	S30A	2/10, n30	√	3 0 0 —
	8	Greenly Company	S31A	2/10, n30	√	7 0 0 —
	13	Charles Company	S32A	2/10, n30	√	1 1 0 0 —
	17	Greenly Company	S33A	2/10, n30	√	2 0 0 0 —
	19	Ralph Company	S34A	2/10, n30	√	4 0 0 —
	23	Greenly Company	S35A	2/10, n30	√	8 0 0 —
	28	Charles Company	S36A	2/10, n30	√	1 5 0 0 —
						7 3 0 0 —
						(118) (422)

The accountant you replaced recorded the sales transactions in the sales journal and included the proper posting references. However, he did not post to the accounts receivable subsidiary ledger and the general ledger.

REQUIRED

1. Using the general ledger account numbers below the Amount column, write the account names and account numbers in the general ledger. List Accounts Receivable first, followed by Sales.
2. Post to the accounts receivable subsidiary ledger. List the customers alphabetically.
3. Post to the general ledger.
4. Prepare a schedule of accounts receivable.

**Objectives
1 through 4**

P 7-3B

Comprehensive Chapter Review Problem   Pearl Typewriter Supply had the following credit transactions during the month of January 19XX:

January 2	Sold $2,900 of merchandise on account to Green Company, invoice number L098. Terms are n30.
January 5	Sold $1,900 of merchandise on credit to Ludwig Company, invoice number L099. Terms are n30.
January 6	Sold to Seale Company $3,700 of machinery, account number 151, on account. Terms are n30. Machinery had a $6,700 balance before the sale.
January 7	Green Company returned $1,100 of inferior merchandise previously purchased January 2. Credit memorandum CM33 is issued.
January 12	Sold $3,800 of merchandise on account to Pait Company, invoice number L100. Terms are n30.
January 18	Sold $2,800 of merchandise on account to Pait Company, invoice number L101. Terms are n30.
January 21	Sold $4,800 of merchandise on credit to Phong Company, invoice number L102. Terms are n30.
January 23	Pait Company returned $400 of damaged merchandise previously purchased January 12. Credit memorandum CM34 is issued.
January 26	Sold $5,100 of merchandise on account to Phong Company, invoice number L103. Terms are n30.
January 28	Sold to Walko Company a $14,500 delivery truck, account number 161, on account. Terms are n30. The delivery truck had a $14,500 balance before the sale.
January 31	Sold $3,400 of merchandise to Asway, Inc. Terms are n30. Invoice number is L104.

REQUIRED

1. Open the previous balances in the Machinery and Delivery Truck accounts. Record the sale of merchandise in a sales journal, page 11.
2. Record the return of merchandise and the sale of assets other than merchandise in a general journal, page 21. Sales Returns and Allowances is account number 432.

3. Post to the accounts receivable subsidiary ledger. List the customers alphabetically.
4. Post to the general ledger. Accounts Receivable is account number 123, and Sales is 431.
5. Prepare a schedule of accounts receivable.

Objectives
1 through 4

P 7-4B

Comprehensive Chapter Review Problem   Mueller Boat Supply had the following credit transactions during the month of November 19XX:

November 2   Sold $1,800 of merchandise on credit to Krell Company, invoice number C016. Terms are 2/10, n30.

November 4   Sold $4,700 of merchandise on account to Pollok Company, invoice number C017. Terms are 2/10, n30.

November 7   Sold to Suman Company $2,000 of merchandise on credit. Terms are 2/10, n30. The invoice number is C018.

November 14   Sold $3,700 of merchandise on credit to Yos Company, invoice number C019. Terms are 2/10, n30.

November 15   Sold to Olson Company $9,000 of office supplies, account number 131, on credit. Terms are n30. Office Supplies had a $15,400 balance before this sale.

November 17   Sold $6,800 of merchandise on account to Pollok Company, invoice number C020. Terms are 2/10, n30.

November 18   Sold $2,100 of merchandise on credit to Suman Company, invoice number C021. Terms are 2/10, n30.

November 20   Sold to Sauceda Company $3,900 of machinery, account number 151, on account. Terms are n30. Machinery had a $12,700 balance before this sale.

November 23   Yos Company returned $900 of damaged merchandise previously purchased November 14. Credit memorandum CM99 is issued.

November 24   Sold $3,800 of merchandise on account to Apte Company, invoice number C022. Terms are 2/10, n30.

November 28   Sold to Wontae Company a $12,900 truck, account number 181, on credit. Terms are n30. The truck had a $12,900 balance before this sale.

November 29   Sold $2,800 of merchandise to Hawley, Inc. Terms are 2/10, n30. Invoice number is C023.

November 29   Suman Company was allowed a $200 credit for defective merchandise previously purchased November 7. Credit memorandum CM100 is issued.

November 30   Sold $8,900 of merchandise on credit to Bandel Company. Terms are 2/10, n30. The invoice number is C024.

REQUIRED
1. Open the previous balances in the Office Supplies, Machinery, and Truck accounts. Record the sale of merchandise in a sales journal, page 12.

2. Record the return of merchandise and the sale of assets, other than merchandise, in a general journal, page 25. Sales Returns and Allowances is account number 441.
3. Post to the accounts receivable subsidiary ledger. List the customers alphabetically.
4. Post to the general ledger. Accounts Receivable is account number 114, and Sales is 440.
5. Prepare a schedule of accounts receivable.

ANSWERS TO SELF-TEST QUESTIONS

1. d 2. c 3. b 4. c 5. a

8

The Purchases Journal and Accounts Payable Subsidiary Ledger

The holy passion of Friendship is of so sweet and steady and loyal and enduring a nature that it will last through a whole lifetime, if not asked to lend money.

MARK TWAIN

LEARNING OBJECTIVES

After reading this chapter, discussing the questions, and working the exercises and problems, you will be able to do the following:

1. Understand and use the purchases journal (pp. 243–44).

2. Understand and use the accounts payable subsidiary ledger (pp. 244–51).

3. Account for purchases returns and allowances (pp. 252–53).

4. Record the purchase of assets other than merchandise on account (pp. 253–56).

In Chapter 7 we examined the sales of merchandise on account for United Auto Supply. In this chapter we will look at the purchases of merchandise on account—what we sold in Chapter 7. Let's begin with a discussion of internal control.

INTERNAL CONTROL

Internal control is the system of policies and procedures adopted by a firm to safeguard assets and promote operational efficiency. In this chapter we are concerned with the internal control over purchases.

Internal Control and Purchases

Most firms will use the following procedures when making purchases:

1. **Purchase Requisition:** a request by a department to purchase certain goods. For example, a department of United Auto Supply has requested the purchase of twenty-five water pumps, which are merchandise inventory. The manager, or another official of the department, approves the purchase requisition and forwards it to the purchasing department. An approved purchase requisition is shown in Exhibit 8-1.

2. **Purchase Order:** a written order for merchandise or other items. Once the purchase has been approved, the firm issues a purchase order to Boyle Manufacturing, requesting that the seller (Boyle Manufacturing) sell the merchandise or other items specified to the buyer (United Auto Supply). The approved purchase order (see Exhibit 8-2) is sent to Boyle Manufacturing, requesting that they sell United Auto Supply twenty-five water pumps at $20 each.

3. **Purchase Invoice:**
   If Boyle Manufacturing accepts the terms of the purchase order, they will sell the merchandise as specified and issue the buyer (United Auto Supply) a purchase invoice, as shown in Exhibit 8-3. The buyer then compares the purchase invoice to the purchase order to see if the order was properly filled. The buyer also makes sure that the merchandise (or other items received) is correct as ordered and in good working order. This purchase invoice is kept in an unpaid-invoice file until it is paid.

EXHIBIT 8-1
Purchase Requisition

Purchase Requisition   No. _W1278_

United Auto Supply
100 Main Street
Houston, Texas 77001

Date Issued: *10/1/XX*   Order From: *Boyle Manufacturing*
Date Required: *10/2/XX*   *P.O. Box 11001*
                                                          New York, NY 10001

Quantity	Description	Amount (each)	Total
25	Water Pump	$20	$500

Ordered
by: *Frank Rylski*   **Date:**   *10/1/XX*
Approved by: _____
Purchase Order Number Issued: *1037*

EXHIBIT 8-2
Purchase Order

Purchase Order   No. _1037_

From: *United Auto Supply*
        100 Main Street
        Houston, Texas 77001

To: *Boyle Manufacturing*
      P.O. Box 11001
      New York, NY 10001

Purchase Requisition Date: *10/1/XX*   **Ship To:**   *above address*
Purchase Order Date: *10/1/XX*
Terms: *2/10, n30*
Ship By: *Rogers Freight*

Quantity	Description	Amount (each)	Total
25	Water Pump	$20	$500

Purchasing Department Manager

EXHIBIT 8-3
Purchase Invoice

Boyle Manufacturing
P.O. Box 11001
New York, NY   10001

Invoice No.   *B6661*

Sold to: *United Auto Supply*
100 Main Street
Houston, Texas   77001

Order Received: *10/2/XX*   **Ship To:**   *above address*

Order Sent: *10/2/XX*

Terms: *2/10, n30*

Purchase Order No.:   *1037*

Shipped By: *Rogers Freight*

Quantity	Description	Amount (each)	Total
25	Water Pump	$20	$500
Tax			0
Total Amount Due			$500

Recording the Purchase in a General Journal

If United Auto Supply recorded the credit sale in a general journal, the purchase would be journalized as shown below.

Purchases is debited for the purchase of merchandise. The corresponding credit is to Accounts Payable. Purchases is part of the cost of goods sold broad classification of accounts used to record the purchase of merchandise inventory. **Cost of goods sold** represents the cost of merchandise inventory sold during an accounting period. However, United Auto Supply would not use a general journal for these reasons.

GENERAL JOURNAL   Page ___1___

Date		Description	Post. Ref.	Debit	Credit
19XX					
Oct.	1	Purchases		5 0 0 —	
		Accounts Payable—Boyle Manufacturing			5 0 0 —
		Invoice Number B6661, Terms 2/10, n30			

1. For each credit purchase, the words Purchases and Accounts Payable must be written.

2. For each credit purchase, both Purchases and Accounts Payable must be posted to the general ledger.

As shown in Chapter 7, to save time and effort, and to increase efficiency, the firm would use special journals.

THE PURCHASES JOURNAL

Objective 1
Understand and use the purchases journal.

The single-column purchases journal in Exhibit 8-4 is used for credit purchases of merchandise only. The credit purchase from Boyle Manufacturing is recorded.

The single-column purchases journal includes a column for the Date, Vendor, Invoice Number, Terms, Post. Ref., and Amount. (The Post. Ref. column will be used later.) "A/P" is an abbreviation for accounts payable. In Chapter 7, "customer" was used to indicate who the firm "sold to." In this chapter we will distinguish the buyer from the seller by using the term "**vendor**," indicating who the firm "purchased from."

A single-column purchases journal is normally used because sales tax charged and paid is considered a cost of acquiring an asset, in this case, merchandise inventory. The final user or consumer normally pays the sales tax. United Auto Supply is buying the merchandise to sell to the final user so no tax is charged. Any acquisition that is not merchandise inventory, such as office supplies, telephone service, and so on, may have a charge for sales tax. Most firms include this sales tax in the cost of the asset or expense. A few firms may actually establish a Sales Tax Expense account. But, in order to simplify this procedure, we will assume that any sales tax is included in the cost.

EXHIBIT 8-4
Single-Column Purchases Journal

PURCHASES JOURNAL   Page ____10____

Date		Vendor	Invoice Number	Terms	Post. Ref.	Amount Purch. (Dr.) A/P (Cr.)
19XX						
Oct.	*1*	*Boyle Manufacturing*	*B6661*	*2/10, n30*		5 0 0 —

Purposes of the Purchases Journal

The purchases journal has the following purposes:

1. To record all credit purchases of merchandise in one journal, thus saving space.
2. To save journalizing time by recording each purchase amount only once on one line.
3. Vendor names, invoice numbers, and terms can be easily identified.
4. The individual credit purchases are added and posted as one total to the general ledger at the end of the accounting period. This total is posted as a debit to Purchases and a credit to Accounts Payable.

Posting from the Purchases Journal

Two of the purposes of the purchases journal are to save space and time. We can see this illustrated in Exhibit 8-5 where the purchases of merchandise on account for October for United Auto Supply are recorded and posted.

There are four steps for posting from the purchases journal to the general ledger, keyed as ①, ②, ③, and ④ in Exhibit 8-5. The steps are as follows:

① The Amount column in the purchases journal is underlined after the final purchase is entered. The purchases are totaled and double underlined.

② The total is posted as a debit to Purchases in the general ledger. "P10" is written in the Post. Ref. column of the general ledger to indicate that the posting is from page 10 of the purchases journal.

③ After posting the debit to Purchases, you would go back to the Amount column in the purchases journal and write "501" in parenthesis below the total.

④ Steps 2 and 3 are repeated for the credit posting to Accounts Payable.

THE ACCOUNTS PAYABLE SUBSIDIARY LEDGER

Objective 2
Understand and use the accounts payable subsidiary ledger.

An **accounts payable subsidiary ledger** (as shown in Exhibit 8-6) is used in conjunction with the purchases journal to identify and accumulate amounts owed to individual vendors. There is usually a separate page in this ledger for each vendor. The vendors' names in the accounts payable subsidiary ledger are often arranged alphabetically, and most accountants use a loose-leaf binder so they can add or remove vendors as needed.

EXHIBIT 8-5
Recording and Posting Credit Merchandise Purchases

PURCHASES JOURNAL   Page _____10_____

Date		Vendor	Invoice Number	Terms	Post. Ref.	Amount Purch. (Dr.) A/P (Cr.)
19XX						
Oct.	1	Boyle Manufacturing	B6661	2/10, n30		5 0 0 —
	5	Hakala Enterprises	X095	n30		2 1 0 0 —
	10	Zamora Warehouse	21087	1/25, n60		1 7 0 0 —
	14	Boyle Manufacturing	B7348	2/10, n30		1 8 0 0 —
	19	Anderson, Inc.	IA566	n30		4 0 0 —
	23	Nguyen Distributors	00982	3/10, n30		1 5 0 0 —
	28	Mehta Manufacturing	786M	4/10, n30		1 9 0 0 —
	31	Anderson, Inc.	IA612	n30		9 0 0 —
					③	10 8 0 0 —
						(501) (201)

①

GENERAL LEDGER ACCOUNTS   ④

Account: Accounts Payable   **Account No.** 201

Date		Item	Post. Ref.	Debit	Credit	Balance Debit	Balance Credit
19XX							
Oct.	31		P10		1 0 8 0 0 —		1 0 8 0 0 —

③

Account: Purchases   **Account No.** 501

Date		Item	Post. Ref.	Debit	Credit	Balance Debit	Balance Credit
19XX							
Oct.	31	②	P10	1 0 8 0 0 —		1 0 8 0 0 —	

Exhibit 8-6 shows the accounts payable subsidiary ledger page for Boyle Manufacturing:

EXHIBIT 8-6
Vendor's Page in Accounts Payable Subsidiary Ledger

ACCOUNTS PAYABLE SUBSIDIARY LEDGER

Vendor: *Boyle Manufacturing*

Date		Item	Post. Ref.	Debit	Credit	Balance
19XX						
Oct.	1		P10		5 0 0 —	5 0 0 —
	14		P10		1 8 0 0 —	2 3 0 0 —

The Control Account

In Chapter 7 the Accounts Receivable account was called a control account. In this chapter the Accounts Payable account in the general ledger is also called a control account. The Accounts Payable balance in the general ledger provides a check or control over the accounts payable subsidiary ledger. The total of all the vendor's balances kept in the accounts payable subsidiary ledger must equal the Accounts Payable account balance in the general ledger when all postings are up to date.

Posting to the Accounts Payable Subsidiary Ledger

There are three steps to follow when posting from the purchases journal to the accounts payable subsidiary ledger, keyed as ①, ②, and ③ in Exhibit 8-7. The posting process is shown for Anderson, Inc. The credit purchases for the other vendors are posted in the same manner. The steps are as follows:

① As purchases of merchandise on account are entered in the purchases journal, they are posted daily or as they occur to the accounts payable subsidiary ledger. When a firm buys merchandise on account, the total purchase amount, including any tax, is entered into the Credit column of the accounts payable subsidiary ledger. A debit is made whenever the firm pays on the account. The Balance column has either a credit or zero balance. (A debit balance would indicate that the firm has paid too much.)

EXHIBIT 8-7
Posting to the Accounts Payable Subsidiary Ledger

PURCHASES JOURNAL
Page __10__

Date	Vendor	Invoice Number	Terms	Post. Ref.	Amount Purch. (Dr.) A/P (Cr.)
19XX					
Oct. 1	Boyle Manufacturing	B6661	2/10, n30	✓	5 0 0 —
5	Hakala Enterprises	X095	n30	✓	2 1 0 0 —
10	Zamora Warehouse	21087	1/25, n60	✓	1 7 0 0 —
14	Boyle Manufacturing	B7348	2/10, n30	✓	1 8 0 0 —
19	Anderson, Inc.	IA566	n30	✓ ③	4 0 0 —
23	Nguyen Distributors	00982	3/10, n30	✓	1 5 0 0 —
28	Mehta Manufacturing	786M	4/10, n30	✓	1 9 0 0 —
31	Anderson, Inc.	IA612	n30	✓	9 0 0 —
					10 8 0 0 —
					(501) (201)

ACCOUNTS PAYABLE SUBSIDIARY LEDGER

Vendor: *Anderson, Inc.*

Date	Item	Post. Ref.	Debit	Credit	Balance
19XX					
Oct. 19	②	P10		① 4 0 0 —	4 0 0 —
31		P10		9 0 0 —	1 3 0 0 —

Vendor: *Boyle Manufacturing*

Date	Item	Post. Ref.	Debit	Credit	Balance
19XX					
Oct. 1		P10		5 0 0 —	5 0 0 —
14		P10		1 8 0 0 —	2 3 0 0 —

(continued)

(Ex. 8-7 concluded)

Vendor: *Hakala Enterprises*

Date		Item	Post. Ref.	Debit	Credit	Balance
19XX						
Oct.	5		P10		2 1 0 0 —	2 1 0 0 —

Vendor: *Mehta Manufacturing*

Date		Item	Post. Ref.	Debit	Credit	Balance
19XX						
Oct.	28		P10		1 9 0 0 —	1 9 0 0 —

Vendor: *Nguyen Distributors*

Date		Item	Post. Ref.	Debit	Credit	Balance
19XX						
Oct.	23		P10		1 5 0 0 —	1 5 0 0 —

Vendor: *Zamora Warehouse*

Date		Item	Post. Ref.	Debit	Credit	Balance
19XX						
Oct.	10		P10		1 7 0 0 —	1 7 0 0 —

② "P10" for purchases journal (P) page 10 is entered in the Post. Ref. column of the vendor's accounts payable subsidiary ledger page after the amount owed has been posted from the purchases journal.

③ Once the posting has been entered into the vendor's accounts payable subsidiary ledger page, a check mark (√) is placed in the Post. Ref. column of the purchases journal. This signifies that the credit purchase amount, including any tax, has been posted to the accounts payable subsidiary ledger for that vendor.

Exhibit 8-7 shows the postings to the accounts payable subsidiary ledger. The accounts payable subsidiary ledger is not, however, posted to the general ledger. A subsidiary ledger (such as the accounts payable subsidiary ledger) supports a book of original entry or journal, which in this case is the purchases journal. By utilizing an accounts payable subsidiary ledger, a firm is able to keep track of the account balances (amounts owed) to its vendors. When a vendor inquires about the balance owed, you can quickly reference that vendor's page in the accounts payable subsidiary ledger and supply the requested information.

Freight In

The merchandise purchased from Boyle Manufacturing is to be delivered by Rogers Freight, terms n30. We will assume that the goods are shipped **FOB shipping point**, which means that the buyer pays the transportation cost from the selling point to the place of delivery. The seller does not pay the transportation cost. FOB is an abbreviation for *free-on-board*. When the buyer pays the transportation cost, an account called **Freight In** is debited. Freight In is a cost of goods sold account that is used to record the transportation cost of merchandise paid for by the buyer.

United Auto Supply's general journal entry to record the transportation charge on the October 1, 19XX, shipment from Boyle Manufacturing is as follows:

GENERAL JOURNAL   Page ___26___

Date		Description	Post. Ref.	Debit	Credit
19XX					
Oct.	1	Freight In	516	3 0 0 —	
		Accounts Payable—Rogers Freight	201/√		3 0 0 —
		Terms n30			

This general journal entry is then posted to the general ledger and accounts payable subsidiary ledger as follows:

GENERAL LEDGER ACCOUNTS

Account: *Accounts Payable* — Account No. 201

Date		Item	Post. Ref.	Debit	Credit	Balance Debit	Balance Credit
19XX							
Oct.	1	*	J26		3 0 0 —		3 0 0 —
	31		P10		1 0 8 0 0 —		1 1 1 0 0 —

Account: *Freight In* — Account No. 516

Date		Item	Post. Ref.	Debit	Credit	Balance Debit	Balance Credit
19XX							
Oct.	1		J26	3 0 0 —		3 0 0 —	

ACCOUNTS PAYABLE SUBSIDIARY LEDGER

Vendor: *Rogers Freight*

Date		Item	Post. Ref.	Debit	Credit	Balance
19XX						
Oct.	1		J26		3 0 0 —	3 0 0 —

Goods are frequently shipped another way—**FOB destination**, where the seller pays the transportation cost from the shipping point to the place of destination. In this book we will assume that all merchandise is shipped FOB shipping point unless stated otherwise.

*Note: Entries are made in date order.

The Schedule of Accounts Payable

A schedule of accounts payable is normally prepared at the end of the accounting period directly from the accounts payable subsidiary ledger. As we see in Exhibit 8-8, each vendor and the balance owed is listed on the schedule. Also shown is the control account, Accounts Payable, in the general ledger. The total of the schedule of accounts payable must equal the total of the control account, Accounts Payable, in the general ledger. If the two do not agree, then a mistake has been made and must be corrected. (Notice that Rogers Freight is included.)

EXHIBIT 8-8
Schedule of Accounts Payable

United Auto Supply
Schedule of Accounts Payable
October 31, 19XX

Vendor	Amount Owed
Anderson, Inc.	$ 1 3 0 0 —
Boyle Manufacturing	2 3 0 0 —
Hakala Enterprises	2 1 0 0 —
Mehta Manufacturing	1 9 0 0 —
Nguyen Distributors	1 5 0 0 —
Rogers Freight	3 0 0 —
Zamora Warehouse	1 7 0 0 —
	$11 1 0 0 —

must equal

GENERAL LEDGER ACCOUNTS

Account: *Accounts Payable*   Account No.   201

Date	Item	Post. Ref.	Debit	Credit	Balance Debit	Balance Credit
19XX						
Oct. 1		J26		3 0 0 —		3 0 0 —
31		P10		1 0 8 0 0 —		1 1 1 0 0 —

THE PURCHASES RETURNS AND ALLOWANCES ACCOUNT

Objective 3
Account for
purchases returns
and allowances.

The **Purchases Returns and Allowances** account is used to record two types of transactions that apply to merchandise previously purchased. A **return** is a physical return of merchandise by the purchaser to the vendor. An **allowance** is granted by the vendor to the purchaser for inferior, defective, or damaged merchandise. Whenever a return or allowance occurs, the purchaser will notify the vendor by sending a prenumbered **debit memorandum**. It is called a debit memorandum because the vendor's account will be debited for the return or allowance. A general journal is used to record the return or allowance of merchandise previously purchased on account. Remember that the purchases journal is only used to record merchandise purchased on account.

The Purchases Returns and Allowances account is a *contra* cost of goods sold account. That is, it reduces cost of goods sold and has a normal credit balance. Purchases Returns and Allowances is included in the cost of goods sold classification of accounts, along with purchases, on the chart of accounts.

Assume that on October 29, 19XX, United Auto Supply returns $400 of defective merchandise previously purchased on account to Zamora Warehouse. Debit memorandum number DM782 is issued to Zamora Warehouse (as shown in Exhibit 8-9). The purchase transaction was originally recorded in the purchases journal (see Exhibit 8-5). Upon receipt of the debit memorandum, Zamora Warehouse will then issue United Auto Supply a credit memorandum, which we discussed in the previous chapter.

Journalizing and Posting Purchases Returns and Allowances

To record a return of merchandise, Accounts Payable is debited, and Purchases Returns and Allowances is credited. In Exhibit 8-10, the return is journalized and posted to the general ledger and accounts payable subsidiary ledger. The journalizing and posting steps are keyed as ①, ②, and ③. These three steps are as follows:

① The return or allowance of a previous credit purchase of merchandise must be recorded in the general journal.

② The debit is posted to both the Accounts Payable account in the general ledger and the vendor's page in the accounts payable subsidiary ledger. "J26" is entered in the Post. Ref. column of the general ledger and accounts payable subsidiary ledger. Once the posting is complete, "201/√" is entered in the Post. Ref. column of the general journal. The term "201" indicates a posting to Accounts

EXHIBIT 8-9
Prenumbered Debit Memorandum

Debit Memorandum   No. _782_

Charge Return   _X_   Cash Return   _____

United Auto Supply
100 Main Street, Houston, Texas   77001

Prepared By: *Carl Moore*
Purchase Date: *10/10/XX*   **Terms:**   *1/25, n60*
Invoice (billing) Date: *10/10/XX*   **Return Date:** *10/29/XX*

Vendor: *Zamora Warehouse*
            300 Travis Road, San Antonio, TX   78201

Return Information

Quantity	Merchandise	Amount (each)	Total Amount
16	*Fuel Pumps*	*$25*	*$400*

Total Amount To Be Debited   *$400*

Payable in the general ledger. The "$\sqrt{}$" indicates a posting to the vendor's account in the accounts payable subsidiary ledger. The slash (/) is used to keep the two references separate.

③ The credit is posted to Purchases Returns and Allowances in the general ledger. "J26" is entered in the Post. Ref. column. Once the posting is complete, "502" is entered in the Post. Ref. column of the general journal.

RECORDING OTHER TRANSACTIONS

Objective 4
Record the purchase of assets other than merchandise on account.

There are other purchase transactions that cannot be recorded in a one-column purchases journal. Any asset (other than merchandise inventory) purchased on account must be recorded using a general journal. For example, let's assume that on October 9, 19XX, United Auto Supply purchased $3,300 of office supplies, which is not merchandise inventory, from

EXHIBIT 8-10
Recording and Posting Purchases Returns and Allowances

① **GENERAL JOURNAL** Page ____26____

Date		Description	Post. Ref.	Debit	Credit
19XX					
Oct.	29	Accounts Payable—Zamora Warehouse	201/✓	4 0 0 — ②	
		Purchases Returns and Allowances	502 ③		4 0 0 —
		Return of Defective Merchandise, Debit Memorandum DM782			

GENERAL LEDGER ACCOUNTS

Account: *Accounts Payable*   Account No.   201

Date	Item	Post. Ref.	Debit	Credit	Balance Debit	Balance Credit
29		J26	4 0 0 —			

Account: *Purchases Returns and Allowances*   Account No.   502

Date		Item	Post. Ref.	Debit	Credit	Balance Debit	Balance Credit
19XX							
Oct.	29		J26		4 0 0 —		4 0 0 —

ACCOUNTS PAYABLE SUBSIDIARY LEDGER

Vendor: *Zamora Warehouse*

Date		Item	Post. Ref.	Debit	Credit	Balance
19XX						
Oct.	10		P10		1 7 0 0 —	1 7 0 0 —
	29		J26	4 0 0 —		1 3 0 0 —

County Office Supplies on account. The terms are **COD**. We will also assume that this transaction is not taxable. COD means that the invoice must be paid when the office supplies are delivered. COD is an abbreviation for *cash-on-delivery*. This transaction would be recorded in the general journal as follows:

GENERAL JOURNAL Page ___26___

Date		Description	Post. Ref.	Debit	Credit
19XX					
Oct.	9	Office Supplies	131	3 3 0 0 —	
		Accounts Payable — County Office Supplies	201/√		3 3 0 0 —
		Terms COD			

For illustration purposes, let's also record this transaction using T accounts:

Office Supplies		Accounts Payable	
(10/9) 3,300			(10/9) 3,300

This general journal entry would then be posted to the general ledger and accounts payable subsidiary ledger as follows:

GENERAL LEDGER ACCOUNTS

Account: *Office Supplies* Account No. 131

Date		Item	Post. Ref.	Debit	Credit	Balance Debit	Balance Credit
19XX							
Oct.	9		J26	3 3 0 0 —		3 3 0 0 —	

(continued)

Account: Accounts Payable					Account No. 201		
Date	Item	Post. Ref.	Debit	Credit	Balance Debit		Credit
19XX							
Oct. 1		J26		3 0 0 —			3 0 0 —
9		J26		3 3 0 0 —			3 6 0 0 —
29		J26	4 0 0 —				3 2 0 0 —
31		P10		1 0 8 0 0 —			1 4 0 0 0 —

ACCOUNTS PAYABLE SUBSIDIARY LEDGER

Vendor: County Office Supplies					
Date	Item	Post. Ref.	Debit	Credit	Balance
19XX					
Oct. 9		J26		3 3 0 0 —	3 3 0 0 —

CHAPTER REVIEW

1. Understand and use the purchases journal (pp. 243–44).
   A single-column purchases journal is used to record the purchase of merchandise on account.

2. Understand and use the accounts payable subsidiary ledger (pp. 244–51).
   An accounts payable subsidiary ledger is used in conjunction with the purchases journal to identify and accumulate amounts owed to individual vendors.

3. Account for purchases returns and allowances (pp. 252–53).
   The Purchases Returns and Allowances account is used to record a return or an allowance that applies to merchandise previously purchased. A return is a physical return of merchandise by the purchaser to the vendor. An allowance is granted by the vendor to the purchaser for inferior, defective, or damaged merchandise. A

prenumbered debit memorandum is given to the vendor by the purchaser for purchases returns and allowances.

4. **Record the purchase of assets other than merchandise on account (pp. 253–56).**
   Any asset (other than merchandise inventory) purchased on account must be recorded using a general journal.

GLOSSARY

Accounts Payable Subsidiary Ledger	Used in conjunction with the purchases journal to identify and accumulate amounts owed to individual vendors. Supports a book of original entry.
COD	Abbreviation for cash-on-delivery. Goods must be paid for when delivered.
Cost of Goods Sold	Represents the cost of merchandise inventory that is sold during an accounting period.
Debit Memorandum	Prenumbered document given to the vendor by the purchaser for purchases returns and allowances.
FOB	Abbreviation for free-on-board.
FOB Destination	Means that the seller will pay the transportation cost from the shipping point to the place of destination.
FOB Shipping Point	Means that the buyer, not the seller, will pay the transportation cost from the selling point to the place of delivery.
Freight In	Cost of goods sold account that is used to record the transportation cost of merchandise paid for by the buyer.
Internal Control	System of policies and procedures adopted by a firm to safeguard assets and promote operational efficiency.
Purchase Invoice	Issued by the seller to the buyer for payment upon acceptance of a purchase order.
Purchase Order	Written order for merchandise or other items.
Purchase Requisition	Request by a department to purchase merchandise or other items.
Purchases	Cost of goods sold account that is used to record the purchase of merchandise inventory.
Purchases Returns and Allowances	Account used to record the return or allowance of merchandise previously purchased.
Schedule of Accounts Payable	Listing of each vendor and the amount owed.
Vendor	Used to indicate who the firm purchased from.

SELF-TEST QUESTIONS FOR REVIEW

(Answers are on p. 271.)

1. A request by a department to purchase certain goods is a
   a. purchase requisition.   b. purchase invoice.
   c. purchase order.   d. debit memorandum.

2. Which of the following accounts will probably have a credit balance after the purchases journal is posted to the general ledger?
   a. Purchases   b. Accounts Payable
   c. Cash   d. Accounts Receivable

3. Which of the following is NOT an asset account?
   a. Prepaid Insurance   b. Accounts Receivable
   c. Freight In   d. Cash

4. Which of the following is a contra cost of goods sold account?
   a. Purchases   b. Accounts Payable
   c. Freight In   d. Purchases Returns and Allowances

5. "DM109" is listed in the description of a transaction. Which of the following accounts is credited for this transaction?
   a. Freight In   b. Purchases
   c. Accounts Payable   d. Purchases Returns and Allowances

PRACTICAL REVIEW PROBLEM

**Objectives
1 through 4**

Recording and Posting Purchases   Mid-Atlantic Sports Supply had the following credit transactions during the month of November 19XX:

November 2   Purchased $400 of merchandise on credit from Babino Company, invoice number B340. Terms are n30.

November 10   Purchased $900 of office supplies, account number 139, on credit. Terms are COD. The vendor is Talmadge, Inc.

November 17   Returned $100 of damaged merchandise previously purchased November 2 from Babino Company. Debit memorandum DM32 is issued.

November 22   Received a freight invoice from Loadstar Freight for the November 2 delivery from Babino Company. Terms are 2/10, n30. The amount is $50.

November 30   Purchased $500 of merchandise on credit from Phu Manufacturing, invoice number L7829. Terms are 1/10, n30.

REQUIRED
1. Record the purchase of merchandise in a purchases journal, page 1.

2. Record the return of merchandise, purchase of assets other than merchandise, and freight in a general journal, page 13. Purchases Returns and Allowances is account number 509, and Freight In is 512.
3. Post to the accounts payable subsidiary ledger. List the vendors alphabetically.
4. Post to the general ledger. Accounts Payable is account number 218, and Purchases is 508.
5. Prepare a schedule of accounts payable.

ANSWER TO PRACTICAL REVIEW PROBLEM

1. **PURCHASES JOURNAL** Page ___1___

Date	Vendor	Invoice Number	Terms	Post. Ref.	Amount Purch. (Dr.) A/P (Cr.)
19XX					
Nov. 2	Babino Company	B340	n30	√	4 0 0 —
30	Phu Manufacturing	L7829	1/10, n30	√	5 0 0 —
					9 0 0 —
					(508) (218)

2. **GENERAL JOURNAL** Page ___13___

Date	Description	Post. Ref.	Debit	Credit
19XX				
Nov. 10	Office Supplies	139	9 0 0 —	
	Accounts Payable—Talmadge, Inc.	218/√		9 0 0 —
	Terms COD			
17	Accounts Payable—Babino Company	218/√	1 0 0 —	
	Purchases Returns and Allowances	509		1 0 0 —
	Return of Damaged Merchandise, Debit Memorandum DM32			
22	Freight In	512	5 0 —	
	Accounts Payable—Loadstar Freight	218/√		5 0 —
	Terms 2/10, n30			

3. ACCOUNTS PAYABLE SUBSIDIARY LEDGER

Vendor: *Babino Company*

Date		Item	Post. Ref.	Debit	Credit	Balance
19XX						
Nov.	2		P1		400 —	400 —
	17		J13	100 —		300 —

Vendor: *Loadstar Freight*

Date		Item	Post. Ref.	Debit	Credit	Balance
19XX						
Nov.	22		J13		50 —	50 —

Vendor: *Phu Manufacturing*

Date		Item	Post. Ref.	Debit	Credit	Balance
19XX						
Nov.	30		P1		500 —	500 —

Vendor: *Talmadge, Inc.*

Date		Item	Post. Ref.	Debit	Credit	Balance
19XX						
Nov.	10		J13		900 —	900 —

4.

GENERAL LEDGER ACCOUNTS

Account: *Office Supplies*   **Account No.** 139

Date	Item	Post. Ref.	Debit	Credit	Balance Debit	Balance Credit
19XX						
Nov. 10		J13	9 0 0 —		9 0 0 —	

Account: *Accounts Payable*   **Account No.** 218

Date	Item	Post. Ref.	Debit	Credit	Balance Debit	Balance Credit
19XX						
Nov. 10		J13		9 0 0 —		9 0 0 —
17		J13	1 0 0 —			8 0 0 —
22		J13		5 0 —		8 5 0 —
30		P1		9 0 0 —		1 7 5 0 —

Account: *Purchases*   **Account No.** 508

Date	Item	Post. Ref.	Debit	Credit	Balance Debit	Balance Credit
19XX						
Nov. 30		P1	9 0 0 —		9 0 0 —	

Account: *Purchases Returns and Allowances*   **Account No.** 509

Date	Item	Post. Ref.	Debit	Credit	Balance Debit	Balance Credit
19XX						
Nov. 17		J13		1 0 0 —		1 0 0 —

(continued)

Account: *Freight In*					Account No. 512	
Date	Item	Post. Ref.	Debit	Credit	Balance Debit	Balance Credit
19XX						
Nov. 22		J13	5 0 —		5 0 —	

5.

Mid-Atlantic Sports Supply
Schedule of Accounts Payable
November 30, 19XX

Vendor	Amount Owed
Babino Company	$ 3 0 0 —
Loadstar Freight	5 0 —
Phu Manufacturing	5 0 0 —
Talmadge, Inc.	9 0 0 —
	$1 7 5 0 —

DISCUSSION QUESTIONS

Q 8-1 What is internal control? Name the procedures that should be followed when making purchases.

Q 8-2 Briefly describe the following: (a) COD; (b) FOB shipping point; and (c) FOB destination.

Q 8-3 Name the two reasons why a merchandising firm would not use a general journal if a purchases journal could be used.

Q 8-4 Define Purchases and Cost of Goods Sold. Also, name the six columns in a purchases journal.

Q 8-5 Name the four purposes of a purchases journal.

Q 8-6 Name the four steps for posting from the purchases journal to the general ledger.

Q 8-7 What is the accounts payable subsidiary ledger used for? Name the three steps to follow when posting to the accounts payable subsidiary ledger.

Q 8-8 Briefly describe the Purchases Returns and Allowances account. What is a debit memorandum? Why is it called a debit memorandum?

Q 8-9   Name the three steps in journalizing and posting the return of merchandise previously purchased on account.

Q 8-10   Which journal and ledgers would the following transaction be recorded in: purchased machinery, which is not merchandise inventory, on account for $790 from Chen Company? Also, give the appropriate accounts that would be debited and credited.

EXERCISES

Objective 1

E 8-1   Recording Purchases   Record this transaction in (a) a general journal, page 9, and then (b) a purchases journal, page 9:

May 4, 19XX   Purchased $700 of merchandise on account from Hauser Enterprises, terms 1/10, 30. Invoice number 197.

Objective 2

E 8-2   Completing Vendor's Page   Complete a vendor's page in the accounts payable subsidiary ledger given the following information:

June 14, 19XX   Purchased $300 of merchandise on account from Newly Manufacturing. The entry was made in page 5 of the purchases journal.

July 23, 19XX   Purchased $900 of merchandise on account from Newly Manufacturing (page 6 of the purchases journal).

Objective 2

E 8-3   Recording Freight   Record the following transaction in a general journal, page 25: A firm received a freight invoice on October 18, 19XX from Quick Transportation. The terms are n30 and the freight charge is $400.

Objective 3

E 8-4   Recording Purchases Returns and Allowances   Record the following transaction in a general journal, page 19: On September 7, 19XX, Tulsa Company returned $600 of defective merchandise previously purchased on account to Portland Distributors. Debit memorandum DM9 is issued to Portland Distributors.

Objective 4

E 8-5   Recording Other Transactions   On March 26, 19XX, Florence Tire Supply purchased $2,300 of store supplies (not merchandise inventory) from WHR Company on account. The terms are COD. Record this transaction using (a) T accounts and then (b) in a general journal, page 47.

Objectives 1 through 4

E 8-6   Describing Transactions   Describe the four transactions recorded in the following T accounts:

Office Supplies	
(b) 1,900	

Accounts Payable	
(d) 200	(a) 3,100
	(b) 1,900
	(c) 400

Purchases	
(a) 3,100	

Purchases Returns and Allowances	
	(d) 200

Freight In	
(c) 400	

Objective 2

E 8-7 Preparing a Schedule of Accounts Payable Prepare a schedule of accounts payable for Robinson Paper Supply given the following vendors and amounts owed: Johnson Limited, $1,100; Tran Enterprises, $2,400; Brinson Company, $4,100; and Michigan Freight, $900. List the vendors alphabetically. The date is December 31, 19XX.

Objective 4

E 8-8 Recording and Posting Other Transactions On January 21, 19XX, a firm purchased a $7,000 copier (not merchandise inventory) from Sanchez Copier Company, terms COD. In your answer, record this transaction in a general journal, page 12, and post to the accounts payable subsidiary ledger and the general ledger. Accounts Payable is account number 205 and Copier is account number 161.

PROBLEM SET A

Objectives 1 and 2

P 8-1A Recording and Posting Purchases Lois Smith is the owner of Smith Plumbing Parts. The firm had the following credit purchases of merchandise during the first half of August 19XX:

Date	Amount	Terms	Invoice Number	Vendor
August 2	$500	n30	498	Zorn Company
August 4	$300	1/10, n30	091	Conner Enterprises
August 9	$700	2/10, n30	H56	HMC, Inc.
August 11	$1,400	n30	506	Zorn Company
August 12	$600	2/10, n30	H61	HMC, Inc.
August 15	$1,700	1/10, n30	098	Conner Enterprises

REQUIRED

1. Record the purchase of merchandise in a purchases journal, page 5.
2. Post to the accounts payable subsidiary ledger. List the vendors alphabetically.

Objectives 1 and 2

P 8-2A Posting Purchases Transactions You are hired as the accountant for Morgan Computer Supply. You find the following purchases journal:

PURCHASES JOURNAL   Page _____6_____

Date	Vendor	Invoice Number	Terms	Post. Ref.	Amount Purch. (Dr.) A/P (Cr.)
19XX					
Nov. 1	Clayton Company	C064	2/10, n30	√	7 0 0 —
5	Whitten Company	816	1/15, n45	√	8 0 0 —
12	Rayburn Manufacturing	0177	n30	√	6 0 0 —
18	Clayton Company	C072	2/10, n30	√	3 0 0 —
20	Rayburn Manufacturing	0186	n30	√	3 4 0 0 —
24	Whitten Company	829	1/15, n45	√	1 6 0 0 —
27	Clayton Company	C081	2/10, n30	√	9 0 0 —
30	Rayburn Manufacturing	0193	n30	√	2 8 0 0 —
					11 1 0 0 —
					(517) (214)

The accountant you replaced recorded the purchases transactions in the purchases journal and included the proper posting references. However, he did not post to the accounts payable subsidiary ledger and the general ledger.

REQUIRED

1. Using the general ledger account numbers below the Amount column, write the account names and account numbers in the general ledger. List Accounts Payable first, followed by Purchases.
2. Post to the accounts payable subsidiary ledger. List the vendors alphabetically.
3. Post to the general ledger.
4. Prepare a schedule of accounts payable.

Objectives 1 through 4

P 8-3A Comprehensive Chapter Review Problem Alvarez Printing Supply had the following credit transactions during the month of January 19XX:

January 2   Purchased $2,900 of merchandise on account from Ramos Company, invoice number R91. Terms are n30.

January 5   Purchased $1,900 of merchandise on credit from Drees Company, invoice number 581. Terms are 1/10, n30.

January 6   Purchased from Yanez Company $1,800 of furniture (account number 151) on account. Terms are n30.

January 7   Returned $400 of inferior merchandise previously purchased January 2 to Ramos Company. Debit memorandum DM87 is issued.

January 12   Received a $100 freight bill from West Coast Transport for the January 5 delivery from Drees Company. Terms are n30.

January 14   Purchased from Drumm Supply $1,900 of store supplies (account number 127) on account. Terms are 1/10, EOM, n30.

January 18   Purchased $2,000 of merchandise on account from Ramos Company, invoice number R98. Terms are n30.

January 21   Purchased $700 of merchandise on credit from Drees Company, invoice number 595. Terms are 1/10, n30.

January 23   Returned $1,600 of damaged merchandise previously purchased January 5 to Drees Company. Debit memorandum DM88 is issued.

January 25   Purchased $1,700 of merchandise on account from Battle Distributors, invoice number 024. Terms are n30.

January 31   Purchased $2,100 of merchandise from Greenwade, Inc. Terms are 2/10, n30. Invoice number is 1637.

REQUIRED

1. Record the purchase of merchandise in a purchases journal, page 10.
2. Record the return of merchandise, purchase of assets other than merchandise, and freight in a general journal, page 19. Purchases Returns and Allowances is account number 516, and Freight In is 522.
3. Post to the accounts payable subsidiary ledger. List the vendors alphabetically.
4. Post to the general ledger. Accounts Payable is account number 213, and Purchases is 515.
5. Prepare a schedule of accounts payable.

**Objectives
1 through 4**

P 8-4A   Comprehensive Chapter Review Problem   Larson Cabinet Supply had the following credit transactions during the month of April 19XX:

April 2   Purchased $4,500 of merchandise on credit from Adams Company, invoice number A047. Terms are 2/10, n30.

April 4   Purchased $7,900 of merchandise on account from Lerman Company, invoice number 342. Terms are 2/10, n30.

April 7   Purchased from Reyna Company $1,800 of merchandise on credit. Terms are n30. The invoice number is 602.

April 8   Received a $550 freight bill from Crosstown Freight for the April 4 delivery from Lerman Company. Terms are 2/10, n30.

April 9   Returned $200 of damaged merchandise previously purchased April 2 to Adams Company. Debit memorandum DM98 is issued.

April 12   Purchased $8,400 of merchandise on credit from Lerman Company, invoice number 358. Terms are 2/10, n30.

April 16   Purchased from Daily Company $800 of office supplies (account number 132) on credit. Terms are 2/10, EOM, n30.

April 17   Purchased $2,900 of merchandise on account from Reyna Company, invoice number 621. Terms are n30.

April 20   Purchased $4,800 of merchandise on credit from Zachery Supply, invoice number 119. Terms are 2/10, n30.

April 21   Received a $350 freight bill from Dartman Delivery for the April 2 delivery from Adams Company. Terms are n30.

April 22   Purchased from Lafoy Company $14,800 of machinery (account number 181) on account. Terms are n30.

April 25   Returned to Reyna Company $400 of inferior merchandise previously purchased April 17. Debit memorandum DM99 is issued.

April 26   Purchased $4,000 of merchandise on credit from Lerman Company, invoice number 373. Terms are 2/10, n30.

April 28   Purchased from Yartosky Company a $13,800 truck (account number 191) on account. Terms are n30.

April 28   Received a $600 freight bill from Fastest Delivery for the April 20 delivery from Zachery Supply. Terms are n30.

April 29   Requested $1,100 allowance for defective merchandise from Lerman Company for the April 26 purchase on credit. Debit memorandum DM100 is issued.

April 30   Purchased $7,900 of merchandise on credit from Bard Company. Terms are 1/10, n30. The invoice number is 0618.

REQUIRED

1. Record the purchase of merchandise in a purchases journal, page 9.
2. Record the return of merchandise, purchase of assets other than merchandise, and freight, in a general journal, page 21. Purchases Returns and Allowances is account number 527, and Freight In is 533.
3. Post to the accounts payable subsidiary ledger. List the vendors alphabetically.
4. Post to the general ledger. Accounts Payable is account number 242, and Purchases is 526.
5. Prepare a schedule of accounts payable.

PROBLEM SET B

Objectives 1
and 2

P 8-1B   Recording and Posting Purchases   H. K. Quan is the owner of Quan Auto Parts. The firm had the following credit purchases of merchandise during the first half of January 19XX:

Date	Amount	Terms	Invoice Number	Vendor
January 1	$1,800	n30	606	Marshall, Inc.
January 3	$500	2/10, n30	B471	Brasher Company
January 8	$600	1/10, n30	092	Gregg Enterprises
January 10	$2,900	n30	611	Marshall, Inc.
January 13	$800	1/10, n30	098	Gregg Enterprises
January 15	$1,000	2/10, n30	B516	Brasher Company

REQUIRED
1. Record the purchase of merchandise in a purchases journal, page 3.
2. Post to the accounts payable subsidiary ledger. List the vendors alphabetically.

Objectives 1
and 2

P 8-2B   Posting Purchases Transactions   You are hired as the accountant for Phillips Uniform Supply. You find the following purchases journal:

PURCHASES JOURNAL   Page ___8___

Date		Vendor	Invoice Number	Terms	Post. Ref.	Amount Purch. (Dr.) A/P (Cr.)
19XX						
Dec.	2	Burrell Company	9861	1/10, n30	√	9 0 0 —
	6	Yong Company	Y046	n30	√	1 3 0 0 —
	11	Larvin Manufacturing	049	2/10, n30	√	8 0 0 —
	17	Burrell Company	9869	1/10, n30	√	4 0 0 —
	19	Larvin Manufacturing	057	2/10, n30	√	2 0 0 0 —
	23	Yong Company	Y061	n30	√	1 9 0 0 —
	29	Burrell Company	9891	1/10, n30	√	6 0 0 —
	31	Larvin Manufacturing	063	2/10, n30	√	1 6 0 0 —
						9 5 0 0 —
						(537) (232)

The accountant you replaced recorded the purchases transactions in the purchases journal and included the proper posting references. However, he did not post to the accounts payable subsidiary ledger and the general ledger.

REQUIRED

1. Using the general ledger account numbers below the Amount column, write the account names and account numbers in the general ledger. List Accounts Payable first, followed by Purchases.
2. Post to the accounts payable subsidiary ledger. List the vendors alphabetically.
3. Post to the general ledger.
4. Prepare a schedule of accounts payable.

Objectives
1 through 4

P 8-3B

Comprehensive Chapter Review Problem Collins Furniture Supply had the following credit transactions during the month of September 19XX:

September 1	Purchased $3,700 of merchandise on account from Zugel Company, invoice number 042. Terms are 2/10, n30.
September 2	Purchased from Break Company $2,700 of equipment (account number 171) on account. Terms are 2/10, EOM, n30.
September 4	Purchased $2,800 of merchandise on credit from Capp Company, invoice number 623. Terms are n30.
September 8	Returned $1,000 of inferior merchandise previously purchased September 1 to Zugel Company. Debit memorandum DM44 is issued.
September 13	Received a $390 freight bill from Charleston Transport for the September 4 delivery from Capp Company. Terms are 2/10, n30.
September 16	Purchased from Tranh Company $4,100 of office supplies (account number 142) on account. Terms are 2/10, EOM, n30.
September 20	Purchased $5,800 of merchandise on account from Zugel Company, invoice number 047. Terms are 2/10, n30.
September 22	Purchased $900 of merchandise on credit from Capp Company, invoice number 637. Terms are n30.
September 27	Returned $300 of damaged merchandise previously purchased September 22 to Capp Company. Debit memorandum DM45 is issued.
September 28	Purchased $3,000 of merchandise on account from Pointer Distributors, invoice number PD34. Terms are n30.
September 30	Purchased $9,100 of merchandise from Kneeland, Inc. Terms are 1/15, n30. Invoice number is K98.

REQUIRED

1. Record the purchase of merchandise in a purchases journal, page 7.

2. Record the return of merchandise, purchase of assets other than merchandise, and freight, in a general journal, page 18. Purchases Returns and Allowances is account number 509, and Freight In is 513.

3. Post to the accounts payable subsidiary ledger. List the vendors alphabetically.

4. Post to the general ledger. Accounts Payable is account number 241, and Purchases is 508.

5. Prepare a schedule of accounts payable.

**Objectives
1 through 4**

P 8-4B

Comprehensive Chapter Review Problem   Owens Cabinet Supply had the following credit transactions during the month of March 19XX:

March 1	Purchased $5,000 of merchandise on credit from Smith Company, invoice number 948. Terms are 1/10, n30.
March 3	Purchased $8,900 of merchandise on account from Abbott Company, invoice number 062. Terms are 1/10, n30.
March 6	Purchased from Zolla Company $6,800 of merchandise on credit. Terms are n30. The invoice number is 491Z.
March 10	Received an $830 freight bill from Knepper Freight for the March 3 delivery from Abbott Company. Terms are n30.
March 11	Returned $300 of damaged merchandise previously purchased March 1 to Smith Company. Debit memorandum DM60 is issued.
March 14	Purchased $4,900 of merchandise on credit from Smith Company, invoice number 962. Terms are 1/10, n30.
March 15	Purchased from Drake Company $2,700 of store supplies (account number 145) on credit. Terms are COD.
March 18	Purchased $7,900 of merchandise on account from Zolla Company, invoice number 502Z. Terms are n30.
March 19	Purchased $3,100 of merchandise on credit from Oakley Supply, invoice number A46. Terms are 2/10, n30.
March 22	Received a $610 freight bill from Nygard Delivery for the March 1 delivery from Smith Company. Terms are 2/10, n30.
March 23	Purchased from Gillam Company $6,800 of equipment (account number 171) on account. Terms are n30.
March 24	Returned to Smith Company $2,600 of defective merchandise previously purchased March 14. Debit memorandum DM61 is issued.
March 27	Purchased $5,800 of merchandise on credit from Oakley Supply, invoice number A57. Terms are 2/10, n30.
March 28	Purchased from Norberg Company a $16,500 delivery van (account number 191) on account. Terms are n30.
March 29	Received a $300 freight bill from Sloan Delivery for the March 19 delivery from Oakley Supply. Terms are 2/10, n30.

March 30   Requested $800 allowance for defective merchandise from Zolla Company for the March 18 purchase on credit. Debit memorandum DM62 is issued.

March 31   Purchased $10,400 of merchandise on credit from Rothman Company. Terms are 1/15, n45. The invoice number is R019.

REQUIRED
1. Record the purchase of merchandise in a purchases journal, page 12.
2. Record the return of merchandise, purchase of assets other than merchandise, and freight, in a general journal, page 35. Purchases Returns and Allowances is account number 526, and Freight In is 531.
3. Post to the accounts payable subsidiary ledger. List the vendors alphabetically.
4. Post to the general ledger. Accounts Payable is account number 235, and Purchases is 525.
5. Prepare a schedule of accounts payable.

ANSWERS TO SELF-TEST QUESTIONS

1. a 2. b 3. c 4. d 5. d

9

The Cash Receipts and Cash Payments Journals

There is no substitute for hard work.

THOMAS ALVA EDISON

LEARNING OBJECTIVES

After reading this chapter, discussing the questions, and working the exercises and problems, you will be able to do the following:

1. Understand and use a cash receipts journal (pp. 274–76).

2. Post from a cash receipts journal to a general ledger (pp. 276–80).

3. Post from a cash receipts journal to an accounts receivable subsidiary ledger (pp. 280–82).

4. Understand and use a cash payments journal (pp. 283–85).

5. Post from a cash payments journal to a general ledger (pp. 285–89).

6. Post from a cash payments journal to an accounts payable subsidiary ledger (pp. 290–92).

■n Chapter 7 we examined the sales and in Chapter 8 we looked at the purchases of merchandise on account for United Auto Supply. In this chapter, we will examine both the receipt of cash and the payment of cash.

THE CASH RECEIPTS JOURNAL

Objective 1
Understand and use a cash receipts journal.

Let's assume that on October 12, 19XX, United Auto Supply received $1,764 from Emma's Auto Repair. This amount is payment in full for the October 4, 19XX, sale of merchandise on account. The amount is calculated as follows:

October 4, 19XX Sale Amount	$1,800
Terms 2/10, n30. Discount of 2 percent	$\times$ .02
Discount Amount	$ 36

$$\text{Cash Received} = \text{Sale Amount} - \text{Discount} = \$1,800 - \$36$$
$$= \$1,764$$

Let's use T accounts to illustrate the discount:

Cash		Sales Discounts		Accounts Receivable	
+	−	+	−	+	−
(10/12) 1,764		(10/12) 36			(10/12) 1,800

If United Auto Supply does not use special journals, then the cash received is recorded in a general journal as follows:

GENERAL JOURNAL   Page ___19___

Date		Description	Post. Ref.	Debit	Credit
19XX					
Oct.	12	Cash		1 7 6 4 —	
		Sales Discounts		3 6 —	
		Accounts Receivable—Emma's Auto Repair			1 8 0 0 —
		2% Discount			

The cash received is recorded by debiting Cash and Sales Discounts and crediting Accounts Receivable. The actual amount of cash received is debited. **Sales Discounts** is a contra revenue account that reduces Sales and is used to keep track of the discounts a firm gives on sales of merchandise. Sales Discounts has a normal debit balance. Accounts Receivable is credited for the amount of cash received plus any discount.

United Auto Supply does not use a general journal to record the receipt of cash for the following reasons:

1. For each receipt of cash, the accounts used must be written.
2. For each receipt of cash, the accounts used must be posted to the general ledger.

Thus, to save time and effort, and to increase efficiency, the firm uses a cash receipts journal to record the receipt of cash.

A **cash receipts journal** is a special journal used to record cash received from any source. Remember that a special journal is a book of original entry that groups similar transactions together.

Purposes of the Cash Receipts Journal

A cash receipts journal has the following purposes:

1. To record all receipts of cash in one journal, which saves time.
2. To save journalizing space by recording each cash receipt using one line. You may have to use more than one line for certain transactions.
3. The customer's name can easily be identified.
4. The individual account columns (except Other Accounts, which is sometimes called Sundry Accounts) are added, totaled, and posted separately to the general ledger at the end of the accounting period.

Structure of the Cash Receipts Journal

The October 12, 19XX, receipt of cash from Emma's Auto Repair is recorded in a cash receipts journal as shown in Exhibit 9-1.

EXHIBIT 9-1
Cash Receipts Journal

CASH RECEIPTS JOURNAL   Page ____10____

| | | | Credits | | | Debits | |
Date	Account Credited	Post. Ref.	Other Accounts	Accounts Receiv.	Sales	Sales Disc.	Cash
19XX							
Oct. 12	Emma's Auto Repair			1 8 0 0 —		3 6 —	1 7 6 4 —

The cash receipts journal illustrated in Exhibit 9-1 has columns for the Date, Account Credited, Post. Ref., Other Accounts (credit), Accounts Receivable (credit), Sales (credit), Sales Discounts (debit), and Cash (debit). (The Post. Ref. column will be used later.)

POSTING FROM THE CASH RECEIPTS JOURNAL TO THE GENERAL LEDGER

Objective 2
Post from a cash receipts journal to a general ledger.

Two of the purposes of the cash receipts journal are to save time and space. To illustrate this, Exhibit 9-2 shows how the following cash receipts for the month of October for United Auto Supply are recorded and posted:

October   3   Cash sale of merchandise inventory, $9,800.

October   5   Sold office supplies, which are not merchandise inventory, $600.

October   8   Borrowed $2,100 from the bank. **Notes Payable,** a liability account, is a formal written promise to pay a certain sum of money at a future date. This amount is credited in the Other Accounts credited column since there is not a listed column for Notes Payable. This note is to be paid in two years, so it is classified as a *long-term liability* (a liability that is due after one year).

EXHIBIT 9-2
Recording and Posting Cash Receipts

CASH RECEIPTS JOURNAL   Page ___10___

| | | | Credits | | | Debits | |
Date	Account Credited	Post. Ref.	Other Accounts	Accounts Receiv.	Sales	Sales Disc.	Cash
19XX							
Oct. 3	Cash Sales				9 8 0 0 —		9 8 0 0 —
5	Office Supplies ①	131	6 0 0 —				6 0 0 —
8	Notes Payable	221	2 1 0 0 —				2 1 0 0 —
12	Emma's Auto Repair			1 8 0 0 —		3 6 —	1 7 6 4 —
14	Montana Company			2 8 0 0 —		5 6 —	2 7 4 4 —
19	Cash Sales				12 0 0 0 —		12 0 0 0 —
25	Lucille Garcia, Capital	301	5 0 0 0 —				5 0 0 0 —
30	Zumwalt Company			1 5 0 0 —		3 0 —	1 4 7 0 —
	②		7 7 0 0 —	6 1 0 0 —	21 8 0 0 —	1 2 2 —	35 4 7 8 —
			(√)	(111)	(401)	(403)	(101)

③   ④

GENERAL LEDGER ACCOUNTS

Account: Cash   Account No.   101

Date	Item	Post. Ref.	Debit	Credit	Balance Debit	Balance Credit
19XX	Previous Balance				7 6 4 1 —	
Oct. 31		CR10	3 5 4 7 8 —		4 3 1 1 9 —	

(continued)

(Ex. 9-2 continued)

Account: Accounts Receivable							Account No.	111
		Post.				Balance		
Date	Item	Ref.	Debit	Credit	Debit		Credit	
19XX	Previous Balance				2 1 3 2 2 —			
Oct. 31		CR10		6 1 0 0 —	1 5 2 2 2 —			

Account: Office Supplies							Account No.	131
		Post.				Balance		
Date	Item	Ref.	Debit	Credit	Debit		Credit	
19XX	Previous Balance				3 3 0 0 —			
Oct. 5		CR10		① 6 0 0 —	2 7 0 0 —			

Account: Notes Payable							Account No.	221
		Post.				Balance		
Date	Item	Ref.	Debit	Credit	Debit		Credit	
19XX	Previous Balance						— 0 —	
Oct. 8		CR10		2 1 0 0 —			2 1 0 0 —	

Account: Lucille Garcia, Capital							Account No.	301
		Post.				Balance		
Date	Item	Ref.	Debit	Credit	Debit		Credit	
19XX	Previous Balance						2 9 1 0 0 —	
Oct. 25		CR10		5 0 0 0 —			3 4 1 0 0 —	

(continued)

(Ex. 9-2 concluded)

Account: *Sales*							Account No. 401	
		Post.				Balance		
Date	Item	Ref.	Debit	Credit	Debit		Credit	
19XX	Previous Balance						1 9 4 0 0 —	
Oct. 31		CR10		2 1 8 0 0 —			4 1 2 0 0 —	

Account: *Sales Discounts*							Account No. 403	
		Post.				Balance		
Date	Item	Ref.	Debit	Credit	Debit		Credit	
19XX	Previous Balance				— 0 —			
Oct. 31		CR10	1 2 2 —		1 2 2 —			

October 12   Received payment in full from Emma's Auto Repair, invoice number 831, less a 2 percent discount. The discount is $36 ($1,800 × .02 = $36). Since this is a full payment, Accounts Receivable is credited for the cash received plus the discount ($1,764 + $36 = $1,800).

October 14   Received payment in full from Montana Company, $2,744, invoice number 832. A 2 percent discount is taken. The discount is $56 ($2,800 × .02 = $56).

October 19   Cash sale of merchandise inventory, $12,000.

October 25   The owner, Lucille Garcia, invested an additional $5,000 in the firm.

October 30   Received $1,470 from Zumwalt Company as payment in full for invoice number 837. A 2 percent discount of $30 ($1,500 × .02 = $30) is taken.

There are four steps for posting from the cash receipts journal to the general ledger, keyed as ①, ②, ③, and ④ in Exhibit 9-2. The posting to Cash is illustrated. The steps are as follows:

① An amount in the Other Accounts credited column is posted daily or as the transaction occurs. "CR10" is entered in the Post. Ref. column of the general ledger. The general ledger account number is then entered in the Post. Ref. column of the cash receipts journal.

(2) The listed columns in the cash receipts journal are totaled and underlined after the final cash receipt is entered for the accounting period. The total is double underlined. These amounts are called *footings*. The debit footings (Cash and Sales Discounts) must equal the credit footings (Other Accounts, Accounts Receivable, and Sales). This process of verifying that the Debit column totals equal the Credit column totals is called **crossfooting**. The column totals are as follows:

Column	Debit	Credit
Other Accounts		7,700
Accounts Receivable		6,100
Sales		21,800
Sales Discounts	122	
Cash	35,478	
Totals	35,600	35,600

(3) The totals are posted to the general ledger. "CR10" is written in the Post. Ref. column of the general ledger to indicate that the posting is from page 10 of the cash receipts journal.

(4) After posting the totals to the general ledger accounts, go back to the cash receipts journal and write the account number in parenthesis below each column. A check mark in parenthesis (√) is placed below the Other Accounts column to show that the individual amounts have been posted to the general ledger.

POSTING TO THE ACCOUNTS RECEIVABLE SUBSIDIARY LEDGER

Objective 3
Post from a cash receipts journal to an accounts receivable subsidiary ledger.

Any amounts received from previous credit transactions must be posted to the accounts receivable subsidiary ledger. These postings will occur daily or as the cash is received. The appropriate postings to the accounts receivable subsidiary ledger are illustrated in Exhibit 9-3.

There are four steps to follow when posting from the cash receipts journal to the accounts receivable subsidiary ledger, keyed as (1), (2), (3), and (4) in Exhibit 9-3. The posting process is shown for Emma's Auto Repair. Cash receipts from other customers are posted in the same manner. The steps are as follows:

(1) As cash receipts of previous credit transactions are recorded in the cash receipts journal, they are posted daily or as they occur to the accounts receivable subsidiary ledger.

EXHIBIT 9-3
Posting to the Accounts Receivable Subsidiary Ledger

CASH RECEIPTS JOURNAL   Page ___10___

Date	Account Credited	Post. Ref.	Credits Other Accounts	Credits Accounts Receiv.	Sales	Debits Sales Disc.	Debits Cash
19XX							
Oct. 3	Cash Sales ④	—			9 8 0 0 —		9 8 0 0 —
5	Office Supplies	131	6 0 0 —				6 0 0 —
8	Notes Payable	221	2 1 0 0 —				2 1 0 0 —
12	Emma's Auto Repair ③ √			1 8 0 0 —		3 6 —	1 7 6 4 —
14	Montana Company	√		2 8 0 0 —		5 6 —	2 7 4 4 —
19	Cash Sales	—			12 0 0 0 —		12 0 0 0 —
25	Lucille Garcia, Capital	301	5 0 0 0 —				5 0 0 0 —
30	Zumwalt Company	√		1 5 0 0 —		3 0 —	1 4 7 0 —
			7 7 0 0 —	6 1 0 0 —	21 8 0 0 —	1 2 2 —	35 4 7 8 —
			(√)	(111)	(401)	(403)	(101)

① **ACCOUNTS RECEIVABLE SUBSIDIARY LEDGER** (partial)

Customer: *Emma's Auto Repair*

Date	Inv. No.	Item	Post. Ref.	Debit	Credit	Balance
19XX						
Oct. 4	831		S10	1 8 0 0 —		1 8 0 0 —
12		②	CR10		1 8 0 0 —	— 0 —

(continued)

(Ex. 9-3 concluded)

Customer: *Montana Company*

Date		Inv. No.	Item	Post. Ref.	Debit	Credit	Balance
19XX							
Oct.	6	832		S10	2 8 0 0 —		2 8 0 0 —
	14			CR10		2 8 0 0 —	— 0 —
	22	836		S10	1 9 0 0 —		1 9 0 0 —

Customer: *Zumwalt Company*

Date		Inv. No.	Item	Post. Ref.	Debit	Credit	Balance
19XX							
Oct.	25	837		S10	1 5 0 0 —		1 5 0 0 —
	30			CR10		1 5 0 0 —	— 0 —

② "CR10" for cash receipts journal (CR), page 10, is entered in the Post. Ref. column of the customer's accounts receivable subsidiary ledger page after the amount received has been posted from the cash receipts journal.

③ Once the posting has been entered into the customer's accounts receivable subsidiary ledger page, a check mark (√) is placed in the Post. Ref. column of the cash receipts journal. This signifies that the credit sale amount, including any tax, has been posted to the accounts receivable subsidiary ledger for that customer.

④ If the Post. Ref. column of the cash receipts journal has not been used, a dash (—) is placed in the Post. Ref. column. This occurs whenever a transaction has not been posted to either the general ledger or accounts receivable subsidiary ledger. (An example would be a cash sale of merchandise.)

THE CASH PAYMENTS JOURNAL

Objective 4
Understand and
use a cash
payments journal.

On October 9, 19XX, United Auto Supply paid $490 to Boyle Manufacturing for invoice number B6661. This amount is payment in full for the October 1, 19XX, purchase of merchandise on account, less a 2 percent discount. The amount is calculated as follows:

October 1, 19XX, Purchase Amount	$500
Terms 2/10, n30. Discount of 2 percent	× .02
Discount Amount	$ 10

Cash paid = Purchase amount − Discount = $500 − $10 = $490

Let's use T accounts to illustrate the purchases discount:

Accounts Payable			Purchases Discounts			Cash	
−	+		−	+		+	−
(10/9) 500				(10/9) 10			(10/9) 490

If United Auto Supply does not use special journals, then the cash paid is recorded in a general journal as follows:

GENERAL JOURNAL   Page __19__

Date		Description	Post. Ref.	Debit	Credit
19XX					
Oct.	9	Accounts Payable—Boyle Manufacturing		5 0 0 —	
		Purchases Discounts			1 0 —
		Cash			4 9 0 —
		2% Discount			

The cash paid is recorded by debiting Accounts Payable and crediting Purchases Discounts and Cash. When a payment is made in full, Accounts Payable is debited for the full, original purchase amount. The actual amount of cash paid is credited. Purchases Discounts is a contra cost of goods sold account that reduces Purchases. This account is used to keep track of the discounts that a firm has taken on purchases of merchandise. Purchases Discounts has a normal credit balance.

United Auto Supply does not use a general journal to record the payment of cash for the following reasons:

1. For each payment of cash, the accounts used must be written.
2. For each payment of cash, the accounts used must be posted to the general ledger.

Thus, a cash payments journal is used to save time and effort, and to increase efficiency. To maintain proper internal control over cash payments, the firm uses a checking account at a bank. Checks (check no.) are prenumbered in consecutive order, and all checks must be accounted for.

A cash payments journal is a special journal used to record cash paid for any purpose.

The Structure of the Cash Payments Journal

The October 9, 19XX, payment of cash to Boyle Manufacturing is recorded in a cash payments journal in Exhibit 9-4:

EXHIBIT 9-4
Cash Payments Journal

CASH PAYMENTS JOURNAL   Page ___10___

Date	Ck. No.	Account Debited	Post. Ref.	Debits			Credits	
				Other Accounts	Accounts Payable	Purchases	Purch. Disc.	Cash
19XX								
Oct. 9	933	Boyle						
		Manufacturing			500—		10—	490—

The cash payments journal has columns for the Date, Check No., Account Debited, Post. Ref., Other Accounts (debit), Accounts Payable (debit), Purchases (debit), Purchases Discounts (credit), and Cash (credit). (The Post. Ref. column will be used later.)

Purposes of the Cash Payments Journal

A cash payments journal has the following purposes:

1. To record all payments of cash in one journal, which saves time.
2. To save journalizing space by recording each cash payment using one line. You may have to use more than one line for certain transactions.

3. The vendor's name can easily be identified.

4. The individual account columns (except Other Accounts) are added, totaled, and posted separately to the general ledger at the end of the accounting period.

POSTING FROM THE CASH PAYMENTS JOURNAL TO THE GENERAL LEDGER

Objective 5
Post from a cash payments journal to a general ledger.

United Auto Supply had twenty cash payments (see p. 286) during October 19XX. These cash payments are recorded in the cash payments journal and posted to the general ledger in Exhibit 9-5.

October 1	Issued check no. 926 for monthly rent, $1,700.
October 2	Bought merchandise, $2,900, check no. 927.
October 4	Paid utilities bill, $195, check no. 928.
October 5	Paid $270 for freight, check no. 929.
October 5	Paid weekly wages $2,450, check no. 930.
October 8	The owner, Lucille Garcia, withdrew $1,200 for her personal use, check no. 931.
October 9	Made an error in writing a vendor's name on check no. 932. Voided the check.
October 9	Paid Boyle Manufacturing $490 for invoice no. B6661, check no. 933. A $10 discount is taken.
October 10	Paid for merchandise inventory, $3,800, check no. 934.
October 11	Paid $225 for freight, check no. 935.
October 12	Paid weekly wages, $2,680, check no. 936.
October 15	Received and paid an advertising bill, $190, check no. 937.
October 17	Paid for merchandise inventory, $5,600, check no. 938.
October 19	Paid weekly wages, $2,380, check no. 939.
October 22	Paid $495 for freight, check no. 940.
October 23	Purchased office equipment for $2,500. Issued check no. 941.
October 25	Paid Nguyen Distributors in full, less a 3 percent discount ($1,500 × .03 = $45), check no. 942. Cash paid is $1,455 ($1,500 − $45).
October 26	Paid weekly wages, $2,560, check no. 943.
October 29	Received and paid a freight bill, $710, check no. 944.
October 30	Paid Zamora Warehouse in full, less a 1 percent discount, check no. 945. The invoice no. was 21087. Terms are 1/25, n60. United Auto Supply returned $400 of merchandise on October 29, 19XX. The discount is based on the original purchase amount less the return ($1,700 − $400 = $1,300 × .01 = $13). $1,287 is paid to the vendor ($1,300 − $13).
October 31	Paid Mehta Manufacturing in full, less a 4 percent discount ($1,900 × .04 = $76), check no. 946. The cash paid is the purchase amount less the discount ($1,900 − $76 = $1,824).

EXHIBIT 9-5
Recording and Posting Cash Payments

CASH PAYMENTS JOURNAL   Page ___10___

Date	Ck. No.	Account Debited	Post. Ref.	Debits Other Accounts	Debits Accounts Payable	Debits Purchases	Credits Purch. Disc.	Credits Cash
19XX								
Oct. 1	926	Rent Expense	601	1 7 0 0 —				1 7 0 0 —
2	927	Cash Purchases				2 9 0 0 —		2 9 0 0 —
4	928	Utilities						
		Expense	631	1 9 5 —				1 9 5 —
5	929	Freight In	516	2 7 0 —				2 7 0 —
5	930	Wages Expense	611	2 4 5 0 —				2 4 5 0 —
8	931	Lucille Garcia,						
		Drawing	311	1 2 0 0 —				1 2 0 0 —
9	932	VOID						
9	933	Boyle						
		Manufacturing			5 0 0 —		1 0 —	4 9 0 —
10	934	Cash Purchases				3 8 0 0 —		3 8 0 0 —
11	935	Freight In	516	2 2 5 —				2 2 5 —
12	936	Wages Expense	611	2 6 8 0 —				2 6 8 0 —
15	937	Advertising						
		Expense	621	1 9 0 —				1 9 0 —
17	938	Cash Purchases				5 6 0 0 —		5 6 0 0 —
19	939	Wages Expense	611	2 3 8 0 —				2 3 8 0 —
22	940	Freight In	516	4 9 5 —				4 9 5 —
23	941	Office						
		Equipment	141	2 5 0 0 —				2 5 0 0 —
25	942	Nguyen						
		Distributors			1 5 0 0 —		4 5 —	1 4 5 5 —
26	943	Wages Expense	611	2 5 6 0 —				2 5 6 0 —
29	944	Freight In	516	7 1 0 —				7 1 0 —
30	945	Zamora						
		Warehouse			1 3 0 0 —		1 3 —	1 2 8 7 —
31	946	Mehta						
		Manufacturing			1 9 0 0 —		7 6 —	1 8 2 4 —
				17 5 5 5 —	5 2 0 0 —	12 3 0 0 —	1 4 4 —	34 9 1 1 —
				(✓)	(201)	(501)	(503)	(101)

③   ④

GENERAL LEDGER ACCOUNTS

Account: *Cash*   Account No.   101

Date	Item	Post. Ref.	Debit	Credit	Balance Debit	Balance Credit
19XX	Previous Balance				7 6 4 1 —	
Oct. 31		CR10	35 4 7 8 —		43 1 1 9 —	
31		CP10		34 9 1 1 —	8 2 0 8 —	

Account: *Office Equipment*   Account No.   141

Date	Item	Post. Ref.	Debit	Credit	Balance Debit	Balance Credit
19XX	Previous Balance				13 0 0 0 —	
Oct. 23		CP10	2 5 0 0 —		15 5 0 0 —	

(continued)

(Ex. 9-5 continued)

Account: *Accounts Payable*   Account No.   *201*

Date		Item	Post. Ref.	Debit	Credit	Balance Debit	Balance Credit
19XX		Previous Balance					1 4 0 0 0 —
Oct.	31		CP10	5 2 0 0 —			8 8 0 0 —

Account: *Lucille Garcia, Drawing*   Account No.   *311*

Date		Item	Post. Ref.	Debit	Credit	Balance Debit	Balance Credit
19XX		Previous Balance				— 0 —	
Oct.	8		CP10	1 2 0 0 —		1 2 0 0 —	

Account: *Purchases*   Account No.   *501*

Date		Item	Post. Ref.	Debit	Credit	Balance Debit	Balance Credit
19XX		Previous Balance				1 0 8 0 0 —	
Oct.	31		CP10	1 2 3 0 0 —		2 3 1 0 0 —	

Account: *Purchases Discounts*   Account No.   *503*

Date		Item	Post. Ref.	Debit	Credit	Balance Debit	Balance Credit
19XX		Previous Balance					— 0 —
Oct.	31		CP10		1 4 4 —		1 4 4 —

(continued)

(Ex. 9-5 continued)

Account: *Freight In*   **Account No.** 516

Date		Item	Post. Ref.	Debit	Credit	Balance Debit	Balance Credit
19XX		Previous Balance				3 0 0 —	
Oct.	5		CP10	2 7 0 —		5 7 0 —	
	11		CP10	2 2 5 —		7 9 5 —	
	22		CP10	4 9 5 —		1 2 9 0 —	
	29		CP10	7 1 0 —		2 0 0 0 —	

Account: *Rent Expense*   **Account No.** 601

Date		Item	Post. Ref.	Debit	Credit	Balance Debit	Balance Credit
19XX		Previous Balance				— 0 —	
Oct.	1		CP10	1 7 0 0 —		1 7 0 0 —	

Account: *Wages Expense*   **Account No.** 611

Date		Item	Post. Ref.	Debit	Credit	Balance Debit	Balance Credit
19XX		Previous Balance				— 0 —	
Oct.	5		CP10	2 4 5 0 —		2 4 5 0 —	
	12		CP10	2 6 8 0 —		5 1 3 0 —	
	19		CP10	2 3 8 0 —		7 5 1 0 —	
	26		CP10	2 5 6 0 —		1 0 0 7 0 —	

Account: *Advertising Expense*   **Account No.** 621

Date		Item	Post. Ref.	Debit	Credit	Balance Debit	Balance Credit
19XX		Previous Balance				— 0 —	
Oct.	15		CP10	1 9 0 —		1 9 0 —	

(continued)

(Ex. 9-5 concluded)

Account: *Utilities Expense*						Account No. *631*	
Date	Item	Post. Ref.	Debit	Credit	Balance		
					Debit	Credit	
19XX	*Previous Balance*				— 0 —		
Oct. *4*		*CP10*	1 9 5 —		1 9 5 —		

There are four steps for posting from the cash payments journal to the general ledger, keyed as ①, ②, ③, and ④ in Exhibit 9-5. The posting to Cash is illustrated. The steps are as follows:

① An amount in the Other Accounts debited column is posted daily or as the transaction occurs. "CP10" is entered in the Post. Ref. column of the general ledger. The general ledger account number is then entered in the Post. Ref. column of the cash payments journal.

② The listed columns in the cash payments journal are totaled and underlined after the final cash payment is entered for the accounting period. The total is double underlined. You should crossfoot the footings to make sure that total debits equal total credits. The totals are as follows:

Column	Debit	Credit
Other Accounts	17,555	
Accounts Payable	5,200	
Purchases	12,300	
Purchases Discounts		144
Cash		34,911
Totals	35,055	35,055

③ The totals are posted to the general ledger. "CP10" is written in the Post. Ref. column of the general ledger to indicate that the posting is from page 10 of the cash payments journal.

④ After posting the totals to the general ledger accounts, go back to the cash payments journal and write the account number in parenthesis below each column. A check mark in parenthesis (√) is placed below the Other Accounts column to show that the individual amounts have been posted to the general ledger.

POSTING TO THE ACCOUNTS PAYABLE SUBSIDIARY LEDGER

Objective 6
Post from a cash payments journal to an accounts payable subsidiary ledger.

When a payment is made on a previous credit transaction, the amount paid is posted to the accounts payable subsidiary ledger. These postings will occur daily (or as the cash is paid). The appropriate postings to the accounts payable subsidiary ledger are illustrated in Exhibit 9-6.

There are four steps to follow when posting from the cash payments journal to the accounts payable subsidiary ledger, keyed as ①, ②, ③, and ④ in Exhibit 9-6. The posting process is shown for Boyle Manufacturing. The cash payments to the other vendors are posted in the same manner. The steps are as follows:

① As cash payments of previous credit transactions are recorded in the cash payments journal, they are posted daily or as they occur to the accounts payable subsidiary ledger.

② "CP10" for cash payments journal (CP), page 10, is entered in the Post. Ref. column of the vendor's accounts payable subsidiary ledger page after the amount paid has been posted from the cash payments journal.

③ Once the posting has been entered into the vendor's accounts payable subsidiary ledger page, a check mark (√) is placed in the Post. Ref. column of the cash payments journal. This signifies that the cash paid has been posted to the accounts payable subsidiary ledger for that vendor.

④ A dash (—) is placed in any Post. Ref. line in the cash payments journal that has not been used. (An example would be a cash purchase of merchandise.)

EXHIBIT 9-6
Posting to the Accounts Payable Subsidiary Ledger

CASH PAYMENTS JOURNAL   Page ___10___

Date	Ck. No.	Account Debited	Post. Ref.	Debits — Other Accounts	Debits — Accounts Payable	Debits — Purchases	Credits — Purch. Disc.	Credits — Cash
19XX								
Oct. 1	926	Rent Expense	601	1 7 0 0 —				1 7 0 0 —
2	927	Cash Purchases	—	④		2 9 0 0 —		2 9 0 0 —
4	928	Utilities Expense	631	1 9 5 —				1 9 5 —
5	929	Freight In	516	2 7 0 —				2 7 0 —
5	930	Wages Expense	611	2 4 5 0 —				2 4 5 0 —
8	931	Lucille Garcia, Drawing	311	1 2 0 0 —				1 2 0 0 —
9	932	VOID						
9	933	Boyle Manufacturing	✓	③	5 0 0 —		1 0 —	4 9 0 —
10	934	Cash Purchases	—			3 8 0 0 —		3 8 0 0 —
11	935	Freight In	516	2 2 5 —				2 2 5 —
12	936	Wages Expense	611	2 6 8 0 —				2 6 8 0 —
15	937	Advertising Expense	621	1 9 0 —				1 9 0 —
17	938	Cash Purchases	—			5 6 0 0 —		5 6 0 0 —
19	939	Wages Expense	611	2 3 8 0 —				2 3 8 0 —
22	940	Freight In	516	4 9 5 —				4 9 5 —
23	941	Office Equipment	141	2 5 0 0 —				2 5 0 0 —
25	942	Nguyen Distributors	✓		1 5 0 0 —		4 5 —	1 4 5 5 —
26	943	Wages Expense	611	2 5 6 0 —				2 5 6 0 —
29	944	Freight In	516	7 1 0 —				7 1 0 —
30	945	Zamora Warehouse	✓		1 3 0 0 —		1 3 —	1 2 8 7 —
31	946	Mehta Manufacturing	✓		1 9 0 0 —		7 6 —	1 8 2 4 —
				17 5 5 5 —	5 2 0 0 —	12 3 0 0 —	1 4 4 —	34 9 1 1 —
				(✓)	(201)	(501)	(503)	(101)

(continued)

(Ex. 9-6 concluded)

① **ACCOUNTS PAYABLE SUBSIDIARY LEDGER** (partial)

Vendor: *Boyle Manufacturing*

Date		Item	Post. Ref.	Debit	Credit	Balance
19XX						
Oct.	1		P10		5 0 0 —	5 0 0 —
	9	②	CP10	5 0 0 —		— 0 —
	14		P10		1 8 0 0 —	1 8 0 0 —

Vendor: *Mehta Manufacturing*

Date		Item	Post. Ref.	Debit	Credit	Balance
19XX						
Oct.	28		P10		1 9 0 0 —	1 9 0 0 —
	31		CP10	1 9 0 0 —		— 0 —

Vendor: *Nguyen Distributors*

Date		Item	Post. Ref.	Debit	Credit	Balance
19XX						
Oct.	23		P10		1 5 0 0 —	1 5 0 0 —
	25		CP10	1 5 0 0 —		— 0 —

Vendor: *Zamora Warehouse*

Date		Item	Post. Ref.	Debit	Credit	Balance
19XX						
Oct.	10		P10		1 7 0 0 —	1 7 0 0 —
	29		J26	4 0 0 —		1 3 0 0 —
	30		CP10	1 3 0 0 —		— 0 —

■■■■■

CHAPTER REVIEW

1. Understand and use a cash receipts journal (pp. 274–76).
   A cash receipts journal is a special journal used to record cash received from any source. This journal is used to save time and effort, and increase efficiency.

2. Post from a cash receipts journal to a general ledger (pp. 276–80).
   There are four steps for posting from the cash receipts journal to the general ledger.

3. Post from a cash receipts journal to an accounts receivable subsidiary ledger (pp. 280–82).
   Any amounts received from previous credit transactions must be posted to the accounts receivable subsidiary ledger. These postings will occur daily or as the cash is received. There are four steps to follow when posting from the cash receipts journal to the accounts receivable subsidiary ledger.

4. Understand and use a cash payments journal (pp. 283–85).
   A cash payments journal is a special journal used to record cash paid for any purpose. A cash payments journal is used to save time and effort, and increase efficiency.

5. Post from a cash payments journal to a general ledger (pp. 285–89).
   There are four steps for posting from the cash payments journal to the general ledger.

6. Post from a cash payments journal to an accounts payable subsidiary ledger (pp. 290–92).
   When a payment is made on a previous credit transaction, the amount paid is posted to the accounts payable subsidiary ledger. These postings will occur daily or as the cash is paid. There are four steps to follow when posting from the cash payments journal to the accounts payable subsidiary ledger.

GLOSSARY

Cash Payments Journal	Special journal used to record cash paid for any purpose.
Cash Receipts Journal	Special journal used to record cash received from any source.

Crossfooting	Process of verifying that Debit column totals equal Credit column totals.
Notes Payable	Formal written promise to pay a certain sum of money at a future date.
Purchases Discounts	Contra cost of goods sold account that reduces purchases.
Sales Discounts	Contra revenue account that reduces sales.

SELF-TEST QUESTIONS FOR REVIEW

(Answers are on p. 307.)

1. Sales Discounts has a normal _____ balance and is a _____ account.
   a. credit; contra asset
   b. debit; contra revenue
   c. debit; contra asset
   d. credit; contra revenue

2. In the cash receipts journal, Notes Payable is credited in the _____ column.
   a. Sales
   b. Accounts Receivable
   c. Cash
   d. Other Accounts

3. A firm purchased merchandise on account for $1,000, less a 3 percent discount. When paid within the discount period, the amount debited to _____ is _____ .
   a. Sales; $1,000
   b. Purchases Discounts; $30
   c. Accounts Payable; $1,000
   d. Cash; $970

4. Which of the following accounts will probably have a credit balance after all postings from a cash payments journal?
   a. Purchases Discounts
   b. Jay Wasserstein, Drawing
   c. Purchases
   d. Freight In

5. After all postings, a _____ is placed in any Post. Ref. column in the cash payments journal that has not been used.
   a. check mark
   b. dash
   c. general ledger number
   d. CP and page number

PRACTICAL REVIEW PROBLEM

**Objectives
1 and 4**

Recording Cash Receipts and Cash Payments   Marion Gurski is the owner of Southern Paper Supply. The firm had the following cash receipts and cash payments during the month of October 19XX:

October   1   Received payment in full from Willsey Company, less a 2 percent discount. The original sale was for $10,000.

October   1   Issued check no. 852 for monthly rent, $1,500.

October	3	Borrowed $7,500 from a bank.
October	7	Paid for merchandise inventory, $5,900, check no. 853.
October	10	Cash sale of merchandise, $8,560.
October	12	Paid for freight, $965, check no. 854.
October	13	Received payment in full from Boyer Company, less a 4 percent discount. The original sale was for $7,900.
October	14	Owner withdrew $1,580 for her personal use, check no. 855.
October	15	Paid wages for two weeks, $3,980, check no. 856.
October	18	Made an error in writing a vendor's name on check no. 857. Voided the check.
October	20	Paid McQueen Manufacturing payment in full, less a 3 percent discount, check no. 858. The original purchase was for $8,800.
October	21	Sold all the firm's store supplies, which are not merchandise, $810.
October	23	Purchased office equipment for $910. Issued check no. 859.
October	26	Owner invested an additional $5,500 in the firm.
October	31	Paid wages for two weeks, $3,900, check no. 860.

REQUIRED

Record the transactions in a cash receipts journal, page 1, or a cash payments journal, page 1.

ANSWER TO PRACTICAL REVIEW PROBLEM

CASH RECEIPTS JOURNAL

Page 1

Date	Account Credited	Post. Ref.	Credits — Other Accounts	Credits — Accounts Receiv.	Credits — Sales	Debits — Sales Disc.	Debits — Cash
19XX							
Oct. 1	Willsey Company			10 0 0 0 —		2 0 0 —	9 8 0 0 —
3	Notes Payable		7 5 0 0 —				7 5 0 0 —
10	Cash Sales				8 5 6 0 —		8 5 6 0 —
13	Boyer Company			7 9 0 0 —		3 1 6 —	7 5 8 4 —
21	Store Supplies		8 1 0 —				8 1 0 —
26	Marion Gurski, Capital		5 5 0 0 —				5 5 0 0 —
			13 8 1 0 —	17 9 0 0 —	8 5 6 0 —	5 1 6 —	39 7 5 4 —

CASH PAYMENTS JOURNAL Page ___1___

Date	Ck. No.	Account Debited	Post. Ref.	Debits			Credits	
				Other Accounts	Accounts Payable	Purchases	Purch. Disc.	Cash
19XX								
Oct. 1	852	*Rent Expense*		1 5 0 0 —				1 5 0 0 —
7	853	*Cash Purchases*				5 9 0 0 —		5 9 0 0 —
12	854	*Freight In*		9 6 5 —				9 6 5 —
14	855	*Marion Gurski,*						
		Drawing		1 5 8 0 —				1 5 8 0 —
15	856	*Wages Expense*		3 9 8 0 —				3 9 8 0 —
18	857	*VOID*						
20	858	*McQueen*						
		Manufacturing			8 8 0 0 —		2 6 4 —	8 5 3 6 —
23	859	*Office*						
		Equipment		9 1 0 —				9 1 0 —
31	860	*Wages Expense*		3 9 0 0 —				3 9 0 0 —
				12 8 3 5 —	8 8 0 0 —	5 9 0 0 —	2 6 4 —	27 2 7 1 —

DISCUSSION QUESTIONS

Q 9-1 What is the sales discounts account? How is a sales discount calculated?

Q 9-2 Give two reasons why a firm would not use a general journal to record the receipt of cash.

Q 9-3 What is a cash receipts journal? Name the four purposes of a cash receipts journal.

Q 9-4 Briefly name the four steps for posting from the cash receipts journal to the general ledger. Also, what is crossfooting?

Q 9-5 Briefly name the four steps for posting from the cash receipts journal to the accounts receivable subsidiary ledger.

Q 9-6 What is the purchases discounts account? How is a purchases discount calculated?

Q 9-7 Name the two reasons why a firm would not use a general journal to record cash payments.

Q 9-8 What is a cash payments journal? Name the four purposes of a cash payments journal.

Q 9-9 How many steps are there for posting from the cash payments journal to the general ledger? Briefly name these steps.

Q 9-10   How many steps are there for posting from the cash payments journal to the accounts payable subsidiary ledger? Briefly name these steps.

EXERCISES

Objective 1

E 9-1   **Recording Receipts**   Record the following transaction using T accounts: A firm received payment in full from a customer, less a 2 percent discount. The original sale amount was $900.

Objectives 2 and 5

E 9-2   **Identifying Special Journals**   Identify the proper special journal for the following transactions. Use CRJ for the cash receipts journal and CPJ for the cash payments journal.

Transactions	Journal (CRJ or CPJ)
a. Cash sale of merchandise inventory.	_____
b. Paid for monthly rent.	_____
c. Borrowed $1,000 from a bank.	_____
d. Bought merchandise, check no. 518.	_____
e. Received payment in full, less a discount.	_____
f. Paid a vendor in full, less a discount.	_____
g. Received and paid a freight bill.	_____
h. The owner invested an additional $10,000 in the firm.	_____

Objective 4

E 9-3   **Recording Payments**   A firm paid a vendor in full, less a 3 percent discount. The original purchase amount was $3,500. Record this transaction in T account form.

Objective 1

E 9-4   **Recording Receipts**   On May 18, 19XX, Akron Cable Supply received payment in full, less a 4 percent discount from Reginald Simpson. The original sale amount was $6,500. Record this transaction in a general journal, page 13.

Objectives 2 and 5

E 9-5   **Describing Transactions**   Describe the following transactions in your own words:
a. A firm debits Cash and credits Sales in a cash receipts journal.
b. A firm debits Accounts Payable and credits both Cash and Purchases Discounts in a cash payments journal.
c. A firm debits Purchases and credits Cash in a cash payments journal.
d. A firm debits Cash and credits Notes Payable in a cash receipts journal.
e. A firm debits Cash and Sales Discounts and credits Accounts Receivable in a cash receipts journal.
f. A firm debits Rent Expense and credits Cash in a cash payments journal.

Objective 4

E 9-6   **Recording Payments**   Record the following transaction in a general journal, page 61: On December 13, 19XX, Culver City Sales paid invoice number X304 in full, less a 5 percent discount. Invoice number X304 is from Augusta Metals Company. The original purchase amount was $19,600.

Objectives 2 and 3

E 9-7   **Recording and Posting Receipts**   A firm had the following cash receipts for the first two days of November 19XX:

November 1   Borrowed $3,000 from a bank.
November 2   Received payment in full from Lim Company, less a 2 percent discount. The original sale amount was $5,000.

In your answer, first open the previous balance in the accounts receivable subsidiary ledger for Lim Company. Second, record the transactions in the cash receipts journal, page 8. Third, post to the general ledger and accounts receivable subsidiary ledger as necessary. Notes Payable is chart-of-accounts number 231.

Objectives 5 and 6

E 9-8   **Recording and Posting Payments**   Ramirez Sales and Service had the following cash payments for the first three days of February 19XX:

February 1   Paid monthly rent, $1,500, check no. 839.
February 2   Bought merchandise, $900, check no. 840.
February 3   Paid Alaska Company in full, less a 3 percent discount, check no. 841. The original purchase amount was $4,200.

In your answer, first open the previous balance in the accounts payable subsidiary ledger for Alaska Company. Second, record the transactions in the cash payments journal, page 2. Third, post to the general ledger and accounts payable subsidiary ledger as necessary. Rent Expense is chart-of-accounts number 601.

PROBLEM SET A

Objectives 1, 2, and 3

P 9-1A   **Recording and Posting Receipts**   D. W. Lindsey is the owner of Lindsey Office Products. The firm had the following cash receipts during the month of August 19XX:

August 2   Borrowed $3,595 from a bank.
August 5   Cash sale of merchandise, $5,900.
August 9   Received payment in full from Klein Company, less a 2 percent discount. The original sale was for $2,800.
August 12   Sold all the firm's office supplies, which are not merchandise, $235.

August 16	Received payment in full from Zwicker Company, less a 3 percent discount. The original sale was for $6,900.
August 19	Cash sale of merchandise, $4,100.
August 24	The owner invested an additional $3,950 in the firm.
August 27	Of an original sale of $8,900, received payment in full, less a 4 percent discount. The customer was Rey Office Supply.
August 31	Received payment in full from Alavi Company, less a 1 percent discount. The original sale was for $9,100.

The firm had the following partial chart-of-accounts numbers:

Cash	106	D. W. Lindsey, Capital	305
Accounts Receivable	117	Sales	404
Office Supplies	125	Sales Discounts	406
Notes Payable	232		

REQUIRED

1. Open the previous balances in the accounts receivable subsidiary ledger as follows: Alavi Company, $9,100; Klein Company, $2,800; Rey Office Supply, $8,900; Zwicker Company, $6,900. Also, open the previous balances in the Accounts Receivable account, $27,700, and the Office Supplies account, $235. Record the transactions in a cash receipts journal, page 9.
2. Post to the accounts receivable subsidiary ledger.
3. Post to the general ledger.

Objectives
4, 5, and 6

P 9-2A **Recording and Posting Payments**   Murray Fabric Supply is owned by Linda Murray. The firm had the following cash payments during December 19XX:

December 1	Issued check no. 178 for monthly rent, $900.
December 3	Paid for merchandise inventory, $4,890, check no. 179.
December 6	Paid for freight, $370, check no. 180.
December 11	Owner withdrew $3,890 for her personal use, check no. 181.
December 14	Made an error in writing a vendor's name on check no. 182. Voided the check.
December 14	Paid Gentry Manufacturing payment in full, less a 2 percent discount, check no. 183. The original purchase was for $6,700.
December 23	Paid Sauceda Distributing payment in full, less a 3 percent discount, check no. 184. The original purchase was for $10,500.
December 29	Purchased office furniture for $3,710. Issued check no. 185.
December 31	Paid monthly wages, $7,300, check no. 186.

The firm had the following partial chart-of-accounts numbers:

Cash	103	Purchases Discounts	506
Office Furniture	151	Freight In	510
Accounts Payable	204	Rent Expense	609
Linda Murray, Drawing	314	Wages Expense	613
Purchases	503		

REQUIRED

1. Open the previous balances in the accounts payable subsidiary ledger as follows: Gentry Manufacturing, $6,700; Sauceda Distributing, $10,500. Also, open the previous balances in the Cash account, $45,000 and the Accounts Payable account, $17,200. Record the transactions in a cash payments journal, page 5.
2. Post to the accounts payable subsidiary ledger.
3. Post to the general ledger.

**Objectives
1 through 6**

P 9-3A   **Comprehensive Chapter Review Problem**   Tim O'Grady is the owner of O'Grady Restaurant Supply. The firm had the following cash receipts during March 19XX:

March 1	Received payment in full from Martinez Company, less a 2 percent discount. The original sale was for $8,300.
March 8	Borrowed $7,510 from the bank.
March 11	Cash sale of merchandise, $6,120.
March 15	Received payment in full from Arellano Company, less a 1 percent discount. The original sale was for $3,700.
March 20	Sold all the firm's store supplies, which are not merchandise, $160.
March 24	Received payment in full from Wells Company, less a 3 percent discount. The original sale was for $2,900.
March 27	Cash sale of merchandise, $5,890.
March 30	Owner invested an additional $4,620 in the firm.
March 31	Of an original sale of $5,800, received payment in full, less a 4 percent discount, from Diab Company.

The firm had the following cash payments during March 19XX:

March 1	Issued check no. 302 for monthly rent, $670.
March 4	Paid for merchandise inventory, $1,870, check no. 303.
March 9	Paid for freight, $400, check no. 304.
March 13	Owner withdrew $3,890 for his personal use, check no. 305.
March 18	Made an error in writing a vendor's name on check no. 306. Voided the check.
March 18	Paid Morris Distributors payment in full, less a 2 percent discount, check no. 307. The original purchase was for $4,800.

March 22	Paid a freight bill, $610, check no. 308.
March 24	Paid Yoong Warehouse payment in full, less a 1 percent discount, check no. 309. The original purchase was for $7,000.
March 28	Purchased office equipment for $1,200. Issued check no. 310.
March 31	Paid monthly wages, $8,500, check no. 311.

The firm had the following partial chart-of-accounts numbers:

Cash	103	Sales	406
Accounts Receivable	109	Sales Discounts	409
Store Supplies	123	Purchases	505
Office Equipment	161	Purchases Discounts	512
Accounts Payable	204	Freight In	518
Notes Payable	231	Rent Expense	603
Tim O'Grady, Capital	314	Wages Expense	615
Tim O'Grady, Drawing	322		

REQUIRED

1. Open the previous balances in the accounts receivable subsidiary ledger as follows: Arellano Company, $3,700; Diab Company, $5,800; Martinez Company, $8,300; Wells Company, $2,900. Open the previous balances in the accounts payable subsidiary ledger as follows: Morris Distributors, $4,800; Yoong Warehouse, $7,000. Also, open the previous balances in the Accounts Receivable account, $20,700, Store Supplies account, $160, and Accounts Payable account, $11,800. Record the transactions in a cash receipts journal, page 7 or a cash payments journal, page 7.
2. Post to the accounts receivable subsidiary ledger or accounts payable subsidiary ledger.
3. Post to the general ledger.

**Objectives
1 through 6**

P 9-4A **Comprehensive Chapter Review Problem** Jose Raya is the owner of
 Ready Book Supply. The firm had the following cash receipts and cash payments during the month of April 19XX:

April 1	Received payment in full from Finke Company, less a 2 percent discount. The original sale was for $12,700.
April 1	Issued check no. 908 for monthly rent, $2,470.
April 3	Borrowed $6,250 from a bank.
April 5	Paid for merchandise inventory, $4,670, check no. 909.
April 9	Cash sale of merchandise, $5,890.
April 11	Paid for freight, $710, check no. 910.
April 12	Received payment in full from DeGeorge Company, less a 1 percent discount. The original sale was for $6,800.
April 13	Owner withdrew $2,670 for his personal use, check no. 911.

April 15	Paid wages for two weeks, $3,600, check no. 912.
April 16	Made an error in writing a vendor's name on check no. 913. Voided the check.
April 17	Paid Insley Manufacturing payment in full, less a 2 percent discount, check no. 914. The original purchase was for $4,800.
April 19	Sold all the firm's office supplies, which are not merchandise, $780.
April 20	Paid a freight bill, $800, check no. 915.
April 22	Paid Prejean Distributors payment in full, less a 3 percent discount, check no. 916. The original purchase was for $5,900.
April 23	Purchased office furniture for $870. Issued check no. 917.
April 24	Received payment in full from Supensky Company, less a 4 percent discount. The original sale was for $13,600.
April 25	Cash sale of merchandise, $4,900.
April 26	Owner invested an additional $6,340 in the firm.
April 27	Paid a utilities bill, check no. 918, $140.
April 29	Of an original sale of $8,100, received payment in full, less a 5 percent discount. The customer was Hosan Company.
April 30	Paid wages for two weeks, $3,815, check no. 919.

The firm had the following partial chart-of-accounts numbers:

Cash	102	Sales	404
Accounts Receivable	104	Sales Discounts	407
Office Supplies	125	Purchases	506
Office Furniture	171	Purchases Discounts	511
Accounts Payable	206	Freight In	519
Notes Payable	243	Rent Expense	602
Jose Raya, Capital	311	Wages Expense	604
Jose Raya, Drawing	321	Utilities Expense	623

REQUIRED
1. Open the previous balances in the accounts receivable subsidiary ledger as follows: DeGeorge Company, $6,800; Finke Company, $12,700; Hosan Company, $8,100; Supensky Company, $13,600. Open the previous balances in the accounts payable subsidiary ledger as follows: Insley Manufacturing, $4,800; Prejean Distributors, $5,900. Also, open the previous balances in the Accounts Receivable account, $41,200, Office Supplies account, $780, and Accounts Payable account, $10,700. Record the transactions in a cash receipts journal, page 4, or a cash payments journal, page 5.
2. Post to the accounts receivable subsidiary ledger or accounts payable subsidiary ledger.
3. Post to the general ledger.

PROBLEM SET B

**Objectives
1, 2, and 3**

P 9-1B **Recording and Posting Receipts** Brenda Richey is the owner of Richey Tool and Craft Supply. The firm had the following cash receipts during July 19XX:

July 3   Borrowed $5,160 from the bank.

July 6   Cash sale of merchandise, $6,000.

July 10   Received payment in full from Murphy Company, less a 2 percent discount. The original sale was for $3,700.

July 13   Sold all the firm's store supplies, which are not merchandise, $580.

July 17   Received payment in full from Capuzzo Company, less a 1 percent discount. The original sale was for $8,100.

July 20   Cash sale of merchandise, $5,900.

July 22   Owner invested an additional $4,170 in the firm.

July 25   Of an original sale of $9,700, received payment in full, less a 5 percent discount. The customer was Clayborn Company.

July 30   Received payment in full from Yao Company, less a 3 percent discount. The original sale was for $3,900.

The firm had the following partial chart-of-accounts numbers:

Cash	103	Brenda Richey, Capital	302
Accounts Receivable	109	Sales	405
Store Supplies	118	Sales Discounts	409
Notes Payable	225		

REQUIRED

1. Open the previous balances in the accounts receivable subsidiary ledger as follows: Capuzzo Company, $8,100; Clayborn Company, $9,700; Murphy Company, $3,700; Yao Company, $3,900. Also, open the previous balances in the Accounts Receivable account, $25,400, and the Store Supplies account, $580. Record the transactions in a cash receipts journal, page 7.
2. Post to the accounts receivable subsidiary ledger.
3. Post to the general ledger.

**Objectives
4, 5, and 6**

P 9-2B **Recording and Posting Payments** Rubio Paint Supply is owned by Luis Rubio. The firm had the following cash payments during January 19XX:

January 1   Issued check no. 784 for monthly rent, $810.

January 4   Paid for merchandise inventory, $6,980, check no. 785.

January 8   Paid for freight, $610, check no. 786.

January 13   Owner withdrew $2,080 for his personal use, check no. 787.

January 15   Made an error in writing a vendor's name on check no. 788. Voided the check.

January 15   Paid Jackson Manufacturing payment in full, less a 1 percent discount, check no. 789. The original purchase was for $8,400.

January 22   Paid Tolson Distributors payment in full, less a 3 percent discount, check no. 790. The original purchase was for $12,600.

January 28   Purchased office equipment for $5,890. Issued check no. 791.

January 31   Paid monthly wages, $8,560, check no. 792.

The firm had the following partial chart-of-accounts numbers:

Cash	104	Purchases Discounts	508
Office Equipment	163	Freight In	513
Accounts Payable	209	Rent Expense	608
Luis Rubio, Drawing	315	Wages Expense	611
Purchases	505		

REQUIRED

1. Open the previous balances in the accounts payable subsidiary ledger as follows: Jackson Manufacturing, $8,400; Tolson Distributors, $12,600. Also, open the previous balances in the Cash account, $60,000 and the Accounts Payable account, $21,000. Record the transactions in a cash payments journal, page 2.
2. Post to the accounts payable subsidiary ledger.
3. Post to the general ledger.

Objectives 1 through 6

P 9-3B   Comprehensive Chapter Review Problem   K. J. Moore is the owner of Moore Vacuum Cleaner Supply. The firm had the following cash receipts during December 19XX:

December 1   Received payment in full from Romero Company, less a 1 percent discount. The original sale was for $4,700.

December 7   Borrowed $6,780 from the bank.

December 10   Cash sale of merchandise, $5,820.

December 14   Received payment in full from Laquire Company, less a 2 percent discount. The original sale was for $2,600.

December 19   Sold all the firm's office supplies, which are not merchandise, $2,670.

December 23   Received payment in full from Aronson Company, less a 3 percent discount. The original sale was for $3,400.

December 26   Cash sale of merchandise, $7,920.

December 30   Owner invested an additional $6,890 in the firm.

December 31   Of an original sale of $1,700, received payment in full, less a 5 percent discount. The customer was Nimmons Company.

The firm had the following cash payments during December 19XX:

December 1	Issued check no. 765 for monthly rent, $890.
December 5	Paid for merchandise inventory, $3,890, check no. 766.
December 8	Paid for freight, $710, check no. 767.
December 14	Owner withdrew $2,710 for her personal use, check no. 768.
December 17	Made an error in writing a vendor's name on check no. 769. Voided the check.
December 17	Paid Wittig Distributors payment in full, less a 1 percent discount, check no. 770. The original purchase was for $4,800.
December 21	Paid a freight bill, $890, check no. 771.
December 23	Paid Calvert Warehouse payment in full, less a 2 percent discount, check no. 772. The original purchase was for $8,200.
December 27	Purchased office furniture for $3,810. Issued check no. 773.
December 31	Paid monthly wages, $5,780, check no. 774.

The firm had the following partial chart-of-accounts numbers:

Cash	105	Sales	404
Accounts Receivable	108	Sales Discounts	407
Office Supplies	122	Purchases	503
Office Furniture	153	Purchases Discounts	508
Accounts Payable	202	Freight In	516
Notes Payable	225	Rent Expense	605
K. J. Moore, Capital	316	Wages Expense	612
K. J. Moore, Drawing	324		

REQUIRED

1. Open the previous balances in the accounts receivable subsidiary ledger as follows: Aronson Company, $3,400; Laquire Company, $2,600; Nimmons Company, $1,700; Romero Company, $4,700. Open the previous balances in the accounts payable subsidiary ledger as follows: Calvert Warehouse, $8,200; Wittig Distributors, $4,800. Also, open the previous balances in the Accounts Receivable account, $12,400, Office Supplies account, $2,670, and Accounts Payable account, $13,000. Record the transactions in a cash receipts journal, page 9, or a cash payments journal, page 11.
2. Post to the accounts receivable subsidiary ledger or accounts payable subsidiary ledger.
3. Post to the general ledger.

**Objectives
1 through 6**

P 9-4B   **Comprehensive Chapter Review Problem**   Andre Lacour is the owner of Eastern Plastic Supply. The firm had the following cash receipts and cash payments during October 19XX:

October 1	Received payment in full from Brock Company, less a 1 percent discount. The original sale was for $15,800.
October 1	Issued check no. 813 for monthly rent, $1,950.
October 3	Borrowed $5,980 from the bank.
October 6	Paid for merchandise inventory, $3,810, check no. 814.
October 8	Cash sale of merchandise, $6,170.
October 12	Paid for freight, $570, check no. 815.
October 14	Received payment in full from Williams Company, less a 2 percent discount. The original sale was for $7,900.
October 14	Owner withdrew $4,810 for his personal use, check no. 816.
October 15	Paid wages for two weeks, $4,415, check no. 817.
October 17	Made an error in writing a vendor's name on check no. 818. Voided the check.
October 17	Paid Carroll Manufacturing payment in full, less a 3 percent discount, check no. 819. The original purchase was for $6,900.
October 18	Sold all the firm's store supplies, which are not merchandise, $810.
October 19	Paid a freight bill, $710, check no. 820.
October 21	Paid Scales Distributors payment in full, less a 5 percent discount, check no. 821. The original purchase was for $7,500.
October 22	Purchased office equipment for $2,600. Issued check no. 822.
October 23	Received payment in full from Chatman Company, less a 6 percent discount. The original sale was for $10,700.
October 24	Cash sale of merchandise, $6,980.
October 25	Owner invested an additional $5,780 in the firm.
October 26	Paid an advertising bill, check no. 823, $610.
October 28	Of an original sale of $9,400, received payment in full, less a 3 percent discount. The customer was Tella Company.
October 31	Paid wages for two weeks, $4,505, check no. 824.

The firm had the following partial chart-of-accounts numbers:

Cash	105	Sales	403
Accounts Receivable	112	Sales Discounts	406
Store Supplies	126	Purchases	508
Office Equipment	153	Purchases Discounts	514
Accounts Payable	205	Freight In	516
Notes Payable	236	Rent Expense	603
Andre Lacour, Capital	306	Wages Expense	606
Andre Lacour, Drawing	313	Advertising Expense	624

REQUIRED
1. Open the previous balances in the accounts receivable subsidiary ledger as follows: Brock Company, $15,800; Chatman Company, $10,700; Tella Company, $9,400; Williams Company, $7,900. Open the previous balances in the accounts payable subsidiary ledger as follows: Carroll Manufacturing, $6,900; Scales Distributors, $7,500. Also, open the previous balances in the Accounts Receivable account, $43,800, Store Supplies account, $810, and Accounts Payable, $14,400. Record the transactions in a cash receipts journal, page 10, or a cash payments journal, page 13.
2. Post to the accounts receivable subsidiary ledger or accounts payable subsidiary ledger.
3. Post to the general ledger.

ANSWERS TO SELF-TEST QUESTIONS

1. b   2. d   3. c   4. a   5. b

SPECIAL JOURNALS REVIEW PROBLEM (CHAPTERS 7–9)

This review problem will test your knowledge of special journals. The working papers are in your Working Papers Manual. The answer to this review problem will be provided by your instructor.

David Trotter is the sole owner of Trotter Paint Supply. He established the following chart of accounts (only those accounts used in this review problem are listed):

Trotter Paint Supply
Chart of Accounts (partial)

Assets (100–199)

101   Cash
111   Accounts Receivable
121   Office Supplies
131   Machinery

Liabilities (200–299)

201   Accounts Payable

Owner's Equity (300–399)

301   David Trotter, Capital
311   David Trotter, Drawing

Revenues (400–499)

401   Sales
402   Sales Returns and Allowances
403   Sales Discounts

Cost of Goods Sold (500–599)

501   Purchases
502   Purchases Returns and Allowances
503   Purchases Discounts
511   Freight In

Expenses (600–699)

601   Wages Expense
611   Rent Expense
621   Utilities Expense

Transactions for the month of May 19XX (all sales of merchandise on account have terms of 2/10, n30):

May	1	The owner started the firm by investing $75,090.
May	1	Paid rent for the month, $1,230, check no. 1.
May	1	Hired a secretary.
May	2	Purchased goods for $780. Issued check no. 2.
May	2	Purchased $5,890 of merchandise on credit from Clancy Enterprises. Terms are 2/10, n30, invoice no. 89.
May	3	Sold $2,710 of merchandise to Drake and Associates, invoice no. T001.
May	4	Purchased $4,760 of merchandise on account from Salcedo Manufacturing. Terms are 2/10, n30, invoice no. 683.
May	5	Purchased $1,730 of office supplies on credit from Caldwell Office Supply. Terms are n30.
May	8	Purchased $6,740 of merchandise on credit from Tranh Paint Brokers. Terms are 3/20, n30, invoice no. 764.
May	9	Sold $1,040 of merchandise to Gayle Dickerson, invoice no. T002.

May 10	Cash sale of merchandise, $3,460.
May 10	Received a $490 freight bill from Branigan Freight, terms n30.
May 11	Purchased $15,640 of machinery on credit from Holman Manufacturing. Terms are n30.
May 11	Paid the May 2 credit purchase from Clancy Enterprises in full, less a 2 percent discount. Issued check no. 3.
May 12	Received payment in full, less a 2 percent discount, from Drake and Associates.
May 12	Paid invoice no. 683 (Salcedo Manufacturing) in full, less a 2 percent discount. Issued check no. 4.
May 15	Paid the secretary's two-week wages, $550. Issued check no. 5.
May 16	Received a utilities bill, $340. The utilities company is State Electric. Terms are n30.
May 17	Sold $2,180 of machinery (not merchandise inventory) on credit to Adams and Daughters. Terms are n30.
May 18	Purchased $2,530 of merchandise on credit from Ullman's Supply. Terms are 2/20, n30, invoice no. U561.
May 22	Sold $3,190 of merchandise to Floyd Martinsen, invoice no. T003.
May 23	Cash sale of merchandise, $2,810.
May 24	Floyd Martinsen returned $680 of inferior paint. Credit memorandum CM1 was issued.
May 25	Returned $1,320 of damaged paint to Ullman's Supply. Issued debit memorandum DM1.
May 26	Purchased goods for $1,620. Issued check no. 6.
May 26	Paid Tranh Paint Brokers in full, less a 3 percent discount. Issued check no. 7.
May 29	Received a transportation charge bill from Branigan Freight, $620. Terms are n30.
May 30	Purchased $10,020 of merchandise on credit from Tranh Paint Brokers. Terms are 3/20, n30, invoice no. 798.
May 30	Sold $2,160 of merchandise to Floyd Martinsen, invoice no. T004.
May 31	Paid the secretary's two-week wages, $550. Issued check no. 8.
May 31	The owner withdrew $1,500. Issued check no. 9.

REQUIRED

1. Record the May 19XX transactions in the proper journals (page 1 for all).
2. Post to the subsidiary ledgers and general ledger as necessary.
3. Prepare a trial balance from the general ledger.
4. Prepare a schedule of accounts receivable and compare the balance to the controlling account.
5. Prepare a schedule of accounts payable and compare the balance to the controlling account.

10

Cash, Petty Cash, and the Change Fund

All wealth is the product of labor.

JOHN LOCKE

LEARNING OBJECTIVES

After reading this chapter, discussing the questions, and working the exercises and problems, you will be able to do the following:

1. Record cash receipts (pp. 312–14).

2. Understand bank transactions (pp. 314–26).

3. Understand and use a petty cash system (pp. 326–31).

4. Understand and use a change fund (pp. 331–33).

A variety of special journals were introduced in the last three chapters, including the sales, purchases, cash receipts, and cash payments journals. Any transaction that could not be entered into these special journals was recorded in the general journal.

In this chapter, we will examine the Cash account for United Auto Supply for October 19XX. A petty cash system and a change fund will also be discussed.

CASH RECEIPTS AND DEPOSITS

Objective 1
Record cash
receipts.

Many merchandising and other firms use cash registers to record sales. Whenever a sale is made, the salesperson or clerk collects the cash, check, or credit card and gives the customer a receipt. At the same time, another receipt or record of the sale is recorded internally in the cash register itself, usually on a roll of paper or tape. Then, at the end of the day, the tape is removed and compared to the actual amount of cash, checks, and/or credit card slips collected.

Cash Receipts

Sometimes the actual amounts collected do not agree with the cash register tape. This could happen for a variety of reasons; for example, the salesperson or clerk could have recorded the sale incorrectly, or, an incorrect amount of change might have been given to the customer. If any errors occur, you must account for the difference—all transactions must be in balance, that is, debit(s) must equal credit(s). Normally, the cash register tape prevails and is recorded as the sale amount. So, when there is a difference between the cash register tape (sales) and the actual amounts collected, the account Cash Short or Over is used.

Assume that on April 10, 19XX, Owens Company had $1,708 in cash and checks. But the cash register tape total was $1,712. Owens is a service-only business and does not use special journals. The general journal entry is as follows:

GENERAL JOURNAL   Page ____4____

Date		Description	Post. Ref.	Debit	Credit
19XX					
Apr.	10	Cash		1 7 0 8 —	
		Cash Short or Over		4 —	
		Sales			1 7 1 2 —
		Cash Sales			

The $4 debit to Cash Short or Over is necessary to balance the transaction. A debit balance in the Cash Short or Over account signifies a miscellaneous *expense*. Miscellaneous *income* occurs whenever a credit balance exists in the Cash Short or Over account.

Let's look at a similar transaction for a merchandising firm that uses special journals. Silva Products, a merchandising firm, had a cash register tape total of $3,487 on December 29, 19XX. Cash and checks on hand totaled $3,489. The entry in the cash receipts journal is as follows:

CASH RECEIPTS JOURNAL   Page ____7____

Date		Account Credited	Post. Ref.	Credits			Debits	
				Other Accounts	Accounts Receiv.	Sales	Sales Disc.	Cash
19XX								
Dec.	29	Cash Short or Over	682	2 —		3 4 8 7 —		3 4 8 9 —

This $2 credit to Cash Short or Over would be classified as miscellaneous income. Silva Products accumulated more cash and checks than could be accounted for on the cash register tape.

Cash and Credit Card Receipts

Lakeside Company, a service-only business, started to use a cash register in March 19XX. At the close of the first day of the month, total collections were $21,480 and the cash register tape was $21,484. Credit card purchases made up $6,000 of the sales, and the firm's bank, Second City Bank, charges 6 percent for credit card deposits. Thus, Lakeside Company receives the cash from the bank less the 6 percent charge. This $360 charge ($6,000 × .06 = $360) is recorded as a debit to Credit Card Expense. The general journal entry is as follows:

GENERAL JOURNAL   Page ____10____

Date		Description	Post. Ref.	Debit	Credit
19XX					
Mar.	1	Cash		21 1 2 0 —	
		Credit Card Expense		3 6 0 —	
		Cash Short or Over		4 —	
		Sales			21 4 8 4 —
		Sales for March 1			

Even though sales were $21,484, the firm increased cash by only $21,120. This $364 difference was the result of cash and other collections ($21,484 − $21,480 = $4) plus the credit card expense of $360. Thus, Cash is debited for $21,120 [$21,484 − ($4 + $360) = $21,484 − $364 = $21,120].

BANK TRANSACTIONS

Objective 2
Understand bank transactions.

Most firms use a checking account for payments (checks) and receipts (deposits) of cash. Using a checking account improves the internal control of cash by minimizing the amount of cash on hand. All checks and deposits are entered in the firm's bank, thus providing a safe depository for cash, checks, change, stocks, bonds, and so on.

Signature Cards

A checking account is established by filling out a signature card (as illustrated in Exhibit 10-1). This card must be signed by the depositor in exactly the same manner as he or she expects to sign checks. A bank teller can then verify the depositor's signature on a check by comparing it to the signature card.

EXHIBIT 10-1
Signature Card

ACCOUNT TITLE	**A/C #**
United Auto Supply	12-34567-8
The "Company"	**TAXPAYER I.D. #** 999-00-9999

☐ Savings   ☐ Money Market Checking   ☐ Checking Plus   **No. of Required** **Date**
☒ Checking   ☐ Money Market Savings   Interest   **Signatures** 1   **Opened** 1/1/XX
☐ Other _____

Specimen Signatures	Authorized Signatures Typed Name
(1) *Lucille Garcia*	Lucille Garcia
(2) *Hu Le*	Hu Le
(3) _____	_____
(4) _____	_____
(5) _____	_____

TO: FIRST CITY NATIONAL BANK OF HOUSTON

The Company is: _____ A Corporation   _____ A Partnership   __X__ A Sole Proprietorship

_____ Unincorporated Association   _____ Other (Specify) _____

Customer Relationship _____

The Company hereby acknowledges receipt of the Rules which govern this account and agrees to abide by those Rules as stated, or as they may be hereafter amended, and all applicable laws or regulations of the State of Texas or the United States of America.
You are hereby authorized to recognize any ___1___ of the signatures above in the payment of funds of the Company.

By: *Lucille Garcia*

Title: Owner
(Pres., V. Pres., or Treasurer)

I certify that the officers or agents whose names appear above have been authorized to sign checks and other orders on behalf of the company. The signatures appearing above are true signatures of such officers or agents.

Hu Le

Title: **SECRETARY**

Address ____ 100 Main Street, Houston, Texas 77001 ____

Mailing Address ____ Same ____

Phone ___999-9999___   Ref. Off. ____   **Initial Deposit** $25,000.00

Account Opened By: Dan Smith, Assistant Cashier   **Approved By:** Joyce Carr, VP

Deposit Slips

A deposit slip or deposit ticket is filled out once all currency, checks, coins, and so on are arranged and endorsed. Currency and coins are usually listed first, followed by checks. Each check should be listed separately, with the appropriate name or company stated. United Auto Supply's October 12, 19XX, deposit is illustrated in Exhibit 10-2.

EXHIBIT 10-2
Deposit Slip

DEPOSIT TICKET

DATE ___October 12___ 19 __XX__

Checks and other items are received for deposit subject to the provisions of the Uniform Commercial Code or any applicable collection agreement.

35-1/1130

First City National Bank
of Houston
P.O. Box 2557, Houston, Texas 77252

FIRST**C**ITY.

UNITED AUTO SUPPLY
100 MAIN ST.
HOUSTON, TEXAS 77001

⑉000067894⑉ 12345678⑉

DELUXE CHECK PRINTERS 60-8E

	DOLLARS	CENTS
CURRENCY		
COIN		
CHECKS _Emma's Auto Repair_	1,764	00
LIST SINGLY • BE SURE EACH ITEM IS ENDORSED		
TOTAL FROM OTHER SIDE		
TOTAL	1,764	00

USE OTHER SIDE FOR ADDITIONAL LISTING

NOT NEGOTIABLE
SAMPLE - VOID
DO NOT CASH!

Endorsements

A check must be *endorsed* before it can be deposited. The check is signed by the payee, who is the person directed to receive the amount written on the face of the check. By endorsing the check, the payee transfers the right to receive the check amount. One type of endorsement is a blank endorsement, where the payee simply signs the back of the check. A blank endorsement is payable to anyone who cashes or deposits the check. Most firms, however, use a restrictive endorsement, where the payee signs the back of the check and then adds such words as "For deposit only," "Pay to the order of," and so on. This restricts the check to be deposited or cashed to a certain bank or individual. An illustration of these two types of endorsements is shown in Exhibit 10-3.

EXHIBIT 10-3
Examples of Endorsements

Backs of Checks (reverse side)

Blank Endorsement	Restrictive Endorsement	Restrictive Endorsement (rubber stamp)
Payee (signed)	*Payee (signed)* *Pay to the order of*	*Pay to the order of City Bank* *For deposit only* *(account number)*

Writing Checks

A check directs a bank to pay a certain sum of money to a particular person or firm (payee). All checks should be accounted for in numerical order. Any voided checks should be recorded and listed as VOID.

A check is completed by filling in the date, who the check is to be paid to ("pay to the order of"), and the amount (in figures and words). The check is then signed by the authorized person. United Auto Supply's check number 933 is illustrated in Exhibit 10-4.

EXHIBIT 10-4
Check

UNITED AUTO SUPPLY
100 MAIN ST. PH 713-999-9999
HOUSTON, TEXAS 77001

933

35-1/1130

October 9 19 *XX*

PAY TO THE ORDER OF *--Boyle Manufacturing--* $ *490.00*

Four hundred ninety-- DOLLARS

First City National Bank
of Houston
P.O. Box 2557, Houston, Texas 77252 **FIRSTCITY.**

NOT NEGOTIABLE
SAMPLE-VOID
DO NOT CASH!

Lucille garcia

FOR

⑈000933⑈ ⑆000067894⑆ 12345678⑈

Bank Statements

Each month, the bank will send a bank statement to the depositor (owner of the account) and return any cancelled checks that have been paid and charged to the depositor's account. The bank statement will show the balance at the beginning of the month, deposits recorded, checks paid, other deposits and payments, and the balance at the end of the month. The bank statement for United Auto Supply for October 31, 19XX, is illustrated in Exhibit 10-5.

General Ledger, Cash Account

The Cash account in the general ledger of United Auto Supply is presented in Exhibit 10-6. The account had an ending balance of $8,208 at October 31, 19XX.

Bank Reconciliation

A bank reconciliation is prepared to account for the difference between the ending balance appearing on the bank statement and the ending balance of Cash in the general ledger. The bank statement (Exhibit 10-5) has an ending balance of $12,623. However, the general ledger shows a balance of $8,208 (Exhibit 10-6). There are a variety of reasons to explain how this discrepancy could occur, some of which follow:

1. **Outstanding Checks:** these are checks issued and recorded by the firm, but not yet cleared or paid by the bank.
2. **Deposits in Transit:** these are deposits recorded by the firm, but not received in sufficient time to be included on the bank statement.
3. **Collections:** a firm will often designate a bank to collect certain notes or payments.
4. **Checks with Non-Sufficient Funds (NSF):** frequently, a firm will receive a non-sufficient funds check and deposit it in their bank account. This is a check that is not paid when the firm's bank presents it for payment to the *maker's* (issuer's) bank. The firm's bank will return the check so the firm can collect the amount due. The NSF check must be reclassified from Cash to Accounts Receivable by a bank reconciliation entry.
5. **Interest Earned:** any interest earned on the checking account must be recorded in the firm's books.
6. **Bank Service Charges:** banks charge their customers for various services such as handling the firm's account, printing checks, stopping payment on checks, and collections.

EXHIBIT 10-5
Bank Statement

Account Statement

First City National Bank of Houston   Statement Date   10/31/XX
P.O. Box 2557   1001 Main   Page 1
Houston, Texas 77001   PH 713-658-6011

   United Auto Supply
   100 Main Street
   Houston, Texas 77001

Account 12-34567-8

Previous Balance	9/30/XX	9,645.00
9	Deposits and Other Items	35,578.00
20	Checks and Other Items	32,593.00
	Service Charge	7.00
	Total Checks and Charges	32,600.00
Ending Balance	10/31/XX	12,623.00

Date Paid	Check Number	Amount	Deposits	Ending Balance
10/01	923	146.00		9,499.00
10/02	924	688.00		8,811.00
10/03	926*	1,700.00	9,800.00	16,911.00
10/05	927	2,900.00	600.00	14,611.00
10/07	929*	270.00		14,341.00
10/09	930	2,450.00	2,100.00	13,991.00
10/13	933*	490.00	1,764.00	15,265.00
10/16	935*	225.00	2,744.00	17,784.00
10/18	934*	3,800.00		13,984.00
10/19	936*	2,608.00		11,376.00
10/22	938*	5,600.00	12,000.00	17,776.00
10/23	939	2,380.00		15,396.00
10/24	940	945.00		14,451.00
10/25	941	2,500.00	5,000.00	16,951.00
10/28	942	1,455.00		15,496.00
10/29	944*	710.00		14,786.00
10/31	946*	1,824.00		
10/31	945*	1,287.00		
10/31			CM 1,500.00	
10/31	SC	7.00		
10/31	RI	600.00		
10/31	DM	15.00	CM 70.00	12,623.00

Codes:	CC	Certified Check	EC	Error Correction
	CM	Credit Memorandum	OD	Overdrawn
	DM	Debit Memorandum	RI	Returned Item
	DC	Deposit Correction	SC	Service Charge

*Check numbers out of sequence.

EXHIBIT 10-6
General Ledger, Cash Account

GENERAL LEDGER ACCOUNTS										
Account: *Cash*								Account No.	*101*	
			Post.						Balance	
Date	Item		Ref.	Debit		Credit		Debit		Credit
19XX	*Previous Balance*							7 6 4 1 —		
Oct.	31		CR10	3 5 4 7 8 —				4 3 1 1 9 —		
	31		CP10			3 4 9 1 1 —		8 2 0 8 —		

7. **Errors:** any error made by either the bank or the firm must be corrected. An error made by the firm is usually corrected by a bank reconciliation entry. An error made by the bank is corrected by contacting the bank and informing them of the error. The error can then be corrected by the bank before the next month's statement.

Steps in Preparing the Bank Reconciliation

A bank reconciliation is prepared as follows:

1. Deposits on the bank statement are compared to the deposits recorded in the cash receipts journal or whatever register the firm uses to record deposits. Any deposits recorded in the cash receipts journal but not on the bank statement are designated as Deposits in Transit.

2. Checks returned with the bank statement should be arranged in numerical order. They should then be compared with the checks listed in the cash payments journal or whatever register the firm uses to record checks. Any checks not returned by the bank should be noted as Outstanding Checks.

3. Any collections, NSF checks, interest earned, and bank service charges listed on the bank statement are compared to the firm's accounting records. For a firm that uses special journals, such as United Auto Supply, this would be the cash receipts and cash payments journals.

4. Any errors, omissions, and/or adjustments that become apparent during the completion of the three previous steps are listed.

Format for a Bank Reconciliation

A format for a bank reconciliation is illustrated in Exhibit 10-7. Any errors or adjustments in the Book Balance section require entries in the general journal to correct the book balance of Cash. Any errors or adjustments in the Bank Balance section do not require entries in the firm's general journal. The bank should be contacted to correct these errors.

EXHIBIT 10-7
Format for a Bank Reconciliation

Name of Firm		
Bank Reconciliation		
Date		
Bank Balance		
Cash Balance per Bank Statement		$ XX
Add: Deposits in Transit	$ XX	
Errors	XX	XX
Subtotal		$ XX
Deduct: Outstanding Checks	$ XX	
Errors	XX	XX
Adjusted Cash Balance per Bank Statement		$ XX
Book Balance		
Cash Balance per General Ledger		$ XX
Add: Collections by the Bank	$ XX	
Errors	XX	XX
Subtotal		$ XX
Deduct: Bank Service Charges	$ XX	
Errors	XX	XX
Adjusted Cash Balance per General Ledger		$ XX

Bank Reconciliation for United Auto Supply

United Auto Supply received a bank statement (see Exhibit 10-5) for October 31, 19XX, and compared it to the general ledger Cash account (see Exhibit 10-6). To find the difference between these two amounts let's look at the cash receipts journal and cash payments journal for October 19XX (as shown in Exhibit 10-8).

As Hu Le, the accountant for United Auto Supply, prepared the bank reconciliation, she noticed the following adjustments and errors:

1. The October 30, 19XX, deposit of $1,470 did not appear on the bank statement.

2. An outstanding check from the September 19XX bank reconciliation, check number 925, for $1,170 was not returned with the October 31, 19XX, bank statement. Also, four checks issued in October 19XX were outstanding: check number 928, $195; check number 931, $1,200; check number 937, $190; and check number 943, $2,560.

3. The bank collected $1,500 for United Auto Supply, of which $1,400 is Notes Receivable and $100 is Interest Income. The bank has a monthly service charge of $7. The deposit made on October 5, 19XX, for $600 was not paid by Duncan Enterprises' bank and was returned as an NSF check. The bank charged United Auto Supply a $15 fee for the returned deposit. The checking account received $70 cash for Interest Income for the month of October 19XX.

EXHIBIT 10-8
Cash Receipts and Cash Payments Journals for United Auto Supply for the Month of October

CASH RECEIPTS JOURNAL   Page ___10___

Date	Account Credited	Post. Ref.	Credits: Other Accounts	Credits: Accounts Receiv.	Credits: Sales	Debits: Sales Disc.	Debits: Cash
19XX							
Oct. 3	Cash Sales	—			9 8 0 0 —		9 8 0 0 —
5	Office Supplies	131	6 0 0 —				6 0 0 —
8	Notes Payable	221	2 1 0 0 —				2 1 0 0 —
12	Emma's Auto Repair	✓		1 8 0 0 —		3 6 —	1 7 6 4 —
14	Montana Company	✓		2 8 0 0 —		5 6 —	2 7 4 4 —
19	Cash Sales	—			12 0 0 0 —		12 0 0 0 —
25	Lucille Garcia, Capital	301	5 0 0 0 —				5 0 0 0 —
30	Zumwalt Company	✓		1 5 0 0 —		3 0 —	1 4 7 0 —
			7 7 0 0 —	6 1 0 0 —	21 8 0 0 —	1 2 2 —	35 4 7 8 —
			(✓)	(111)	(401)	(403)	(101)

(continued)

(Ex. 10-8 concluded)

CASH PAYMENTS JOURNAL

Date	Ck. No.	Account Debited	Post. Ref.	Debits — Other Accounts	Debits — Accounts Payable	Debits — Purchases	Credits — Purch. Disc.	Credits — Cash
19XX								
Oct 1	926	Rent Expense	601	1 7 0 0 —				1 7 0 0 —
2	927	Cash Purchases	—			2 9 0 0 —		2 9 0 0 —
4	928	Utilities Expense	631	1 9 5 —				1 9 5 —
5	929	Freight In	516	2 7 0 —				2 7 0 —
5	930	Wages Expense	611	2 4 5 0 —				2 4 5 0 —
8	931	Lucille Garcia, Drawing	311	1 2 0 0 —				1 2 0 0 —
9	932	VOID						
9	933	Boyle Manufacturing	✓		5 0 0 —		1 0 —	4 9 0 —
10	934	Cash Purchases	—			3 8 0 0 —		3 8 0 0 —
11	935	Freight In	516	2 2 5 —				2 2 5 —
12	936	Wages Expense	611	2 6 8 0 —				2 6 8 0 —
15	937	Advertising Expense	621	1 9 0 —				1 9 0 —
17	938	Cash Purchases	—			5 6 0 0 —		5 6 0 0 —
19	939	Wages Expense	611	2 3 8 0 —				2 3 8 0 —
22	940	Freight In	516	4 9 5 —				4 9 5 —
23	941	Office Equipment	141	2 5 0 0 —				2 5 0 0 —
25	942	Nguyen Distributors	✓		1 5 0 0 —		4 5 —	1 4 5 5 —
26	943	Wages Expense	611	2 5 6 0 —				2 5 6 0 —
29	944	Freight In	516	7 1 0 —				7 1 0 —
30	945	Zamora Warehouse	✓		1 3 0 0 —		1 3 —	1 2 8 7 —
31	946	Mehta Manufacturing	✓		1 9 0 0 —		7 6 —	1 8 2 4 —
				17 5 5 5 —	5 2 0 0 —	12 3 0 0 —	1 4 4 —	34 9 1 1 —
				(✓)	(201)	(501)	(503)	(101)

4. Check number 936 was incorrectly recorded in the cash payments journal as $2,680. The correct amount was $2,608, which cleared the bank on October 19, 19XX. Check number 940 was also incorrectly recorded in the cash payments journal. The correct amount was $945, which cleared the bank on October 24, 19XX. The incorrect amount written in the cash payments journal was $495.

The completed bank reconciliation is shown in Exhibit 10-9.

EXHIBIT 10-9
Completed Bank Reconciliation

United Auto Supply
Bank Reconciliation
October 31, 19XX

Bank Balance			
Cash Balance per Bank Statement			$12 6 2 3 —
Add: Deposits in Transit			1 4 7 0 —
Subtotal			$14 0 9 3 —
Deduct: Outstanding Checks as Listed:			
Check Number 925	$ 1 1 7 0 —		
Check Number 928	1 9 5 —		
Check Number 931	1 2 0 0 —		
Check Number 937	1 9 0 —		
Check Number 943	2 5 6 0 —	5 3 1 5 —	
Adjusted Cash Balance per Bank Statement		$ 8 7 7 8 —	
Book Balance			
Cash Balance per General Ledger		$ 8 2 0 8 —	
Add: Collection of Note	$ 1 4 0 0 —		
Collection of Interest on Note	1 0 0 —		
Interest on Checking Account	7 0 —		
Correction of Check Number 936	7 2 —	1 6 4 2 —	
Subtotal		$ 9 8 5 0 —	
Deduct: Bank Service Charge	$ 7 —		
Returned Check, NSF Check	6 0 0 —		
Fee for Returned Check	1 5 —		
Correction of Check Number 940	4 5 0 —	1 0 7 2 —	
Adjusted Cash Balance per General Ledger		$ 8 7 7 8 —	

Bank Reconciliation Entries

Once you are satisfied that the Adjusted Cash Balance per the General Ledger equals the Adjusted Cash Balance per the Bank Statement you can make bank reconciliation entries in the general journal, not the special journals. There is no actual payment or receipt of cash as there is in the cash payments and cash receipts journals. The Bank Reconciliation general journal entries for United Auto Supply are shown in Exhibit 10-10.

EXHIBIT 10-10
Bank Reconciliation Entries

GENERAL JOURNAL   Page ___27___

Date		Description	Post. Ref.	Debit	Credit
		Bank Reconciliation Entries			
19XX					
Oct.	31	Cash		1500 —	
		Notes Receivable			1400 —
		Interest Income			100 —
		Collection of Note by Bank			
	31	Cash		70 —	
		Interest Income			70 —
		Checking Account Interest			
	31	Cash		72 —	
		Wages Expense			72 —
		Correction of Check Number 936			
	31	Bank Service Expense		7 —	
		Cash			7 —
		Service Charge on Checking Account			
	31	Accounts Receivable—Duncan Enterprises		615 —	
		Cash			615 —
		NSF Check of $600 and $15 Fee by Bank			
	31	Freight In		450 —	
		Cash			450 —
		Correction of Check Number 940			

United Auto Supply would attempt to collect $615 ($600 + $15) from Duncan Enterprises to cover both the original receipt and the fee charged by the bank. The $615 should also be posted to the accounts receivable subsidiary ledger for Duncan Enterprises.

General Ledger (Cash) after Bank Reconciliation Entries

The adjusted cash balance of $8,778 would appear on the balance sheet for Cash at October 31, 19XX. Let's look at the Cash account in the general ledger (Exhibit 10-11) after the bank reconciliation entries have been posted.

EXHIBIT 10-11
General Ledger, Cash Account

GENERAL LEDGER ACCOUNTS

Account: *Cash*　　　　　　　　　　　　　　　　　　　Account No.   101

Date	Item	Post. Ref.	Debit	Credit	Balance Debit	Balance Credit
19XX	*Previous Balance*				7641—	
Oct. 31		CR10	35478—		43119—	
31		CP10		34911—	8208—	
31		J27	1500—		9708—	
31		J27	70—		9778—	
31		J27	72—		9850—	
31		J27		7—	9843—	
31		J27		615—	9228—	
31		J27		450—	8778—	

THE PETTY CASH SYSTEM

Objective 3
Understand and use a petty cash system.

For internal cash control purposes, all payments should be made by checks. However, for some small or urgent expenditures, it is not feasible to make all payments by check. Some of these cash payments could include washing the firm's automobile, paying taxi fare, buying a few postage stamps, and so on.

Most firms will set up a petty cash fund to pay these small expenditures when it is inconvenient to pay them with a check. A petty cash fund that is established for a fixed amount is referred to as an imprest system (Petty cash is an asset account.)

Establishing the Petty Cash Fund

On November 18, 19XX, Lucille Garcia, the owner of United Auto Supply, decided to establish a petty cash fund for $150, check number 967. She felt that this amount should cover small cash expenditures for an estimated one to two weeks. This transaction would be recorded in the cash payments journal as follows:

CASH PAYMENTS JOURNAL   Page ___11___

				Debits			Credits	
Date	Ck. No.	Account Debited	Post. Ref.	Other Accounts	Accounts Payable	Purchases	Purch. Disc.	Cash
19XX								
Nov. 18	967	Petty Cash	102	1 5 0 —				1 5 0 —

Petty Cash Disbursements

A petty cash voucher, as illustrated in Exhibit 10-12, should be prepared for each expenditure. The custodian of the petty cash fund enters the date, purpose, and amount. The petty cash voucher is signed by the person receiving the payment. For internal control purposes, petty cash vouchers should be prenumbered, and all supporting documentation, such as receipts, should be attached. Lucille Garcia makes Hu Le the custodian of the petty cash fund. In Exhibit 10-12, the first voucher is issued for $2 for washing the firm's automobile.

EXHIBIT 10-12
Prenumbered Petty Cash Voucher

Petty Cash Voucher

Date: *November 19, 19XX*   No. *001*

For: *Car Wash*

Charge to: *Miscellaneous Expense*

Amount: $2.00

Frank Rylski
Received by

Petty Cash Reimbursements

The custodian has the responsibility of monitoring the fund's balance, keeping track of the petty cash vouchers and the cash balance of the fund by means of a petty cash disbursements record (as shown in Exhibit 10-13). When the petty cash fund becomes low, it is replenished by a check from the firm's bank account. Each voucher is accounted for, and the disbursements are classified in the appropriate account category. Hu Le, the custodian, decides to replenish the fund on November 28, 19XX. The fund has a cash balance on hand of $54, and petty cash vouchers 001–004 total $95. The total amount accounted for is thus $149 ($54 + $95).

EXHIBIT 10-13
Petty Cash Disbursements Record

PETTY CASH DISBURSEMENTS RECORD   Page ___1___

Date	Voucher Number	Account Charged	Amount	Fund Balance	Comments
11/18				150.00	Established Fund Check
					Number 967
11/19	001	Miscellaneous Expense	2.00	148.00	
11/20	002	Office Supplies	26.00	122.00	
11/21	003	Freight In	25.00	97.00	
11/25	004	Postage Expense	42.00	55.00	
11/28				150.00*	Replenished Fund Check
					Number 989

*Check number 989 is for $96, which replenishes the fund to $150 (see Exhibit 10-14).

Petty Cash Reconciliation

The difference of $1 ($150 − $149) is charged to Cash Short or Over. Exhibit 10-14 shows the petty cash reconciliation for November 28, 19XX:

EXHIBIT 10-14
Petty Cash Reconciliation

United Auto Supply
Petty Cash Reconciliation
November 28, 19XX

Beginning Balance, November 18, 19XX		$150 —
Less: Disbursements (vouchers)	$ 95 —	
Cash on Hand	54 —	149 —
Difference, Cash Short or Over		$ 1 —

Replenishing the Petty Cash Fund

The entry in the cash payments journal to replenish the petty cash fund would be as follows:

CASH PAYMENTS JOURNAL   Page ___11___

| Date | Ck. No. | Account Debited | Post. Ref. | Debits | | | Credits | |
				Other Accounts	Accounts Payable	Purchases	Purch. Disc.	Cash
19XX								
Nov. 28	989	Miscellaneous						
		Expense	691	2 —				
		Office Supplies	131	26 —				
		Freight In	516	25 —				
		Postage						
		Expense	681	42 —				
		Cash Short						
		or Over	682	1 —				96 —

Petty Cash Account

The account, Petty Cash, is not debited or credited except in the following situations:

1. The petty cash fund is first established.

2. The amount of the fund increases. For example, if United Auto Supply increased the size of the fund to $200, a debit is made to Petty Cash for $50 and a credit is made to Cash for $50. This entry in the cash payments journal would be as follows:

CASH PAYMENTS JOURNAL   Page _____12_____

| Date | Ck. No. | Account Debited | Post. Ref. | Debits | | | Credits | |
				Other Accounts	Accounts Payable	Purchases	Purch. Disc.	Cash
19XX								
Dec. 1	997	Petty Cash	102	5 0 —				5 0 —

3. The amount of the fund decreases. For example, if United Auto Supply decreased the size of the fund from $150 to $125, a debit is made to Cash for $25 and a credit is made to Petty Cash for $25. This entry in the cash receipts journal would be as follows:

CASH RECEIPTS JOURNAL   Page _____12_____

| Date | Account Credited | Post. Ref. | Credits | | | Debits | |
			Other Accounts	Accounts Receiv.	Sales	Sales Disc.	Cash
19XX							
Dec. 1	Petty Cash	102	2 5 —				2 5 —

4. The petty cash fund is eliminated. In this case, Cash is debited and Petty Cash is credited. If United Auto Supply eliminated the $150 petty cash fund, the entry in the cash receipts journal would be as follows:

CASH RECEIPTS JOURNAL   Page ___12___

| | | | | Credits | | | Debits | |
Date	Account Credited	Post. Ref.	Other Accounts	Accounts Receiv.	Sales	Sales Disc.	Cash
19XX							
Dec. 1	Petty Cash	102	1 5 0 —				1 5 0 —

THE CHANGE FUND

Objective 4
Understand and use a change fund.

    At the beginning of this chapter we said that many firms use cash registers to record sales. These firms will establish a change fund in the cash register drawer when the following situations occur: (1) there are numerous cash transactions, and (2) the business must be able to make change.

    A change fund is a fixed amount of cash that is placed in the cash register drawer. It is used to make change for those customers who pay cash. Before establishing the change fund, the firm must first determine the size of the fund and the denominations of coins and bills. For example, a business that establishes a $50 change fund may want $20 of coins and $30 of small bills in their cash register drawer. Let's now examine how a change fund is established.

Establishing the Change Fund

    On November 25, 19XX, United Auto Supply decided to establish a $100 change fund. This transaction may be illustrated using T accounts as follows:

Change Fund			Cash	
+	−		+	−
100				100

This transaction would be recorded in the cash payments journal, check number 975, as follows:

CASH PAYMENTS JOURNAL   Page ____11____

| | | | | Debits | | | Credits | |
| | | | | | | | | |
Date	Ck. No.	Account Debited	Post. Ref.	Other Accounts	Accounts Payable	Purchases	Purch. Disc.	Cash
19XX								
Nov. 25	975	Change Fund		1 0 0 —				1 0 0 —

Like the petty cash fund, the account Change Fund will not be debited or credited again unless the firm decided to change the size of the change fund.

Recording Cash Sales

At the end of the business day on November 25, 19XX, United Auto Supply has $410 of cash. The firm's accountant retains the amount of the change fund in convenient denominations, $30 of change and $70 of small bills (total of $100), and deposits the remainder in a bank. This is determined as follows:

Total cash in cash register drawer	$410
Less: Change fund balance	100
Deposit in bank	$310

This transaction can be shown using T accounts as follows:

Cash		Sales	
+	−	−	+
310			310

The cash received is recorded in the cash receipts journal:

CASH RECEIPTS JOURNAL   Page ___11___

Date	Account Credited	Post. Ref.	Credits			Debits	
			Other Accounts	Accounts Receiv.	Sales	Sales Disc.	Cash
19XX							
Nov. 25	Cash Sales				3 1 0 —		3 1 0 —

Financial Statement Presentation

The Change Fund account is an asset. It is presented on the balance sheet below Cash. The Change Fund account will follow the Petty Cash account if the Petty Cash account balance is larger than the Change Fund account balance. In Exhibit 10-15, Cash, Petty Cash, and Change Fund are shown on a partial balance sheet for United Auto Supply.

EXHIBIT 10-15
Cash, Petty Cash, and Change Fund

United Auto Supply
Balance Sheet (partial)
November 30, 19XX

Assets		
Cash	$10 0 0 0 —	
Petty Cash	1 5 0 —	
Change Fund	1 0 0 —	

CHAPTER REVIEW

1. **Record cash receipts (pp. 312–14).**
   Many merchandising and other firms use cash registers to record sales. When there is a difference between the cash register tape (sales) and the actual amounts collected, the account Cash Short or Over is used.

2. **Understand bank transactions (pp. 314–26).**
   A checking account improves the internal control of cash by minimizing the amount of cash on hand. A checking account is established by filling out a signature card. A bank reconciliation is prepared to account for the difference between the ending balance appearing on the bank statement and the ending balance of Cash in the general ledger.

3. **Understand and use a petty cash system (pp. 326–31).**
   A petty cash fund can be established to pay small expenditures when it is inconvenient to pay them with a check. Petty Cash is an asset account.

4. **Understand and use a change fund (pp. 331–33).**
   A change fund is a fixed amount of cash that is placed in a cash register drawer. It is established when there are numerous cash transactions and the firm must be able to make change. Like Petty Cash, the account Change Fund is an asset account.

GLOSSARY

Bank Reconciliation	Prepared by the depositor to account for the differences between the bank statement balance and the book balance of Cash.
Bank Statement	Summary of a depositor's Cash account.
Blank Endorsement	Payee signs the back of the check. Payable to anyone who cashes or deposits the check.
Cash Short or Over	Account that is used to balance an accounting entry.
Change Fund	A fixed amount of cash that is placed in a cash register drawer.
Check	Form that directs a bank to pay a certain sum of money.
Deposit Slip	Form used to deposit money in a bank account.
Depositor	Individual or firm that controls or owns a bank account.
Deposits In Transit	Money that has been deposited in a bank account but is not listed on a bank statement.

Imprest System	Petty cash fund established for a fixed amount.
Outstanding Checks	Checks that have been issued by the depositor, but have not been paid by the bank.
Payee	Person directed to receive the amount written on the face of a check.
Petty Cash Disbursements Record	Means of accounting for petty cash payments and reimbursements.
Petty Cash Fund	Cash account used to pay small expenditures when it is inconvenient to pay them with a check.
Petty Cash Reconciliation	Prepared by the custodian of the petty cash fund to account for disbursements and cash on hand.
Petty Cash Voucher	Prenumbered form used to record petty cash payments.
Restrictive Endorsement	Check can only be deposited or cashed by a certain bank or person.
Signature Card	Form authorizing the appropriate personnel to sign checks for the firm.

SELF-TEST QUESTIONS FOR REVIEW

(Answers are on p. 349.)

1. Cash Short or Over is credited in a transaction. This is
   a. a miscellaneous expense.
   b. the cost of goods sold.
   c. an asset.
   d. a miscellaneous income.

2. Which of the following is added in the book balance section of a bank reconciliation?
   a. Bank service charges
   b. Outstanding checks
   c. Collections by the bank
   d. Deposits in transit

3. "Collection of Note by Bank" is written as a description for a bank reconciliation entry. _____ is debited.
   a. Cash
   b. Notes Receivable
   c. Interest Income
   d. Accounts Receivable

4. Cash is debited and Petty Cash is credited. This transaction could
   a. establish a change fund.
   b. eliminate a petty cash fund.
   c. increase a petty cash fund.
   d. establish a petty cash fund.

5. Consider the following accounts and account balances (all are normal): Cash, $20,000; Petty Cash, $500; and Change Fund, $700. The balance sheet presentation order is _____ first and _____ third.
   a. Cash; Petty Cash
   b. Petty Cash; Change Fund
   c. Cash; Change Fund
   d. Change Fund; Petty Cash

PRACTICAL REVIEW PROBLEM

Objectives 3
and 4

Using a Petty Cash System and Change Fund   Goldsmith Paint Supply had the following petty cash, change fund, and cash sales transactions for the week ended April 30, 19XX:

April 26	Established a petty cash fund for $160 (check number 278).
April 27	Established a change fund for $80 (check number 279).
April 27	Cash count, $560.
April 28	Cash count, $430.
April 28	Reimbursed the petty cash fund, check number 280. Cash on hand is $22 and April 27 petty cash vouchers total $136. Voucher 1 ($70) is for store supplies and the remainder is for postage (voucher 2).
April 29	Cash count, $610.
April 30	Increased the petty cash fund to $250, check number 281.
April 30	Cash count, $520.
April 30	Received and reconciled the bank statement. The adjusted Cash balance per the bank statement is $11,070.

REQUIRED

1. Record transactions in the cash payments journal (page 7) or the cash receipts journal (page 4).
2. Prepare a petty cash disbursements record, page 1.
3. Prepare a petty cash reconciliation when the petty cash fund is replenished.
4. Prepare a partial balance sheet on April 30, 19XX, for Cash, Petty Cash, and Change Fund.

ANSWER TO PRACTICAL REVIEW PROBLEM

1.   **CASH PAYMENTS JOURNAL**   Page _____7_____

Date	Ck. No.	Account Debited	Post. Ref.	Debits — Other Accounts	Debits — Accounts Payable	Debits — Purchases	Credits — Purch. Disc.	Credits — Cash
19XX								
Apr. 26	278	Petty Cash		1 6 0 —				1 6 0 —
27	279	Change Fund		8 0 —				8 0 —
28	280	Store Supplies		7 0 —				
		Postage						
		Expense		6 6 —				
		Cash Short						
		or Over		2 —				1 3 8 —
30	281	Petty Cash		9 0 —				9 0 —

CASH RECEIPTS JOURNAL

Page ___4___

| Date | Account Credited | Post. Ref. | Credits | | | Debits | | |
			Other Accounts	Accounts Receiv.	Sales	Sales Disc.	Cash	
19XX								
Apr. 27	Cash Sales				480 —		480 —	*
28	Cash Sales				350 —		350 —	*
29	Cash Sales				530 —		530 —	*
30	Cash Sales				440 —		440 —	*

2.   **PETTY CASH DISBURSEMENTS RECORD**   Page ___1___

Date	Voucher Number	Account Charged	Amount	Fund Balance	Comments
4/26				160.00	Established Fund
					Check Number 278
4/27	1	Store Supplies	70.00	90.00	
4/27	2	Postage Expense	66.00	24.00	
4/28			**	160.00	Replenished Fund
					Check Number 280
4/30				250.00	Increased Fund
					Check Number 281

3.   Goldsmith Paint Supply
                  Petty Cash Reconciliation
                     April 28, 19XX

Beginning Balance, April 26, 19XX			$160 —
Less: Disbursements (vouchers)	$136 —		
Cash on Hand		22 —	158 —
Difference, Cash Short or Over			$ 2 —

*Cash count less change fund.

**Check number 280 is for $138, which replenishes the fund to $160 (see petty cash reconciliation—requirement 3).

4.

Goldsmith Paint Supply
Balance Sheet (partial)
April 30, 19XX

Assets					
Cash		$11 0 7 0	—		
Petty Cash		2 5 0	—		
Change Fund		8 0	—		

DISCUSSION QUESTIONS

Q 10-1   When is the Cash Short or Over account needed?

Q 10-2   Describe the following in your own words: (a) signature card; (b) deposit slip; (c) check; and (d) bank statement.

Q 10-3   When is a bank reconciliation necessary? What is the purpose of a bank reconciliation?

Q 10-4   Give five reasons for preparing a bank reconciliation.

Q 10-5   Briefly explain the four steps in preparing a bank reconciliation.

Q 10-6   When are bank reconciliation entries necessary? Name at least four possible bank reconciliation entries that could be journalized in the general journal.

Q 10-7   Why is a petty cash system necessary?

Q 10-8   Briefly describe the process of setting up and replenishing the petty cash fund. When is the account Petty Cash used?

Q 10-9   Name the two situations in which a firm will establish a change fund.

Q 10-10   A firm has a $100 change fund. Cash at the end of a business day totals $270. What is the cash deposit for the day?

EXERCISES

Objective 1

E 10-1   **Recording Sales**   McCormick Company had total collections of $35,810 for March 19XX. The cash register tape totaled $35,822. A total of $11,500 of the sales were by credit cards, and the firm's bank charges 8 percent for credit card deposits. Prepare a general journal entry to record the March 31, 19XX, sales.

Objective 2

E 10-2   **Preparing a Bank Reconciliation**   Prepare a bank reconciliation for Silberg Company for January 31, 19XX, given the following information:
a. The cash balance per the general ledger is $9,000.
b. The cash balance per the bank statement is $10,000.
c. Interest earned for January 19XX is $50.

d. Bank service charges are $10.

e. Outstanding checks total $960.

Objective 1   **E 10-3**   **Recording Sales**   Bennet Company had a cash register tape of $19,416 and cash and checks on hand of $19,421 on September 30, 19XX. Prepare a general journal entry to record the September sales. Also, prepare an entry in a cash receipts journal to record the sales if the firm used special journals.

Objective 2   **E 10-4**   **Recording Bank Reconciliation Entries**   Prepare general journal entries to record the following bank reconciliation adjustments, if necessary:

a. Collection of a note by the bank for $6,500 of which $360 is interest.

b. A deposit in transit was identified for $1,200.

c. Four outstanding checks were identified: number A901, $180; number A902, $799; number A908, $1,647; and number A910, $63.

d. Interest earned for the month is $19.

e. An NSF check for $700 from Jackowski Company was returned by the bank. The bank charged a $20 fee. The check was for credit purchases.

Objective 3   **E 10-5**   **Recording Petty Cash Transactions**   Prepare the following entries in a cash payments journal, page 4, for Milligan Company:

a. On April 14, 19XX, the firm established a petty cash fund for $75, check number 781.

b. The firm reimbursed the fund on April 18, 19XX, check number 782. Vouchers totaled $68, and cash on hand was $6. All the vouchers were issued for office supplies.

c. On April 23, 19XX, the firm increased the fund to $125, check number 783.

Objective 2   **E 10-6**   **Completing a Bank Reconciliation**   Fill in the missing numbers and descriptions for the following bank reconciliation:

Bank Balance

Cash Balance per Bank Statement	$1,700
Add: Deposit in Transit	300
Subtotal	$ (a)
Deduct: Outstanding checks	(b)
(c)	$ (d)

Book Balance

Cash Balance per General Ledger		$ (e)
Add: Collection of Note	$ (f)	
Interest Earned	25	795
Subtotal		$ (g)
Deduct: Bank Service Charge		10
(h)		$1,480

Objective 3   E 10-7   Preparing a Petty Cash Reconciliation   Prepare a petty cash reconciliation for Kite Software Supply for February 28, 19XX. Also, prepare an entry in the cash payments journal, page 5, for the reimbursement of the petty cash fund (check number 019) given the following information:

a. The petty cash fund was established on February 4, 19XX, for $165.
b. On February 28, 19XX, cash on hand is $20.
c. The following vouchers were issued: number A19, $22, for Freight In; number A20, $14, for Postage Expense; number A21, $55, for Office Supplies; and number A22, $50, for Miscellaneous Expense.

Objective 4   E 10-8   Recording Change Fund Transactions   Consider the following transactions:

a. On November 14, 19XX, Ky Paper Supply establishes a $170 change fund. Record this transaction, first using T accounts and then using a cash payments journal, page 3 (check number 421).
b. At the end of a business day (November 21, 19XX) Ky Paper Supply has $1,260 of cash. Assuming a $170 change fund, record this transaction in a cash receipts journal, page 3.

PROBLEM SET A

Objective 1   P 10-1A   Recording Deposits   Manning Company's bank fluctuates the rate of credit card percentage charges. The company had the following sales activity for October 19XX:

Date	Cash Register Tape Total	Collections			Credit Card Charge
		Cash	Credit Card	Total	
19XX					
10/3	*$ 12,000*	*$11,000*	*$ 1,000*	*$ 12,000*	*6%*
10/11	*74,010*	*67,000*	*7,000*	*74,000*	*10*
10/19	*90,005*	*90,000*	*—0—*	*90,000*	*7*
10/25	*113,616*	*75,610*	*38,000*	*113,610*	*5*
10/30	*49,082*	*40,500*	*8,600*	*49,100*	*8*

REQUIRED
Prepare general journal entries (page 19) to record the deposits.

Objective 2   P 10-2A   Preparing a Bank Reconciliation   The May 19XX bank statement for Hanson's Marine Supply and the May accounting records reveal the following information:

● Bank statement balance, $25,890.

● Cash account balance, $25,630.

- Outstanding checks: No. 319, $420; No. 331, $190; and No. 337, $60.
- The May 31, 19XX deposit of $1,750 did not appear on the bank statement.
- The bank collected $1,840 of which $1,800 is Notes Receivable and the remainder is Interest Income.
- A deposit made May 14, 19XX for $780 was not paid by Flannagan Enterprises' bank and was returned as an NSF check. The bank charged a $10 fee for the returned deposit.
- Check no. 324 cleared the bank correctly for $250. The check was written erroneously for $520 for transportation costs.
- Monthly service charge, $20.
- Checking account interest income for the month of May, $40.

REQUIRED
1. Prepare a bank reconciliation.
2. Journalize all bank reconciliation entries in the general journal, page 10.

Objectives 3 and 4

P 10-3A   **Using a Petty Cash System and Change Fund**   Yolanda's Dress Supply had the following petty cash, change fund, and cash sales transactions for the week ended March 31, 19XX:

March 27	Established a petty cash fund for $120 (check number 814).
March 28	Established a change fund for $90 (check number 815).
March 28	Cash count, $1,620.
March 29	Cash count, $1,310.
March 29	Reimbursed the petty cash fund, check number 816. Cash on hand is $36 and March 28 petty cash vouchers total $83. Voucher 1 ($60) is for office supplies and the remainder is for postage (voucher 2).
March 30	Cash count, $1,540.
March 30	Increased the petty cash fund to $200, check number 817.
March 31	Cash count, $1,790.
March 31	Received and reconciled the bank statement. The adjusted Cash balance per the bank statement is $15,630.

REQUIRED (see Practical Review Problem)
1. Record transactions in the cash payments journal (page 4) or the cash receipts journal (page 3).
2. Prepare a petty cash disbursements record, page 1.
3. Prepare a petty cash reconciliation when the petty cash fund is replenished.
4. Prepare a partial balance sheet on March 31, 19XX, for Cash, Petty Cash, and Change Fund.

Objective 2   P 10-4A   **Comprehensive Bank Reconciliation Problem**   Sorensen Company
received the following bank statement on January 31, 19XX:

Previous Balance	12/31/XX				3,336.00
5	Deposits and Other Items				5,336.00
6	Checks and Other Items				2,069.00
	Service Charge				8.00
	Total Checks and Charges				2,077.00
Ending Balance	**1/31/XX**				**6,595.00**

Date Paid	Check Number	Amount	Deposits		Ending Balance
1/2			2,150.00		5,486.00
1/4	796	759.00			4,727.00
1/11	797	388.00	513.00		4,852.00
1/19	800*	198.00	1,095.00		5,749.00
1/28	802*	195.00			5,554.00
1/31	SC	8.00			
1/31	RI	513.00			
1/31	DM	16.00			
1/31			CM	1,565.00	
1/31			CM	13.00	6,595.00

Codes:	CC	Certified Check	EC	Error Correction
	CM	Credit Memorandum	OD	Overdrawn
	DM	Debit Memorandum	RI	Returned Item
	DC	Deposit Correction	SC	Service Charge

*Check numbers out of sequence.

Referring to the bank statement: SC 8.00 is a service charge on the
checking account; RI 513.00 is an NSF check; DM 16.00 is a fee charged
by the bank for the NSF check; CM 1,565.00 is a collection of a note
which includes $115 interest income; and CM 13.00 is checking account
interest income.

The Cash account in the general ledger is as follows:

GENERAL LEDGER ACCOUNT

Account: *Cash*   Account No.   102

Date		Item	Post. Ref.	Debit	Credit	Balance Debit	Balance Credit
19XX		*Previous Balance*				2 9 4 8 —	
Jan.	*31*		CR8	4 1 5 0 —		7 0 9 8 —	
	31		CP9		3 1 7 1 —	3 9 2 7 —	

The cash receipts journal is as follows:

CASH RECEIPTS JOURNAL   Page ____8____

Date		Account Credited	Post. Ref.	Credits Other Accounts	Credits Accounts Receiv.	Credits Sales	Debits Sales Disc.	Debits Cash
19XX								
Jan.	*2*	*Cash Sales*	—			2 1 5 0 —		2 1 5 0 —
	11	*Kay Sawyer*	√		5 1 3 —			5 1 3 —
	19	*Cash Sales*	—			1 0 9 5 —		1 0 9 5 —
	31	*Larry Caesia*	√		4 0 0 —		8 —	3 9 2 —
					9 1 3 —	3 2 4 5 —	8 —	4 1 5 0 —
					(108)	(401)	(403)	(102)

The cash payments journal is as follows:

CASH PAYMENTS JOURNAL

Page _____ 9 _____

Date	Ck. No.	Account Debited	Post. Ref.	Debits — Other Accounts	Debits — Accounts Payable	Debits — Purchases	Credits — Purch. Disc.	Credits — Cash
19XX								
Jan. 1	796	Rent Expense	601	7 9 5 —				7 9 5 —
5	797	Goyle						
		Manufacturing	✓		4 0 0 —		1 2 —	3 8 8 —
10	798	VOID						
10	799	Finn						
		Distributors	✓		2 1 9 —			2 1 9 —
16	800	Advertising						
		Expense	621	1 9 8 —				1 9 8 —
21	801	Thomas						
		Warehouse	✓		8 0 0 —		2 4 —	7 7 6 —
27	802	Cash Purchases	—			1 9 5 —		1 9 5 —
31	803	Wages Expense	611	6 0 0 —				6 0 0 —
				1 5 9 3 —	1 4 1 9 —	1 9 5 —	3 6 —	3 1 7 1 —
				(✓)	(202)	(503)	(505)	(102)

Check number 789 for $388 is outstanding from the previous month's bank reconciliation. Check number 796 was incorrectly recorded in the cash payments journal as $795. The check cleared the bank correctly at $759.

REQUIRED

1. Prepare a bank reconciliation.
2. Journalize all bank reconciliation entries in the general journal, page 16.
3. Post the bank reconciliation entries to the cash account in the general ledger (include all previous balances).

PROBLEM SET B

Objective 1

P 10-1B   Recording Deposits   Schneider Company's bank fluctuates the rate of credit card percentage charges. The following sales activity was recorded for Schneider Company for January 19XX:

Date	Cash Register Tape Total	Collections			Credit Card Charge
		Cash	Credit Card	Total	
19XX					
1/5	*$ 14,000*	*$ 12,000*	*$ 2,000*	*$ 14,000*	*9%*
1/9	*60,910*	*51,000*	*9,900*	*60,900*	*10*
1/20	*103,008*	*75,600*	*27,400*	*103,000*	*5*
1/24	*154,995*	*107,010*	*48,000*	*155,010*	*8*
1/29	*99,000*	*99,050*	*—0—*	*99,050*	*4*

REQUIRED

Prepare general journal entries (page 21) to record the deposits.

Objective 2

P 10-2B   Preparing a Bank Reconciliation   The July 19XX bank statement for Keller's Pipe Supply and the July accounting records reveal the following information:

- Bank statement balance, $42,670.
- Cash account balance, $41,100.
- Outstanding checks: No. 809, $1,610; No. 868, $680; and No. 902, $2,140.
- The July 31, 19XX deposit of $4,690 did not appear on the bank statement.
- The bank collected $3,060 of which $2,550 is Notes Receivable and the remainder is Interest Income.
- A deposit made July 22, 19XX for $1,530 was not paid by Kim Yiung Enterprises' bank and was returned as an NSF check. The bank charged a $20 fee for the returned deposit.
- Check no. 876 cleared the bank correctly for $2,470. The check was written erroneously for $2,740 for transportation charges.
- Monthly service charge, $20.
- Checking account interest income for the month of July, $70.

REQUIRED

1. Prepare a bank reconciliation.
2. Journalize all bank reconciliation entries in the general journal, page 16.

Objectives 3 and 4

P 10-3B   **Using a Petty Cash System and Change Fund**   Hammond Valve Supply had the following petty cash, change fund, and cash sales transactions for the week ended August 31, 19XX:

August 27   Established a petty cash fund for $210 (check number 93).

August 28   Established a change fund for $130 (check number 94).

August 28   Cash count, $560.

August 29   Cash count, $840.

August 29   Reimbursed the petty cash fund, check number 95. Cash on hand is $42 and August 28 petty cash vouchers total $166. Voucher 1 ($80) is for postage and the remainder is for office supplies (voucher 2).

August 30   Cash count, $730.

August 30   Increased the petty cash fund to $280, check number 96.

August 31   Cash count, $650.

August 31   Received and reconciled the bank statement. The adjusted Cash balance per the bank statement is $13,510.

REQUIRED (see Practical Review Problem)
1. Record transactions in the cash payments journal (page 9) or the cash receipts journal (page 8).
2. Prepare a petty cash disbursements record, page 1.
3. Prepare a petty cash reconciliation when the petty cash fund is replenished.
4. Prepare a partial balance sheet on August 31, 19XX, for Cash, Petty Cash, and Change Fund.

Objective 2

P 10-4B   **Comprehensive Bank Reconciliation Problem**   Rodriguez Company received the following bank statement on April 30, 19XX:

Previous Balance	3/31/XX			5,831.00
6	Deposits and Other Items			7,365.00
6	Checks and Other Items			3,891.00
	Service Charge			9.00
	Total Checks and Charges			3,900.00
Ending Balance	4/30/XX			9,296.00

Date Paid	Check Number	Amount	Deposits	Ending Balance
4/2	B20	684.00	2,468.00	7,615.00
4/5	B22*	978.00		6,637.00
4/12	B24*	768.00	847.00	6,716.00
4/18			1,408.00	8,124.00
4/27	B26*	602.00	735.00	8,257.00
4/30	SC	9.00		
4/30	RI	847.00		
4/30	DM	12.00		
4/30			CM 1,893.00	
4/30			CM 14.00	9,296.00

Codes:	CC	Certified Check	EC	Error Correction
	CM	Credit Memorandum	OD	Overdrawn
	DM	Debit Memorandum	RI	Returned Item
	DC	Deposit Correction	SC	Service Charge

*Check numbers out of sequence.

Referring to the bank statement: SC 9.00 is a service charge on the checking account; RI 847.00 is an NSF check; DM 12.00 is a fee charged by the bank for the NSF check; CM 1,893.00 is a collection of a note which includes $198.00 interest income; and CM 14.00 is checking account interest income.

The cash account in the general ledger is as follows:

GENERAL LEDGER ACCOUNT

Account: *Cash*   Account No.   104

Date	Item	Post. Ref.	Debit	Credit	Balance Debit	Balance Credit
19XX	*Previous Balance*				5 4 4 5 —	
Apr. 30		CR6	6 3 4 0 —		1 1 7 8 5 —	
30		CP7		4 4 5 3 —	7 3 3 2 —	

The cash receipts journal is as follows:

CASH RECEIPTS JOURNAL   Page ____6____

Date	Account Credited	Post. Ref.	Credits Other Accounts	Credits Accounts Receiv.	Credits Sales	Debits Sales Disc.	Debits Cash
19XX							
Apr. 2	*Cash Sales*	—			2 4 6 8 —		2 4 6 8 —
11	*Larry Lymons*	✓		8 4 7 —			8 4 7 —
18	*Cash Sales*	—			1 4 0 8 —		1 4 0 8 —
26	*Pat Wagler*	✓		7 5 0 —		1 5 —	7 3 5 —
30	*Alvin Slater*	✓		9 0 0 —		1 8 —	8 8 2 —
				2 4 9 7 —	3 8 7 6 —	3 3 —	6 3 4 0 —
				(113)	(407)	(409)	(104)

The cash payments journal is as follows:

CASH PAYMENTS JOURNAL   Page ____7____

Date	Ck. No.	Account Debited	Post. Ref.	Debits: Other Accounts	Debits: Accounts Payable	Debits: Purchases	Credits: Purch. Disc.	Credits: Cash
19XX								
Apr. 1	B20	Rent Expense	603	6 8 4 —				6 8 4 —
3	B21	Evans Company	√		4 0 0 —		4 —	3 9 6 —
6	B22	Cash Purchases	—			9 8 7 —		9 8 7 —
11	B23	VOID						
11	B24	Tumnan Enterprises	√		8 0 0 —		3 2 —	7 6 8 —
19	B25	Utilities Expense	628	1 7 9 —				1 7 9 —
25	B26	Cash Purchases	—			6 0 2 —		6 0 2 —
30	B27	Wages Expense	605	8 3 7 —				8 3 7 —
				1 7 0 0 —	1 2 0 0 —	1 5 8 9 —	3 6 —	4 4 5 3 —
				(√)	(201)	(502)	(505)	(104)

Check number B16 for $386 is outstanding from the previous month's bank reconciliation. Check number B22 was incorrectly recorded in the cash payments journal as $987. The check cleared the bank correctly at $978.

REQUIRED
1. Prepare a bank reconciliation.
2. Journalize all bank reconciliation entries in the general journal, page 16.
3. Post the bank reconciliation entries to the Cash account in the general ledger (include all previous balances).

ANSWERS TO SELF-TEST QUESTIONS

1. d   2. c   3. a   4. b   5. a

REVIEW OF ACCOUNTS

The highlighted accounts were added in Chapters 7–10.

Account	Normal Balance	Increased by A	Decreased by A	Classification	Financial Statement	Nominal or Real
Cash	Debit	Debit	Credit	Asset	Balance Sheet	Real
Petty Cash	Debit	Debit	Credit	Asset	Balance Sheet	Real
Change Fund	Debit	Debit	Credit	Asset	Balance Sheet	Real
Accounts Receivable	Debit	Debit	Credit	Asset	Balance Sheet	Real
Notes Receivable	Debit	Debit	Credit	Asset	Balance Sheet	Real
Office Supplies	Debit	Debit	Credit	Asset	Balance Sheet	Real
Prepaid Insurance	Debit	Debit	Credit	Asset	Balance Sheet	Real
Furniture	Debit	Debit	Credit	Asset	Balance Sheet	Real
Equipment	Debit	Debit	Credit	Asset	Balance Sheet	Real
Automobile	Debit	Debit	Credit	Asset	Balance Sheet	Real
Truck	Debit	Debit	Credit	Asset	Balance Sheet	Real
Accumulated Depreciation, Asset	Credit	Credit	Debit	Asset (Contra)	Balance Sheet	Real
Accounts Payable	Credit	Credit	Debit	Liability	Balance Sheet	Real
Notes Payable	Credit	Credit	Debit	Liability	Balance Sheet	Real
Wages Payable	Credit	Credit	Debit	Liability	Balance Sheet	Real
Owner, Capital	Credit	Credit	Debit	Owner's Equity	Statement of Owner's Equity and Balance Sheet	Real
Owner, Drawing	Debit	Debit	Credit	Owner's Equity (Contra)	Statement of Owner's Equity	Nominal
Income Summary	(used only during closing)			Owner's Equity	(used only during closing)	Nominal
Sales	Credit	Credit	Debit	Revenue	Income Statement	Nominal
Sales Returns and Allowances	Debit	Debit	Credit	Revenue (Contra)	Income Statement	Nominal
Sales Discounts	Debit	Debit	Credit	Revenue (Contra)	Income Statement	Nominal

Cash Short or Over*	Credit	Credit	Debit	Revenue	Income Statement	Nominal
Auditing Fees	Credit	Credit	Debit	Revenue	Income Statement	Nominal
Tax Services	Credit	Credit	Debit	Revenue	Income Statement	Nominal
Service Fees	Credit	Credit	Debit	Revenue	Income Statement	Nominal
Legal Fees	Credit	Credit	Debit	Revenue	Income Statement	Nominal
Interest Income	Credit	Credit	Debit	Revenue	Income Statement	Nominal
Purchases	Debit	Debit	Credit	COGS**	Income Statement	Nominal
Purchases Returns and Allowances	Credit	Credit	Debit	COGS** (Contra)	Income Statement	Nominal
Purchases Discounts	Credit	Credit	Debit	COGS** (Contra)	Income Statement	Nominal
Freight In	Debit	Debit	Credit	COGS**	Income Statement	Nominal
Wages Expense	Debit	Debit	Credit	Expense	Income Statement	Nominal
Advertising Expense	Debit	Debit	Credit	Expense	Income Statement	Nominal
Rent Expense	Debit	Debit	Credit	Expense	Income Statement	Nominal
Utilities Expense	Debit	Debit	Credit	Expense	Income Statement	Nominal
Office Supplies Expense	Debit	Debit	Credit	Expense	Income Statement	Nominal
Insurance Expense	Debit	Debit	Credit	Expense	Income Statement	Nominal
Depreciation Expense, Asset	Debit	Debit	Credit	Expense	Income Statement	Nominal
Cash Short or Over*	Debit	Debit	Credit	Expense	Income Statement	Nominal
Credit Card Expense	Debit	Debit	Credit	Expense	Income Statement	Nominal
Bank Service Expense	Debit	Debit	Credit	Expense	Income Statement	Nominal
Postage Expense	Debit	Debit	Credit	Expense	Income Statement	Nominal
Miscellaneous Expense	Debit	Debit	Credit	Expense	Income Statement	Nominal

*Cash Short or Over could be either a revenue or expense depending on the account balance.

**COGS is an abbreviation for cost of goods sold.

11

Adjustments and Worksheets for a Merchandising Firm

Money is the seed of money, and the first guinea is sometimes more difficult to acquire than the second million.

GEORGE GRENVILLE

LEARNING OBJECTIVES

After reading this chapter, discussing the questions, and working the exercises and problems, you will be able to do the following:

1. Calculate adjustments including (pp. 354–58):
    a. Merchandise Inventory.
    b. Deferrals.
    c. Accruals.

2. Prepare a worksheet for a merchandising firm (pp. 358–68).

3. Journalize and post adjusting entries (pp. 368–72).

n Chapter 6 we completed the discussion of a service operation or firm, and the accounting records of the service firm were cleared for the next accounting period. Revenues, expenses, Drawing, and Income Summary were closed to Capital. Then, after the closing entries were journalized and posted, a post-closing trial balance was prepared.

In Chapters 7 through 10 we recorded the transactions for United Auto Supply, a merchandising firm. In this chapter we will begin the closing process by preparing adjusting entries and a worksheet. In the next chapter, financial statements will be prepared, along with closing entries and a post-closing trial balance.

MERCHANDISE INVENTORY ADJUSTMENTS

Objective 1
Calculate
adjustments.

Remember that United Auto Supply uses the *periodic* method to account for merchandise inventory. When using this method, you must count the actual amount of merchandise inventory on hand at the end of the accounting period. This actual amount becomes the *ending balance* of Merchandise Inventory for the accounting period. Therefore, the *beginning balance* must be eliminated. So the first adjustment is to eliminate beginning Merchandise. (These adjusting entries will be identified in order by a, b, and so on.)

Beginning Merchandise Inventory (a) United Auto Supply started the October 19XX accounting period with $8,209 of merchandise inventory. An adjustment is necessary to eliminate Merchandise Inventory for October 19XX.

We will use the Income Summary account when adjusting for Merchandise Inventory because the adjustment is part of the closing process, and the accounting records must be properly set for the next accounting period. When the periodic method is used, Merchandise Inventory must be adjusted to reflect its actual balance at the end of the accounting period. Therefore, the beginning balance of Merchandise Inventory must be closed, and the ending balance must be opened. Let's use T accounts to illustrate the adjustment for beginning Merchandise Inventory:

Merchandise Inventory		Income Summary	
(10/1) Balance 8,209	(a) 8,209	(a) 8,209	
Balance after closing beginning inventory —0—		8,209	

This adjustment clears the beginning Merchandise Inventory balance.

Ending Merchandise Inventory (b)   On October 31, 19XX, the end of the accounting period, Frank Rylski counted the auto parts (merchandise inventory) on hand. He determined that $8,285 of inventory was on hand. Since United Auto Supply uses the periodic method of accounting for Merchandise Inventory, we must make an adjustment so this balance can be reflected in the accounting records. Let's use T accounts to illustrate the adjustment for ending Merchandise Inventory:

Merchandise Inventory		Income Summary	
(b) 8,285			(b) 8,285

Merchandise inventory is a balance sheet account, so by making this adjusting entry we will place the correct amount of Merchandise Inventory in the balance sheet. Let's now account for the *deferral* type of adjusting entries for United Auto Supply.

DEFERRAL ADJUSTMENTS

From Chapter 4 we remember that a deferral is necessary whenever one or both of the following situations occur:

1. Expenses have been paid to apply to future accounting periods.
2. Revenues have been received to apply to future accounting periods.

Office Supplies Adjustment (c)   On October 31, 19XX, United Auto Supply's accountant, Hu Le, counted $2,500 of office supplies on hand at the end of the accounting period. She made the following calculation:

Office Supplies Available to be Used	$2,700
Less: October 31, 19XX, Count (Ending Balance)	2,500
Office Supplies Used (Expensed) for the Month	$ 200

To record this adjustment, Office Supplies Expense is debited $200, and Office Supplies is credited $200. Let's use T accounts to illustrate this adjusting entry:

Office Supplies Expense	Office Supplies
(c) 200	(c) 200

Prepaid Insurance Adjustment (d)   United Auto Supply paid $1,800 for a twelve-month insurance policy on January 1, 19XX. In October 19XX, $150 is allocated as follows:

$$\$1,800 \div 12 \text{ Months} = \$150 \text{ per Month Expense Allocation}$$

T accounts may be used to show this adjusting entry:

Insurance Expense	Prepaid Insurance
(d) 150	(d) 150

Depreciation Adjustment: Office Equipment (e)   United Auto Supply uses the straight-line depreciation method where an equal amount of Depreciation Expense is allocated to each accounting period over that asset's useful life. Office equipment costs $15,500 and is estimated to have a $1,100 salvage value at the end of its useful life of four years. In October 19XX, $300 is allocated as follows:

$$\text{Office Equipment Depreciation Expense for October 19XX} = \frac{\$15,500 - \$1,100}{48 \text{ Months}}$$

$$= \frac{\$14,400}{48 \text{ Months}}$$

$$= \$300$$

Let's again use T accounts to illustrate this adjusting entry:

Depreciation Expense, Office Equipment	Accumulated Depreciation, Office Equipment
(e) 300	(e) 300

Earned Revenue Adjustment (f)   Many firms receive payment for revenues in advance, before the revenues are actually earned. For example, theaters sell season tickets in advance, and magazine subscriptions are paid for in advance. On September 1, 19XX, United Auto Supply received $3,000 from Hobbs Car Sales for future sales of merchandise. The entry to record this receipt of cash is as follows:

CASH RECEIPTS JOURNAL   Page ____9____

Date		Account Credited	Post. Ref.	Credits			Debits	
				Other Accounts	Accounts Receiv.	Sales	Sales Disc.	Cash
19XX								
Sep.	1	Unearned Sales						
		Revenue	231	3 0 0 0 —				3 0 0 0 —

Cash is received and is debited. **Unearned Sales Revenue** is a liability account and is credited. This account indicates that the firm has an obligation to deliver merchandise inventory in the future.

United Auto Supply delivers $1,500 of the merchandise in October 19XX. We'll use T accounts again to demonstrate this adjusting entry:

Unearned Sales Revenue		Sales
	(10/1 Bal.) 3,000	
(f) 1,500		(f) 1,500
	(10/31 Bal.) 1,500	

ACCRUAL ADJUSTMENTS

From Chapter 4 we remember that an accrual is necessary whenever one or both of the following situations occur:

1. Expenses are incurred but unrecorded.
2. Revenues are earned but unrecorded.

The accrual adjustment that will be examined for United Auto Supply is for an expense that has been incurred but is not yet recorded.

Wages Expense Adjustment (g)   United Auto Supply pays its employees every week on Friday. October 31, 19XX, the last day of the accounting period, was on a Wednesday:

October 19XX

S	M	T	W	T	F	S
	1	2	3	4	5	6
7	8	9	10	11	12	13
14	15	16	17	18	19	20
21	22	23	24	25	26	27
28	29	30	(31)	1	(2)	

Last Day of Accounting Period ⟶

(2) ⟵ Payday

If an adjusting entry is not made, then five days (Saturday to Wednesday) of Wages Expense will be entered in the November accounting records. An accrual type of adjusting entry is necessary, since the actual cash payment of wages and salaries will not be made until Friday, November 2, 19XX. Let's use T accounts to demonstrate this adjusting entry:

Wages Expense	Wages Payable
(g) 1,600	(g) 1,600

THE WORKSHEET

Objective 2
Prepare a worksheet for a merchandising firm.

The trial balance is prepared directly from the general ledger accounts. It is entered on a ten-column worksheet in Exhibit 11-1. (Notice that Merchandise Inventory, a balance sheet account, is included.)

Trial Balance Columns of the Worksheet

In Exhibit 11-1, the trial balance as of October 31, 19XX, before adjustments, is entered on the worksheet. You should add the columns again to make sure that total debits equal total credits before you go on.

Adjustments Columns of the Worksheet

In Exhibit 11-2, the adjustments prepared earlier in this chapter are entered on the worksheet. Each adjustment is consecutively lettered. Some adjustments may need accounts that have not been previously used in the Trial Balance. These accounts should be listed below the Trial Balance in order of usage. But do not try to list these added accounts in chart-of-accounts order, since this is unnecessary, and, if you have a large number of Adjustments, an error could easily occur.

The two Adjustments columns must be totaled, and total debits must equal total credits before you continue to the Adjusted Trial Balance.

Adjusted Trial Balance Columns

Once the Trial Balance and Adjustments columns are entered and totaled, the Adjusted Trial Balance columns are prepared (see Exhibit 11-3). This step is crucial, as an error here can cause the Income Statement and Balance Sheet columns to be incorrect. Those accounts with no adjustments (such as Cash, Sales Discounts, and so on) should be extended to the proper Adjusted Trial Balance column with their balance "as is." Those accounts that have adjustments (such as Prepaid Insurance, Wages Expense, and so on) should be added or subtracted. The resulting balances are extended to the Adjusted Trial Balance. The Adjusted Trial Balance columns are then added, and total debits must equal total credits before you proceed to the next step. At this time it would also be a good idea to make sure that all account balances are normal, that is, Cash is a debit, Notes Payable is a credit, and so on.

Income Statement and Balance Sheet Columns

In Exhibit 11-4 we will extend the Adjusted Trial Balance account balances to the appropriate Debit or Credit column of the Income Statement or Balance Sheet columns. We have done this before in Chapter 4, so you should be familiar with this procedure. However, since we have not prepared a worksheet with Merchandise Inventory, we should examine the steps to account for merchandise inventory on the worksheet:

1. Determine the ending balance of Merchandise Inventory for the accounting period.
2. Enter the adjusting entry for beginning Merchandise Inventory on the worksheet. The beginning Merchandise Inventory balance is debited to Income Summary and credited to Merchandise Inventory. At this time Merchandise Inventory will have a zero balance.
3. Enter the adjusting entry for ending Merchandise Inventory on the worksheet. The ending Merchandise Inventory balance is debited to Merchandise Inventory and credited to Income Summary.
4. The balances of Merchandise Inventory (second line below Cash) are added and subtracted. The resulting balance is the ending Merchandise Inventory balance for the accounting period. This amount is extended to the Debit column of the Adjusted Trial Balance and Balance Sheet.
5. The Income Summary debit and credit amounts are extended "as is" to the Adjusted Trial Balance and Income Statement columns.

Account	Trial Balance		Adjustments	
	Debit	Credit	Debit	Credit
Cash	8 7 7 8 —			
Accounts Receivable	15 8 3 7 —			
Merchandise Inventory	8 2 0 9 —			
Office Supplies	2 7 0 0 —			
Prepaid Insurance	4 5 0 —			
Office Equipment	15 5 0 0 —			
Accumulated Depreciation, Office Equipment		6 0 0 —		
Accounts Payable		8 8 0 0 —		
Notes Payable (long term)		2 1 0 0 —		
Unearned Sales Revenue		3 0 0 0 —		
Lucille Garcia, Capital		34 1 0 0 —		
Lucille Garcia, Drawing	1 2 0 0 —			
Sales		41 2 0 0 —		
Sales Returns and Allowances	7 8 —			
Sales Discounts	1 2 2 —			
Interest Income		1 7 0 —		
Purchases	23 1 0 0 —			
Purchases Returns and Allowances		4 0 0 —		
Purchases Discounts		1 4 4 —		
Freight In	2 4 5 0 —			
Rent Expense	1 7 0 0 —			
Wages Expense	9 9 9 8 —			
Advertising Expense	1 9 0 —			
Utilities Expense	1 9 5 —			
Bank Service Expense	7 —			
Totals	90 5 1 4 —	90 5 1 4 —		

11-1
the Worksheet

Supply

sheet

October 31, 19XX

Adjusted Trial Balance		Income Statement		Balance Sheet	
Debit	Credit	Debit	Credit	Debit	Credit

Account	Trial Balance		Adjustments	
	Debit	Credit	Debit	Credit
Cash	8 7 7 8 —			
Accounts Receivable	15 8 3 7 —			
Merchandise Inventory	8 2 0 9 —		(b) 8 2 8 5 —	(a) 8 2 0 9 —
Office Supplies	2 7 0 0 —			(c) 2 0 0 —
Prepaid Insurance	4 5 0 —			(d) 1 5 0 —
Office Equipment	15 5 0 0 —			
Accumulated Depreciation, Office Equipment		6 0 0 —		(e) 3 0 0 —
Accounts Payable		8 8 0 0 —		
Notes Payable (long term)		2 1 0 0 —		
Unearned Sales Revenue		3 0 0 0 —	(f) 1 5 0 0 —	
Lucille Garcia, Capital		34 1 0 0 —		
Lucille Garcia, Drawing	1 2 0 0 —			
Sales		41 2 0 0 —		(f) 1 5 0 0 —
Sales Returns and Allowances	7 8 —			
Sales Discounts	1 2 2 —			
Interest Income		1 7 0 —		
Purchases	23 1 0 0 —			
Purchases Returns and Allowances		4 0 0 —		
Purchases Discounts		1 4 4 —		
Freight In	2 4 5 0 —			
Rent Expense	1 7 0 0 —			
Wages Expense	9 9 9 8 —		(g) 1 6 0 0 —	
Advertising Expense	1 9 0 —			
Utilities Expense	1 9 5 —			
Bank Service Expense	7 —			
Totals	90 5 1 4 —	90 5 1 4 —		
Income Summary			(a) 8 2 0 9 —	(b) 8 2 8 5 —
Office Supplies Expense			(c) 2 0 0 —	
Insurance Expense			(d) 1 5 0 —	
Depreciation Expense, Office Equipment			(e) 3 0 0 —	
Wages Payable				(g) 1 6 0 0 —
			20 2 4 4 —	20 2 4 4 —

11-2
on the Worksheet

Supply

sheet

October 31, 19XX

Adjusted Trial Balance		Income Statement		Balance Sheet	
Debit	Credit	Debit	Credit	Debit	Credit

EXHIBIT
Adjusted Trial Balance Columns

United Auto
Work
For the Month Ended

Account	Trial Balance Debit	Trial Balance Credit	Adjustments Debit	Adjustments Credit
Cash	8 7 7 8 —			
Accounts Receivable	15 8 3 7 —			
Merchandise Inventory	8 2 0 9 —		(b) 8 2 8 5 —	(a) 8 2 0 9 —
Office Supplies	2 7 0 0 —			(c) 2 0 0 —
Prepaid Insurance	4 5 0 —			(d) 1 5 0 —
Office Equipment	15 5 0 0 —			
Accumulated Depreciation, Office Equipment		6 0 0 —		(e) 3 0 0 —
Accounts Payable		8 8 0 0 —		
Notes Payable (long term)		2 1 0 0 —		
Unearned Sales Revenue		3 0 0 0 —	(f) 1 5 0 0 —	
Lucille Garcia, Capital		34 1 0 0 —		
Lucille Garcia, Drawing	1 2 0 0 —			
Sales		41 2 0 0 —		(f) 1 5 0 0 —
Sales Returns and Allowances	7 8 —			
Sales Discounts	1 2 2 —			
Interest Income		1 7 0 —		
Purchases	23 1 0 0 —			
Purchases Returns and Allowances		4 0 0 —		
Purchases Discounts		1 4 4 —		
Freight In	2 4 5 0 —			
Rent Expense	1 7 0 0 —			
Wages Expense	9 9 9 8 —		(g) 1 6 0 0 —	
Advertising Expense	1 9 0 —			
Utilities Expense	1 9 5 —			
Bank Service Expense	7 —			
Totals	90 5 1 4 —	90 5 1 4 —		
Income Summary			(a) 8 2 0 9 —	(b) 8 2 8 5 —
Office Supplies Expense			(c) 2 0 0 —	
Insurance Expense			(d) 1 5 0 —	
Depreciation Expense, Office Equipment			(e) 3 0 0 —	
Wages Payable				(g) 1 6 0 0 —
			20 2 4 4 —	20 2 4 4 —

11-3
on the Worksheet

Supply

sheet

October 31, 19XX

Adjusted Trial Balance		Income Statement		Balance Sheet	
Debit	Credit	Debit	Credit	Debit	Credit
8 7 7 8 —					
15 8 3 7 —					
8 2 8 5 —					
2 5 0 0 —					
3 0 0 —					
15 5 0 0 —					
	9 0 0 —				
	8 8 0 0 —				
	2 1 0 0 —				
	1 5 0 0 —				
	34 1 0 0 —				
1 2 0 0 —					
	42 7 0 0 —				
7 8 —					
1 2 2 —					
	1 7 0 —				
23 1 0 0 —					
	4 0 0 —				
	1 4 4 —				
2 4 5 0 —					
1 7 0 0 —					
11 5 9 8 —					
1 9 0 —					
1 9 5 —					
7 —					
8 2 0 9 —	8 2 8 5 —				
2 0 0 —					
1 5 0 —					
3 0 0 —					
	1 6 0 0 —				
100 6 9 9 —	100 6 9 9 —				

EXHIBIT
Income Statement and

United Auto
Work
For the Month Ended

Account	Trial Balance				Adjustments				
	Debit			Credit		Debit		Credit	
Cash	8 7 7 8 —								
Accounts Receivable	15 8 3 7 —								
Merchandise Inventory	8 2 0 9 —				(b) 8 2 8 5 —		(a) 8 2 0 9 —	
Office Supplies	2 7 0 0 —						(c) 2 0 0 —	
Prepaid Insurance	4 5 0 —						(d) 1 5 0 —	
Office Equipment	15 5 0 0 —							
Accumulated Depreciation, Office Equipment			6 0 0 —				(e) 3 0 0 —	
Accounts Payable			8 8 0 0 —					
Notes Payable (long term)			2 1 0 0 —					
Unearned Sales Revenue			3 0 0 0 —	(f) 1 5 0 0 —				
Lucille Garcia, Capital			34 1 0 0 —					
Lucille Garcia, Drawing	1 2 0 0 —							
Sales			41 2 0 0 —				(f) 1 5 0 0 —	
Sales Returns and Allowances	7 8 —							
Sales Discounts	1 2 2 —							
Interest Income			1 7 0 —					
Purchases	23 1 0 0 —							
Purchases Returns and Allowances			4 0 0 —					
Purchases Discounts			1 4 4 —					
Freight In	2 4 5 0 —							
Rent Expense	1 7 0 0 —							
Wages Expense	9 9 9 8 —				(g) 1 6 0 0 —			
Advertising Expense	1 9 0 —							
Utilities Expense	1 9 5 —							
Bank Service Expense	7 —							
Totals	90 5 1 4 —		90 5 1 4 —					
Income Summary					(a) 8 2 0 9 —		(b) 8 2 8 5 —	
Office Supplies Expense					(c) 2 0 0 —			
Insurance Expense					(d) 1 5 0 —			
Depreciation Expense, Office Equipment					(e) 3 0 0 —			
Wages Payable							(g) 1 6 0 0 —	
					20 2 4 4 —		20 2 4 4 —	
Net Income								

11-4
Balance Sheet Columns

Supply

sheet

October 31, 19XX

Adjusted Trial Balance		Income Statement		Balance Sheet	
Debit	Credit	Debit	Credit	Debit	Credit
8 7 7 8 —				8 7 7 8 —	
15 8 3 7 —				15 8 3 7 —	
8 2 8 5 —				8 2 8 5 —	
2 5 0 0 —				2 5 0 0 —	
3 0 0 —				3 0 0 —	
15 5 0 0 —				15 5 0 0 —	
	9 0 0 —				9 0 0 —
	8 8 0 0 —				8 8 0 0 —
	2 1 0 0 —				2 1 0 0 —
	1 5 0 0 —				1 5 0 0 —
	34 1 0 0 —				34 1 0 0 —
1 2 0 0 —				1 2 0 0 —	
	42 7 0 0 —		42 7 0 0 —		
7 8 —		7 8 —			
1 2 2 —		1 2 2 —			
	1 7 0 —		1 7 0 —		
23 1 0 0 —		23 1 0 0 —			
	4 0 0 —		4 0 0 —		
	1 4 4 —		1 4 4 —		
2 4 5 0 —		2 4 5 0 —			
1 7 0 0 —		1 7 0 0 —			
11 5 9 8 —		11 5 9 8 —			
1 9 0 —		1 9 0 —			
1 9 5 —		1 9 5 —			
7 —		7 —			
8 2 0 9 —	8 2 8 5 —	8 2 0 9 —	8 2 8 5 —		
2 0 0 —		2 0 0 —			
1 5 0 —		1 5 0 —			
3 0 0 —		3 0 0 —			
	1 6 0 0 —				1 6 0 0 —
100 6 9 9 —	100 6 9 9 —	48 2 9 9 —	51 6 9 9 —	52 4 0 0 —	49 0 0 0 —
		3 4 0 0 —			3 4 0 0 —
		51 6 9 9 —	51 6 9 9 —	52 4 0 0 —	52 4 0 0 —

Referring to Exhibit 11-4, the Income Statement and Balance Sheet columns are added and totaled. Net income or net loss places the worksheet in balance.

Finding and Correcting Worksheet Errors

In Chapter 4 we examined some errors that could occur when the worksheet is prepared. Whenever you discover an error, you should follow these steps:

1. Read the columns to make sure the error was not due to incorrect addition.
2. Make sure that net income or net loss is correct. The net income or net loss should place the worksheet in balance.
3. Check to see if all account balances are normal, that is, Cash has a debit balance, Notes Payable a credit balance, and so on.
4. Also check to see if beginning and ending Merchandise Inventory were properly eliminated and restated, respectively.

You must correct any errors before you prepare financial statements.

JOURNALIZING AND POSTING ADJUSTMENTS

Objective 3
Journalize and post adjusting entries.

Adjusting entries provide a means of placing assets, liabilities, owner's equity, revenue, cost of goods sold, and expense accounts at their proper balances for the accounting period. Adjusting entries are not journalized and posted until the worksheet is complete. This way you can see the "full picture" of how the financial statements will look. By looking at the completed worksheet, you can determine if any additional accounts are to be adjusted. Once you are satisfied with the account balances on the worksheet, you can journalize and post adjusting entries. The adjusting entries are taken directly from the Adjustments columns of the worksheet. The adjusting entries as calculated earlier in this chapter are as follows:

a. Adjust Beginning Inventory.
b. Adjust Ending Inventory.
c. Adjust Office Supplies.
d. Adjust Prepaid Insurance.
e. Adjust Office Equipment.
f. Adjust Unearned Revenue.
g. Adjust Wages Expense.

These seven adjusting entries are journalized in the general journal in Exhibit 11-5 and posted to the general ledger in Exhibit 11-6. You should

EXHIBIT 11-5
Journalizing Adjusting Entries

GENERAL JOURNAL   Page ___28___

Date		Description	Post. Ref.	Debit	Credit
		Adjusting Entries			
19XX					
Oct.	31	Income Summary	321	8 2 0 9 —	
		Merchandise Inventory	121		8 2 0 9 —
	31	Merchandise Inventory	121	8 2 8 5 —	
		Income Summary	321		8 2 8 5 —
	31	Office Supplies Expense	641	2 0 0 —	
		Office Supplies	131		2 0 0 —
	31	Insurance Expense	651	1 5 0 —	
		Prepaid Insurance	135		1 5 0 —
	31	Depreciation Expense, Office Equipment	661	3 0 0 —	
		Accumulated Depreciation, Office Equipment	142		3 0 0 —
	31	Unearned Sales Revenue	231	1 5 0 0 —	
		Sales	401		1 5 0 0 —
	31	Wages Expense	611	1 6 0 0 —	
		Wages Payable	211		1 6 0 0 —

indicate in the general journal and general ledger that these entries and postings are from adjusting entries. In the general journal you would write "Adjusting Entries" in the Description column before the first adjustment is entered. You would not need to write a description for each adjusting entry since you have indicated that they are adjusting entries. When you post the adjusting entry to the general ledger you would write "Adjusting" in the Item column. You are then able to distinguish adjusting entries from other entries.

These adjusting entries are posted to the general ledger in Exhibit 11-6, but only those general ledger accounts that are used for this posting process are listed.

EXHIBIT 11-6
General Ledger Accounts Used to Post Adjusting Entries

Account: *Merchandise Inventory*   **Account No.** *121*

Date		Item	Post. Ref.	Debit	Credit	Balance Debit	Balance Credit
19XX		Previous Balance				8 2 0 9 —	
Oct.	31	Adjusting	J28		8 2 0 9 —	— 0 —	
	31	Adjusting	J28	8 2 8 5 —		8 2 8 5 —	

Account: *Office Supplies*   **Account No.** *131*

Date		Item	Post. Ref.	Debit	Credit	Balance Debit	Balance Credit
19XX		Previous Balance				2 7 0 0 —	
Oct.	31	Adjusting	J28		2 0 0 —	2 5 0 0 —	

Account: *Prepaid Insurance*   **Account No.** *135*

Date		Item	Post. Ref.	Debit	Credit	Balance Debit	Balance Credit
19XX		Previous Balance				4 5 0 —	
Oct.	31	Adjusting	J28		1 5 0 —	3 0 0 —	

Account: *Accumulated Depreciation, Office Equipment*   **Account No.** *142*

Date		Item	Post. Ref.	Debit	Credit	Balance Debit	Balance Credit
19XX		Previous Balance					6 0 0 —
Oct.	31	Adjusting	J28		3 0 0 —		9 0 0 —

(continued)

(Ex. 11-6 continued)

Account: Wages Payable								Account No. 211	
Date	Item	Post. Ref.	Debit	Credit	Balance Debit		Balance Credit		
19XX	Previous Balance						— 0 —		
Oct. 31	Adjusting	J28		1600 —			1600 —		

Account: Unearned Sales Revenue								Account No. 231	
Date	Item	Post. Ref.	Debit	Credit	Balance Debit		Balance Credit		
19XX	Previous Balance						3000 —		
Oct. 31	Adjusting	J28	1500 —				1500 —		

Account: Income Summary								Account No. 321	
Date	Item	Post. Ref.	Debit	Credit	Balance Debit		Balance Credit		
19XX	Previous Balance				— 0 —		— 0 —		
Oct. 31	Adjusting	J28	8209 —		8209 —				
31	Adjusting	J28		8285 —			76 —		

Account: Sales								Account No. 401	
Date	Item	Post. Ref.	Debit	Credit	Balance Debit		Balance Credit		
19XX	Previous Balance						41200 —		
Oct. 31	Adjusting	J28		1500 —			42700 —		

(continued)

(Ex. 11-6 concluded)

Account: Wages Expense						Account No. 611
Date	Item	Post. Ref.	Debit	Credit	Balance Debit	Balance Credit
19XX	Previous Balance				9 9 9 8 —	
Oct. 31	Adjusting	J28	1 6 0 0 —		1 1 5 9 8 —	

Account: Office Supplies Expense						Account No. 641
Date	Item	Post. Ref.	Debit	Credit	Balance Debit	Balance Credit
19XX	Previous Balance				— 0 —	
Oct. 31	Adjusting	J28	2 0 0 —		2 0 0 —	

Account: Insurance Expense						Account No. 651
Date	Item	Post. Ref.	Debit	Credit	Balance Debit	Balance Credit
19XX	Previous Balance				— 0 —	
Oct. 31	Adjusting	J28	1 5 0 —		1 5 0 —	

Account: Depreciation Expense, Office Equipment						Account No. 661
Date	Item	Post. Ref.	Debit	Credit	Balance Debit	Balance Credit
19XX	Previous Balance				— 0 —	
Oct. 31	Adjusting	J28	3 0 0 —		3 0 0 —	

CHAPTER REVIEW

1. **Calculate adjustments (pp. 354–58).**
   When the periodic inventory method is used, you must count the actual amount of merchandise inventory on hand at the end of the accounting period. This actual amount becomes the ending balance of Merchandise Inventory for the accounting period. Therefore, the beginning balance of Merchandise Inventory must be eliminated.

   Many firms receive payment for revenues in advance, before the revenues are actually earned. This is a "deferral-revenue" type of adjustment.

2. **Prepare a worksheet for a merchandising firm (pp. 358–68).**
   A worksheet is prepared for a merchandising firm by (a) listing the trial balance on the worksheet; (b) entering the adjustments in the Adjustments columns; (c) extending the Trial Balance columns and the Adjustments columns to the Adjusted Trial Balance columns; and (d) extending the account balances to the appropriate Income Statement and Balance Sheet columns.

3. **Journalize and post adjusting entries (pp. 368–72).**
   Adjusting entries are not journalized and posted until the worksheet is complete. This way you can see the "full picture" of how the financial statements will look. By looking at the completed worksheet, you can determine if any additional accounts are to be adjusted. Once you are satisfied with the account balances on the worksheet, you can journalize and post adjusting entries. The adjusting entries are taken directly from the Adjustments columns of the worksheet.

GLOSSARY

Unearned Sales Revenue Obligation to deliver merchandise inventory in the future. A liability account.

SELF-TEST QUESTIONS FOR REVIEW

(Answers are on p. 391.)

1. Which of the following accounts is debited in the adjusting entry to eliminate merchandise inventory?
   a. Merchandise Inventory
   b. Income Summary
   c. Owner, Capital
   d. Accounts Receivable
2. Cash would probably be listed on which of the following columns on a completed ten-column worksheet?
   a. Trial Balance, Credit
   b. Balance Sheet, Credit
   c. Balance Sheet, Debit
   d. Income Statement, Debit
3. The account _____ is credited in the adjusting entry to adjust Unearned Revenue.
   a. Sales
   b. Wages Payable
   c. Income Summary
   d. Unearned Sales Revenue
4. Which of the following is an accrual adjustment?
   a. Adjust Office Supplies
   b. Adjust Prepaid Insurance
   c. Adjust Unearned Revenue
   d. Adjust Wages Expense
5. The account _____ is debited in the adjusting entry to adjust ending Merchandise Inventory.
   a. Owner, Capital
   b. Merchandise Inventory
   c. Income Summary
   d. Accounts Payable

PRACTICAL REVIEW PROBLEM

Objective 2

Completing a Worksheet   H. M. Tovar is the owner of Tovar Clothing Store. He had the following partial worksheet.

Tovar Clothing Store
Worksheet (partial)
For the Month Ended April 30, 19XX

Account	Trial Balance Debit	Trial Balance Credit	Adjusted Trial Balance Debit	Adjusted Trial Balance Credit
Cash	2 5 1 8 —		2 5 1 8 —	
Merchandise Inventory	1 2 1 6 —		2 5 8 8 —	
Office Supplies	1 4 1 2 —		1 2 6 8 —	
Prepaid Insurance	1 8 0 0 —		1 5 1 2 —	
Furniture	12 0 0 0 —		12 0 0 0 —	
Notes Payable (long-term)		5 8 0 0 —		5 8 0 0 —
Unearned Sales Revenue		3 8 8 3 —		3 6 2 0 —
H. M. Tovar, Capital		9 3 2 4 —		9 3 2 4 —
H. M. Tovar, Drawing	1 0 9 9 —		1 0 9 9 —	
Sales		5 9 6 9 —		6 2 3 2 —
Sales Returns and Allowances	2 1 7 —		2 1 7 —	
Sales Discounts	6 4 —		6 4 —	
Purchases	3 6 6 2 —		3 6 6 2 —	
Purchases Returns and Allowances		1 2 6 —		1 2 6 —
Purchases Discounts		9 8 —		9 8 —
Freight In	1 0 0 —		1 0 0 —	
Wages Expense	1 1 1 2 —		1 3 9 0 —	
Totals	25 2 0 0 —	25 2 0 0 —		
Income Summary			1 2 1 6 —	2 5 8 8 —
Office Supplies Expense			1 4 4 —	
Insurance Expense			2 8 8 —	
Depreciation Expense, Furniture			1 1 0 —	
Accumulated Depreciation, Furniture				1 1 0 —
Wages Payable				2 7 8 —
			28 1 7 6 —	28 1 7 6 —
Net Income				

REQUIRED

1. Using the Trial Balance and Adjusted Trial Balance columns, calculate and place adjusting entries in the Adjustments columns of the worksheet (use the sequence as illustrated in the chapter).

2. Complete the worksheet.

ANSWER TO PRACTICAL REVIEW PROBLEM

1 and 2.

Tovar Clothing
Work
For the Month Ended

Account	Trial Balance Debit	Trial Balance Credit	Adjustments Debit	Adjustments Credit
Cash	2518 —			
Merchandise Inventory	1216 —		(b) 2588 —	(a) 1216 —
Office Supplies	1412 —			(c) 144 —
Prepaid Insurance	1800 —			(d) 288 —
Furniture	12000 —			
Notes Payable (long-term)		5800 —		
Unearned Sales Revenue		3883 —	(f) 263 —	
H. M. Tovar, Capital		9324 —		
H. M. Tovar, Drawing	1099 —			
Sales		5969 —		(f) 263 —
Sales Returns and Allowances	217 —			
Sales Discounts	64 —			
Purchases	3662 —			
Purchases Returns and Allowances		126 —		
Purchases Discounts		98 —		
Freight In	100 —			
Wages Expense	1112 —		(g) 278 —	
Totals	25200 —	25200 —		
Income Summary			(a) 1216 —	(b) 2588 —
Office Supplies Expense			(c) 144 —	
Insurance Expense			(d) 288 —	
Depreciation Expense, Furniture			(e) 110 —	
Accumulated Depreciation, Furniture				(e) 110 —
Wages Payable				(g) 278 —
			4887 —	4887 —
Net Income				

Store

sheet

April 30, 19XX

Adjusted Trial Balance		Income Statement		Balance Sheet	
Debit	Credit	Debit	Credit	Debit	Credit
2 5 1 8 —				2 5 1 8 —	
2 5 8 8 —				2 5 8 8 —	
1 2 6 8 —				1 2 6 8 —	
1 5 1 2 —				1 5 1 2 —	
12 0 0 0 —				12 0 0 0 —	
	5 8 0 0 —				5 8 0 0 —
	3 6 2 0 —				3 6 2 0 —
	9 3 2 4 —				9 3 2 4 —
1 0 9 9 —				1 0 9 9 —	
	6 2 3 2 —		6 2 3 2 —		
2 1 7 —		2 1 7 —			
6 4 —		6 4 —			
3 6 6 2 —		3 6 6 2 —			
	1 2 6 —		1 2 6 —		
	9 8 —		9 8 —		
1 0 0 —		1 0 0 —			
1 3 9 0 —		1 3 9 0 —			
1 2 1 6 —	2 5 8 8 —	1 2 1 6 —	2 5 8 8 —		
1 4 4 —		1 4 4 —			
2 8 8 —		2 8 8 —			
1 1 0 —		1 1 0 —			
	1 1 0 —				1 1 0 —
	2 7 8 —				2 7 8 —
28 1 7 6 —	28 1 7 6 —	7 1 9 1 —	9 0 4 4 —	20 9 8 5 —	19 1 3 2 —
		1 8 5 3 —			1 8 5 3 —
		9 0 4 4 —	9 0 4 4 —	20 9 8 5 —	20 9 8 5 —

DISCUSSION QUESTIONS

Q 11-1 Briefly explain the adjusting entries that are necessary to close and open Merchandise Inventory.

Q 11-2 Why is Income Summary used to record the opening and closing balances of Merchandise Inventory in an accounting period?

Q 11-3 How are adjustments for beginning and ending Merchandise Inventory entered on the worksheet?

Q 11-4 Explain why the Adjusted Trial Balance columns are necessary to complete a worksheet.

Q 11-5 Name and briefly discuss the three types of adjusting entries discussed in this chapter. (Hint: One type is accruals).

Q 11-6 Name the columns used in a worksheet for a merchandising firm, starting with the Trial Balance columns.

Q 11-7 Briefly describe the procedure (steps) in preparing a worksheet, starting with the Trial Balance.

Q 11-8 If you were the accountant for a merchandising firm, what adjusting entries would you probably have at the end of each accounting period?

Q 11-9 Name and briefly discuss the procedures (steps) for finding and correcting worksheet errors.

Q 11-10 Name the five steps to account for Merchandise Inventory on the worksheet.

EXERCISES

Objective 1   E 11-1 Adjusting Merchandise Inventory Use T accounts to record the following adjustments: (a) beginning merchandise inventory was $75,000 and (b) ending merchandise inventory is $80,000.

Objective 2   E 11-2 Determining Account Placements   Find the placement (Column, Debit or Credit) of the following accounts on a completed worksheet for a merchandising firm. Assume adjustments for merchandise inventory and earned sales revenue. The first is completed for you.

0. Cash—Trial Balance, Debit; Adjusted Trial Balance, Debit; and Balance Sheet, Debit.
a. Merchandise Inventory.
b. Notes Payable (long-term).
c. Unearned Sales Revenue.
d. Sales.
e. Income Summary.

Objective 3   **E 11-3**   **Describing Adjusting Entries** Describe in your own words the following adjusting entries (in random order) for April 30, 19XX:

GENERAL JOURNAL   Page _____5_____

Date		Description	Post. Ref.	Debit	Credit
		Adjusting Entries			
19XX					
Apr.	30	Unearned Sales Revenue	231	6 0 0 —	
		Sales	401		6 0 0 —
	30	Income Summary	322	3 8 0 0 —	
		Merchandise Inventory	129		3 8 0 0 —
	30	Depreciation Expense, Truck	678	3 0 0 —	
		Accumulated Depreciation, Truck	146		3 0 0 —
	30	Wages Expense	603	1 9 0 0 —	
		Wages Payable	222		1 9 0 0 —
	30	Insurance Expense	641	2 0 0 —	
		Prepaid Insurance	125		2 0 0 —
	30	Merchandise Inventory	129	4 9 0 0 —	
		Income Summary	322		4 9 0 0 —
	30	Office Supplies Expense	666	4 0 0 —	
		Office Supplies	131		4 0 0 —

Objective 1   **E 11-4**   **Adjusting Equipment and Earned Revenue** Consider the following adjustments for the month ended January 31, 19XX:

a. Equipment costs $18,840 and is estimated to have a $3,000 salvage value at the end of its useful life of six years. Illustrate this adjustment using T accounts. (Use the straight-line method.)

b. On January 3, 19XX, a firm received $3,800 from Parsons, Inc. for future sales of merchandise. During the month, the firm delivers $1,200 of merchandise to Parsons, Inc. In your answer (a) record the receipt of cash in a cash receipts journal, page 4, and (b) illustrate the adjusting entry using T accounts.

Objective 1   **E 11-5   Illustrating Adjusting Entries**   Use T accounts to illustrate the following adjustments:
a. Store Supplies used, $400.
b. Adjust Prepaid Insurance, $100.
c. Depreciation of truck, $200.
d. A total of $700 of previously Unearned Sales Revenue was earned.
e. Accrued Wages Expense, $900.

Objective 2   **E 11-6   Completing a Worksheet**   Complete a worksheet for Clancy Enterprises for August 31, 19XX. Notice that the adjusting entries are included.

Clancy Enterprises
Worksheet (partial)
For the Month Ended August 31, 19XX

Account	Trial Balance Debit	Trial Balance Credit	Adjustments Debit	Adjustments Credit
Cash	3 8 —			
Merchandise Inventory	1 8 —		(b) 2 2 —	(a) 1 8 —
Unearned Sales Revenue		2 1 —	(c) 5 —	
Oliver Clancy, Capital		2 9 —		
Oliver Clancy, Drawing	5 —			
Sales		9 6 —		(c) 5 —
Sales Returns and Allowances	8 —			
Sales Discounts	4 —			
Purchases	6 7 —			
Purchases Returns and Allowances		9 —		
Purchases Discounts		5 —		
Freight In	6 —			
Wages Expense	1 4 —		(d) 3 —	
Totals	1 6 0 —	1 6 0 —		
Income Summary			(a) 1 8 —	(b) 2 2 —
Wages Payable				(d) 3 —

Objective 3   **E 11-7   Journalizing Adjusting Entries**   Record the following adjusting entries in a general journal, page 19, for the month ended June 30, 19XX:
a. Merchandise Inventory on June 1, 19XX, was $9,200.
b. Merchandise Inventory on June 30, 19XX, was $7,900.

c. Office Supplies used during the month, $400.

d. Insurance Expense was $200 for the month.

e. Depreciation of an automobile, $300.

f. Earned $2,100 of previously unearned sales revenues.

g. Wages Expense incurred, but not paid, $3,400.

Objective 2   **E 11-8**   **Completing a Worksheet**   Complete the worksheet for Robinson Supply for April 30, 19XX, using the following adjusting entries and Trial Balance:

a. April 1, 19XX, Merchandise Inventory was $18.

b. April 30, 19XX, Merchandise Inventory was $19.

c. Depreciation Expense, Truck, $2.

d. Unearned Sales Revenue of $11 was earned.

e. Wages Expense incurred but not paid was $17.

Robinson Supply

Worksheet (partial)

For the Month Ended April 30, 19XX

Account	Trial Balance	
	Debit	**Credit**
Cash	4 4 —	
Accounts Receivable	2 1 —	
Merchandise Inventory	1 8 —	
Truck	9 6 —	
Accumulated Depreciation, Truck		1 2 —
Unearned Sales Revenue		1 5 —
G. W. Robinson, Capital		1 4 0 —
G. W. Robinson, Drawing	1 3 —	
Sales		1 1 3 —
Sales Returns and Allowances	6 —	
Sales Discounts	3 —	
Purchases	5 3 —	
Purchases Returns and Allowances		7 —
Purchases Discounts		4 —
Freight In	3 —	
Wages Expense	3 4 —	
Totals	2 9 1 —	2 9 1 —

PROBLEM SET A

Objective 2   P 11-1A   Completing a Worksheet   Gunnels Pharmacy is owned by David Gunnels. He had the following Trial Balance and Adjustments columns of the worksheet for October 31, 19XX:

Gunnels Pharmacy

Worksheet (partial)

For the Month Ended October 31, 19XX

Account	Trial Balance Debit	Trial Balance Credit	Adjustments Debit	Adjustments Credit
Cash	21 9 0 0 —			
Accounts Receivable	17 4 0 0 —			
Merchandise Inventory	9 6 0 0 —		(b) 9 8 0 0 —	(a) 9 6 0 0 —
Office Supplies	5 7 0 0 —			(c) 2 2 0 0 —
Prepaid Insurance	3 8 0 0 —			(d) 5 0 0 —
Delivery Truck	26 3 0 0 —			
Accumulated Depreciation, Delivery Truck		5 4 0 0 —		(e) 2 0 0 —
Accounts Payable		16 3 0 0 —		
Unearned Sales Revenue		2 8 0 0 —	(f) 1 7 0 0 —	
David Gunnels, Capital		56 0 0 0 —		
David Gunnels, Drawing	1 5 0 0 —			
Sales		29 7 0 0 —		(f) 1 7 0 0 —
Sales Returns and Allowances	1 6 0 0 —			
Purchases	15 1 0 0 —			
Purchases Returns and Allowances		9 0 0 —		
Freight In	1 2 0 0 —			
Wages Expense	6 3 0 0 —		(g) 8 0 0 —	
Rent Expense	7 0 0 —			
Totals	111 1 0 0 —	111 1 0 0 —		
Income Summary			(a) 9 6 0 0 —	(b) 9 8 0 0 —
Office Supplies Expense			(c) 2 2 0 0 —	
Insurance Expense			(d) 5 0 0 —	
Depreciation Expense, Delivery Truck			(e) 2 0 0 —	
Wages Payable				(g) 8 0 0 —
			24 8 0 0 —	24 8 0 0 —

REQUIRED

Complete the worksheet.

Objective 3   **P 11-2A**   **Journalizing and Posting Adjustments**   Sawyer Software Supply had the following adjustments and partial chart-of-accounts numbers for the month ended April 30, 19XX.

Adjustments:

a. April 1, 19XX, Merchandise Inventory was $5,700.

b. April 30, 19XX, Merchandise Inventory was $6,100.

c. Office Supplies used during the month, $500.

d. Insurance Expense was $100 for the month.

e. Depreciation of office equipment, $200.

f. Unearned Sales Revenue earned during the month was $900.

g. Accrued Wages Expense, $1,900.

Partial chart-of-accounts numbers (previous balances in parenthesis):

Merchandise Inventory, 131 ($5,700); Office Supplies, 141 ($3,200); Prepaid Insurance, 145 ($2,100); Accumulated Depreciation, Office Equipment, 152 ($1,200); Wages Payable, 211 ($–0–); Unearned Sales Revenue, 241 ($4,600); Income Summary, 331 ($–0–); Sales, 401 ($21,300); Wages Expense, 621 ($3,900); Office Supplies Expense, 651 ($–0–); Insurance Expense, 661 ($–0–); and Depreciation Expense, Office Equipment, 671 ($–0–).

REQUIRED

1. Enter the account names, account numbers, and previous balances in the general ledger.

2. Journalize the adjusting entries in the general journal, page 21.

3. Post the adjusting entries to the general ledger.

Objectives 2 and 3   **P 11-3A**   **Completing a Worksheet and Journalizing Adjustments**   Howard Flowers is the owner of Flowers Music Store. He had the following partial worksheet:

Flowers Music Store
Worksheet (partial)
For the Month Ended March 31, 19XX

Account	Trial Balance Debit	Trial Balance Credit	Adjusted Trial Balance Debit	Adjusted Trial Balance Credit
Cash	5 0 5 0 —		5 0 5 0 —	
Accounts Receivable	1 2 5 0 —		1 2 5 0 —	
Merchandise Inventory	3 9 4 0 —		4 8 9 0 —	
Office Supplies	1 9 8 0 —		9 6 0 —	
Prepaid Insurance	9 5 0 —		7 6 0 —	
Computer	17 5 0 0 —		17 5 0 0 —	
Accumulated Depreciation, Computer		7 5 0 —		1 0 0 0 —
Accounts Payable		3 4 8 0 —		3 4 8 0 —
Unearned Sales Revenue		1 2 8 0 —		5 2 0 —
Howard Flowers, Capital		24 7 2 0 —		24 7 2 0 —
Howard Flowers, Drawing	8 9 0 —		8 9 0 —	
Sales		12 8 9 0 —		13 6 5 0 —
Sales Discounts	2 8 0 —		2 8 0 —	
Purchases	7 6 3 0 —		7 6 3 0 —	
Purchases Discounts		3 8 0 —		3 8 0 —
Freight In	5 8 0 —		5 8 0 —	
Wages Expense	2 8 9 0 —		3 6 3 0 —	
Rent Expense	5 6 0 —		5 6 0 —	
Totals	43 5 0 0 —	43 5 0 0 —		
Income Summary			3 9 4 0 —	4 8 9 0 —
Office Supplies Expense			1 0 2 0 —	
Insurance Expense			1 9 0 —	
Depreciation Expense, Computer			2 5 0 —	
Wages Payable				7 4 0 —
			49 3 8 0 —	49 3 8 0 —
Net Income				

REQUIRED
1. Using the Trial Balance and Adjusted Trial Balance columns, calculate and place adjusting entries in the Adjustments columns of the worksheet (use the sequence as illustrated in the chapter). See the Practical Review Problem if you need help.
2. Complete the worksheet.
3. Journalize the adjusting entries in the general journal, page 26. DO NOT post to the general ledger.

Objectives 1, 2,
and 3

P 11-4A Comprehensive Chapter Review Problem   Elaine Dixon owns Midwest Card Store. She had the following Trial Balance columns of the worksheet and adjusting entries for January 31, 19XX:

Midwest Card Store

Worksheet (partial)

For the Month Ended January 31, 19XX

Account	Trial Balance Debit	Trial Balance Credit
Cash	14 045 —	
Accounts Receivable	2 781 —	
Merchandise Inventory	6 999 —	
Office Supplies	1 612 —	
Prepaid Insurance	2 567 —	
Equipment	17 000 —	
Accumulated Depreciation, Equipment		1 500 —
Accounts Payable		1 003 —
Unearned Sales Revenue		5 770 —
Elaine Dixon, Capital		35 397 —
Elaine Dixon, Drawing	1 200 —	
Sales		13 453 —
Sales Returns and Allowances	335 —	
Sales Discounts	421 —	
Interest Income		1 813 —
Purchases	9 073 —	
Purchases Returns and Allowances		666 —
Purchases Discounts		954 —
Freight In	299 —	
Wages Expense	3 899 —	
Advertising Expense	325 —	
Totals	60 556 —	60 556 —

Adjusting entries:

a. Merchandise Inventory for January 1, 19XX, was $6,999.

b. Merchandise Inventory for January 31, 19XX, was $8,452.

c. An actual count of office supplies on January 31, 19XX revealed $789 on hand.

d. A total of $77 of Prepaid Insurance was used during the month.

e. Equipment cost $17,000 and will have a useful life of ten years. The salvage value is $2,000, and the straight-line method of depreciation is used.

f. A total of $609 of Unearned Sales Revenue was earned during the month.

g. Accrued Wages Expense was $700.

The chart-of-accounts numbers (partial) are: 112, Merchandise Inventory; 125, Office Supplies; 134, Prepaid Insurance; 146, Accumulated Depreciation, Equipment; 208, Wages Payable; 214, Unearned Sales Revenue; 324, Income Summary; 405, Sales; 605, Wages Expense; 631, Office Supplies Expense; 641, Insurance Expense; 651, Depreciation Expense, Equipment.

REQUIRED

1. Complete the worksheet.

2. Journalize the adjusting entries in a general journal, page 36.

3. From the Trial Balance columns on the worksheet, open the previous account balances in the general ledger (include account names and numbers). Post the adjusting entries to the general ledger.

PROBLEM SET B

Objective 2   **P 11-1B**   **Completing a Worksheet**   Torres Marine is owned by Gloria Torres. She had the following Trial Balance and Adjustments columns of the worksheet for January 31, 19XX:

Torres Marine

Worksheet (partial)

For the Month Ended January 31, 19XX

Account	Trial Balance Debit	Trial Balance Credit	Adjustments Debit	Adjustments Credit
Cash	42 7 0 0 —			
Accounts Receivable	25 1 0 0 —			
Merchandise Inventory	31 9 0 0 —		(b) 36 2 0 0 —	(a) 31 9 0 0 —
Office Supplies	12 4 0 0 —			(c) 4 6 0 0 —
Prepaid Insurance	7 6 0 0 —			(d) 3 0 0 —
Automobile	19 3 0 0 —			
Accumulated Depreciation, Automobile		5 6 0 0 —		(e) 4 0 0 —
Accounts Payable		18 5 0 0 —		
Unearned Sales Revenue		7 2 0 0 —	(f) 3 1 0 0 —	
Gloria Torres, Capital		96 3 0 0 —		
Gloria Torres, Drawing	1 3 0 0 —			
Sales		95 8 0 0 —		(f) 3 1 0 0 —
Sales Returns and Allowances	2 1 0 0 —			
Purchases	41 8 0 0 —			
Purchases Returns and Allowances		3 6 0 0 —		
Freight In	3 9 0 0 —			
Wages Expense	36 1 0 0 —		(g) 4 7 0 0 —	
Rent Expense	2 8 0 0 —			
Totals	227 0 0 0 —	227 0 0 0 —		
Income Summary			(a) 31 9 0 0 —	(b) 36 2 0 0 —
Office Supplies Expense			(c) 4 6 0 0 —	
Insurance Expense			(d) 3 0 0 —	
Depreciation Expense, Automobile			(e) 4 0 0 —	
Wages Payable				(g) 4 7 0 0 —
			81 2 0 0 —	81 2 0 0 —

REQUIRED

Complete the worksheet.

Objective 3

P 11-2B **Journalizing and Posting Adjustments** Berkowitz Engine Supply had the following adjustments and partial chart-of-accounts numbers for the month ended November 30, 19XX.

Adjustments:

a. November 1, 19XX, Merchandise Inventory was $9,200.
b. November 30, 19XX, Merchandise Inventory was $9,800.
c. Store Supplies used during the month, $700.
d. Insurance Expense was $200 for the month.
e. Depreciation of office furniture, $300.
f. Unearned Sales Revenue earned during the month was $1,600.
g. Accrued Wages Expense, $3,900.

Partial chart-of-accounts numbers (previous balances in parenthesis):

Merchandise Inventory, 141 ($9,200); Store Supplies, 151 ($6,400); Prepaid Insurance, 153 ($3,500); Accumulated Depreciation, Office Furniture, 162 ($1,800); Wages Payable, 221 ($–0–); Unearned Sales Revenue, 251 ($5,100); Income Summary, 321 ($–0–); Sales, 401 ($31,600); Wages Expense, 631 ($6,700); Store Supplies Expense, 661 ($–0–); Insurance Expense, 671 ($–0–); and Depreciation Expense, Office Furniture, 681 ($–0–).

REQUIRED

1. Enter the account names, account numbers, and previous balances in the general ledger.
2. Journalize the adjusting entries in the general journal, page 34.
3. Post the adjusting entries to the general ledger.

Objectives 2
and 3

P 11-3B Completing a Worksheet and Journalizing Adjustments   P. K. Andrews is the owner of Andrews Grocery Store. She had the following partial worksheet:

Andrews Grocery Store
Worksheet (partial)
For the Month Ended February 28, 19XX

Account	Trial Balance		Adjusted Trial Balance	
	Debit	**Credit**	**Debit**	**Credit**
Cash	7 3 2 0 —		7 3 2 0 —	
Accounts Receivable	1 9 1 0 —		1 9 1 0 —	
Merchandise Inventory	4 7 1 0 —		5 8 2 0 —	
Office Supplies	2 0 8 0 —		1 1 2 0 —	
Prepaid Insurance	2 1 3 0 —		1 8 1 0 —	
Equipment	14 1 4 0 —		14 1 4 0 —	
Accumulated Depreciation, Equipment		4 5 0 —		5 4 0 —
Accounts Payable		2 7 8 0 —		2 7 8 0 —
Unearned Sales Revenue		3 8 7 0 —		2 9 6 0 —
P. K. Andrews, Capital		24 2 5 0 —		24 2 5 0 —
P. K. Andrews, Drawing	9 8 0 —		9 8 0 —	
Sales		16 9 8 0 —		17 8 9 0 —
Sales Discounts	5 1 0 —		5 1 0 —	
Purchases	9 5 6 0 —		9 5 6 0 —	
Purchases Discounts		4 1 0 —		4 1 0 —
Freight In	6 7 0 —		6 7 0 —	
Wages Expense	3 9 0 0 —		4 4 6 0 —	
Rent Expense	8 3 0 —		8 3 0 —	
Totals	48 7 4 0 —	48 7 4 0 —		
Income Summary			4 7 1 0 —	5 8 2 0 —
Office Supplies Expense			9 6 0 —	
Insurance Expense			3 2 0 —	
Depreciation Expense, Equipment			9 0 —	
Wages Payable				5 6 0 —
			55 2 1 0 —	55 2 1 0 —
Net Income				

REQUIRED

1. Using the Trial Balance and Adjusted Trial Balance columns, calculate and place adjusting entries in the Adjustments columns of the worksheet (use the sequence as illustrated in the chapter). See the Practical Review Problem if you need help.
2. Complete the worksheet.
3. Journalize the adjusting entries in the general journal, page 14. DO NOT post to the general ledger.

Objectives 1, 2, and 3

P 11-4B **Comprehensive Chapter Review Problem** Calvin Milton owns Spring River Grocery. He had the following Trial Balance columns and adjusting entries of the worksheet for October 31, 19XX:

Spring River Grocery
Worksheet (partial)
For the Month Ended October 31, 19XX

Account	Trial Balance Debit	Trial Balance Credit
Cash	10 7 5 6 —	
Accounts Receivable	9 8 7 1 —	
Merchandise Inventory	7 9 0 3 —	
Office Supplies	2 7 8 8 —	
Prepaid Insurance	1 5 6 0 —	
Automobile	17 7 0 0 —	
Accumulated Depreciation, Automobile		3 7 8 0 —
Accounts Payable		2 1 6 7 —
Unearned Sales Revenue		3 8 9 1 —
Calvin Milton, Capital		35 6 6 4 —
Calvin Milton, Drawing	1 5 6 0 —	
Sales		17 2 4 7 —
Sales Returns and Allowances	4 1 9 —	
Sales Discounts	3 4 1 —	
Interest Income		9 1 4 —
Purchases	8 0 7 7 —	
Purchases Returns and Allowances		4 1 7 —
Purchases Discounts		5 1 5 —
Freight In	3 1 4 —	
Wages Expense	2 8 9 1 —	
Advertising Expense	4 1 5 —	
Totals	64 5 9 5 —	64 5 9 5 —

Adjusting entries:

a. Merchandise Inventory for October 1, 19XX, was $7,903.
b. Merchandise Inventory for October 31, 19XX, was $6,912.
c. An actual count of office supplies on October 31, 19XX, revealed $1,562 on hand.
d. A total of $98 of Prepaid Insurance was used during the month.
e. An automobile cost $17,700 and will have a useful life of 5 years. The salvage value is $1,500, and the straight-line method of depreciation is used.
f. Unearned Sales Revenue of $824 was earned during the month.
g. Accrued Wages Expense was $715.

The chart-of-accounts numbers (partial) are: 116, Merchandise Inventory; 128, Office Supplies; 132, Prepaid Insurance; 146, Accumulated Depreciation, Automobile; 208, Wages Payable; 219, Unearned Sales Revenue; 324, Income Summary; 403, Sales; 603, Wages Expense; 631, Office Supplies Expense; 641, Insurance Expense; 651, Depreciation Expense, Automobile.

REQUIRED
1. Complete the worksheet.
2. Journalize the adjusting entries in a general journal, page 39.
3. From the Trial Balance columns of the worksheet, open the previous account balances in the general ledger (include account names and numbers). Post the adjusting entries to the general ledger.

ANSWERS TO SELF-TEST QUESTIONS

1. b   2. c   3. a   4. d   5. b

12

Financial Statements and Closing Entries for a Merchandising Firm

Blessed is the man who has both mind and money, for he employs the latter well.

MENANDER

LEARNING OBJECTIVES

After reading this chapter, discussing the questions, and working the exercises and problems, you will be able to do the following:

Chapter 11 began the closing process for United Auto Supply by adjusting Merchandise Inventory. In this chapter we will finish the closing process by preparing closing entries and a post-closing trial balance. Financial statements will be prepared and analyzed to measure performance and to state the firm's financial position. You will also have the option of using *reversing entries* for certain adjusting entries.

PREPARING FINANCIAL STATEMENTS

Objective 1
Prepare financial
statements.

We completed the worksheet for United Auto Supply for the month ended October 31, 19XX, in Chapter 11. The Income Statement and Balance Sheet columns of this worksheet are illustrated in Exhibit 12-1 to help us prepare financial statements. Included in Exhibit 12-1 is the owner's Capital account in the general ledger. The first financial statement that we will prepare is the income statement. We will then prepare the statement of owner's equity, followed by the balance sheet.

THE INCOME STATEMENT

We are now ready to prepare a detailed income statement, so-called because each unique part is stated separately. For example, revenues are classified as either a part of Sales or listed under the caption "Other Revenue." Costs and expenses are separated into two categories: Cost of Goods Sold or Operating Expenses. Let's examine each part of the detailed income statement.

Revenues from Sales   The revenues section of the income statement for a merchandising firm will be different than one for a service-type firm in three ways:

1. Revenues for a merchandising firm consist of sales of resalable merchandise versus service revenues for a service firm.

2. Sales Returns and Allowances and Sales Discounts must be subtracted from Sales, if appropriate, to arrive at Net (final) Sales.

3. Any other type of revenue earned other than sales of merchandise inventory must be listed under Other Revenue at the end of the

EXHIBIT 12-1
Income Statement and Balance Sheet Columns of the Worksheet
United Auto Supply
Worksheet
For the Month Ended October 31, 19XX

Account	Income Statement Debit	Income Statement Credit	Balance Sheet Debit	Balance Sheet Credit
Cash			8 778 —	
Accounts Receivable			15 837 —	
Merchandise Inventory			8 285 —	
Office Supplies			2 500 —	
Prepaid Insurance			300 —	
Office Equipment			15 500 —	
Accumulated Depreciation, Office Equipment				900 —
Accounts Payable				8 800 —
Notes Payable (long term)				2 100 —
Unearned Sales Revenue				1 500 —
Lucille Garcia, Capital				34 100 —
Lucille Garcia, Drawing			1 200 —	
Sales		42 700 —		
Sales Returns and Allowances	78 —			
Sales Discounts	1 22 —			
Interest Income		1 70 —		
Purchases	23 100 —			
Purchases Returns and Allowances		400 —		
Purchases Discounts		1 44 —		
Freight In	2 450 —			
Rent Expense	1 700 —			
Wages Expense	11 598 —			
Advertising Expense	1 90 —			
Utilities Expense	1 95 —			
Bank Service Expense	7 —			
Totals				
Income Summary	8 209 —	8 285 —		
Office Supplies Expense	2 00 —			
Insurance Expense	1 50 —			
Depreciation Expense, Office Equipment	3 00 —			
Wages Payable				1 600 —
	48 299 —	51 699 —	52 400 —	49 000 —
Net Income	3 400 —			3 400 —
	51 699 —	51 699 —	52 400 —	52 400 —

(continued)

(Ex. 12-1 concluded)

GENERAL LEDGER ACCOUNT						
Account: *Lucille Garcia, Capital*						Account No. *301*
		Post.			**Balance**	
Date	**Item**	**Ref.**	**Debit**	**Credit**	**Debit**	**Credit**
19XX	*Previous Balance*					2 9 1 0 0 —
Oct. 25		*CR10*		5 0 0 0 —		3 4 1 0 0 —

income statement. This is because Cost of Goods Sold is subtracted from Net Sales to arrive at the gross profit on sales. This proper matching of revenues (Net Sales) and costs (Cost of Goods Sold) is consistent with the Matching Principle. Remember that with the Matching Principle we wanted to get a proper matching of the appropriate revenues and the associated costs or expenses.

Using the Income Statement columns in Exhibit 12-1, the Revenue from Sales section for United Auto Supply for October 19XX is as follows:

United Auto Supply
Income Statement (partial)
For the Month Ended October 31, 19XX

Revenue from Sales			
Sales		$42 7 0 0 —	
Less: Sales Returns and Allowances	$ 7 8 —		
Sales Discounts	1 2 2 —	2 0 0 —	
Net Sales			$42 5 0 0 —

The two contra accounts, Sales Returns and Allowances and Sales Discounts, are summed. They are then subtracted from Sales to arrive at the final or Net Sales amount.

Cost of Goods Sold   The Cost of Goods Sold section of the income statement is used by a merchandising firm to comply with the Matching

Principle. Remember that the Matching Principle requires that the associated costs be allocated or matched to the revenues for an accounting period. Therefore, Cost of Goods Sold represents the cost of the merchandise sold in the accounting period. The format to arrive at Cost of Goods Sold is as follows:

Cost of Goods Sold
 Merchandise Inventory, Beginning Date $XX
 Purchases $XX
 Less: Purchases Returns and Allowances   XX
     Purchases Discounts   XX
 Net Purchases   XX
 Freight In   XX
 Cost of Goods Available for Sale $XX
 Less: Merchandise Inventory, Ending Date   XX
  Cost of Goods Sold   XX

As you can see, in the Cost of Goods Sold format, four amount columns are used. Starting from the right is Cost of Goods Sold, determined by subtracting the amount of Merchandise Inventory on hand at the end of the accounting period from the total amount of Cost of Goods Available for Sale. The Cost of Goods Available for Sale is either sold (Cost of Goods Sold) or unsold (Merchandise Inventory, Ending Date).

Cost of Goods Available for Sale is calculated by adding the beginning Merchandise Inventory, Net Purchases, and Freight In. Net Purchases results from subtracting the two contra accounts, Purchases Returns and Allowances and Purchases Discounts, from Purchases.

This detailed listing of the Cost of Goods Sold section should enable the reader to go into as much depth as necessary. One person may only want to examine the total of Cost of Goods Sold while another may want to see Net Purchases. The income statement provides an uncluttered and informative form for the reader.

Using the Income Statement columns in Exhibit 12-1, the Cost of Goods Sold section of the income statement for United Auto Supply can be prepared. On October 31, 19XX, the end of the accounting period, Frank Rylski counted the auto parts (Merchandise Inventory). He determined that $8,285 of inventory was on hand. This is the ending Merchandise Inventory for this accounting period, and it will be the beginning Merchandise

Inventory for the next accounting period. This section of the income statement for October 19XX is prepared as follows:

<table>
<tr><td colspan="4" align="center">**United Auto Supply**</td></tr>
<tr><td colspan="4" align="center">**Income Statement (partial)**</td></tr>
<tr><td colspan="4" align="center">**For the Month Ended October 31, 19XX**</td></tr>
<tr><td>Cost of Goods Sold</td><td></td><td></td><td></td></tr>
<tr><td> Merchandise Inventory, October 1</td><td></td><td>$8 2 0 9 —</td><td></td></tr>
<tr><td> Purchases</td><td>$23 1 0 0 —</td><td></td><td></td></tr>
<tr><td> Less: Purchases Returns and Allowances</td><td>4 0 0 —</td><td></td><td></td></tr>
<tr><td>   Purchases Discounts</td><td>1 4 4 —</td><td></td><td></td></tr>
<tr><td> Net Purchases</td><td></td><td>22 5 5 6 —</td><td></td></tr>
<tr><td> Freight In</td><td></td><td>2 4 5 0 —</td><td></td></tr>
<tr><td> Cost of Goods Available for Sale</td><td></td><td>$33 2 1 5 —</td><td></td></tr>
<tr><td> Less: Merchandise Inventory, October 31</td><td></td><td>8 2 8 5 —</td><td></td></tr>
<tr><td>   Cost of Goods Sold</td><td></td><td></td><td>24 9 3 0 —</td></tr>
</table>

A detailed income statement for United Auto Supply is completed in Exhibit 12-2.

Gross Profit on Sales   Subtracting Cost of Goods Sold from Net Sales on the income statement yields **Gross Profit on Sales.** (see Exhibit 12-2). This balance represents the profit from sales after the appropriate cost of those sales has been applied. This balance is very important because a firm must sell its merchandise at a price that is high enough to cover the cost of sales (Cost of Goods Sold) and operating expenses. However, the firm's merchandise must also be competitively priced.

Operating Expenses   Expenses that occur in the normal course of business are called **Operating Expenses.** They are needed to conduct everyday business activities. The Operating Expenses for United Auto Supply (see Exhibit 12-2) total $14,340.

Income from Operations   Total Operating Expenses are subtracted from Gross Profit on Sales to arrive at **Income from Operations** (see Exhibit 12-2). This amount represents the profit or loss from normal business activities; that is, what the firm is primarily in business for.

EXHIBIT 12-2
Completed Detailed Income Statement

United Auto Supply

Income Statement

For the Month Ended October 31, 19XX

Revenue from Sales				
Sales			$42 7 0 0 —	
Less: Sales Returns and Allowances	$ 7 8 —			
Sales Discounts	1 2 2 —		2 0 0 —	
Net Sales				$42 5 0 0 —
Cost of Goods Sold				
Merchandise Inventory, October 1		$8 2 0 9 —		
Purchases	$23 1 0 0 —			
Less: Purchases Returns and Allowances	4 0 0 —			
Purchases Discounts	1 4 4 —			
Net Purchases		22 5 5 6 —		
Freight In		2 4 5 0 —		
Cost of Goods Available for Sale			$33 2 1 5 —	
Less: Merchandise Inventory, October 31			8 2 8 5 —	
Cost of Goods Sold				24 9 3 0 —
Gross Profit on Sales				$17 5 7 0 —
Operating Expenses				
Rent Expense			$ 1 7 0 0 —	
Wages Expense			11 5 9 8 —	
Advertising Expense			1 9 0 —	
Utilities Expense			1 9 5 —	
Bank Service Expense			7 —	
Office Supplies Expense			2 0 0 —	
Insurance Expense			1 5 0 —	
Depreciation Expense, Office Equipment			3 0 0 —	
Total Operating Expenses				14 3 4 0 —
Income from Operations				$3 2 3 0 —
Other Revenue				
Interest Income				1 7 0 —
Net Income				$3 4 0 0 —

Other Revenue Any other types of revenues for a merchandising firm (such as interest income, dividend income, revenues from performing services, and so on) are included under Other Revenue. For example, a grocery store is in business to sell food. But, this store would likely have interest income from checking and savings accounts, dividend income from stock investments, and so on. These transactions are not part of the normal course of business, food sales, but occur as a result of being in business and making various decisions. Therefore, the firm would separate these revenue accounts from grocery sales. United Auto Supply had interest income from its bank checking account and a note. This $170 is listed under Other Revenue.

Net Income Net income is determined by adding Other Revenue and Income from Operations. In Exhibit 12-2, we see that Net Income for United Auto Supply is $3,400.

THE STATEMENT OF OWNER'S EQUITY

We will use the Balance Sheet columns of the worksheet and the owner's Capital account in the general ledger to prepare a statement of owner's equity. Exhibit 12-3 shows a statement of owner's equity for United Auto Supply:

EXHIBIT 12-3
Statement of Owner's Equity

United Auto Supply
Statement of Owner's Equity
For the Month Ended October 31, 19XX

Lucille Garcia, Capital, October 1						$29	1	0	0	—
Add: Net Income for October						3	4	0	0	—
Additional Investment						5	0	0	0	—
Subtotal						$37	5	0	0	—
Less: Lucille Garcia, Drawing						1	2	0	0	—
Lucille Garcia, Capital, October 31						$36	3	0	0	—

THE BALANCE SHEET

A balance sheet can be prepared after the income statement and statement of owner's equity. We will use the Balance Sheet columns in Exhibit 12-1 and the statement of owner's equity to prepare the balance sheet. The balance sheet prepared in Exhibit 12-4 is called a **classified balance sheet** because it separates (or classifies) various accounts. The assets of the firm are divided into two categories: Current Assets, and Property, Plant, and Equipment. Three other asset categories—Investments, Intangible Assets, and Other Assets—are also commonly used, but are not applicable to United Auto Supply at this time. Liabilities are separated into two categories: Current and Long-term.

Assets

Current Assets   Considered to be the most liquid assets, **Current Assets** will be realized into cash within the normal cycle of a business, which is generally twelve months. Current Assets are listed in order of their *liquidity,* that is, their convertibility into cash. Cash would obviously be listed first. Accounts Receivable is usually realized (cash collected) within a month or a few months. Merchandise Inventory would be sold for cash or on account. Office Supplies and Prepaid Expenses are considered to be Current Assets because cash is paid to buy these assets, which will be used up or consumed within the normal cycle of a business.

Investments   If applicable, **Investments** would be listed next. Investments are long-term assets that will not be used by the firm within the normal cycle of business. Some examples would include land held for future use, equipment not used in the business, and so on.

Property, Plant, and Equipment   Under this heading you would find long-term assets that are used in the continuing operations of the firm. Accumulated Depreciation is placed below each depreciable asset to present the book value of that asset. Office Equipment, in Exhibit 12-4, would have a book value of $14,600 ($15,500 − $900).

Intangible Assets   Following Property, Plant, and Equipment are **Intangible Assets**. These are long-term assets that have a value but do not have any physical substance. The value is based on the privileges or rights that belong to the owner. Some examples would include patents, copyrights, and trademarks.

EXHIBIT 12-4
Classified Balance Sheet

United Auto Supply
Balance Sheet
October 31, 19XX

Assets						
Current Assets						
Cash	$ 8 7 7 8	—				
Accounts Receivable	15 8 3 7	—				
Merchandise Inventory	8 2 8 5	—				
Office Supplies	2 5 0 0	—				
Prepaid Insurance	3 0 0	—				
Total Current Assets			$35 7 0 0	—		
Property, Plant, and Equipment						
Office Equipment	$15 5 0 0	—				
Less: Accumulated Depreciation	9 0 0	—	14 6 0 0	—		
Total Assets			$50 3 0 0	—		
Liabilities						
Current Liabilities						
Accounts Payable	$ 8 8 0 0	—				
Wages Payable	1 6 0 0	—				
Unearned Sales Revenue ~~Current portion Mortage payable~~	1 5 0 0	—	*1000*		
Total Current Liabilities			$11 9 0 0	—		
Long-term Liabilities						
~~Notes Payable~~ Morgatage payable			2 1 0 0	—		
Total Liabilities			$14 0 0 0	—		
Owner's Equity						
Lucille Garcia, Capital			36 3 0 0	—		
Total Liabilities and Owner's Equity			$50 3 0 0	—		

Other Assets   If applicable, **Other Assets** would be listed next. This category would include any other assets that cannot be placed into the first four categories. United Auto Supply does not need this category because all its assets can be classified using the other categories.

Liabilities

Current Liabilities   Obligations or debts that are due to be paid within the normal cycle (one year) of a business are called **Current Liabilities**. Accounts Payable, Wages Payable, and Unearned Sales Revenue are some examples.

Long-Term Liabilities   Obligations or debts that are due to be paid in more than one year, or the normal cycle, are called **Long-Term Liabilities**. Some examples would include Notes Payable (long-term), Mortgages Payable, and Bonds Payable.

ANALYZING FINANCIAL STATEMENTS

Objective 2
Analyze financial
statements.

The preparation of the detailed income statement and classified balance sheet will help us to analyze the financial statements of United Auto Supply. Financial statements must be analyzed to determine whether certain relationships or trends are favorable or unfavorable. We will look at three types of analysis: working capital; current ratio; and profit margin.

Working Capital

Working Capital is the amount by which current assets exceed current liabilities. United Auto Supply's working capital would be:

Current Assets	$35,700
Less: Current Liabilities	11,900
Working Capital	$23,800

This indicates that the firm is able to pay its current obligations with current assets and still have $23,800 remaining.

Current Ratio

Another way of stating working capital is by the **current ratio**, which is current assets divided by current liabilities:

$$\text{Current Ratio} = \frac{\text{Current Assets}}{\text{Current Liabilities}}$$

For United Auto Supply this would be:

$$\text{Current Ratio} = \frac{\$35,700}{\$11,900} = 3 \text{ times}$$

This indicates that the firm would be able to pay its current obligations or debts 3 times with current assets.

Profit Margin

The profit margin is determined by dividing net income by net sales:

$$\text{Profit Margin} = \frac{\text{Net Income}}{\text{Net Sales}}$$

This ratio shows the percentage of profit from net sales. For United Auto Supply this would be:

$$\text{Profit Margin} = \frac{\$3,400}{\$42,500} = .08 = 8\%$$

This indicates that net income is 8 percent of net sales, or 8 cents of every net sales dollar is realized in net income.

Converting Decimals to Percents

To convert a decimal number to a percent, move the decimal point two places to the right and add the percent sign. For example, .04 is converted to 4%, .12 would be converted to 12%, .25 to 25%, and so on.

CLOSING ENTRIES

Objective 3
Prepare and
journalize closing
entries.

We prepared closing entries in Chapter 6 for a service-type firm. In this chapter we will prepare closing entries for the merchandising firm, United Auto Supply. We will again prepare the same four closing entries. However, we now have additional *nominal* accounts which must be cleared at the end of the accounting period, such as Sales Discounts, Purchases Returns and Allowances, and so on. Thus, to include these additional accounts we will clear all temporary accounts with credit balances in the first closing entry. Those temporary or nominal accounts with debit balances will be cleared in the second closing entry. Income Summary is closed to Capital in the third closing entry, and Drawing is cleared to Capital in the fourth.

Close Revenues and Other Credits to Income Summary (1)   For a merchandising firm, the first closing entry clears all revenue accounts and any other credit balances (nominal accounts only) to Income Summary. The first closing entry for United Auto Supply would be as follows:

GENERAL JOURNAL   Page ___29___

Date		Description	Post. Ref.	Debit	Credit
		Closing Entries			
19XX					
Oct.	31	Sales		42 7 0 0 —	
		Interest Income		1 7 0 —	
		Purchases Returns and Allowances		4 0 0 —	
		Purchases Discounts		1 4 4 —	
		Income Summary			43 4 1 4 —

Close Expenses and Other Debits to Income Summary (2)   The second closing entry for a merchandising firm clears all expense accounts and any other debit balances (nominal accounts only) to Income Summary. The second closing entry for United Auto Supply would be as follows:

Date		Description	Post. Ref.	Debit	Credit
	31	Income Summary		40 0 9 0 —	
		Sales Returns and Allowances			7 8 —
		Sales Discounts			1 2 2 —
		Purchases			23 1 0 0 —
		Freight In			2 4 5 0 —
		Rent Expense			1 7 0 0 —
		Wages Expense			11 5 9 8 —
		Advertising Expense			1 9 0 —
		Utilities Expense			1 9 5 —
		Bank Service Expense			7 —
		Office Supplies Expense			2 0 0 —
		Insurance Expense			1 5 0 —
		Depreciation Expense, Office Equipment			3 0 0 —

Close Income Summary to Capital (3) You should post the first two closing entries to the Income Summary account before journalizing the third closing entry. The resulting balance confirms the net income or net loss for the accounting period.

The third closing entry is to clear the Income Summary account to the owner's Capital account. Let's use a T account to illustrate the activity in the Income Summary account after the adjusting entry for Merchandise Inventory (see Chapter 11) and the two preceding closing entries:

Income Summary

(10/31) Adjusting Entry (beginning Merchandise Inventory)	8,209		
		8,285	(10/31) Adjusting Entry (ending Merchandise Inventory)
		43,414	(10/31) Closing Entry (clear credits)
(10/31) Closing Entry (clear debits)	40,090		
		3,400	Balance to be cleared to owner's Capital

United Auto Supply had a Net Income of $3,400 for October 19XX, which corresponds to the balance of the Income Summary account. The third closing entry for United Auto Supply would be as follows:

31	Income Summary		3 4 0 0 —		
	Lucille Garcia, Capital			3 4 0 0 —	

Once again, let's use a T account to illustrate the activity in the Income Summary account after the third closing entry is posted:

Income Summary

(10/31) Adjusting Entry (beginning Merchandise Inventory)	8,209		
		8,285	(10/31) Adjusting Entry (ending Merchandise Inventory)
		43,414	(10/31) Closing Entry (clear credits)
(10/31) Closing Entry (clear debits)	40,090		
(10/31) Closing Entry (clear Income Summary)	3,400		
(10/31) Final Balance	—0—	—0—	

Now, let's use a T account to illustrate the activity in the owner's Capital account after the third closing entry is posted:

Lucille Garcia, Capital

		34,100	(10/25) Previous Balance
		3,400	(10/31) Third closing entry posted
		37,500	(10/31) Balance after third closing entry

Close Drawing to Capital (4) The owner's Drawing account is cleared in the last closing entry by debiting the owner's Capital account and crediting the owner's Drawing account. The fourth and final closing entry for United Auto Supply is as follows:

31	*Lucille Garcia, Capital*		1 2 0 0 —	
	Lucille Garcia, Drawing			1 2 0 0 —

Once again we'll use a T account to demonstrate the activity in the owner's Capital account after the fourth closing entry is posted:

Lucille Garcia, Capital

		34,100	(10/25) Previous Balance
		3,400	(10/31) Third closing entry posted
(10/31) Fourth closing entry posted	1,200		
		36,300	(10/31) Final Balance

THE POST-CLOSING TRIAL BALANCE

Objective 4
Prepare a post-closing trial balance.

As we discussed in Chapter 6, an accountant may be very confident that all appropriate closing entries have been properly journalized and posted. But to insure that the accounting records, in particular the general ledger, are ready for the start of the next accounting period, a post-closing trial balance must be prepared. The post-closing trial balance for a merchandising firm has the following purposes:

1. All nominal accounts are closed.
2. Total debits equal total credits.
3. All account balances are normal.
4. Ending Merchandise Inventory is correct.

The post-closing trial balance for a merchandising firm is very similar to the post-closing trial balance prepared in Chapter 6 for a service-type firm. The general ledger accounts are listed in chart-of-accounts order. Any account that has a zero balance is not listed. The post-closing trial balance for United Auto Supply at the end of the accounting period, October 19XX, is shown on page 409.

Now that the post-closing trial balance has been prepared, let's see if the four purposes have been met. First, we can see that no nominal accounts are listed. This indicates that all nominal accounts have zero balances. Next, we see that total debits equal total credits. Then, looking at the accounts and account balances we see that all account balances are normal; that is, Accounts Receivable has a debit balance, Accounts Payable a credit balance, and so on. Finally, we see that ending Merchandise Inventory has the correct balance. Therefore, the accounting records are

United Auto Supply
Post-Closing Trial Balance
October 31, 19XX

Accounts	Debit	Credit
Cash	8 7 7 8 —	
Accounts Receivable	15 8 3 7 —	
Merchandise Inventory	8 2 8 5 —	
Office Supplies	2 5 0 0 —	
Prepaid Insurance	3 0 0 —	
Office Equipment	15 5 0 0 —	
Accumulated Depreciation, Office Equipment		9 0 0 —
Accounts Payable		8 8 0 0 —
Wages Payable		1 6 0 0 —
Notes Payable (long-term)		2 1 0 0 —
Unearned Sales Revenue		1 5 0 0 —
Lucille Garcia, Capital		36 3 0 0 —
Totals	51 2 0 0 —	51 2 0 0 —

properly set for the next accounting period. You should always thoroughly examine the accounting records to make sure that all journal entries, postings, descriptions, and so on, are correct before you go on to the next accounting period.

REVERSING ENTRIES

Objective 5
Prepare and journalize reversing entries (Optional).

Some adjusting entries made in the previous accounting period may be reversed at the beginning of the current accounting period. A *reversing entry* reverses or "turns around" a previous adjusting entry.

Reversing entries have the following purposes:

1. To facilitate recording revenues in the proper accounting period.
2. To facilitate recording expenses in the proper accounting period.
3. To ensure that transactions are recorded in a smooth and routine manner between two accounting periods.

Since the accounting records for United Auto Supply are now closed, the current accounting period is November 19XX. Reversing entries are not necessary or required. They are simply another tool you may utilize to make your work as an accountant easier and possibly reduce errors.

Let's follow the process in Exhibit 12-5 for the use of reversing entries. In this example we will assume that a $961 Wages Expense adjustment was recorded May 31, 19XX. A total of $1,200 Cash will be paid June 5, 19XX. A total of $239 Wages Expense is to be allocated to June, and $961 to May.

EXHIBIT 12-5
Reversing Entry Thought and Procedure Process

REVERSING ENTRY PROCESS

General Journal Entry			Affect on Accounts			
			Wages Expense		Wages Payable	
			+	−	−	+
Adjusting	Dr.	Cr.				
(5/31) Wages Expense	961		961			
Wages Payable		961				961
Closing						
(5/31) Income Summary	961					
Wages Expense		961		961		
Account Balance after Closing Entry			—0—			961
Reversing						
(6/1) Wages Payable	961				961	
Wages Expense		961		961		
Account Balance after Reversing Entry			961 (a)			—0— (b)
Payment of Cash						
(6/5) Wages Expense	1,200		1,200			
Cash		1,200				
Account Balance after Payment Entry			(c) 239			—0—

(a) This balance is not normal. This will remind you that another entry must be made to bring the account balance back to normal.
(b) No liability for new accounting period.
(c) Cash paid for Wages Expense is apportioned to the correct accounting period. Total cash paid of $1,200 for Wages Expense (debit) minus May Wages Expense of $961 (credit) equals June Wages Expense of $239. Or, $1,200 debit minus $961 credit equals a $239 debit balance.

T accounts are used to show the account balances after each entry is made. The "+" indicates that the account has increased. Remember that the plus side is the normal side. The "−" indicates that the account has decreased. An account with a minus balance is not considered to be normal.

Any adjustment (adjusting entry) that will not be realized into cash paid or received in the following accounting period should not be reversed. Therefore, the *deferral* type of adjusting entry that we examined in Chapters 4 and 11 would not be reversed. An *accrual* type of adjusting entry may be reversed depending on whether cash is to be received or paid in the next accounting period following the one in which the adjusting entry is made.

Remember that if you do not use reversing entries then you must go back and look in the accounting records to see, in this example, how much of the $1,200 Wages Expense is to be allocated to June 19XX. This may not appear to be a problem. But imagine if you were an accountant working in a large firm with numerous transactions and with many employees working with the accounting records. This review could then be quite difficult and time consuming.

CHAPTER REVIEW

1. **Prepare financial statements (pp. 394–403).**
   The Income Statement and Balance Sheet columns of the worksheet were used to prepare financial statements. The financial statements were prepared in this order: (a) income statement; (b) statement of owner's equity; and (c) balance sheet.

2. **Analyze financial statements (pp. 403–404).**
   Financial statements are analyzed to determine whether certain relationships or trends are favorable or unfavorable. The types of analysis that were examined in this chapter include (a) working capital; (b) current ratio; and (c) profit margin.

3. **Prepare and journalize closing entries (pp. 404–408).**
   All temporary accounts with credit balances are cleared in the first closing entry. Those temporary or nominal accounts with debit balances are closed in the second closing entry. Income Summary is cleared to Capital in the third closing entry. Finally, Drawing is closed to Capital in the fourth closing entry.

4. **Prepare a post-closing trial balance (pp. 408–409).**
   A post-closing trial balance is prepared to ensure that the accounting records, in particular the general ledger, are ready for the start of the next accounting period.

5. Prepare and journalize reversing entries (Optional)
(pp. 409–411).
A reversing entry reverses or "turns around" a previous adjusting entry. Reversing entries are another tool an accountant may use to make his or her work easier and reduce errors.

GLOSSARY

Classified Balance Sheet	Balance Sheet that separates each unique category of accounts.
Current Assets	Assets that are realized into cash within the normal cycle of a business.
Current Liabilities	Obligations or debts that are due within the normal cycle of a business.
Current Ratio	Current Assets divided by Current Liabilities.
Detailed Income Statement	An income statement that separates each unique category of accounts.
Gross Profit on Sales	Net Sales minus Cost of Goods Sold.
Income from Operations	Gross Profit on Sales minus Total Operating Expenses.
Intangible Assets	Long-term assets that have a value but do not have any physical substance.
Investments	Long-term assets that will not be used in the normal cycle of a business.
Long-Term Liabilities	Obligations or debts that are due in more than one year.
Normal Course of Business	The main profit-making or business activity or activities of a firm.
Normal Cycle of Business ✓	One year (12 months) for most firms.
Other Assets	Any asset that cannot be categorized into the four major categories of assets.
Profit Margin	Net Income divided by Net sales.
Property, Plant, and Equipment	Long-term assets that are used in the continuing operations of a business.
Reversing Entry	Turns around a previous adjusting entry.
Working Capital	Current Assets minus Current Liabilities.

SELF-TEST QUESTIONS FOR REVIEW

(Answers are on p. 428.)

1. On a detailed income statement, Interest Income is included with
   a. Revenue from Sales.   b. Cost of Goods Sold.
   c. Operating Expenses.   d. Other Revenue.

2. Which of the following categories immediately follows Property, Plant, and Equipment on a classified balance sheet?
   a. Current Assets   b. Intangible Assets
   c. Investments   d. Other Assets

3. _____ is subtracted to find working capital.
   a. Current Liabilities   b. Net Income
   c. Current Assets   d. Net Sales

4. Close Income Summary to Capital is the _____ closing entry.
   a. first   b. second
   c. third   d. fourth

5. Which of the following accounts could be found in the credit column on a post-closing trial balance (assume all balances are normal)?
   a. Accounts Receivable   b. Merchandise Inventory
   c. Income Summary   d. Unearned Sales Revenue

PRACTICAL REVIEW PROBLEM

Objectives 3 and 4

Journalizing Closing Entries and Preparing a Post-Closing Trial Balance Frances Carter is the accountant for Lewistown Furniture Store. She finds the following accounts and account balances (all are normal) before closing entries at July 31, 19XX:

Cash	$34,870
Accounts Receivable	19,320
Merchandise Inventory	29,130
Office Supplies	4,650
Prepaid Insurance	3,240
Office Equipment	46,780
Accumulated Depreciation, Office Equipment	6,900
Accounts Payable	16,310
Notes Payable (long-term)	5,430
Unearned Sales Revenue	7,120
Felix Franks, Capital	94,120
Felix Franks, Drawing	1,460
Sales	46,690
Sales Returns and Allowances	2,360
Sales Discounts	1,050
Interest Income	340
Purchases	22,130
Purchases Returns and Allowances	1,810
Purchases Discounts	520
Freight In	3,090
Rent Expense	1,580
Wages Expense	13,420
Advertising Expense	870
Utilities Expense	230

Bank Service Expense	20	
Income Summary	2,540 (credit)	
Office Supplies Expense	710	
Insurance Expense	250	
Depreciation Expense, Office Equipment	300	
Wages Payable	3,680	

REQUIRED

1. Journalize the closing entries in a general journal, page 35.
2. Prepare a post-closing trial balance.

ANSWER TO PRACTICAL REVIEW PROBLEM

1.   **GENERAL JOURNAL**   Page ___35___

Date	Description	Post. Ref.	Debit	Credit
	Closing Entries			
19XX				
July 31	Sales		46 690 —	
	Interest Income		3 40 —	
	Purchases Returns and Allowances		1 8 10 —	
	Purchases Discounts		5 20 —	
	Income Summary			49 360 —
31	Income Summary		46 010 —	
	Sales Returns and Allowances			2 360 —
	Sales Discounts			1 0 50 —
	Purchases			22 130 —
	Freight In			3 0 90 —
	Rent Expense			1 5 80 —
	Wages Expense			13 420 —
	Advertising Expense			8 70 —
	Utilities Expense			2 30 —
	Bank Service Expense			20 —
	Office Supplies Expense			7 10 —
	Insurance Expense			2 50 —
	Depreciation Expense, Office Equipment			3 00 —
31	Income Summary		5 890 —	
	Felix Franks, Capital			5 890 —
31	Felix Franks, Capital		1 460 —	
	Felix Franks, Drawing			1 460 —

2.

Lewistown Furniture Store									
Post-Closing Trial Balance									
July 31, 19XX									
Accounts	Debit					Credit			
Cash	34	8	7	0	—				
Accounts Receivable	19	3	2	0	—				
Merchandise Inventory	29	1	3	0	—				
Office Supplies	4	6	5	0	—				
Prepaid Insurance	3	2	4	0	—				
Office Equipment	46	7	8	0	—				
Accumulated Depreciation, Office Equipment						6	9	0	0	—
Accounts Payable						16	3	1	0	—
Wages Payable						3	6	8	0	—
Notes Payable (long-term)						5	4	3	0	—
Unearned Sales Revenue						7	1	2	0	—
Felix Franks, Capital						98	5	5	0	—
Totals	137	9	9	0	—	137	9	9	0	—

*$94,120 + $5,890 − $1,460 = $98,550.

DISCUSSION QUESTIONS

Q 12-1   Briefly describe a detailed income statement.

Q 12-2   In what two categories are costs and expenses separated in a detailed income statement?

Q 12-3   Briefly describe a classified balance sheet.

Q 12-4   Explain how assets and liability accounts are categorized in a classified balance sheet.

Q 12-5   Why must a post-closing trial balance be prepared for a merchandising firm as well as a service-type firm?

Q 12-6   Name and give the formulas for the three analyses in this chapter.

Q 12-7   Explain the first closing entry for a merchandising firm. Identify, in your answer, some accounts that you would expect to find in this entry.

Q 12-8   Explain the second closing entry for a merchandising firm. Identify, in your answer, some accounts that you would expect to find in this entry.

Q 12-9   Explain the third and fourth closing entries for a merchandising firm. Name the accounts that you would most likely find in these two entries.

Q 12-10   What type of adjusting entries can be reversed for a merchandising
(Optional)   firm? What type cannot be reversed? Explain your answers.

EXERCISES

Objective 1

E 12-1 Completing an Income Statement Fill in the missing amounts in the following detailed income statement. [Hint: (b) is $400 − $300 = $100.]

Barfield Equipment Sales
Income Statement
For the Month Ended November 30, 19XX

Revenues from Sales			
Sales			$ (a)
Less: Sales Returns and Allowances		$ 300	
Sales Discounts		(b)	400
Net Sales			$8,900
Cost of Goods Sold			
Merchandise Inventory, November 1		$3,100	
Purchases	$5,700		
Less: Purchases Returns & Allowances	500		
Purchases Discounts	200		
Net Purchases		(c)	
Freight In		100	
Cost of Goods Available for Sale		$ (d)	
Less: Merchandise Inventory, November 30		3,600	
Cost of Goods Sold			(e)
Gross Profit on Sales			(f)
Operating Expenses			
Wages Expense		$1,900	
Depreciation Expense, Truck		200	
Total Operating Expenses			(g)
Income from Operations			(h)
Other Revenue			
Interest Income			800
Net Income			$3,000

Objective 2   E 12-2   Analyzing Financial Statements   Determine (a) working capital; (b) current ratio; and (c) profit margin given the following information: Net Sales, $34,600; Current Assets, $89,400; Net Income, $5,190; and Current Liabilities, $29,800.

Objective 1   E 12-3   Completing a Balance Sheet   Fill in the missing amounts in the following classified balance sheet. [Hint: (b) is $16,800 − $16,000 = $800]:

Mendoza Sales
Balance Sheet
January 31, 19XX

Assets

Current Assets
Cash	$ (a)	
Accounts Receivable	2,450	
Merchandise Inventory	4,860	
Prepaid Insurance	2,530	
Total Current Assets		$18,110

Property, Plant, and Equipment
Truck	$16,800	
Less: Accumulated Depreciation	(b)	16,000
Total Assets		(c)

Liabilities

Current Liabilities
Wages Payable	$ 3,660	
Unearned Sales Revenue	990	
Total Current Liabilities		(d)

Long-term Liabilities
Notes Payable		12,770
Total Liabilities		(e)

Owner's Equity

Hector Mendoza, Capital		(f)
Total Liabilities and Owner's Equity		(g)

Objective 3   **E 12-4   Completing Closing Entries**   Complete the following closing entries:

GENERAL JOURNAL

Page _____29_____

Date		Description	Post. Ref.	Debit	Credit
		Closing Entries			
19XX					
Apr.	30	Sales		22 6 0 0 —	
		Interest Income		1 1 0 0 —	
		Purchases Returns and Allowances		9 0 0 —	
		Purchases Discounts		2 0 0 —	
		(a)			(b)
	30	(c)		(d)	
		Sales Returns and Allowances			1 4 0 0 —
		Sales Discounts			8 0 0 —
		Purchases			11 8 0 0 —
		Freight In			4 0 0 —
		Wages Expense			4 8 0 0 —
		Depreciation Expense, Store Equipment			3 0 0 —
	30	(e)		8 2 0 0 —	
		Gayle Gilder, Capital			8 2 0 0 —
	30	(f)		7 0 0 —	
		(g)			7 0 0 —

Objective 1   **E 12-5   Preparing an Income Statement**   Prepare a detailed income statement given the Income Statement columns from the worksheet for Ramsey Company (p. 419).

Objective 4   **E 12-6   Completing a Post-Closing Trial Balance**   Complete the post-closing trial balance on August 31, 19XX, for Kelso's Magazine Stand (p. 419).

Ramsey Company
Worksheet
For the Month Ended October 31, 19XX

Account	Income Statement	
	Debit	**Credit**
Sales		14 0 4 0 —
Sales Returns and Allowances	6 1 0 —	
Sales Discounts	8 8 0 —	
Interest Income		4 3 0 —
Purchases	7 8 5 0 —	
Purchases Returns and Allowances		4 5 0 —
Purchases Discounts		1 9 0 —
Freight In	4 2 0 —	
Wages Expense	2 8 8 0 —	
Telephone Expense	4 4 0 —	
Income Summary	4 3 3 0 —	5 3 8 0 —
Depreciation Expense, Machinery	3 3 0 —	
	17 7 4 0 —	20 4 9 0 —
Net Income	2 7 5 0 —	
	20 4 9 0 —	20 4 9 0 —

	(a)
	(b)
	(c)

(d)	(e)	(f)
Cash	13 9 0 0 —	
Accounts Receivable	16 1 0 0 —	
Merchandise Inventory	12 7 0 0 —	
Wages Payable		4 8 0 0 —
Unearned Sales Revenue		2 7 0 0 —
Doris Kelso, Capital		(g)
Totals	(h)	(i)

Objective 3   **E 12-7**   **Journalizing Closing Entries**   The accountant for Lopez Sports Supply finds the following selected accounts and account balances (all are normal) for the month ended February 28, 19XX:

L. T. Lopez, Capital, $45,670; L. T. Lopez, Drawing, $2,010; Income Summary, $2,560 credit balance; Sales, $31,940; Sales Returns and Allowances, $280; Sales Discounts, $190; Interest Income, $1,360; Purchases, $19,530; Purchases Returns and Allowances, $1,710; Purchases Discounts, $230; Freight In, $1,650; Rent Expense, $1,350; Wages Expense, $9,770; Advertising Expense, $340.

Journalize the closing entries in the general journal, page 17, as follows: Close revenues and other credits, close expenses and other debits, close Income Summary (include the previous credit balance), and close drawing.

Objective 5   **E 12-8**   **Journalizing Reversing Entries**   A $1,950 Wages Expense adjustment
(Optional)   was recorded December 31, 19XX. A total of $4,180 cash will be paid January 4, 19XX. Record the following entries in a general journal:
a. December 31, 19XX, adjusting entry.
b. December 31, 19XX, closing entry (for Wages Expense).
c. January 1, 19XX, reversing entry.
d. January 4, 19XX, payment of cash.

PROBLEM SET A

Objective 1   **P 12-1A**   **Preparing Financial Statements**   Lori Hayes owns and operates Hayes Equipment Sales. The owner invested $1,000 during the month, which is included in the owner's Capital account on the worksheet. Lori had the following worksheet (partial) for June 30, 19XX (p. 421).

REQUIRED
1. Prepare financial statements including the (a) detailed income statement; (b) statement of owner's equity; and (c) classified balance sheet.

Objectives 3   **P 12-2A**   **Journalizing Closing Entries and Preparing a Post-Closing Trial Balance**   Billy Simmons is the accountant for North Central Apparel Store. He finds the following accounts and account balances (all are normal) before closing entries at December 31, 19XX:

Cash	$25,120
Accounts Receivable	8,350
Merchandise Inventory	18,430
Office Supplies	3,890
Prepaid Insurance	2,160

Hayes Equipment Sales
Worksheet
For the Month Ended June 30, 19XX

Account	Income Statement Debit	Income Statement Credit	Balance Sheet Debit	Balance Sheet Credit
Cash			9 7 0 0 —	
Accounts Receivable			12 3 0 0 —	
Merchandise Inventory			8 7 0 0 —	
Truck			21 6 0 0 —	
Accumulated Depreciation, Truck				8 0 0 —
Notes Payable (long-term)				14 7 0 0 —
Unearned Sales Revenue				2 9 0 0 —
Lori Hayes, Capital				32 5 0 0 —
Lori Hayes, Drawing			2 1 0 0 —	
Sales		13 2 0 0 —		
Sales Returns and Allowances	3 0 0 —			
Sales Discounts	4 0 0 —			
Interest Income		6 0 0 —		
Purchases	6 7 0 0 —			
Purchases Returns and Allowances		7 0 0 —		
Purchases Discounts		1 0 0 —		
Freight In	2 0 0 —			
Rent Expense	9 0 0 —			
Wages Expense	3 5 0 0 —			
Telephone Expense	5 0 0 —			
Income Summary	8 9 0 0 —	8 7 0 0 —		
Depreciation Expense, Truck	1 0 0 —			
Wages Payable				1 7 0 0 —
	21 5 0 0 —	23 3 0 0 —	54 4 0 0 —	52 6 0 0 —
Net Income	1 8 0 0 —			1 8 0 0 —
	23 3 0 0 —	23 3 0 0 —	54 4 0 0 —	54 4 0 0 —

Office Equipment	35,240
Accumulated Depreciation, Office Equipment	5,500
Accounts Payable	7,280
Notes Payable (long-term)	4,210
Unearned Sales Revenue	5,090
Mary Konacek, Capital	65,720
Mary Konacek, Drawing	930
Sales	30,240
Sales Returns and Allowances	720
Sales Discounts	810
Interest Income	290
Purchases	13,620
Purchases Returns and Allowances	730
Purchases Discounts	240
Freight In	1,670
Rent Expense	1,850
Wages Expense	6,790
Advertising Expense	540
Utilities Expense	290
Bank Service Expense	10
Income Summary	1,060 (credit)
Office Supplies Expense	580
Insurance Expense	150
Depreciation Expense, Office Equipment	500
Wages Payable	1,290

REQUIRED
1. Journalize the closing entries in a general journal, page 22.
2. Prepare a post-closing trial balance. See the Practical Review Problem if you need help.

Objectives 1 and 2

P 12-3A

Preparing and Analyzing Financial Statements   Rudy Luna owns and operates Northern Furniture Sales. He invested $2,980 during the month, which is included in the owner's Capital account on the worksheet. Rudy had the following worksheet (partial) for August 31, 19XX (p. 423).

REQUIRED
1. Prepare financial statements including the (a) detailed income statement; (b) statement of owner's equity; and (c) classified balance sheet.
2. Analyze financial statements by calculating (a) working capital; (b) current ratio; and (c) profit margin.

Northern Furniture Sales
Worksheet
For the Month Ended August 31, 19XX

Account	Income Statement Debit	Income Statement Credit	Balance Sheet Debit	Balance Sheet Credit
Cash			12 8 9 0 —	
Accounts Receivable			9 6 7 0 —	
Merchandise Inventory			14 8 9 0 —	
Prepaid Insurance			3 4 5 0 —	
Automobile			18 7 8 0 —	
Accumulated Depreciation, Automobile				2 3 8 0 —
Accounts Payable				13 5 6 0 —
Notes Payable (long-term)				9 4 5 0 —
Unearned Sales Revenue				1 2 2 0 —
Rudy Luna, Capital				26 0 8 0 —
Rudy Luna, Drawing			3 5 7 0 —	
Sales		33 5 5 0 —		
Sales Returns and Allowances	5 2 0 —			
Sales Discounts	4 3 0 —			
Interest Income		6 3 0 —		
Purchases	18 1 6 0 —			
Purchases Returns and Allowances		7 1 0 —		
Purchases Discounts		2 8 0 —		
Freight In	1 3 4 0 —			
Rent Expense	1 2 8 0 —			
Wages Expense	9 3 4 0 —			
Utilities Expense	1 2 0 —			
Income Summary	13 5 6 0 —	14 8 9 0 —		
Insurance Expense	1 9 0 —			
Depreciation Expense, Automobile	2 3 0 —			
Wages Payable				5 6 7 0 —
	45 1 7 0 —	50 0 6 0 —	63 2 5 0 —	58 3 6 0 —
Net Income	4 8 9 0 —			4 8 9 0 —
	50 0 6 0 —	50 0 6 0 —	63 2 5 0 —	63 2 5 0 —

Objectives 1
through 5

P 12-4A

Comprehensive Chapter Review Problem   Brown's Health Store is owned and operated by Shirley Brown. She invested $1,380 during the month, which is included in the owner's Capital account. The following accounts and account balances (all are normal) were taken from the Income Statement and Balance Sheet columns of her completed worksheet for the month ended October 31, 19XX:

Cash, $9,712; Accounts Receivable, $11,782; Merchandise Inventory, $18,091; Prepaid Insurance, $1,488; Office Equipment, $35,891; Accumulated Depreciation, Office Equipment, $3,480; Accounts Payable, $4,453; Notes Payable (long-term), $18,715; Unearned Sales Revenue, $4,672; Shirley Brown, Capital, $36,423; Shirley Brown, Drawing, $2,168; Sales, $35,458; Sales Returns and Allowances, $561; Sales Discounts, $782; Interest Income, $892; Purchases, $14,570; Purchases Returns and Allowances, $781; Purchases Discounts, $452; Freight In, $987; Rent Expense, $1,515; Wages Expense, $9,561; Advertising Expense, $782; Income Summary, $19,564 debit and $18,091 credit; Wages Payable, $4,566; Insurance Expense, $181; and Depreciation Expense, Office Equipment, $348.

REQUIRED
1. Prepare financial statements including the (a) detailed income statement; (b) statement of owner's equity; and (c) classified balance sheet.
2. Analyze financial statements by calculating (a) working capital; (b) current ratio; and (c) profit margin.
3. Prepare and journalize (page 42) closing entries. DO NOT post to the general ledger.
4. Prepare a post-closing trial balance.
   (Optional)
5. Prepare and journalize (page 43) the reversing entry for Wages Payable on November 1, 19XX. DO NOT post to the general ledger.
6. The firm paid wages on November 6, 19XX, $6,019. Record this transaction in a general journal, page 43. DO NOT post to the general ledger.

PROBLEM SET B

Objective 1

P 12-1B

Preparing Financial Statements   Dai Phan owns and operates Eastside Equipment Sales. The owner invested $1,500 during the month, which is included in Capital on the worksheet. Dai had the following worksheet (partial) for July 31, 19XX (p. 425).

REQUIRED
Prepare financial statements including the (a) detailed income statement; (b) statement of owner's equity; and (c) classified balance sheet.

Eastside Equipment Sales
Worksheet
For the Month Ended July 31, 19XX

Account	Income Statement Debit	Income Statement Credit	Balance Sheet Debit	Balance Sheet Credit
Cash			7 9 0 0 —	
Accounts Receivable			6 4 0 0 —	
Merchandise Inventory			5 8 0 0 —	
Automobile			12 3 0 0 —	
Accumulated Depreciation, Automobile				1 2 0 0 —
Notes Payable (long-term)				9 5 0 0 —
Unearned Sales Revenue				5 2 0 0 —
Dai Phan, Capital				17 4 0 0 —
Dai Phan, Drawing			3 7 0 0 —	
Sales		18 4 0 0 —		
Sales Returns and Allowances	6 0 0 —			
Sales Discounts	2 0 0 —			
Interest Income		5 0 0 —		
Purchases	13 4 0 0 —			
Purchases Returns and Allowances		4 0 0 —		
Purchases Discounts		7 0 0 —		
Freight In	9 0 0 —			
Rent Expense	8 0 0 —			
Wages Expense	2 1 0 0 —			
Telephone Expense	1 0 0 —			
Income Summary	6 1 0 0 —	5 8 0 0 —		
Depreciation Expense, Automobile	3 0 0 —			
Wages Payable				1 5 0 0 —
	24 5 0 0 —	25 8 0 0 —	36 1 0 0 —	34 8 0 0 —
Net Income	1 3 0 0 —			1 3 0 0 —
	25 8 0 0 —	25 8 0 0 —	36 1 0 0 —	36 1 0 0 —

Objectives 3
and 4

P 12-2B   **Journalizing Closing Entries and Preparing a Post-Closing Trial Balance**   Emily O'Connor is the accountant for Washington Paper Supply. She finds the following accounts and account balances (all are normal) before closing entries at July 31, 19XX:

Cash	$43,270
Accounts Receivable	23,610
Merchandise Inventory	31,560
Office Supplies	9,340
Prepaid Insurance	5,350
Office Furniture	46,810
Accumulated Depreciation, Office Furniture	6,500
Accounts Payable	17,010
Notes Payable (long-term)	10,320
Unearned Sales Revenue	6,490
H. L. Powers, Capital	106,020
H. L. Powers, Drawing	1,350
Sales	74,520
Sales Returns and Allowances	2,670
Sales Discounts	1,420
Interest Income	860
Purchases	35,710
Purchases Returns and Allowances	1,970
Purchases Discounts	1,020
Freight In	2,830
Rent Expense	2,560
Wages Expense	22,490
Advertising Expense	2,410
Utilities Expense	960
Bank Service Expense	30
Income Summary	4,120 (credit)
Office Supplies Expense	1,420
Insurance Expense	250
Depreciation Expense, Office Furniture	500
Wages Payable	5,710

REQUIRED
1. Journalize the closing entries in a general journal, page 45.
2. Prepare a post-closing trial balance. See the Practical Review Problem if you need help.

Objectives 1
and 2

P 12-3B   **Preparing and Analyzing Financial Statements**   Virginia Cook owns and operates Falls City Sales. She invested $2,670 during the month, which is included in Capital on the worksheet. She had the following worksheet (partial) for September 30, 19XX (p. 427).

Falls City Sales
Worksheet
For the Month Ended September 30, 19XX

Account	Income Statement Debit	Income Statement Credit	Balance Sheet Debit	Balance Sheet Credit
Cash			10 9 1 0 —	
Accounts Receivable			16 6 7 0 —	
Merchandise Inventory			12 3 4 0 —	
Prepaid Insurance			2 1 3 0 —	
Computer			12 3 2 0 —	
Accumulated Depreciation, Computer				1 7 1 0 —
Accounts Payable				5 5 6 0 —
Notes Payable (long-term)				8 9 1 0 —
Unearned Sales Revenue				1 5 3 0 —
Virginia Cook, Capital				35 3 0 0 —
Virginia Cook, Drawing			2 8 9 0 —	
Sales		12 7 1 0 —		
Sales Returns and Allowances	2 1 0 —			
Sales Discounts	7 8 0 —			
Interest Income		5 6 0 —		
Purchases	6 2 9 0 —			
Purchases Returns and Allowances		3 4 0 —		
Purchases Discounts		5 3 0 —		
Freight In	6 3 0 —			
Rent Expense	1 1 0 0 —			
Wages Expense	2 3 4 0 —			
Utilities Expense	1 4 0 —			
Income Summary	11 7 1 0 —	12 3 4 0 —		
Insurance Expense	1 6 0 —			
Depreciation Expense, Computer	1 9 0 —			
Wages Payable				1 3 2 0 —
	23 5 5 0 —	26 4 8 0 —	57 2 6 0 —	54 3 3 0 —
Net Income	2 9 3 0 —			2 9 3 0 —
	26 4 8 0 —	26 4 8 0 —	57 2 6 0 —	57 2 6 0 —

REQUIRED

1. Prepare financial statements including the (a) detailed income statement; (b) statement of owner's equity; and (c) classified balance sheet.
2. Analyze financial statements by calculating (a) working capital; (b) current ratio; and (c) profit margin.

Objectives 1 through 5

P 12-4B

Comprehensive Chapter Review Problem   Flanders Grocery Store is owned and operated by Harvey Flanders. He invested $3,788 during the month, which is included in the owner's Capital account. The following accounts and account balances (all are normal) were taken from the Income Statement and Balance Sheet columns of his completed worksheet for the month ended February 28, 19XX:

Cash, $13,909; Accounts Receivable, $15,803; Merchandise Inventory, $31,823; Prepaid Insurance, $2,431; Office Equipment, $18,008; Accumulated Depreciation, Office Equipment, $2,090; Accounts Payable, $12,563; Notes Payable (long-term), $12,872; Unearned Sales Revenue, $3,947; Harvey Flanders, Capital, $42,086; Harvey Flanders, Drawing, $2,891; Sales, $44,984; Sales Returns and Allowances, $892; Sales Discounts, $792; Interest Income, $453; Purchases, $22,423; Purchases Returns and Allowances, $891; Purchases Discounts, $908; Freight In, $1,063; Rent Expense, $1,210; Wages Expense, $13,451; Advertising Expense, $689; Income Summary, $31,617 debit and $31,823 credit; Wages Payable, $4,812; Insurance Expense, $218; and Depreciation Expense, Office Equipment, $209.

REQUIRED

1. Prepare financial statements including the (a) detailed income statement; (b) statement of owner's equity; and (c) classified balance sheet.
2. Analyze financial statements by calculating (a) working capital; (b) current ratio; and (c) profit margin.
3. Prepare and journalize (page 39) closing entries. DO NOT post to the general ledger.
4. Prepare a post-closing trial balance.
(Optional)
5. Prepare and journalize (page 40) the reversing entry for Wages Payable on March 1, 19XX. DO NOT post to the general ledger.
6. Paid wages on March 5, 19XX, $7,214. Record this transaction in a general journal, page 40. DO NOT post to the general ledger.

ANSWERS TO SELF-TEST QUESTIONS

1. d   2. b   3. a   4. c   5. d

ACCOUNTING CYCLE REVIEW, CHAPTERS 7–12 (MERCHANDISING FIRM)

A review of the accounting cycle was introduced after Chapter 6 for a service firm. We will now examine the accounting cycle for a merchandising firm. Chapter 12 completed the accounting cycle for the merchandising firm United Auto Supply. This review section contains the following diagrams of the accounting cycle:

(A) An overview of the accounting cycle

(B) T account: applying debits and credits

(C) Posting

(D) Worksheet

(E) Financial statements (placed after Diagram C—on p. 433)

(F) Adjusting entries

(G) Closing entry sequence

Follow the arrows, where indicated, for the proper sequence.

DIAGRAM A
Accounting Cycle—Overview

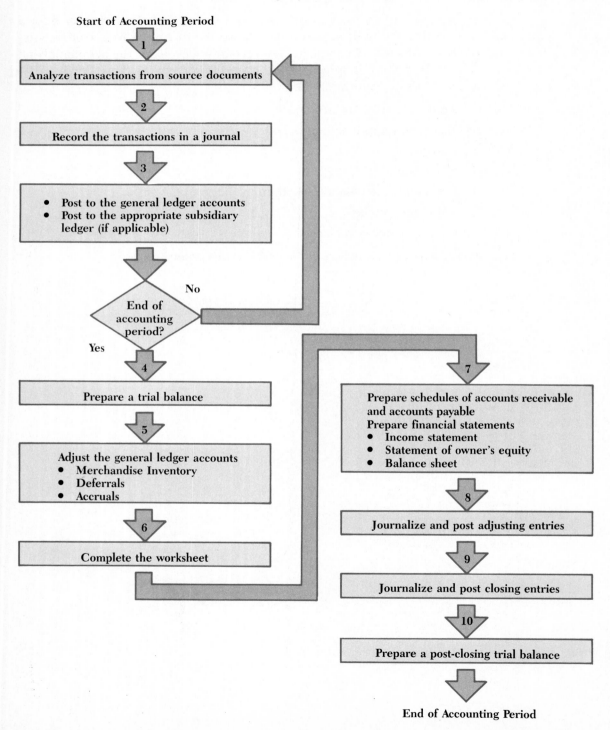

DIAGRAM B
T Account: Applying Debits and Credits

Account Title

Debit Side	Credit Side
Increase Asset	Decrease Asset
Decrease Contra Asset	Increase Contra Asset
Decrease Liability	Increase Liability
Decrease Owner's Capital	Increase Owner's Capital
Increase Owner's Drawing	Decrease Owner's Drawing
Decrease Revenues (sales)	Increase Revenues (sales)
Increase Contra Revenues or Contra Sales	Decrease Contra Revenues or Contra Sales
Increase Cost of Goods Sold	Decrease Cost of Goods Sold
Decrease Contra Cost of Goods Sold	Increase Contra Cost of Goods Sold
Increase Expenses	Decrease Expenses

DIAGRAM C
Posting (see Chapters 7–9)

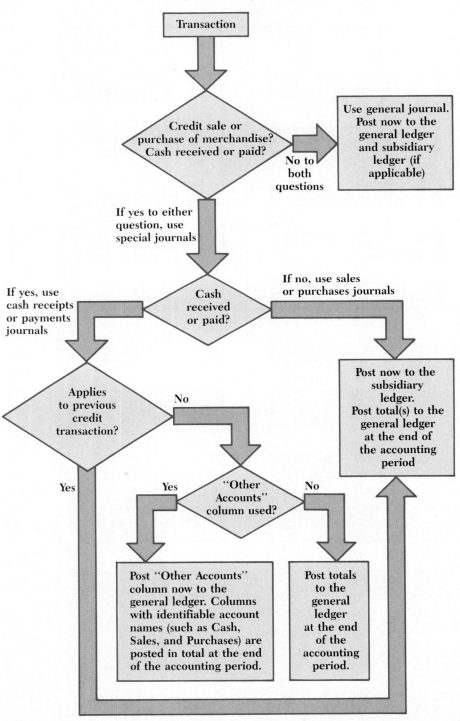

Transaction

Credit sale or purchase of merchandise? Cash received or paid?

No to both questions → Use general journal. Post now to the general ledger and subsidiary ledger (if applicable)

If yes to either question, use special journals

If yes, use cash receipts or payments journals

Cash received or paid?

If no, use sales or purchases journals

Applies to previous credit transaction?

No

Post now to the subsidiary ledger. Post total(s) to the general ledger at the end of the accounting period

Yes

Yes

"Other Accounts" column used?

No

Post "Other Accounts" column now to the general ledger. Columns with identifiable account names (such as Cash, Sales, and Purchases) are posted in total at the end of the accounting period.

Post totals to the general ledger at the end of the accounting period.

DIAGRAM E
Financial Statements (see Chapter 12)

Complete worksheet

1

Prepare income statement for the accounting period
Net Sales − Cost of Goods Sold = Gross Profit on Sales
− Operating Expenses = Income from Operations
+ Other Revenue = Net Income

2

Prepare statement of owner's equity for the accounting period
Beginning Capital + Net Income
+ Additional Investment(s) − Drawing = Ending Capital

3

Prepare balance sheet at end of accounting period
Assets = Liabilities + Owner's Equity

Accounting Period—Typically a Month, Quarter, or Year

DIAGRAM D
Completing the Worksheet (see Chapter 11)

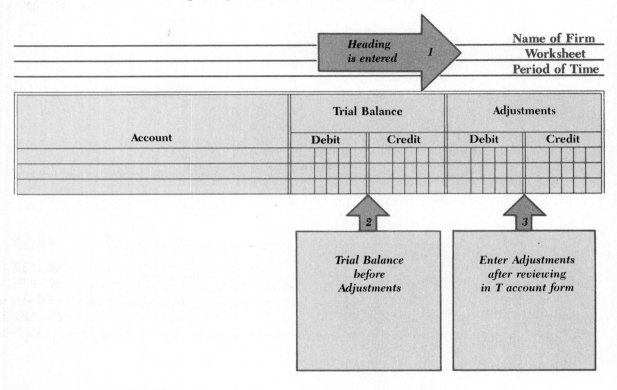

Adjusted Trial Balance		Income Statement		Balance Sheet	
Debit	**Credit**	**Debit**	**Credit**	**Debit**	**Credit**

4

Add, subtract, or extend "as is" Trial Balance and Adjustments columns

5

Extend revenues, expenses, and Income Summary to Income Statement columns

6

Extend assets, liabilities, Capital, and Drawing to Balance Sheet columns

DIAGRAM F
Journalizing and Posting Adjusting Entries (see Chapter 11)

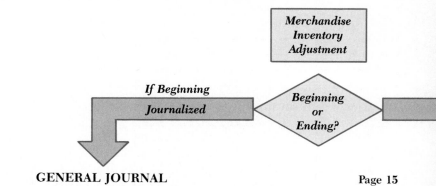

GENERAL JOURNAL   Page 15

Date		Description	Post. Ref.	Debit	Credit
		Adjusting Entries			
19XX					
Apr.	30	Income Summary	331	1 0 0 0 0 —	
		Merchandise Inventory	121		1 0 0 0 0 —

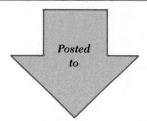

Posted
to

GENERAL LEDGER ACCOUNTS

Account: Merchandise Inventory   Account No. 121

Date		Item	Post. Ref.	Debit	Credit	Balance Debit	Balance Credit
19XX		Previous Balance				1 0 0 0 0 —	
Apr.	30	Adjusting	J15		1 0 0 0 0 —	— 0 —	

Account: Income Summary   Account No. 331

Date		Item	Post. Ref.	Debit	Credit	Balance Debit	Balance Credit
19XX							
Apr.	30	Adjusting	J15	1 0 0 0 0 —		1 0 0 0 0 —	

If Ending

Journalized

GENERAL JOURNAL

Page 15

Date		Description	Post. Ref.	Debit	Credit
		Adjusting Entries			
19XX					
Apr.	*30*	*Merchandise Inventory*	*121*	*12 0 0 0 —*	
		Income Summary	*331*		*12 0 0 0 —*

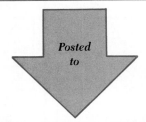

Posted
to

GENERAL LEDGER ACCOUNTS

Account: Merchandise Inventory   Account No. 121

Date		Item	Post. Ref.	Debit	Credit	Balance Debit	Balance Credit
19XX		*Previous Balance*				*1 0 0 0 0 —*	
Apr.	*30*	*Adjusting*	*J15*		*1 0 0 0 0 —*	*— 0 —*	
	30	*Adjusting*	*J15*	*1 2 0 0 0 —*		*1 2 0 0 0*	

Account: Income Summary   Account No. 331

Date		Item	Post. Ref.	Debit	Credit	Balance Debit	Balance Credit
19XX							
Apr.	*30*	*Adjusting*	*J15*	*1 0 0 0 0 —*		*1 0 0 0 0 —*	
	30	*Adjusting*	*J15*		*1 2 0 0 0 —*		*2 0 0 0 —*

DIAGRAM G
Closing Entry Sequence (see Chapter 12)

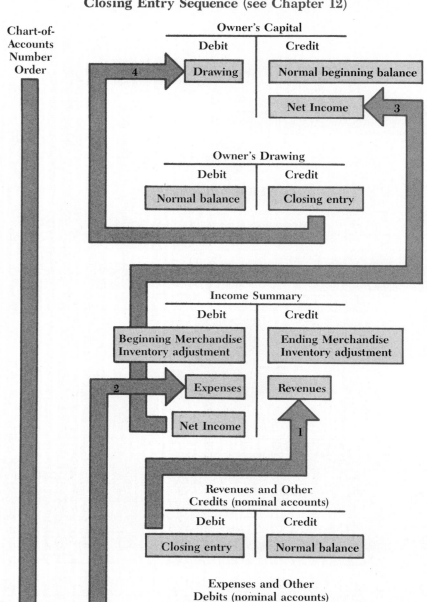

APPENDIX B
The Electronic Spreadsheet

An accountant can analyze financial statements manually by preparing a worksheet. She would write the account names and numbers in columns and manually add, subtract, multiply, or divide the numbers. But, what if her manager asks her to project net income if sales increase by 10 percent? Or, what is net income if sales decrease by 5 percent? In each situation, the accountant must manually recalculate the numbers or create a new worksheet—a tedious, expensive, and time-consuming task!

Today, much of this tiresome work is performed by using an electronic spreadsheet. The electronic spreadsheet is created by using a microcomputer and spreadsheet software. In Appendix A we asked three questions concerning computers and accounting. In this appendix we will continue our discussion of computers and accounting by focusing on the electronic spreadsheet.

WHAT IS AN ELECTRONIC SPREADSHEET?

Definition

In Appendix A we learned that an electronic spreadsheet is a computerized version of the worksheet. A spreadsheet is laid out just as a manual worksheet but performs all the mathematical calculations that are normally done by hand.

Calculations

The electronic spreadsheet adds, subtracts, multiplies, and divides instantly. It also can be used to compute averages, square roots, and other mathematical calculations.

HOW DOES AN ELECTRONIC SPREADSHEET WORK?

Structure

The electronic spreadsheet is simply a large blank page made up of columns and rows. Remember that the electronic spreadsheet uses the power of the microcomputer to perform mathematical calculations instantly and accurately. In Exhibit B-1 we see that the *columns* are shown as the letters A through H across the top. *Rows* are identified by 1 through 20 down the left side. The intersection of each column and row is called a

EXHIBIT B-1
Structure of Electronic Spreadsheet

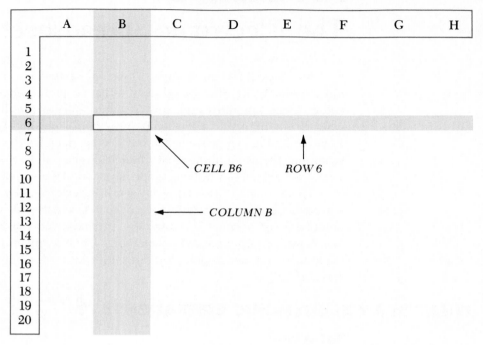

cell. In Exhibit B-1 we see that cell B6 is the intersection of column B and row 6.

Most popular spreadsheet software programs contain many columns and rows. In fact, some electronic spreadsheet packages can store millions of cells—a printout larger than any manual worksheet!

Cell Contents

A cell can contain a label, number, or formula. A *label* is a description, such as Revenue. 80,000 would be an example of a number. *Formulas* are programmed instructions, such as Revenues minus Expenses equals Net Income. This formula could be expressed as $+B4-B5$ (subtract cell B5 from B4).

HOW ARE ELECTRONIC SPREADSHEETS USED BY ACCOUNTANTS?

Common Uses

Accountants use electronic spreadsheets to prepare financial statements, make forecasts of sales and expenses, prepare budgets, evaluate alternatives, maintain and update inventories, and perform other mathematical calculations as necessary.

Application

A simple application of an electronic spreadsheet is shown in Exhibit B-2. Since a spreadsheet is a large blank page, the accountant enters all labels, numbers, and formulas in the appropriate cells. The spreadsheet to the left in Exhibit B-2 shows the labels, numbers, and formula as entered by the spreadsheet creator, such as an accountant. The electronic spreadsheet to the right in Exhibit B-2 illustrates the display to be used by a spreadsheet user, such as a department manager. The income statement has revenue of 100,000 (cell B4) and an 80,000 expense (cell B5). As in a manual worksheet, the expense is subtracted from revenue to obtain net income. On the electronic spreadsheet this formula is entered as $+B4-B5$ in cell B6 (left spreadsheet—Exhibit B-2). $+B4-B5$ means that the expense (80,000 in cell B5) is subtracted from revenue (100,000 in cell B4). Net income would then show the number 20,000 $(100,000 - 80,000)$ in cell B6 (right spreadsheet—Exhibit B-2).

EXHIBIT B-2
Simple Income Statement

Entered

	A	B	C
1	Preparer's Name:	Nora Gold	
2	Spreadsheet Title:	Income	
3		Statement	
4	Revenue	100,000	
5	Expense	80,000	
6	Net Income	+ B4-B5	
7			
8			

Displayed

	A	B	C
1	Preparer's Name:	Nora Gold	
2	Spreadsheet Title:	Income	
3		Statement	
4	Revenue	100,000	
5	Expense	80,000	
6	Net Income	20,000	
7			
8			

TEXTBOOK USE

The *Study Guide*, by the author, which accompanies this textbook, contains a section on the electronic spreadsheet. This section includes full instructions to work selected problems for the remainder of this textbook (starting with Chapter 13) using the electronic spreadsheet. Brief notes on how to work the selected problems appear on page 524.

13

Payroll: Employee Earnings and Deductions

If making money is a slow process, losing it is quickly done.

IHARA SAIKAKU

LEARNING OBJECTIVES

After reading this chapter, discussing the questions, and working the exercises and problems, you will be able to do the following:

1. Understand employee payroll accounting (pp. 444–45).

2. Calculate gross and net pay (pp. 446–51).

3. Prepare an employee compensation record and a payroll register (pp. 451–55).

In Chapter 10 we discussed the cash transactions for United Auto Supply for October 19XX. In this chapter we'll examine payroll. Payroll is a major expense for most firms. In fact, in many service businesses, such as law, accounting, banking, and brokerage, payroll costs represent half or more of operating expenses.

EMPLOYEE PAYROLL ACCOUNTING

Objective 1
Understand employee payroll accounting.

Payroll accounting has three objectives:

1. To compute the amount of wages or salaries due employees.
2. To pay the wages or salaries promptly.
3. To complete various government reports.

We will examine the first two objectives in this chapter. The various government reports will be examined in Chapter 14.

The Employer/Employee Relationship An **employer** is a person or firm who hires an **employee** to perform designated services. The employer usually provides the place of work for the employee and usually has the right to hire, fire, and control the work of the employee.

An **independent contractor** is in business for him- or herself; examples are attorneys, dentists, and certified public accountants. An independent contractor is hired by a person or firm to perform designated services. However, the person or firm does not have the right to control or supervise the independent contractor.

Hourly Wages and Salaries **Wages** are the earnings of employees who are paid on an hourly or piecework basis. A few examples of this type of worker are automobile assembly line workers, machinists, and steel workers. **Salaries** are the earnings of employees who are paid on a monthly or annual basis. Some examples of this type of worker are teachers, store managers, and police officers.

Payroll Tax Laws

Certain laws passed by the U.S. Congress affect the amount a person is paid. Three of the major payroll-related laws are the Fair Labor Standards Act, the Federal Insurance Contributions Act, and the Sixteenth Amendment to the Constitution.

Fair Labor Standards Act   The Fair Labor Standards Act (FLSA), commonly known as the Federal Wage and Hour Law, was established in 1938. It is administered by the Wage and Hour Division of the U.S. Department of Labor. This act states that overtime pay is required for all hours worked in excess of forty during a workweek. For any hours over forty, the required overtime pay is equal to time and one-half (1.5) the employee's regular hourly rate of pay.

For example, assume that Donna Newhart's regular rate of pay is $10.10 per hour. Her overtime rate would be $10.10 times 1.5, which is $15.15 per hour.

Federal Insurance Contributions Act   The Federal Insurance Contributions Act (FICA), commonly known as the Social Security Act, was enacted in 1935. This act, with all its amendments, provides for a federal system of old age, survivors, disability, and hospital insurance. Both the employee and employer must contribute an equal amount to this fund. We will assume in this chapter that the rate is 7.65 percent each for employers and employees to a maximum amount of $51,300 per year. Thus, an employee and employer could each contribute a maximum of $3,924.45 ($51,300 × .0765). If an employee is paid more than $51,300, no additional FICA taxes are withheld.

For example, assume that Gene Morgan has year-to-date earnings of $26,500. His FICA tax would be $2,027.25 ($26,500 × .0765). Gene's employer would contribute an equal amount. A co-worker of Gene's, Mary Lopez, has year-to-date earnings of $52,500. She and her employer would each contribute $3,924.45 ($51,300 × .0765). No contributions are made after $51,300; therefore, the difference of $1,200 ($52,500 − $51,300) is exempt from FICA taxes.

Sixteenth Amendment   On March 1, 1913, the Sixteenth Amendment to the Constitution was enacted to allow income (earnings) to be taxed by the federal government. Until 1943 employees paid the amount due at the end of the year. But with the passage of the Current Tax Payment Act of 1943 employers were required to withhold federal income taxes from the wages and salaries paid their employees on a "pay-as-you-go" basis.

CALCULATING THE GROSS PAYROLL

Objective 2
Calculate gross
and net pay.

The total amount earned by all employees before deductions is called the **gross payroll** or **gross pay.** The gross payroll involves the earnings of those employees paid on an hourly and piecework basis (wages) and those paid on a monthly or annual basis (salary). Let's first calculate the gross pay of an hourly worker for United Auto Supply for the week ended January 31, 19XX.

Wage Earners   Carl Moore is an hourly worker who is paid $10.50 per hour. United Auto Supply pays time and one-half for hours worked in excess of forty for the week. He works forty-two hours during the week, so his gross pay is calculated as follows:

	40 Hours at Straight Time	40 × $10.50 = $420.00
	2 Hours Overtime	2 × 15.75 = 31.50
Total	42 Hours	$451.50

The $15.75 overtime rate is calculated by multiplying the regular hourly rate times one and one-half ($10.50 × 1.5 = $15.75).

Overtime is calculated for a specific workweek only, even if an employee is paid every two weeks. For example, if an employee worked thirty-seven hours one week and forty-four hours the next, the four hours in the second week would be considered overtime. The weeks are not averaged together.

Salaried Earners   Hu Le, the accountant for United Auto Supply, is a salaried employee who is paid $27,300 per year. The gross earnings per pay period are computed as follows:

Pay Period	Number of Pay Periods in a Year	Gross Pay Per Period
Monthly	12 months	$27,300 ÷ 12 = $2,275
Bi-weekly	26 weeks	$27,300 ÷ 26 = $1,050
Weekly	52 weeks	$27,300 ÷ 52 = $ 525

Piece Rate   Some employees are paid on a unit-of-production basis called **piece rate.** For example, Larry Hayes, a factory worker, is paid $0.26 for each unit produced. If he produces 1,340 units, then his pay is $348.40 (1,340 units × $0.26).

Commission   Many salespeople are paid on a **commission** basis. For example, Sarah McNutt, a lumber salesperson, is paid 4 percent of her sales. She sells $11,762 of lumber, so her pay is $470.48 ($11,762 × .04).

CALCULATING NET PAY

An employee does not usually receive his or her gross (total) earnings as **net pay.** Net pay is the actual cash amount that an employee receives in the form of a paycheck. The difference is due to deductions applied to the employee's gross pay. These deductions may be voluntary (such as charitable contributions, savings bonds, life insurance, and so on), or they could be involuntary (such as FICA tax, federal income tax, state income tax, and so on).

The largest deduction for most employees is their estimated liability for federal income tax. Since March 1, 1913, income has been taxed by the federal government. Employers are required to withhold federal income taxes from the wages and salaries paid their employees on a "pay-as-you-go" basis. This amount is then forwarded to the Internal Revenue Service. Exhibit 13-1 shows a withholding table for married employees who are paid weekly. This withholding table is found in *Circular E, Employer's Tax Guide*, which is obtained from the IRS. This guide tells employers about their tax responsibilities to their employees.

Hu Le is married and claims four withholding allowances (dependents). Her weekly pay is $525. Therefore, the federal income tax to be withheld by United Auto Supply for Hu is $45 (see Exhibit 13-1). The $45 is determined by finding the wages in the left-hand column (525) and then matching that with the withholding allowances at the top (4). Her $525 falls between the "At least" $520 "But less than" $530, so the rate is $45. To know how much federal income tax to withhold from an employee's salary or wages, the employer should have a **Form W-4, Employee's Withholding Allowance Certificate,** on file for each employee. The amount to be withheld is determined by the employee's gross wages or salary and the information submitted by the employee on Form W-4 (see Exhibit 13-2). This information includes the employee's marital status, the number of withholding allowances claimed, the employee's request to have additional tax withheld, and the employee's claim to exemption from withholdings.

Hu Le's take-home or net pay for the week ended December 31, 19XX, is computed as follows:

Gross Earnings (Pay)		$525.00
Less Deductions:		
FICA Tax ($525 × 7.65%)	$40.16*	
Federal Income Tax	45.00	
Medical Insurance	12.00	
Total Deductions		97.16
Net (Take-home) Pay		$427.84

*Rounded to the cent. See page 450 for rounding steps.

EXHIBIT 13-1
Circular E: Married Persons—Weekly Payroll

MARRIED Persons—WEEKLY Payroll Period

And the wages are—		And the number of withholding allowances claimed is—										
At least	But less than	0	1	2	3	4	5	6	7	8	9	10
		The amount of income tax to be withheld shall be—										
$0	$70	$0	$0	$0	$0	$0	$0	$0	$0	$0	$0	$0
70	75	1	0	0	0	0	0	0	0	0	0	0
75	80	2	0	0	0	0	0	0	0	0	0	0
80	85	3	0	0	0	0	0	0	0	0	0	0
85	90	3	0	0	0	0	0	0	0	0	0	0
90	95	4	0	0	0	0	0	0	0	0	0	0
95	100	5	0	0	0	0	0	0	0	0	0	0
100	105	6	0	0	0	0	0	0	0	0	0	0
105	110	6	0	0	0	0	0	0	0	0	0	0
110	115	7	1	0	0	0	0	0	0	0	0	0
115	120	8	2	0	0	0	0	0	0	0	0	0
120	125	9	3	0	0	0	0	0	0	0	0	0
125	130	9	3	0	0	0	0	0	0	0	0	0
130	135	10	4	0	0	0	0	0	0	0	0	0
135	140	11	5	0	0	0	0	0	0	0	0	0
140	145	12	6	0	0	0	0	0	0	0	0	0
145	150	12	6	0	0	0	0	0	0	0	0	0
150	155	13	7	1	0	0	0	0	0	0	0	0
155	160	14	8	2	0	0	0	0	0	0	0	0
160	165	15	9	3	0	0	0	0	0	0	0	0
165	170	15	9	3	0	0	0	0	0	0	0	0
170	175	16	10	4	0	0	0	0	0	0	0	0
175	180	17	11	5	0	0	0	0	0	0	0	0
180	185	18	12	6	0	0	0	0	0	0	0	0
185	190	18	12	6	1	0	0	0	0	0	0	0
190	195	19	13	7	1	0	0	0	0	0	0	0
195	200	20	14	8	2	0	0	0	0	0	0	0
200	210	21	15	9	3	0	0	0	0	0	0	0
210	220	22	17	11	5	0	0	0	0	0	0	0
220	230	24	18	12	6	0	0	0	0	0	0	0
230	240	25	20	14	8	2	0	0	0	0	0	0
240	250	27	21	15	9	3	0	0	0	0	0	0
250	260	28	23	17	11	5	0	0	0	0	0	0
260	270	30	24	18	12	6	0	0	0	0	0	0
270	280	31	26	20	14	8	2	0	0	0	0	0
280	290	33	27	21	15	9	3	0	0	0	0	0
290	300	34	29	23	17	11	5	0	0	0	0	0
300	310	36	30	24	18	12	6	0	0	0	0	0
310	320	37	32	26	20	14	8	2	0	0	0	0
320	330	39	33	27	21	15	9	3	0	0	0	0
330	340	40	35	29	23	17	11	5	0	0	0	0
340	350	42	36	30	24	18	12	6	1	0	0	0
350	360	43	38	32	26	20	14	8	2	0	0	0
360	370	45	39	33	27	21	15	9	4	0	0	0
370	380	46	41	35	29	23	17	11	5	0	0	0
380	390	48	42	36	30	24	18	12	7	1	0	0
390	400	49	44	38	32	26	20	14	8	2	0	0
400	410	51	45	39	33	27	21	15	10	4	0	0
410	420	52	47	41	35	29	23	17	11	5	0	0
420	430	54	48	42	36	30	24	18	13	7	1	0
430	440	55	50	44	38	32	26	20	14	8	2	0
440	450	57	51	45	39	33	27	21	16	10	4	0
450	460	58	53	47	41	35	29	23	17	11	5	0
460	470	60	54	48	42	36	30	24	19	13	7	1
470	480	61	56	50	44	38	32	26	20	14	8	2
480	490	63	57	51	45	39	33	27	22	16	10	4
490	500	64	59	53	47	41	35	29	23	17	11	5
500	510	66	60	54	48	42	36	30	25	19	13	7
510	520	67	62	56	50	44	38	32	26	20	14	8
520	530	69	63	57	51	45	39	33	28	22	16	10
530	540	70	65	59	53	47	41	35	29	23	17	11
540	550	72	66	60	54	48	42	36	31	25	19	13
550	560	73	68	62	56	50	44	38	32	26	20	14
560	570	75	69	63	57	51	45	39	34	28	22	16
570	580	76	71	65	59	53	47	41	35	29	23	17
580	590	78	72	66	60	54	48	42	37	31	25	19
590	600	79	74	68	62	56	50	44	38	32	26	20
600	610	81	75	69	63	57	51	45	40	34	28	22
610	620	82	77	71	65	59	53	47	41	35	29	23
620	630	84	78	72	66	60	54	48	43	37	31	25

(Continued on next page)

MARRIED Persons—WEEKLY Payroll Period

And the wages are—		And the number of withholding allowances claimed is—										
At least	But less than	0	1	2	3	4	5	6	7	8	9	10
		The amount of income tax to be withheld shall be—										
$630	$640	$85	$80	$74	$68	$62	$56	$50	$44	$38	$32	$26
640	650	87	81	75	69	63	57	51	46	40	34	28
650	660	88	83	77	71	65	59	53	47	41	35	29
660	670	90	84	78	72	66	60	54	49	43	37	31
670	680	91	86	80	74	68	62	56	50	44	38	32
680	690	93	87	81	75	69	63	57	52	46	40	34
690	700	95	89	83	77	71	65	59	53	47	41	35
700	710	98	90	84	78	72	66	60	55	49	43	37
710	720	101	92	86	80	74	68	62	56	50	44	38
720	730	104	93	87	81	75	69	63	58	52	46	40
730	740	106	95	89	83	77	71	65	59	53	47	41
740	750	109	98	90	84	78	72	66	61	55	49	43
750	760	112	101	92	86	80	74	68	62	56	50	44
760	770	115	104	93	87	81	75	69	64	58	52	46
770	780	118	107	95	89	83	77	71	65	59	53	47
780	790	120	109	98	90	84	78	72	67	61	55	49
790	800	123	112	101	92	86	80	74	68	62	56	50
800	810	126	115	104	93	87	81	75	70	64	58	52
810	820	129	118	107	96	89	83	77	71	65	59	53
820	830	132	121	109	98	90	84	78	73	67	61	55
830	840	134	123	112	101	92	86	80	74	68	62	56
840	850	137	126	115	104	93	87	81	76	70	64	58
850	860	140	129	118	107	96	89	83	77	71	65	59
860	870	143	132	121	110	99	90	84	79	73	67	61
870	880	146	135	123	112	101	92	86	80	74	68	62
880	890	148	137	126	115	104	93	87	82	76	70	64
890	900	151	140	129	118	107	96	89	83	77	71	65
900	910	154	143	132	121	110	99	90	85	79	73	67
910	920	157	146	135	124	113	102	92	86	80	74	68
920	930	160	149	137	126	115	104	93	88	82	76	70
930	940	162	151	140	129	118	107	96	89	83	77	71
940	950	165	154	143	132	121	110	99	91	85	79	73
950	960	168	157	146	135	124	113	102	92	86	80	74
960	970	171	160	149	138	127	116	105	94	88	82	76
970	980	174	163	151	140	129	118	107	96	89	83	77
980	990	176	165	154	143	132	121	110	99	91	85	79
990	1,000	179	168	157	146	135	124	113	102	92	86	80
1,000	1,010	182	171	160	149	138	127	116	105	94	88	82
1,010	1,020	185	174	163	152	141	130	119	107	96	89	83
1,020	1,030	188	177	165	154	143	132	121	110	99	91	85
1,030	1,040	190	179	168	157	146	135	124	113	102	92	86
1,040	1,050	193	182	171	160	149	138	127	116	105	94	88
1,050	1,060	196	185	174	163	152	141	130	119	108	97	89
1,060	1,070	199	188	177	166	155	144	133	121	110	99	91
1,070	1,080	202	191	179	168	157	146	135	124	113	102	92
1,080	1,090	204	193	182	171	160	149	138	127	116	105	94
1,090	1,100	207	196	185	174	163	152	141	130	119	108	97
1,100	1,110	210	199	188	177	166	155	144	133	122	111	100
1,110	1,120	213	202	191	180	169	158	147	135	124	113	102
1,120	1,130	216	205	193	182	171	160	149	138	127	116	105
1,130	1,140	218	207	196	185	174	163	152	141	130	119	108
1,140	1,150	221	210	199	188	177	166	155	144	133	122	111
1,150	1,160	224	213	202	191	180	169	158	147	136	125	114
1,160	1,170	227	216	205	194	183	172	161	149	138	127	116
1,170	1,180	230	219	207	196	185	174	163	152	141	130	119
1,180	1,190	232	221	210	199	188	177	166	155	144	133	122
1,190	1,200	235	224	213	202	191	180	169	158	147	136	125
1,200	1,210	238	227	216	205	194	183	172	161	150	139	128
1,210	1,220	241	230	219	208	197	186	175	163	152	141	130
1,220	1,230	244	233	221	210	199	188	177	166	155	144	133
1,230	1,240	246	235	224	213	202	191	180	169	158	147	136
1,240	1,250	249	238	227	216	205	194	183	172	161	150	139
1,250	1,260	252	241	230	219	208	197	186	175	164	153	142
1,260	1,270	255	244	233	222	211	200	189	177	166	155	144
1,270	1,280	258	247	235	224	213	202	191	180	169	158	147
1,280	1,290	260	249	238	227	216	205	194	183	172	161	150

EXHIBIT 13-2
W-4: Employee's Withholding Allowance Certificate

Form **W-4** Department of the Treasury Internal Revenue Service	**Employee's Withholding Allowance Certificate** ▶ **For Privacy Act and Paperwork Reduction Act Notice, see reverse.**	OMB No. 1545-0010

1 Type or print your first name and middle initial _Hu_	Last name _Le_	**2** Your social security number _400-00-0000_

Home address (number and street or rural route) _12 G Avenue_	**3** Marital status	☐ Single ☒ Married
City or town, state, and ZIP code _Houston, Texas 77002_		☐ Married, but withhold at higher Single rate. **Note:** If married, but legally separated, or spouse is a nonresident alien, check the Single box.

4 Total number of allowances you are claiming (from line G above or from the Worksheets on back if they apply) . . . **4** | _4_

5 Additional amount, if any, you want deducted from each pay . . . . **5** $ _-0-_

6 I claim exemption from withholding and I certify that I meet **ALL** of the following conditions for exemption:
- Last year I had a right to a refund of **ALL** Federal income tax withheld because I had **NO** tax liability; **AND**
- This year I expect a refund of **ALL** Federal income tax withheld because I expect to have **NO** tax liability; **AND**
- This year if my income exceeds $500 and includes nonwage income, another person cannot claim me as a dependent.

If you meet all of the above conditions, enter the year effective and "EXEMPT" here . . . . . ▶ **6** | 19

7 Are you a full-time student? (**Note:** Full-time students are not automatically exempt.) . . . . **7** ☐ Yes ☒ No

Under penalties of perjury, I certify that I am entitled to the number of withholding allowances claimed on this certificate or entitled to claim exempt status.

Employee's signature ▶ _Hu Le_   Date ▶ _February 1_ , 19 _XX_

8 Employer's name and address (**Employer:** Complete 8 and 10 **only if sending to IRS**)	**9** Office code (optional)	**10** Employer identification number

---

Rounding to the Cent

There are three steps to follow when rounding to the cent (two places). First, identify the digit to be rounded, which is the cent (two places to the right of the decimal point). Second, if the digit to the right of the cent is 5 or more, increase the cent by one. If 4 or less, the cent is not changed. And third, change all of the digits to the right of the cent to zeros. For example, $12.6891 is rounded to $12.69, $6.9954 is rounded to $7.00, $547.01462 is rounded to $547.01, and so on.

Payroll Deductions An employee may have deductions other than the ones previously listed. A **deduction** is an amount that reduces an employee's take-home or net pay. Some of these deductions may include:

1. State income tax.
2. City income tax.
3. Purchase of U.S. savings bonds.
4. Union dues.

5. Life insurance premiums.

6. Contributions to charities.

7. Loan payments to a company credit union.

8. Savings through a company credit union.

EMPLOYEE COMPENSATION RECORDS

Objective 3
Prepare an employee compensation record and a payroll register.

An employer must keep a record of earnings and withholdings for each employee. United Auto Supply would have an **employee compensation record** for each employee. The one for Hu Le is shown in Exhibit 13-3:

EXHIBIT 13-3
Employee Compensation Record

EMPLOYEE COMPENSATION RECORD

Employee's Name _____ *Hu Le* _____ Social Security No. _____ *400-00-0000* _____
Address _*12 G Avenue*_ Male _____ Female _*X*_ Weekly Pay Rate _*$525.00*_
*Houston, Texas 77002* Married _*X*_ Single _____ Hourly Equivalent _*$13.13*_
Date of Birth _*April 5, 1952*_ Withholding Allowances _*4*_
Position _*Accountant*_ Date of Employment _*February 1, 19XX*_
Date Employment Ended _____

| Pay Period Ending | Total Hours | Earnings | | | Deductions | | | | Net Pay | Cumulative Gross Earnings |
		Regular	Overtime	Total	FICA Tax	FIT Tax	Medical Insurance	Total Deductions		
12/10	40	525.00	0.00	525.00	40.16	45.00	12.00	97.16	427.84	24,675.00
12/17	40	525.00	0.00	525.00	40.16	45.00	12.00	97.16	427.84	25,200.00
12/24	40	525.00	0.00	525.00	40.16	45.00	12.00	97.16	427.84	25,725.00
12/31	40	525.00	0.00	525.00	40.16	45.00	12.00	97.16	427.84	26,250.00

PAYROLL REGISTERS

The employer would also prepare a **payroll register** for each payroll period which summarizes the payroll for *all* employees. The payroll register is prepared using each employee's compensation record. Exhibit 13-4

EXHIBIT 13-4
Payroll Register

PAYROLL REGISTER
For the Week Ended   December 31, 19XX

| Employee | Total Hours | Earnings ② | | | Deductions ④ | | | | Net Pay ⑦ | Distribution |
		Regular	Overtime	Total	FICA Tax	FIT Tax	Medical Insurance	Total Deductions		Wages Expense
Le, H. ①	40	525.00	0.00	525.00	40.16	45.00	12.00	97.16	427.84	525.00
Moore, C.	42	420.00	31.50	451.50	34.54	47.00	11.00	92.54	358.96	451.50
Rylski, F.	40	640.00	0.00	640.00	48.96	69.00	13.00	130.96	509.04	640.00
Vega, B.	43	568.00	63.90	631.90	48.34	56.00	10.00	114.34	517.56	631.90
Totals ③		2,153.00	95.40	2,248.40	172.00	217.00	46.00	435.00	1,813.40	2,248.40
					⑤	⑥			⑧	⑨

shows a payroll register for United Auto Supply for the week ended December 31, 19XX.

Completing the Payroll Register

There are nine steps to follow when completing the payroll register. The steps are keyed to Exhibit 13-4 as follows:

① Use one line for each employee for each payroll period.

② Calculate Total Earnings for each employee, including any overtime pay. Total the Earnings columns.

③ Verify that Regular Earnings and Overtime Earnings equal Total Earnings as follows:

Total Regular Earnings	$2,153.00
Total Overtime Earnings	95.40
Total Earnings	$2,248.40

④ Determine the Deductions for each employee.

⑤ Total the Deductions columns.

⑥ Verify that the Deductions columns equal the Total Deductions column as follows:

Total FICA Tax	$172.00
Total FIT Tax	217.00
Total Medical Insurance	46.00
Total Deductions	$435.00

⑦ Calculate the Net Pay for each employee by subtracting the employee's Total Deductions from the employee's Total Earnings. Total the Net Pay column.

⑧ Verify that Total Deductions subtracted from Total Earnings equals Total Net Pay as follows:

Total Earnings	$2,248.40
Less: Total Deductions	435.00
Total Net Pay	$1,813.40

⑨ Record the distribution.

Recording the Payroll

The payroll entry is recorded in the general journal using the information from the payroll register. Since payroll calculations are usually made before paychecks are distributed to employees, the accountant credits Wages Payable rather than Cash. Using the information from the payroll register in Exhibit 13-4, the payroll entry is journalized in Exhibit 13-5:

EXHIBIT 13-5
Payroll Entry

GENERAL JOURNAL   Page ___40___

Date		Description	Post. Ref.	Debit	Credit
19XX					
Dec.	31	Wages Expense ①		2 2 4 8 40	
		FICA Tax Payable			1 7 2 —
		② Federal Income Tax Payable			2 1 7 —
		Medical Insurance Payable			4 6 —
		③ Wages Payable			1 8 1 3 40
		Employee's Payroll for the Week Ended December 31, 19XX			

There are three steps to follow when preparing the payroll entry from the payroll register. These steps are keyed in Exhibit 13-5. The amounts are taken from the payroll register (Exhibit 13-4). For United Auto Supply, the steps are as follows:

1. The Total Earnings from the payroll register is listed as Wages Expense in the payroll entry. This amount is debited.

2. Each of the Deductions is credited in the payroll entry. The Deductions represent liabilities that must be paid at a later date to the appropriate authorities.

3. The Total Net Pay amount in the payroll register is recorded as Wages Payable in the payroll entry. This amount is a liability and is credited. Wages Payable (Net Pay) is the total amount the employees will receive in cash for this payroll period. Remember that employees have deductions withheld, thus reducing the amount of money they will actually receive.

Payroll Checking Accounts

Many firms maintain a special payroll checking account at a bank. The purposes for this account are as follows:

1. Payroll checks can be issued separately from other check payments, such as rent expense, purchases of merchandise, and so on. This makes it easier for many firms with a large number of employees to reconcile bank checking accounts.

2. Only the Total Net Pay amount is deposited in the special payroll checking account, thus providing greater internal control over Cash. The special payroll checking account should have a zero balance after all payroll checks have cleared the bank.

3. Only a few employees, such as the payroll accountant, will know what other employees are paid. Thus, by having a special payroll checking account, there is more privacy.

SELF-TEST QUESTIONS FOR REVIEW

(Answers are on p. 467.)

1. What of the following, enacted on March 1, 1913, pertains to taxes?
   a. Fair Labor Standards Act
   b. Social Security Act
   c. Sixteenth Amendment
   d. Current Tax Payment Act

2. A person is paid 5 percent of her sales. This is an example of
   a. a commission.
   b. piece work.
   c. wages.
   d. a salary.

3. The FICA tax rate used in the chapter is _____ for the employee and _____ for the employer.
   a. 7.65%; none
   b. none; 7.65%
   c. 7.65%; 7.15%
   d. 7.65%; 7.65%

4. "Record the distribution" is step ____ of completing the payroll register.
   a. 3
   b. 5
   c. 1
   d. 9

5. _____ is debited and _____ is credited when depositing money in a special payroll checking account.
   a. Cash; Wages Expense
   b. Wages Payable; Cash
   c. Cash; Wages Payable
   d. Accounts Payable; Cash

PRACTICAL REVIEW PROBLEM

Objective 3

Completing Employee Compensation Records Saunders Fuel Supply has two employees. This information was collected to complete the employee compensation records for the week ended October 23, 19XX (both are married):

	Maria D'Amico	Fred Walters
Social Security Numbers	111-11-0000	222-22-0000
Addresses	195 Canal	401 Santa Ana
	Modesto, California	Modesto, California
	95354	95350
Weekly or Hourly Pay Rate	$710/week	$10.60/hour
Withholding Allowances	2	4
Cumulative Gross Earnings (including this pay period)	$31,950	$19,060
Position	Office Manager	Bookkeeper
Medical Insurance Deductions	$46	$52
Employment Date	February 2, 19XX	March 9, 19XX
Birth Date	April 6, 1948	July 18, 1951
Overtime Earnings	$–0–	6 hours

Other Payroll Data:

a. The FICA tax rate is 7.65 percent of the first $51,300 of earnings for each employee.

b. Use Exhibit 13-1 to determine federal income taxes.

c. The firm pays overtime pay at time and one-half (1.5) for any hours worked in excess of forty per workweek.

REQUIRED

Complete an employee compensation record for each employee. Round all amounts to the cent. For purposes of simplicity, assume that there are no state or city income taxes.

ANSWER TO PRACTICAL REVIEW PROBLEM

EMPLOYEE COMPENSATION RECORD

Employee's Name ___Maria D'Amico___   Social Security No. ___111-11-0000___   ①

Address ___195 Canal___   Male _____ Female __X__ Weekly Pay Rate ___$710.00___

___Modesto, California 95354___   Married __X__ Single _____ Hourly Equivalent ___$17.75___

Date of Birth ___April 6, 1948___   Withholding Allowances __2__

Position ___Office Manager___   Date of Employment ___February 2, 19XX___

Date Employment Ended _____

Pay Period Ending	Total Hours	Earnings			Deductions			Total Deduc-tions	Net Pay	Cumulative Gross Earnings
		Regular	Overtime	Total	FICA Tax	FIT Tax	Medical Insur-ance			
10/23	40	710.00	0.00	710.00	54.32	86.00	46.00	186.32	523.68	31,950.00

EMPLOYEE COMPENSATION RECORD

Employee's Name _____ *Fred Walters* _____   Social Security No. _____ *222-22-0000* _____

Address _____ *401 Santa Ana* _____   Male __*X*__ Female _____ Weekly Pay Rate __*$424.00*__ ②

_____ *Modesto, California 95350* _____   Married __*X*__ Single _____ Hourly Equivalent __*$10.60*__

Date of Birth __*July 18, 1951*__   Withholding Allowances __*4*__

Position __*Bookkeeper*__   Date of Employment _____ *March 9, 19XX* _____

Date Employment Ended _____

| Pay Period Ending | Total Hours | Earnings | | | Deductions | | | | Net Pay | Cumulative Gross Earnings |
		Regular	Overtime	Total	FICA Tax	FIT Tax	Medical Insurance	Total Deductions		
10/23	46	424.00	95.40 ③	519.40	39.73 ④	44.00	52.00	135.73	383.67	19,060.00

① $710 ÷ 40 = $17.75.

② $10.60 × 40 = $424.

③ $10.60 × 1.5 = $15.90 × 6 = $95.40.

④ Example of rounding: $519.40 × 0.765 = $39.7341 = $39.73 rounded to the cent.

DISCUSSION QUESTIONS

Q 13-1   What are the three objectives of payroll accounting?

Q 13-2   Identify and briefly explain the major payroll laws.

Q 13-3   In your own words, explain the reason(s) for paying employees time and a half. Is this beneficial for both the employee and employer?

Q 13-4   How is net pay calculated? Could gross pay ever equal net pay?

Q 13-5   What is the purpose of an employee compensation record and a payroll register? Are they related? If yes, explain how.

Q 13-6   Name at least five payroll deductions.

Q 13-7   Name the steps in completing the payroll register.

Q 13-8   Name the steps to follow when preparing the payroll entry from the payroll register.

Q 13-9   What is the largest deduction for most employees from their paychecks? What type of deductions do you have or have you had from *your* paycheck?

Q 13-10   Name the three reasons why a firm would have a special payroll checking account.

EXERCISES

Objective 2   **E 13-1**   **Categorizing Deductions**   Categorize the following deductions as voluntary (V) or involuntary (I):

a. FICA tax
b. Savings bonds
c. Life insurance
d. State income tax
e. Charitable contributions
f. Federal income tax
g. Savings through a company credit union
h. City income tax

Objective 2   **E 13-2**   **Calculating Gross Pay**   Calculate the gross pay for the following employees:

a. D. Bui is paid time and a half for all hours over forty. She works forty-five hours during a workweek, and her regular pay is $10 per hour.
b. F. Young is paid weekly. His gross earnings for the year (52 weeks) are $21,320.
c. J. Rojas is paid 5 percent of her sales. She sells $10,740.

Objective 3   **E 13-3**   **Completing an Employee Compensation Record**   Complete an employee compensation record using the following information: The employee is Jack Allbright and his social security number is 500-00-0000. Jack's address is 7100 South Phillips, Chicago, Illinois, 60649. He is single and has zero withholding allowances. He was employed as an accountant for the firm on March 7, 19XX, at a weekly (40 hours) rate of $600. For the pay period ending June 7, 19XX, Jack worked 40 hours with no overtime hours. His FICA tax is $45.90, FIT tax is $81, and medical insurance is $20. Jack was born June 16, 1960. His cumulative gross earnings are $6,000 (as of June 7, 19XX). For purposes of simplicity, assume that there are no state or city income taxes.

Objective 1   **E 13-4**   **Calculating FICA Taxes**   Calculate FICA taxes for the following employees using a rate of 7.65 percent (maximum of $51,300):

a. Phyllis Martin has weekly wages of $700 (all wages subject to FICA taxes).
b. John O'Shea has year-to-date earnings of $50,000 before the current month's salary of $5,000. Determine how much of the $5,000 is subject to FICA taxes and then calculate the FICA tax.
c. Joe Campos has year-to-date earnings of $52,000 before the current week's commission of $2,000. Determine how much of the $2,000 is subject to FICA taxes and then calculate the FICA tax.

Objective 2   **E 13-5**   **Determining Federal Income Taxes**   Use Exhibit 13-1 to determine the federal income taxes for the following employees (all are married):
   a. K. Parker has weekly wages of $805 and claims 3 withholding allowances.
   b. R. Pacetti has weekly wages of $978 and claims 2 withholding allowances.
   c. A. Schmidt has weekly wages of $460 and claims 0 withholding allowances.

Objective 3   **E 13-6**   **Completing a Payroll Register**   Complete the following payroll register:

PAYROLL REGISTER
For the Week Ended _April 18, 19XX_

Employee	Total Hours	Regular	Overtime	Total	FICA Tax	FIT Tax	Medical Insurance	Total Deductions	Net Pay	Wages Expense
			Earnings			Deductions				Distribution
Bond, I.	40	700.00	0.00	(a)	53.55	90.00	20.00	(b)	(c)	(d)
Jacks, L.	46	600.00	135.00	(e)	56.23	65.00	30.00	(f)	(g)	(h)
Stone, A.	48	400.00	120.00	(i)	39.78	45.00	10.00	(j)	(k)	(l)
Totals		(m)	(n)	(o)	(p)	(q)	(r)	(s)	(t)	(u)

Objective 2   **E 13-7**   **Calculating Net Pay**   Assuming a FICA rate of 7.65 percent, calculate the net pay for the following employees (use Exhibit 13-1 for federal income taxes):
   a. Jules Polasky is married and claims 4 withholding allowances. His weekly pay is $715 (all subject to FICA taxes) and he has $20 for medical insurance withheld.
   b. Marla Sommers is married and her weekly pay is $820 ($200 subject to FICA taxes). She claims 5 withholding allowances. Marla also has union dues ($15), savings bonds ($25), and medical insurance ($30) withheld.

Objective 3   **E 13-8**   **Recording Payroll and Depositing Funds**   Wagner Company had the following employee payroll amounts for the week ended February 9, 19XX:

Total earnings, $12,500; FICA tax withheld, $900; federal income tax withheld, $3,100; and medical insurance withheld, $400. In your answer, (a) record this payroll transaction in a general journal, page 19, and (b) deposit the necessary funds in a special payroll checking account, using a cash payments journal, page 11 (check number 317). The payment is made February 9, 19XX.

PROBLEM SET A

Objective 2

P 13-1A **Calculating Gross Pay and FICA Taxes** Consider the following five employees:

a. Vera Darnell is a salaried employee who earns $29,380 per year (52 weeks). All of her weekly salary is subject to FICA taxes.

b. Roger Weston is an hourly worker who is paid $11.50 per hour. His firm pays time and one-half for hours worked in excess of forty for the week. He works fifty hours during the week. All wages are subject to FICA taxes.

c. Juan Morales is a factory worker who is paid $0.35 for each unit produced. He produces 1,200 units during a week and all his pay is subject to FICA taxes.

d. Before this pay period, Mai Wilson had year-to-date earnings of $51,000. She is a carpet salesperson who is paid 6 percent of her sales. She sells $21,700 during a week.

e. Mike Hannigan is a salaried employee who earns $54,184 per year (52 weeks). Before this pay period, Mike had year-to-date earnings of $52,100.

REQUIRED (if necessary, round to the cent)
1. Calculate the weekly gross pay for each employee.
2. Calculate the FICA tax, if any, for each employee for his or her weekly earnings. Assume FICA is a rate of 7.65 percent (first $51,300 of wages).

Objective 3

P 13-2A **Completing Employee Compensation Records** Graber Marine Supply has two employees. The following information was collected to complete the employee compensation records for the week ended August 17, 19XX (both are married):

	Marilyn Adams	George Potosky
Social Security Numbers	233-00-3333	255-00-5555
Addresses	610 Third Avenue Cleveland, Ohio 44112	19001 Day Street Cleveland, Ohio 44129
Weekly or Hourly Pay Rate	$580/week	$11.80/hour
Withholding Allowances	4	3
Cumulative Gross Earnings (including this pay period)	$8,120	$12,880
Position	Bookkeeper	Driver
Medical Insurance Deductions	$31	$27
Employment Date	May 13, 19XX	March 5, 19XX
Birth Date	June 12, 1954	April 7, 1956
Overtime Earnings	$–0–	4 hours

Other Payroll Data:

a. The FICA tax rate is 7.65 percent of the first $51,300 of earnings for each employee.

b. Use Exhibit 13-1 to determine federal income taxes.

c. The firm pays overtime pay at time and one-half (1.5) for any hours worked in excess of forty per workweek.

REQUIRED

Complete an employee compensation record for each employee. Round all amounts to the cent. See the Practical Review Problem if you need help. For purposes of simplicity, assume that there are no state or city income taxes.

Objective 3   **P 13-3A**   **Preparing a Payroll Register and Recording Payroll**   Morganstein Computer Supply has four employees. The firm's accountant accumulated employee's payroll data from the employee compensation records (by employee) as follows for the week ended November 15, 19XX:

a. Alex Pitts has regular earnings of $416.00 and overtime earnings of $62.40. His deductions are FICA tax, $36.60, federal income tax, $32.00, and medical insurance, $19.80. He worked 44 hours during the week.

b. Fran Clark worked 42 hours during the week. She had these deductions: federal income tax, $30.00, FICA tax, $26.32, and medical insurance, $16.25. Her overtime earnings were $24.00 and her regular earnings were $320.00.

c. Oscar Vargas is a salaried employee who worked 40 hours during the week at $695.00. He had $24.90 deducted for medical insurance, $53.17 for FICA tax, and $65.00 for federal income tax.

d. I. H. Tran had the following deductions: medical insurance, $22.35, federal income tax, $39.00, and FICA tax, $40.39. She is an employee who receives a salary of $528.00. She worked 40 hours during the week.

REQUIRED

1. Prepare a payroll register. List employees in alphabetical order, by last name. Use the first letter of the employee's first name. Calculate total earnings, total deductions, and net pay for each employee. Total the appropriate columns. All earnings are distributed as Wages Expense.

2. Record the employee's payroll in a general journal, page 56.

Objectives 1, 2, and 3   **P 13-4A**   **Comprehensive Chapter Review Problem**   Gallagher Beverage Supply has two employees, Floyd Givens and Nancy Ruiz. Floyd's social security number is 299-00-0000. Floyd's address is 1390 Lake Street, Rochester, New York, 14615. He is married and has two withholding allowances. Floyd was born December 5, 1932, and he is employed as a bookkeeper. He was employed April 2, 19XX, at a weekly (40 hours) rate of $715. For the pay period ending August 13, 19XX, Floyd worked

40 hours with no overtime hours. His medical insurance is $24. His cumulative gross earnings are $13,585 (as of August 13, 19XX). Nancy's address is 150 Walnut Drive, Rochester, New York, 14608. Her cumulative gross earnings are $29,640 (as of August 13, 19XX). She was employed February 9, 19XX, at an hourly rate of $22.80. For the pay period ending August 13, 19XX, Nancy worked 43 hours (3 overtime hours). Nancy's social security number is 199-00-0000. Her medical insurance is $28. She is married and has three withholding allowances. Nancy was born September 1, 1952. She is employed as a driver.

REQUIRED

1. Complete an employee's compensation record for each employee for the week ended August 13, 19XX. Calculate FICA taxes using a FICA tax rate of 7.65 percent (maximum of $51,300). Using Exhibit 13-1, determine the federal income tax for each employee. Round all amounts to the cent. For purposes of simplicity, assume that there are no state or city income taxes.
2. Using the information in 1, prepare a payroll register (list employees alphabetically).
3. Prepare a general journal entry, page 43, to record the employee's payroll.
4. Using a cash payments journal, page 16, make the necessary deposit in a special payroll checking account. Check number 324 is issued (August 13, 19XX).

PROBLEM SET B

Objective 2   **P 13-1B**   **Calculating Gross Pay and FICA Taxes**   Consider the following five employees:

a. Paul Gooding is a salaried employee who earns $24,180 per year (52 weeks). All of his weekly salary is subject to FICA taxes.
b. Linda Archer is an hourly worker who is paid $12.50 per hour. Her firm pays time and one-half for hours worked in excess of forty for the week. She works forty-five hours during the week. All wages are subject to FICA taxes.
c. Simon Cooper is a factory worker who is paid $0.25 for each unit produced. He produces 1,500 units during a week and all his pay is subject to FICA taxes.
d. Before this pay period, Luci Lopez had year-to-date earnings of $50,200. She is a furniture salesperson who is paid 7 percent of her sales. She sells $21,400 during a week.
e. P. K. Chen is a salaried employee who earns $54,912 per year (52 weeks). Before this pay period, P. K. had year-to-date earnings of $51,900.

REQUIRED (if necessary, round to the cent)
1. Calculate the weekly gross pay for each employee.
2. Calculate the FICA tax, if any, for each employee for his or her weekly earnings. Assume FICA is a rate of 7.65 percent (first $51,300 of wages).

Objective 3

P 13-2B   Completing Employee Compensation Records   Ochoa Medical Supply has two employees. The following information was collected to complete the employee compensation records for the week ended October 24, 19XX (both are married):

	Tom French	Cathy Phillips
Social Security Numbers	466-00-6666	488-00-8888
Addresses	307 Palm Street	215 First Avenue
	Cocoa, Florida	Cocoa, Florida
	32922	32927
Weekly or Hourly Pay Rate	$10.20/hour	$640/week
Withholding Allowances	5	6
Cumulative Gross Earnings (including this pay period)	$16,720	$19,840
Position	Supply Clerk	Store Manager
Medical Insurance Deductions	$61	$68
Employment Date	January 4, 19XX	March 1, 19XX
Birth Date	August 30, 1939	June 14, 1947
Overtime Earnings	2 hours	$–0–

Other Payroll Data:
a. The FICA tax rate is 7.65 percent of the first $51,300 of earnings for each employee.
b. Use Exhibit 13-1 to determine federal income taxes.
c. The firm pays overtime pay at time and one-half (1.5) for any hours worked in excess of forty per workweek.

REQUIRED
Complete an employee compensation record for each employee. Round all amounts to the cent. See the Practical Review Problem if you need help. For purposes of simplicity, assume that there are no state or city income taxes.

Objective 3

P 13-3B   Preparing a Payroll Register and Recording Payroll   Hernandez Beauty Supply has four employees. The firm's accountant accumulated employee's payroll data from the employee compensation records (by employee) as follows for the week ended October 7, 19XX:
a. Walt Hardy has regular earnings of $380.00 and overtime earnings of $42.75. His deductions are FICA tax, $32.34, federal income tax, $30.00, and medical insurance, $31.75. He worked 43 hours during the week.

b. Paula Reyes worked 45 hours during the week. She had these deductions: federal income tax, $53.00, FICA tax, $38.15, and medical insurance, $24.15. Her overtime earnings were $78.75 and her regular earnings were $420.00.

c. Bob Miller is a salaried employee who worked 40 hours during the week at $819.00. He had $36.60 deducted for medical insurance, $62.65 for FICA tax, and $83.00 for federal income tax.

d. Joann Dixon had the following deductions: medical insurance, $29.50, federal income tax, $81.00, and FICA tax, $55.46. She is an employee who receives a salary of $725.00. She worked 40 hours during the week.

REQUIRED

1. Prepare a payroll register. List employees in alphabetical order, by last name. Use the first letter of the employee's first name. Calculate total earnings, total deductions, and net pay for each employee. Total the appropriate columns. All earnings are distributed as Wages Expense.

2. Record the employee's payroll in a general journal, page 24.

Objectives 1, 2, and 3

P 13-4B   Comprehensive Chapter Review Problem   Sullivan Paper Distributors has two employees, Hazel Newly and Earl Fine. Hazel's social security number is 433-00-3333. Hazel's address is 1600 Union Avenue, Tulsa, Oklahoma, 74107. She is married and has four withholding allowances. She was employed January 5, 19XX, at a weekly (40 hours) rate of $605. For the pay period ending October 21, 19XX, Hazel worked 40 hours with no overtime hours. Her medical insurance is $32. She was born April 29, 1945, and is employed as an accountant. Her cumulative gross earnings are $24,200 (as of October 21, 19XX). Earl's address is 2100 Garrison Place, Tulsa, Oklahoma, 74108. He was born January 8, 1962. His cumulative gross earnings are $22,188 (as of October 21, 19XX). He was employed January 2, 19XX at an hourly rate of $12.90. For the pay period ending October 21, 19XX, Earl worked 44 hours (4 overtime hours). Earl's social security number is 477-77-0000. He is employed as a dispatcher. His medical insurance is $35. He is married and has five withholding allowances.

REQUIRED

1. Complete an employee's compensation record for each employee for the week ended October 21, 19XX. Calculate FICA taxes using a FICA tax rate of 7.65 percent (maximum of $51,300). Using Exhibit 13-1, determine the federal income tax for each employee. Round all amounts to the cent. For purposes of simplicity, assume that there are no state or city income taxes.

2. Using the information in 1, prepare a payroll register (list employees alphabetically.

ANSWERS TO SELF-TEST QUESTIONS

3. Prepare a general journal entry, page 22, to record the employee's payroll.
4. Using a cash payments journal, page 14, make the necessary deposit in a special payroll checking account. Check number 561 is issued (October 21, 19XX).

ANSWERS TO SELF-TEST QUESTIONS

1. c   2. a   3. d   4. d   5. b

14

————————————————————————————————— ■ ■ ■ ■ ■ ■

Payroll: Employer's Taxes and Reports

Remember that time is money.

BENJAMIN FRANKLIN

LEARNING OBJECTIVES

After reading this chapter, discussing the questions, and working the exercises and problems, you will be able to do the following:

1. Understand and compute employer's payroll taxes (pp. 470–73).

2. Prepare Form 941 (pp. 473–77).

3. Prepare Form 940 (pp. 477–80).

4. Record the payment of payroll liabilities (pp. 480–83).

5. Calculate and record worker's compensation insurance (pp. 483–85).

Employers are responsible for collecting payroll taxes and then remitting those taxes to the proper tax authorities. In Chapter 13 we saw that payroll taxes and other deductions were withheld from an employee's pay. In this chapter we will examine the *employer's* payroll taxes. We will also look at how these payroll taxes are deposited and reported.

Applications for Employer Identification Numbers

Objective 1
Understand and compute employer's payroll taxes.

An application for an employer identification number must be filed by every employer of one or more persons. The application is completed on **Form SS-4,** which is available at any IRS or Social Security Office. The employer identification number must be included on all correspondence, forms, and returns submitted to the IRS relating to payroll taxes.

EMPLOYER'S PAYROLL TAXES

In order to compute the employer's payroll taxes, the payroll register must be expanded. This is shown in Exhibit 14-1, where there are three additional columns for Year-to-Date Earnings, FICA (social security) Taxable Earnings, and Federal (FUTA) and State (SUTA) Unemployment Taxable Earnings.

Year-to-Date Earnings

Referring to Exhibit 14-1, the Year-to-Date Earnings column represents the total earnings of the employee up to and including this payroll period. This amount becomes the basis for computing the employer's payroll taxes.

FICA (Social Security) Tax

We will assume that the employer must pay the same FICA tax as the employee. In this book we are using a rate of 7.65 percent of the first $51,300 of earnings for a calendar year (January 1 to December 31). Remember that payroll taxes are based on a calendar year, not a fiscal year. (The employer's FICA tax, as well as the federal income tax, are reported to the IRS on Form 941, which we will examine later.)

EXHIBIT 14-1
Expanded Payroll Register

PAYROLL REGISTER
For the Week Ended _December 31, 19XX_

| | | Earnings | | | Deductions | | | | | Distribution | | Taxable Earnings | |
Employee	Total Hours	Regular	Over-time	Total	FICA Tax	FIT Tax	Medical Insur-ance	Total Deduc-tions	Net Pay	Wages Expense	Year To Date Earnings	FICA Tax	FUTA/ SUTA
Le, H.	40	525.00	0.00	525.00	40.16	45.00	12.00	97.16	427.84	525.00	26,250.00	525.00	0.00
Moore, C.	42	420.00	31.50	451.50	34.54	47.00	11.00	92.54	358.96	451.50	7,000.00	451.50	451.50
Rylski, F.	40	640.00	0.00	640.00	48.96	69.00	13.00	130.96	509.04	640.00	7,340.00	640.00	300.00
Vega, B.	43	568.00	63.90	631.90	48.34	56.00	10.00	114.34	517.56	631.90	32,180.00	631.90	0.00
Totals		2,153.00	95.40	2,248.40	172.00	217.00	46.00	435.00	1,813.40	2,248.40	72,770.00	2,248.40	751.50

① FUTA/SUTA is an abbreviation for federal unemployment tax, and state unemployment tax.

② Over $7,000 limit.

③ ($7,340 − $640 = $6,700. $7,000 limit − $6,700 = $300 taxable earnings).

United Auto Supply paid $172.00 of FICA tax for the week ended December 31, 19XX ($2,248.40 × .0765 = $172.00). The employee's contribution was also $172.00.

Using T accounts, the entry to record the employer's portion of the FICA tax is as follows:

Payroll Tax Expense		FICA Tax Payable	
+	−	−	+
(12/31) 172.00			(12/31) 172.00

Federal and State Unemployment Taxes

The **Federal Unemployment Tax Act (FUTA)** allows the state and federal government to cooperate in establishing and administering an unemployment tax program. This program provides unemployment compensation to workers who have lost their jobs. The various states create the actual employment insurance systems, while the federal government approves the state laws and pays the administrative costs of the state programs.

Under this dual system, the employer is first subject to a tax levied by the state. This tax then becomes a credit against a separate federal tax. (A firm could be exempt from the state tax but would still have to pay the federal tax.) The federal unemployment tax is reported on Form 940, Employer's Annual Federal Unemployment (FUTA) Tax Return. This form covers one calendar year and is due January 31 of the following year.

We will assume that the maximum amount of wages subject to Federal Unemployment (FUTA) Tax is $7,000 and that the FUTA tax rate is 6.2 percent. We will also assume that the credit against the FUTA tax for payments to state unemployment funds is a maximum of 5.4 percent. Thus, the net federal unemployment tax could be 0.8 percent (.008) assuming a state unemployment rate of 5.4 percent (6.2% − 5.4% = 0.8%). United Auto Supply pays state unemployment taxes of 5.4 percent and federal unemployment taxes of 0.8 percent. These taxes are paid only by the employer and are not deducted from wages paid to employees.

Calculating the Federal Unemployment Tax

Assuming a rate of 0.8 percent (.008), and taxable earnings of $751.50 (see Exhibit 14-1), the federal unemployment tax is calculated as follows:

$$\$751.50 \times .008 = \$6.01$$

As shown in Exhibit 14-1, Hu Le and Bernita Vega have already earned more than $7,000, so any additional earnings are not subject to federal unemployment taxes. Using T accounts, this tax is recorded as follows:

Payroll Tax Expense		Federal Unemployment Tax Payable	
+	−	−	+
(12/31) 6.01			(12/31) 6.01

Calculating State Unemployment Tax

Assuming a rate of 5.4 percent (.054), and taxable wages of $760 (see Exhibit 14-1), the state unemployment tax is calculated as follows:

$$\$751.50 \times .054 = \$40.58$$

As shown in Exhibit 14-1, some of the employees have already earned more than $7,000, so any additional earnings are not subject to state unemployment taxes. Using T accounts, this tax is recorded as follows:

Payroll Tax Expense		State Unemployment Tax Payable	
+	−	−	+
(12/31) 40.58			(12/31) 40.58

Recording the Employer's Payroll Taxes

The three employer's payroll taxes that we have just discussed would be recorded in the accounting records together, using a general journal. Since United Auto Supply pays its employees weekly, this payroll tax entry is also made weekly. Of course, the amounts will probably change, since total earnings and the earnings subject to unemployment taxes will change.

GENERAL JOURNAL   Page ___40___

Date		Description	Post. Ref.	Debit	Credit
19XX					
Dec.	31	Payroll Tax Expense		2 1 8 59	
		FICA Tax Payable			1 7 2 —
		Federal Unemployment Tax Payable			6 01
		State Unemployment Tax Payable			4 0 58
		Employer's Payroll Taxes for the Week Ended			
		December 31, 19XX			

FORM 941

Objective 2
Prepare Form 941.

An employer who is required to withhold federal income taxes and/or social security (FICA) taxes must file a return reporting the amounts withheld. Form 941, **Employer's Quarterly Federal Tax Return,** normally is used for this purpose.

When to File

Form 941 is due by the last day of the month after each quarter ends:

Quarters	Ending Date	Due Date*
January, February, March	March 31	April 30
April, May, June	June 30	July 31
July, August, September	September 30	October 31
October, November, December	December 31	January 31

When Deposits Are Due

The amount of taxes that a firm owes determines the frequency of deposits. These taxes are owed when the wages are paid, not when the payroll period ends. The following rules indicate when deposits are due:

1. If at the end of any eighth-month period the total undeposited taxes are $3,000 or more, the taxes are to be deposited within three banking days after the end of the eighth-month period. (Exhibit 14-3 gives the eighth-month periods "1st through 3rd," "4th through 7th," and so on).

2. If at the end of any month the total undeposited taxes are $500 or more but less than $3,000, the taxes must be deposited within fifteen days after the end of the month.

3. If at the end of any month the total undeposited taxes are less than $500, a deposit is not required. The taxes are carried over to the following month.

4. If at the end of the quarter the total undeposited taxes are less than $500, the taxes do not have to be deposited. However, these taxes must be paid by the due date of Form 941. An employer may pay the taxes with Form 941 or deposit them by the due date of the return.

How to Make Deposits

An employer must deposit income tax withheld, and both the employer and employee social security taxes with an authorized financial institution or a Federal Reserve Bank or branch. Exhibit 14-2 illustrates **Form 8109-B, Federal Tax Deposit Coupon,** which must be included with each deposit to indicate the type of tax being deposited.

*If the due date for a return falls on a Saturday, Sunday, or legal holiday, the due date is the next regular workday.

EXHIBIT 14-2
Form 8109-B

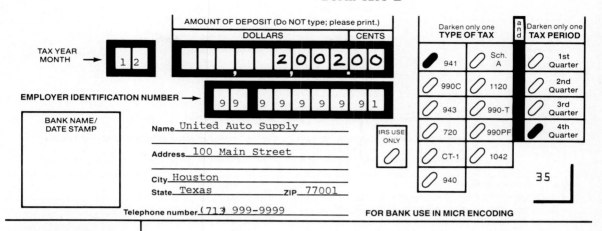

Federal Tax Deposit Coupon
Form 8109-B

Completing Form 941

United Auto Supply completed Form 941 for the quarter ended December 31, 19XX (see Exhibit 14-3).

In the heading, the trade name is United Auto Supply. The address is 100 Main Street, Houston, Texas, 77001. The quarter ended December 31, 19XX, and the employer identification number is 99-9999991.

Here is a description of the process for completing Form 941:

Line 2	Enter the total of all wages paid, tips reported, and other compensation paid to employees. The total for October through December 19XX is $20,000.
Line 3	Enter the income tax withheld. United Auto Supply withheld $2,480.
Line 5	The firm had no adjustments so the amount withheld is $2,480.
Line 6	The total wages subject to social security taxes is entered. This amount is $20,000 multiplied by 15.3 percent, which equals $3,060. This is the total of both the employee's and employer's contributions.
Line 8	This is the total of lines 6, 7a, and 7b, which is $3,060.
Line 10	The firm had no adjustments, so the total is $3,060.

EXHIBIT 14-3

Form 941

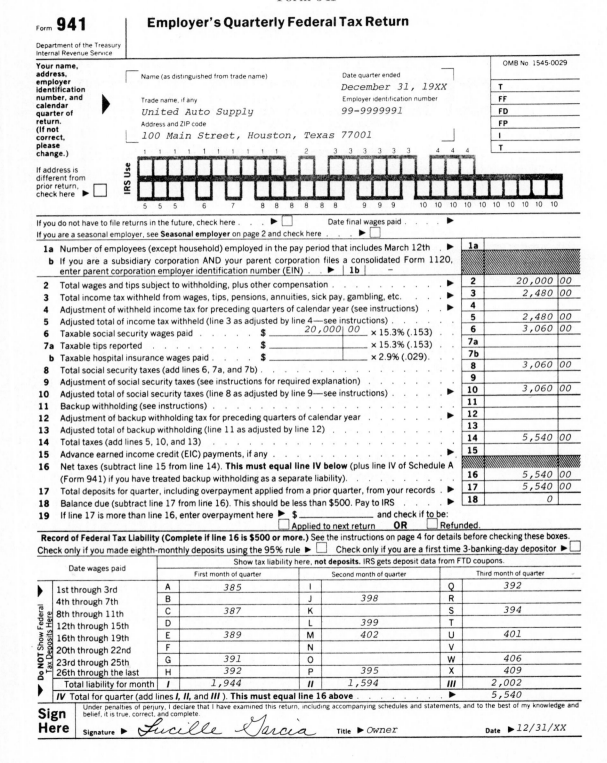

Form 941

Department of the Treasury
Internal Revenue Service

Employer's Quarterly Federal Tax Return

Your name, address, employer identification number, and calendar quarter of return. (If not correct, please change.)

Name (as distinguished from trade name)	Date quarter ended *December 31, 19XX*
Trade name, if any *United Auto Supply*	Employer identification number *99-9999991*
Address and ZIP code *100 Main Street, Houston, Texas 77001*	

OMB No 1545-0029

T	
FF	
FD	
FP	
I	
T	

If address is different from prior return, check here ▶ ☐

IRS Use

If you do not have to file returns in the future, check here . . . ▶ ☐   Date final wages paid . . . . ▶
If you are a seasonal employer, see **Seasonal employer** on page 2 and check here . . . ▶ ☐

1a	Number of employees (except household) employed in the pay period that includes March 12th ▶	**1a**
b	If you are a subsidiary corporation AND your parent corporation files a consolidated Form 1120, enter parent corporation employer identification number (EIN) . ▶ **1b** –	
2	Total wages and tips subject to withholding, plus other compensation . . . . ▶	**2** 20,000 00
3	Total income tax withheld from wages, tips, pensions, annuities, sick pay, gambling, etc. . . ▶	**3** 2,480 00
4	Adjustment of withheld income tax for preceding quarters of calendar year (see instructions) . .	**4**
5	Adjusted total of income tax withheld (line 3 as adjusted by line 4—see instructions) . . .	**5** 2,480 00
6	Taxable social security wages paid . . . . . $ _20,000 00_ × 15.3% (.153) .	**6** 3,060 00
7a	Taxable tips reported . . . . $ _____ × 15.3% (.153) .	**7a**
b	Taxable hospital insurance wages paid . . . . $ _____ × 2.9% (.029).	**7b**
8	Total social security taxes (add lines 6, 7a, and 7b)	**8** 3,060 00
9	Adjustment of social security taxes (see instructions for required explanation)	**9**
10	Adjusted total of social security taxes (line 8 as adjusted by line 9—see instructions) . . . ▶	**10** 3,060 00
11	Backup withholding (see instructions)	**11**
12	Adjustment of backup withholding tax for preceding quarters of calendar year . . . . . ▶	**12**
13	Adjusted total of backup withholding (line 11 as adjusted by line 12)	**13**
14	Total taxes (add lines 5, 10, and 13)	**14** 5,540 00
15	Advance earned income credit (EIC) payments, if any . . . . ▶	**15**
16	Net taxes (subtract line 15 from line 14). **This must equal line IV below** (plus line IV of Schedule A (Form 941) if you have treated backup withholding as a separate liability).	**16** 5,540 00
17	Total deposits for quarter, including overpayment applied from a prior quarter, from your records . ▶	**17** 5,540 00
18	Balance due (subtract line 17 from line 16). This should be less than $500. Pay to IRS . . ▶	**18** 0
19	If line 17 is more than line 16, enter overpayment here ▶ $ _____ and check if to be: ☐ Applied to next return **OR** ☐ Refunded.	

Record of Federal Tax Liability (Complete if line 16 is $500 or more.) See the instructions on page 4 for details before checking these boxes.
Check only if you made eighth-monthly deposits using the 95% rule ▶ ☐   Check only if you are a first time 3-banking-day depositor ▶ ☐

Show tax liability here, **not deposits.** IRS gets deposit data from FTD coupons.

Date wages paid		First month of quarter		Second month of quarter		Third month of quarter
1st through 3rd	A	385	I		Q	392
4th through 7th	B		J	398	R	
8th through 11th	C	387	K		S	394
12th through 15th	D		L	399	T	
16th through 19th	E	389	M	402	U	401
20th through 22nd	F		N		V	
23rd through 25th	G	391	O		W	406
26th through the last	H	392	P	395	X	409
Total liability for month	**I**	1,944	**II**	1,594	**III**	2,002
IV Total for quarter (add lines **I**, **II**, and **III**). **This must equal line 16 above** . . . . ▶						5,540

Do NOT Show Federal Tax Deposits Here

Sign Here
Under penalties of perjury, I declare that I have examined this return, including accompanying schedules and statements, and to the best of my knowledge and belief, it is true, correct, and complete.

Signature ▶ *Lucille Garcia*   Title ▶ *Owner*   Date ▶ *12/31/XX*

Line 14   Lines 5, 10, and 13 are added. The firm's total taxes are $5,540 (lines 5 and 10).

Line 16   The net taxes are $5,540.

Line 17   Enter the total deposits for the quarter including any overpayment applied from the previous quarter. United Auto Supply deposited the correct amount of $5,540.

Line 18   The balance due is zero.

Record of federal tax liability.

If the taxes for the quarter (line 16) are less than $500, the employer does not have to complete the Record. The employer may pay the taxes with Form 941 or deposit them by the due date of the return. If the taxes for the quarter are $500 or more, the employer must complete the Record. The firm has a tax liability of $5,540, which was deposited as required.

FORM 940

Depositing the Tax

Objective 3
Prepare Form
940.

For deposit purposes, FUTA tax is figured quarterly. Multiply 0.8 percent (.008) times the wages subject to FUTA taxes for the quarter. If this amount (plus any amount not yet deposited for any earlier quarter) is more than $100, the deposit is made during the first month after the quarter. But if the amount is $100 or less, it is added to the amount to be deposited in the next quarter.

Deposits are made at a Federal Reserve Bank or other authorized financial institution. Each deposit must be accompanied by a federal tax deposit (FTD) coupon. Form 8109, Federal Tax Deposit Coupon Book, is sent to the employer automatically after he or she has applied for an employer identification number (see Exhibit 14-2).

Completing Form 940

United Auto Supply completed Form 940 (Exhibit 14-4) for the 19XX calendar year on January 31, 19XX. The heading includes the trade name, address, and employer identification number. All filers must complete questions A and B and Part I. The firm signified that it has paid all required amounts to its state unemployment funds. The amount of contributions was $1,512 for the year. For question B, the firm is required to pay contributions to more than one state.

EXHIBIT 14-4
Form 940

Form **940**	Employer's Annual Federal Unemployment (FUTA) Tax Return	OMB No. 1545-0028

Department of the Treasury
Internal Revenue Service

If incorrect, make any necessary change. ▶

Name (as distinguished from trade name)

Calendar year
19XX

Trade name, if any
United Auto Supply

Address and ZIP code
100 Main Street, Houston, Texas 77001

Employer identification number
99 - 9999991

	T
	FF
	FD
	FP
	I
	T

A Did you pay all required contributions to state unemployment funds by the due date of Form 940? (See instructions if none required.) . . . ☒ **Yes** ☐ **No**

If you checked the "Yes" box, enter the amount of contributions paid to state unemployment funds . . . . . . ▶ $ _____*1,512*|*00*

B Are you required to pay contributions to only one state? . . . . ☐ **Yes** ☒ **No**

If you checked the "Yes" box: (1) Enter the name of the state where you are required to pay contributions . . . . . . ▶ _____

(2) Enter your state reporting number(s) as shown on state unemployment tax return. ▶ _____

C If any part of wages taxable for FUTA tax is exempt from state unemployment tax, check the box. (See the Specific Instructions on page 2.) . . . . ☐

Note: *If you checked the "Yes" boxes in both questions A and B and did not check the box in C above, you may be able to use Form 940-EZ.*

Part I — Computation of Taxable Wages (to be completed by all taxpayers)

1	Total payments (including exempt payments) during the calendar year for services of employees	**1**	72,770	00
2	Exempt payments. (Explain each exemption shown, attaching additional sheets if necessary.) ▶ _____	**2** (Amount paid)		
3	Payments for services of more than $7,000. Enter only the excess over the first $7,000 paid to individual employees not including exempt amounts shown on line 2. Do not use the state wage limitation.	**3** 44,770 00		
4	Total exempt payments (add lines 2 and 3)	**4**	44,770	00
5	**Total taxable wages** (subtract line 4 from line 1). (If any part is exempt from state contributions, see instructions.) ▶	**5**	28,000	00

Part II — Tax Due or Refund (Complete if you checked the "Yes" boxes in both questions A and B and did not check the box in C above.)

1	**Total FUTA tax.** Multiply the wages in Part I, line 5, by .008 and enter here	**1**	
2	Total FUTA tax deposited for the year, including any overpayment applied from a prior year (from your records) . .	**2**	
3	**Balance due** (subtract line 2 from line 1). This should be $100 or less. Pay to IRS . . . . . ▶	**3**	
4	**Overpayment** (subtract line 1 from line 2). Check if it is to be: ☐ Applied to next return, or ☐ Refunded ▶	**4**	

Part III — Tax Due or Refund (Complete if you checked the "No" box in either question A or B or you checked the box in C above. Also complete Part V.)

1	Gross FUTA tax. Multiply the wages in Part I, line 5, by .062		**1**	1,736	00
2	Maximum credit. Multiply the wages in Part I, line 5, by .054	**2** 1,512 00			
3	**Credit allowable:** Enter the smaller of the amount in Part V, line 11, or Part III, line 2	**3** 1,512 00			
4	**Total FUTA tax** (subtract line 3 from line 1)		**4**	224	00
5	Total FUTA tax deposited for the year, including any overpayment applied from a prior year (from your records)		**5**	224	00
6	**Balance due** (subtract line 5 from line 4). This should be $100 or less. Pay to IRS . . . . . ▶		**6**	0	
7	**Overpayment** (subtract line 4 from line 5). Check if it is to be: ☐ Applied to next return, or ☐ Refunded ▶		**7**		

Part IV — Record of Quarterly Federal Tax Liability for Unemployment Tax (Do not include state liability.)

Quarter	First	Second	Third	Fourth	Total for Year
Liability for quarter	79.00	67.00	48.00	30.00	224.00

Part V — Computation of Tentative Credit (Complete if you checked the "No" box in either question A or B or you checked the box in C above—see instructions.)

Name of state 1	State reporting number(s) as shown on employer's state contribution returns 2	Taxable payroll (as defined in state act) 3	State experience rate period 4 From—	To—	State experience rate 5	Contributions if rate had been 5.4% (col. 3 x .054) 6	Contributions payable at experience rate (col. 3 x col. 5) 7	Additional credit (col. 6 minus col.7) If 0 or less, enter 0. 8	Contributions actually paid to the state 9
CA	12345	9,900	1/1	12/31	5.4				534.60
IL	00000	8,600	1/1	12/31	5.4				464.40
TX	99999	9,500	1/1	12/31	5.4				513.00
10 Totals ▶		28,000							1,512.00
11 Total tentative credit (add line 10, columns 8 and 9 only—see instructions for limitations) . . . . . ▶									1,512 00

If you will not have to file returns in the future, write "Final" here (see general instruction "Who Must File") and sign the return. ▶

Under penalties of perjury, I declare that I have examined this return, including accompanying schedules and statements, and to the best of my knowledge and belief, it is true, correct, and complete, and that no part of any payment made to a state unemployment fund claimed as a credit was or is to be deducted from the payments to employees.

Signature ▶ *Lucille Garcia* Title (Owner, etc.) ▶ *Owner* Date ▶ *1/31/XX*

Form **940**

Here is the process of completing Form 940 (this f[...]
from time to time):

Part I   **Computation of Taxable Wages and Credit Re[...]**

Line 1   Enter the total payments made to employees d[...]
          calendar year, even if they are not taxable. The f[...]
          $72,770.

Line 3   Enter the total amounts of more than $7,000 that wer[...]
          each employee. The excess was $44,770 ($72,770 − $28[...]
          ($28,000 is $7,000 times four employees.)

Line 4   The total exempt payments are $44,770.

Line 5   The firm had $28,000 in taxable wages ($72,770 − $44,770).

Part II   **Tax Due or Refund.**
          This part is used only if questions A and B were both checked
          "Yes" and the firm did not check the box in C. This does not
          apply to United Auto Supply.

Part III **Tax Due or Refund.**
          This part is completed only if the employer does not qualify
          to use Part II.

Line 1   The firm would multiply $28,000 (line 5, Part I) by .062,
          which equals $1,736.

Line 2   United Auto Supply would multiply $28,000 (line 5, Part I) by
          .054, which equals $1,512. This credit is for payment to state
          unemployment funds.

Line 3   Enter the smaller of (1) Part V, line 11, total tentative credit,
          or (2) Part III, line 2, 5.4 percent of taxable FUTA wages. As
          both are the same, this would be $1,512.

Line 4   The total FUTA tax is $224, which is line 3 subtracted from
          line 1.

Line 5 $224 of FUTA taxes were deposited for the year by the firm.

Line 6   The balance due is 0.

Part IV   **Record of Federal Tax Liability.**
          This part must be completed if the total tax (Part II, line 1 or
          Part III, line 4) is over $100. The firm had the following
          liabilities for the first through fourth quarters: $79, $67, $48,
          and $30 for a total of $224.

Part V   **Computation of Tentative Credit.**
          This schedule must be completed if the employer checked the
          "No" box in either question A or B, or if the employer checked
          the box in C.

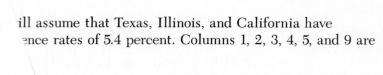

ill assume that Texas, Illinois, and California have
ence rates of 5.4 percent. Columns 1, 2, 3, 4, 5, and 9 are

er the name of the state or states to which the firm
required to pay contributions. California, Illinois,
exas are listed.

he state reporting number assigned to the
er when he or she registered with that state as an
employer. Assume that California is 12345, Illinois is
00000, and Texas is 99999.

Column 3	Enter the taxable payroll on which the employer is required to pay state unemployment taxes. The firm had $9,900 in California, $8,600 in Illinois, and $9,500 in Texas.
Columns 4 and 5	The rate for all three states is assumed to be 5.4 percent, and the period is 1/1 to 12/31.
Column 9	Enter the contributions paid to the state unemployment fund. The firm paid California $534.60, Illinois $464.40, and Texas $513.00.
Line 10	The totals are $28,000 for column 3 and $1,512 for column 9.
Line 11	The total is $1,512.

THE PAYMENT OF PAYROLL LIABILITIES

Objective 4
Record the
payment of payroll
liabilities.

Both FICA taxes and federal income taxes must be computed and
filed on Form 941 (see Exhibit 14-3). If at the end of any month the total
undeposited taxes are more than $500 but less than $3,000, the taxes must
be paid and deposited within fifteen days after the end of the month.
Therefore, United Auto Supply makes a payment of $2,002 on January 10,
19XX (see Exhibits 14-2 and 14-3). This includes the employee's FICA tax
liability, the employer's FICA tax liability, and the employee's federal income tax withholdings. These liabilities are debited when payment is made.

Payments for the employer's state and federal unemployment tax liabilities were made on January 31, 19XX, for the quarter ended December 31,
19XX. The firm pays $202.50 ($3,750 × 5.4 percent) to the state unemployment commissions of Texas, Illinois and California. The firm pays the
federal unemployment taxes of $30 ($3,750 × .8 percent) to the Federal Reserve Bank.

Finally, the firm must remit the amounts deducted and collected for medical insurance payable ($552 is paid to Roberts Insurance Company on January 31, 19XX).

The payments are recorded and paid as follows:

CASH PAYMENTS JOURNAL   Page ___1___

Date	Ck. No.	Account Debited	Post. Ref.	Other Accounts	Accounts Payable	Purchases	Purch. Disc.	Cash
				Debits			**Credits**	
19XX								
Jan. 10		FICA Tax						
		Payable		1 2 2 4 —				
		Federal Income						
		Tax Payable		7 7 8 —				2 0 0 2 —
	31	State						
		Unemployment						
		Tax Payable		2 0 2 50				2 0 2 50
	31	Federal						
		Unemployment						
		Tax Payable		3 0 —				3 0 —
	31	Medical						
		Insurance						
		Payable		5 5 2 —				5 5 2 —

Form W-2

The employer must give copies B and C of Form W-2, Wage and Tax Statement, to each employee. Hu Le's Form W-2, as illustrated in Exhibit 14-5, shows: (a) total wages and other compensation paid; (b) amounts deducted for income tax; (c) amounts deducted for social security tax (FICA); and other disclosures, if applicable. The employer must give each employee the statement by January 31 following the end of the calendar year covered. If the employment ends before the close of the year, the employee may request the form earlier. In this case, the employer must give the employee the statement within thirty days of the employee's written request, if the thirty-day period ends before January.

EXHIBIT 14-5
Form W-2—Wage and Tax Statement—Copy B

1 Control number		
	OMB No. 1545-0008	

2 Employer's name, address, and ZIP code	6 Statutory employee ☐ Deceased ☐ Pension plan ☐ Legal rep. ☐ 942 emp. ☐ Subtotal ☐ Deferred compensation ☐ Void ☐

United Auto Supply
100 Main Street
Houston, Texas   77001

	7 Allocated tips — —	8 Advance EIC payment — —

9 Federal income tax withheld 2,250.00	10 Wages, tips, other compensation 26,250.00

3 Employer's identification number 99-9999991	4 Employer's state I.D. number 99999	11 Social security tax withheld 2,008.00	12 Social security wages 26,250.00
5 Employee's social security number 400-00-0000		13 Social security tips — —	14 Nonqualified plans — —

19 Employee's name, address and ZIP code	15 Dependent care benefits — —	16 Fringe benefits incl. in Box 10 — —

Hu Le
12 G Avenue
Houston, Texas   77002

	17	18 Other

20	21	22	23

24 State income tax — —	25 State wages, tips, etc. — —	26 Name of state — —	27 Local income tax — —	28 Local wages, tips, etc. — —	29 Name of locality — —

Copy B To be filed with employee's FEDERAL tax return   Dept. of the Treasury—Internal Revenue Service

Form **W-2 Wage and Tax Statement**

This information is being furnished to the Internal Revenue Service

Form W-3

Each year, the employer must file **Form W-3, Transmittal of Income and Tax Statements,** to transmit Copy A of Forms W-2 to the Social Security Administration. Form W-3, as shown in Exhibit 14-6, and Copy A of Forms W-2 must be filed by the last day of February after the calendar year for which the Forms W-2 are prepared. The Social Security Administration will process these forms and give the Internal Revenue Service the income tax data that it needs from these forms.

EXHIBIT 14-6
Form W-3—Transmittal of Income and Tax Statements

DO NOT STAPLE

1 Control number	33333	For Official Use Only ▶ OMB No. 1545-0008		

☐ Kind of Payer ▶	2 941/941E ☒ Military ☐ 943 ☐ CT-1 ☐ 942 ☐ Medicare gov't. emp. ☐	3 Employer's state I.D. number — —	5 Total number of statements
		4 — —	4

6 Establishment number — —	7 Allocated tips — —	8 Advance EIC payments — —
9 Federal income tax withheld **9,411.00**	**10** Wages, tips, and other compensation **72,770.00**	**11** Social security tax withheld **5,566.91**
12 Social security wages **72,770.00**	**13** Social security tips — —	**14** Nonqualified plans — —
15 Dependent care benefits — —	**16** Adjusted total social security wages and tips	**17** Deferred compensation — —
18 Employer's identification number **99— 9999991**		**19** Other EIN used this year — —
20 Employer's name **United Auto Supply**		**21** Gross annuity, pension, etc. (Form W-2P) — —
		23 Taxable amount (Form W-2P) — —
100 Main Street **Houston, Texas 77001**		**24** Income tax withheld by third-party payer — —
22 Employer's address and ZIP code (If available, place label over boxes 18 and 20.)		

Under penalties of perjury, I declare that I have examined this return and accompanying documents, and to the best of my knowledge and belief, they are true, correct, and complete.

Signature ▶ *Lucille Garcia*   Title ▶ *Owner*   Date ▶ *1/31/XX*

Telephone number (optional) *713-999-9999*

Form **W-3 Transmittal of Income and Tax Statements**

Department of the Treasury
Internal Revenue Service

WORKER'S COMPENSATION INSURANCE

Objective 5
Calculate and
record worker's
compensation
insurance.

Employees and their dependents are protected against losses due to injury or death during employment by **worker's compensation insurance**. The employer pays the premium in advance, based on the estimated payroll for the year. The insurance premiums are usually stated in terms of each $100 of weekly wages paid to employees. Most states require employers to provide the insurance through plans administered by the state or through private insurance agencies approved by the state. Premium rates vary among the types of jobs and the firm's historical number of accidents.

At United Auto Supply, there are two different grades (types) of work—office clerical and sales. At the beginning of the year, the firm's accountant estimated the annual premium as follows:

Grade of Work	Estimated Payroll	Rate Per Hundred	Premium
Office Clerical	$30,000	.13	$ 39.00*
Sales	$40,000	.70	280.00**
Total Estimated Premium			$319.00

The amount paid at the beginning of the year was recorded as follows:

CASH PAYMENTS JOURNAL   Page ____1____

				Debits			Credits	
Date	Ck. No.	Account Debited	Post. Ref.	Other Accounts	Accounts Payable	Purchases	Purch. Disc.	Cash
19XX								
Jan. 1		Prepaid						
		Insurance		3 1 9 —				3 1 9 —

At the end of the year, the accountant analyzed the payroll data for the year, and the actual payroll for the year was as follows:

Grade of Work	Actual Payroll	Rate Per Hundred	Premium
Office Clerical	$32,500	.13	$ 42.25
Sales	$40,750	.70	285.25
Total Actual Premium			$327.50
Less: Estimated Premium Paid January 1			319.00
Balance of Premium Due			$ 8.50

*$30,000 × .0013 = $39.00.
**$40,000 × .007 = $280.00.

The additional premium is $8.50, which was paid as follows:

CASH PAYMENTS JOURNAL   Page ___12___

| Date | Ck. No. | Account Debited | Post. Ref. | Debits | | | Credits | |
				Other Accounts	Accounts Payable	Purchases	Purch. Disc.	Cash
19XX								
Dec. 31		Insurance						
		Expense		8 50				8 50

If the firm had overpaid its insurance obligation then it would be due a refund.

CHAPTER REVIEW

1. **Understand and compute employer's payroll taxes (pp. 470–73).**
   Employers are responsible for collecting payroll taxes and then remitting the taxes to the proper tax authorities. The payroll register must be expanded to include the employer's payroll taxes.

2. **Prepare Form 941 (pp. 473–77).**
   An employer who is required to withhold federal income taxes and/or social security (FICA) taxes must file a return reporting the amounts withheld. Form 941, Employer's Quarterly Federal Tax Return, normally is used for this purpose.

3. **Prepare Form 940 (pp. 477–80).**
   The Employer's Annual Federal Unemployment (FUTA) Tax Return (Form 940) is a form that reports the amount of unemployment taxes owed and paid.

4. **Record the payment of payroll liabilities (pp. 480–83).**
   The employer is responsible for paying payroll liabilities to the appropriate authorities. The employer must give copies B and C of Form W-2, Wage and Tax Statement, to each employee. Each year, the employer must file Form W-3, Transmittal of Income and Tax Statements, to transmit Copy A of Forms W-2 to the Social Security Administration.

5. Calculate and record worker's compensation insurance
(pp. 483–85).
Worker's compensation insurance protects employees and their
dependents against losses due to injury or death during employment.
The employer pays the premium in advance, based on the estimated
payroll for the year. Most states require employers to provide worker's
compensation insurance through plans administered by the state or
through private insurance agencies approved by the state.

GLOSSARY

Employer's Annual Federal Unemployment (FUTA) Tax Return (Form 940)	Form that states the amount of federal unemployment taxes owed and paid.
Employer's Quarterly Federal Tax Return (Form 941)	Form that reports amounts withheld for federal income taxes and/or social security (FICA) taxes and the employer's matching social security tax.
Federal Tax Deposit Coupon (Form 8109–B)	Form that indicates the type of tax being deposited. It must be included with each income tax and social security tax deposit.
Federal Unemployment Tax Act (FUTA)	Act that provides for the state and federal government to cooperate in establishing and administering an unemployment tax program.
Form SS-4	Used to apply for an employer identification number.
Form W-2	Called the Wage and Tax Statement. Shows wages paid, income tax deductions, social security tax deductions, and other disclosures, if applicable.
Form W-3	Used to transmit Copy A of Forms W-2 to the Social Security Administration.
State Unemployment Tax (SUTA)	Tax paid by the employer to cooperate with the federal government in establishing and administering the unemployment tax program.
Worker's Compensation Insurance	Protects employees and their dependents against losses due to injury or death during employment.

SELF-TEST QUESTIONS FOR REVIEW

(Answers are on page 496.)

1. An employee contributes $1,000 for FICA taxes. Her employer will contribute
   a. exactly $1,000.   b. more than $1,000.
   c. less than $1,000.   d. exactly $2,000.

2. The federal unemployment tax rate used in the chapter is
   a. 5.4 percent.   b. 8.0 percent.
   c. 0.8 percent.   d. 0.54 percent.

3. A description for a transaction reads: "Employer's Payroll Taxes for the Week Ended May 21, 19XX." The account debited for this transaction is
   a. Wages Payable.   b. Payroll Tax Expense.
   c. Wages Expense.   d. Cash.

4. Form 941 is due by April 19XX. This due date pertains to the quarter ended
   a. December.   b. June.
   c. September.   d. March.

5. _____ is debited and _____ is credited when paying for worker's compensation insurance at the beginning of the year.
   a. Prepaid Insurance; Cash   b. Cash; Prepaid Insurance
   c. Cash; Insurance Expense   d. Insurance Expense; Cash

PRACTICAL REVIEW PROBLEM

Objective 5

Calculating and Recording Worker's Compensation Insurance .The accountant for Smythe Company accumulated the following data for worker's compensation insurance for the year ended December 31, 19XX:

a. The company has five different grades (types) of work:

Grade of Work	Rate per Hundred	Estimated Payroll
Office Clerical	.12	$76,000
Office Sales	.15	27,000
Outside Sales	.60	48,000
Drivers	1.20	31,000
Manufacturing	1.40	59,000

b. The actual payroll for the year is:

Grade of Work	Rate per Hundred	Actual Payroll
Office Clerical	.12	$81,300
Office Sales	.15	22,800
Outside Sales	.60	49,300
Drivers	1.20	30,900
Manufacturing	1.40	59,100

REQUIRED
1. Calculate the estimated premium.
2. Record the payment on January 1, 19XX, to Johnson Insurance Agency in a cash payments journal, page 1.
3. Calculate the actual premium.
4. Record the payment of the additional premium on December 31, 19XX, to Johnson Insurance Agency, page 12.

ANSWER TO PRACTICAL REVIEW PROBLEM

1. Calculate the estimated premium.

Grade of Work	Estimated Payroll	Rate per Hundred	Premium
Office Clerical	$76,000	.12	$ 91.20
Office Sales	27,000	.15	40.50
Outside Sales	48,000	.60	288.00
Drivers	31,000	1.20	372.00
Manufacturing	59,000	1.40	826.00
Total Estimated Payroll			$1,617.70

2. Record the payment on January 1, 19XX.

CASH PAYMENTS JOURNAL   Page ___1___

Date	Ck. No.	Account Debited	Post. Ref.	Debits — Other Accounts	Debits — Accounts Payable	Purchases	Credits — Purch. Disc.	Cash
19XX								
Jan. 1		Prepaid						
		Insurance		1 6 1 7 70				1 6 1 7 70

3. Calculate the actual premium.

Grade of Work	Actual Payroll	Rate per Hundred	Premium
Office Clerical	$81,300	.12	$ 97.56
Office Sales	22,800	.15	34.20
Outside Sales	49,300	.60	295.80
Drivers	30,900	1.20	370.80
Manufacturing	59,100	1.40	827.40
Total Actual Premium			$1,625.76
Less: Estimated Premium Paid January 1			1,617.70
Balance of Premium Due			$ 8.06

4. Record the payment of the additional premium on December 31, 19XX.

CASH PAYMENTS JOURNAL   Page ___12___

				Debits			Credits	
Date	Ck. No.	Account Debited	Post. Ref.	Other Accounts	Accounts Payable	Purchases	Purch. Disc.	Cash
19XX								
Dec. 31		Insurance						
		Expense		8 06				8 06

DISCUSSION QUESTIONS

Q 14-1   Briefly explain what Form SS-4 is used for.

Q 14-2   Briefly explain the provisions of the Federal Unemployment Tax Act.

Q 14-3   What is Form 941 used for? What period of time does it cover? When is it due?

Q 14-4   What is Form 940 used for? What period of time does it cover? When is it due?

Q 14-5   Briefly explain what Form 8109–B is used for.

Q 14-6   For deposit purposes, when is FUTA tax figured? Where and when are deposits made?

Q 14-7   Name the accounts that are debited or credited for the following payroll payments: (a) payment of FICA and federal income taxes; (b) payment of state and federal unemployment taxes; and (c) payment of medical insurance.

Q 14-8   What is the purpose of Forms W-2 and W-3?

Q 14-9   What is the purpose of worker's compensation insurance? How is it administered?

Q 14-10   How do the premium rates for worker's compensation insurance vary? Name at least two different grades (types) of work.

EXERCISES

Objective 1

E 14-1   **Calculating and Recording Payroll Taxes**   Record each of the following payroll taxes separately using T accounts:

Payroll Tax	Taxable Earnings	Rate
FICA Tax	$57,800	7.65%
Federal Unemployment Tax	13,200	0.80
State Unemployment Tax	13,200	5.40

Objective 2

E 14-2   **Determining Form 941 Filings and Deposits**   Determine (a) the ending date of the quarter; (b) the due date of Form 941 for that quarter; and (c) when the Form 941 taxes must be deposited given the following situation: For Adamle Company, Form 941 is prepared for the quarter that begins in January and at the end of January the total undeposited taxes are $1,500.

Objective 3

E 14-3   **Completing Form 940**   Referring to Form 940 in Exhibit 14-4, fill in the blanks for Nelson Equipment Sales: Part I, line 1, $100,000; line 3, $60,000; line 4, __(a)__; line 5, __(b)__; Part III, line 1, __(c)__; line 2, __(d)__, and line 4, __(e)__.

Objective 4

E 14-4 **Paying Payroll Liabilities** Record the payment of the following payroll taxes and deductions during 19XX in a cash payments journal:

Tax or Deduction	Date Paid	Amount
FICA Tax	March 31	$4,000
Federal Income Tax	March 31	3,000
Federal Unemployment Tax	April 30	60
State Unemployment Tax	April 30	405
Life Insurance	May 15	967

Objective 5

E 14-5 **Calculating Worker's Compensation Insurance** Calculate the estimated worker's compensation insurance premium given the following information:

Grade of Work	Rate per Hundred	Estimated Payroll
Office Clerical	.11	$15,000
Office Sales	.18	18,000
Manufacturing	1.20	34,000
Drivers	1.10	27,000

Objective 1

E 14-6 **Recording Payroll Taxes** Record the following payroll taxes in a general journal, page 74, for the week ending March 12, 19XX:

Payroll Tax	Taxable Earnings	Rate
FICA Tax	$65,320	7.65%
Federal Unemployment Tax	45,760	0.80
State Unemployment Tax	45,760	5.40

Objective 2

E 14-7 **Determining Form 941 Taxes and Deposits** Referring to Form 941 in Exhibit 14-3, determine (1) the total tax to be deposited and (2) by when the deposit is due for the following business firms:

	Pena Supply	Taylor Company	City Food Store
a. Line 3	$200	$1,400	$ 3,700
b. Line 6	900	8,400	18,900

Objective 5

E 14-8 **Recording Worker's Compensation Insurance** On January 1, 19XX, Mancuso Feed Supply estimated that its worker's compensation insurance premium for the year was $870. At the end of the year, on December 31, 19XX, the firm calculated the actual premium of $930. From this information, (a) record the estimated premium in a cash payments journal, page 1 (January 1, 19XX); (b) calculate the balance of premium due; and (c) record the additional premium in a cash payments journal, page 12 (December 31, 19XX).

PROBLEM SET A

Objective 1

P 14-1A Calculating and Recording Payroll Taxes Logan Plastic Supply had the following payroll taxes during the first two weeks of September 19XX:

Week Ending	Payroll Tax	Taxable Earnings	Rate
September 7	FICA Tax	$107,400	7.65%
September 7	Federal Unemployment Tax	75,300	0.80
September 7	State Unemployment Tax	75,300	5.40
September 14	FICA Tax	112,700	7.65
September 14	Federal Unemployment Tax	63,900	0.80
September 14	State Unemployment Tax	63,900	5.40

REQUIRED
1. Calculate the payroll taxes for each week separately in T account form.
2. Prepare general journal entries to record the payroll at the end of each week (use the information in 1).

Objective 2

P 14-2A Preparing Form 941 The accountant for Springtime Video Store located at 2400 Monterey Road, San Jose, California, 95111, is accumulating the necessary data to complete Form 941 for the quarter ended December 31, 19XX. The employer's identification number is 44-4444441. The data for lines 2 through 18 are:

Total wages subject to withholding, $35,000; total income tax withheld from wages, $3,200; taxable social security wages paid, $35,000.

The data for the record of federal tax liability are:

• First month—1st, 609; 8th, 612; 15th, 610; 22nd, 613; 29th, 615.
• Second month—5th, 598; 12th, 601; 19th, 609; 26th, 613.
• Third month—3rd, 616; 10th, 610; 17th, 612; 24th, 617; 31th, 620.

The owner, Joyce Parsons, signs the form December 31, 19XX.

REQUIRED
Complete Form 941.

Objective 3

P 14-3A Preparing Form 940 John Emerson is the accountant for Pembrook Clothing Store. The firm's address is 650 First Street, Minneapolis, Minnesota, 55403, and the employer's identification , number is 00-2345678. John accumulated the following data to complete Form 940 for the year ended December 31, 19XX:

• Questions—The firm checked the "Yes" box for question A and entered the amount from line 11 (Part V). The firm checked the "No" box for question B and did not check box C.

- Part I—Total payments, $96,800; payments for services of more than $7,000, $54,800.
- Part II—Not used.
- Part III—Used.
- Part IV—First quarter, $171; second quarter, $102; third quarter, $42; and fourth quarter, $21.
- Part V—The period for all three states is 1/1 to 12/31, and the experience rate for all states is 5.4 percent. The states are:

State	Reporting Number	Taxable Payroll
Minnesota (MN)	432-876	$17,000
Wisconsin (WI)	1234567	15,000
Wyoming (WY)	909-128	10,000

The owner, Mariano Reyes, signs the form January 31, 19XX.

REQUIRED
Complete Form 940.

Objective 5

P 14-4A **Calculating and Recording Worker's Compensation Insurance** The accountant for Fulton Company accumulated the following data for worker's compensation insurance for the year ended December 31, 19XX:

a. The company has five different grades (types) of work:

Grade of Work	Rate per Hundred	Estimated Payroll
Office Clerical	.16	$123,000
Office Sales	.18	165,000
Outside Sales	.80	218,000
Drivers	1.30	98,000
Production	1.50	146,000

b. The actual payroll for the year is as follows:

Grade of Work	Rate per Hundred	Actual Payroll
Office Clerical	.16	$125,700
Office Sales	.18	171,800
Outside Sales	.80	214,670
Drivers	1.30	99,690
Production	1.50	148,580

REQUIRED
1. Calculate the estimated premium.
2. Record the payment on January 1, 19XX, to Robbins Insurance Agency in a cash payments journal, page 1.

3. Calculate the actual premium.
4. Record the payment of the additional premium on December 31, 19XX, to Robbins Insurance Agency (page 12).

PROBLEM SET B

Objective 1

P 14-1B   **Calculating and Recording Payroll Taxes**   Ramirez Medical Supply had the following payroll taxes during the first two weeks of November 19XX:

Week Ending	Payroll Tax	Taxable Earnings	Rate
November 7	FICA Tax	$156,100	7.65%
November 7	Federal Unemployment Tax	52,700	0.80
November 7	State Unemployment Tax	52,700	5.40
November 14	FICA Tax	167,400	7.65
November 14	Federal Unemployment Tax	41,600	0.80
November 14	State Unemployment Tax	41,600	5.40

REQUIRED
1. Calculate the payroll taxes for each week separately in T account form.
2. Prepare general journal entries to record the payroll at the end of each week (use the information in 1).

Objective 2

P 14-2B   **Preparing Form 941**   The accountant for Augusta Metal Supply located at 2600 Smith Creek Avenue, Augusta, Georgia, 30904, is accumulating the necessary data to complete Form 941 for the quarter ended December 31, 19XX. The employer's identification number is 55-5555551. The data for lines 2 through 18 are:

Total wages subject to withholding, $45,000; total income tax withheld from wages, $4,660; taxable social security wages paid, $45,000.

The data for the record of federal tax liability are:

• First month—1st, 815; 8th, 817; 15th, 820; 22nd, 814; 29th, 822.
• Second month—5th, 825; 12th, 822; 19th, 827; 26th, 826.
• Third month—3rd, 829; 10th, 830; 17th, 835; 24th, 832; 31th, 831.

The owner, Gary Franklin, signs the form December 31, 19XX.

REQUIRED
Complete Form 941.

Objective 3

P 14-3B   **Preparing Form 940**   Paula McCune is the accountant for Sequoia Typewriter Supply. The firm's address is 718 Spruce Street, Tampa, Florida, 33617 and the employer's identification number is 87-1231230.

Paula accumulated the following data to complete Form 940 for the year ended December 31, 19XX:

- Questions—The firm checked the "Yes" box for question A and entered the amount from line 11 (Part V). The firm checked the "No" box for question B and did not check box C.
- Part I—Total payments, $87,400; payments for services of more than $7,000, $52,400.
- Part II—Not used.
- Part III—Used.
- Part IV—First quarter, $130; second quarter, $100; third quarter, $40; and fourth quarter, $10.
- Part V—The period for all three states is 1/1 to 12/31, and the experience rate for all states is 5.4 percent. The states are:

State	Reporting Number	Taxable Payroll
Florida (FL)	909-123	$18,000
Massachusetts (MA)	4448888	10,000
Washington (WA)	616-919	7,000

The owner, Monica Wilson, signs the form January 31, 19XX.

REQUIRED
Complete Form 940.

Objective 5

P 14-4B   Calculating and Recording Worker's Compensation Insurance   The accountant for Ellington Company accumulated the following data for worker's compensation insurance for the year ended December 31, 19XX:

a. The company has five different grades (types) of work:

Grade of Work	Rate per Hundred	Estimated Payroll
Office Clerical	.12	$235,000
Office Sales	.19	199,000
Outside Sales	.90	327,000
Drivers	1.40	134,000
Production	1.70	289,000

b. The actual payroll for the year is as follows:

Grade of Work	Rate per Hundred	Actual Payroll
Office Clerical	.12	$236,400
Office Sales	.19	198,600
Outside Sales	.90	329,450
Drivers	1.40	132,780
Production	1.70	293,410

REQUIRED
1. Calculate the estimated premium.
2. Record the payment on January 2, 19XX, to Pham Insurance Agency in a cash payments journal, page 1.
3. Calculate the actual premium.
4. Record the payment of the additional premium on December 31, 19XX, to Pham Insurance Agency (page 12).

ANSWERS TO SELF-TEST QUESTIONS

1. a   2. c   3. b   4. d   5. a

PAYROLL REVIEW PROBLEM (CHAPTERS 13 AND 14)

This review problem will test your knowledge of payroll. The working papers are in your *Working Papers* manual. The answer to this review problem will be provided by your instructor.

Denise Smithfield is the payroll accountant for Liberty Plumbing Supply. She reviews the following general payroll information:

- The owner of Liberty Plumbing Supply is Gayle Parker.
- The firm is located at 3794 Las Olas, El Paso, Texas 79951.
- State unemployment taxes are 5.4 percent of the first $7,000 of taxable income for each employee.
- The employer's identification number is 88-0945121.
- FICA tax is 7.65 percent of the first $51,300 of earnings for each employee. Both the employer and employees pay the same amount.   3924.45
- Federal unemployment taxes are 0.8 percent of the first $7,000 of taxable income for each employee.   5600.⁰⁰
- Liberty Plumbing Supply uses a special payroll checking account.

Denise accumulates the following data from a completed payroll register for the week ended June 30, 19XX:

- The firm has five employees. 10,000
- Regular earnings were $1,700 for the week and overtime earnings were $300 for the week.   2000
- Medical insurance deductions total $108.
- All earnings are taxable for FICA tax purposes.
- Federal income tax deductions total $295.
- $1,000 of earnings are taxable for both federal and state unemployment taxes.

Ms. Smithfield also reviews payroll information for the quarter that ends June 30, 19XX, and finds (Form 941):

- Total wages subject to withholding total $30,000.
- Total income tax withheld from wages total $3,750.

• Taxable social security wages paid total $30,000.

The data for the record of federal tax liability is (Form 941):

• First month—2nd, 590; 9th, 592; 16th, 594; 23rd, 596; 30th, 595.
• Second month—7th, 597; 14th, 598; 21st, 594; 28th, 593.
• Third month—4th, 596; 11th, 597; 18th, 599; 25th, 598; 30th, 601.

The owner signs Form 941 on July 31, 19XX.

REQUIRED

1. Record the employee's and the employer's payroll in a general journal, page 18, for the week ended June 30, 19XX.
2. Make the necessary deposit in a special payroll checking account to pay employees. Use a cash payments journal, page 6. Check number 794 is issued.
3. Complete Form 941 for the quarter ended June 30, 19XX.

APPENDIX C
The Combined Journal

Many individuals and small firms do not need to keep elaborate accounting records. For example, a dentist, attorney, or investor may only have a few repetitive transactions each accounting period and may employ only one bookkeeper or accountant. Thus, setting up special journals, or even the general journal, may be too time-consuming and even inappropriate. To save posting time the individual or firm may decide to set up a **combined journal**

DESIGNING THE COMBINED JOURNAL

Much care and thought should be given to the design of the combined journal. First, you should write down all of the frequent transactions you will normally have each accounting period—Accounts Payable, Accounts Receivable, Cash, and so on. Then you should decide on the number of columns needed to record these transactions.

Let's look at a combined journal designed by the accountant for Donna Mathews, Medical Doctor. (We will not use cents in this appendix, only whole dollars; therefore, a cents column is not included on this combined journal.)

COMBINED JOURNAL
Page _____

Date	Explanation	Ck. No.	P.R.	Other Accounts Dr.	Other Accounts Cr.	Accounts Receivable Dr.	Accounts Receivable Cr.	Accounts Payable Dr.	Accounts Payable Cr.	Med. Fees Cr.	Cash Dr.	Cash Cr.

As we can see, the accountant listed columns for the Date, Explanation, Ck. No. (check number), P. R. (posting reference), Other Accounts, Accounts Receivable, Accounts Payable, Med. Fees (medical fees—revenue), and Cash. "Dr." is the abbreviation for debit. "Cr." is the abbreviation for credit. Any other transactions would be recorded in the Other Accounts column. You can use as many columns as you need. However, if the journal is too large, it may become difficult to use.

Transactions

Let's record the following transactions in the combined journal and then post to the general ledger for the month of August 19XX:

COMBINED JOURNAL

Page ____1____

Date	Explanation	Ck. No.	P.R.	Other Accounts Dr.	Other Accounts Cr.	Accounts Receivable Dr.	Accounts Receivable Cr.	Accounts Payable Dr.	Accounts Payable Cr.	Med. Fees Cr.	Cash Dr.	Cash Cr.
19XX												
Aug. 1	Donna Mathews, Capital		301		5,000						5,000	
3			—							100	100	
6	Medical Supplies		112	215					215			
10			—			34				34		
15	Wages Expense	1	501	400								400
19	Medical Supplies	2	112	321								321
26			—			97				97		
28		3	—					215				215
31			—				97				97	
31	Donna Mathews, Drawing	4	302	100								100
				1,036	5,000	131	97	215	215	231	5,197	1,036
				(√)	(√)	(110)	(110)	(201)	(201)	(401)	(101)	(101)

August 1   The owner, Donna Mathews, started her medical practice and deposited $5,000 in a bank account. Cash is account number 101, and Donna Mathews, Capital, is number 301.

August 3   Examined a patient and received $100 for Medical Fees, account number 401.

August 6	Bought $215 of Medical Supplies, account number 112, on account. Accounts Payable is account number 201.
August 10	Billed a patient $34 for an ear examination. Accounts Receivable is account number 110.
August 15	Paid Wages Expense, account number 501, $400. Check number 1 is issued.
August 19	Bought $321 of Medical Supplies for cash, check number 2.
August 26	Billed a patient $97 for a physical examination.
August 28	Paid $215, check number 3, to pay for the August 6 purchase of Medical Supplies.
August 31	Received $97 from a patient to apply to the August 26 examination.
August 31	The owner, Dr. Mathews, withdrew $100 for personal use, check number 4. Donna Mathews, Drawing, is account number 302.

As we post to the general ledger we will use "CJ" as the abbreviation for combined journal. CJ1 would indicate a posting from page 1 of the combined journal:

GENERAL LEDGER ACCOUNTS

Account: *Cash* Account No. 101

Date		Item	Post. Ref.	Debit	Credit	Balance Debit	Balance Credit
19XX							
Aug.	31		CJ1	5 1 9 7 —		5 1 9 7 —	
	31		CJ1		1 0 3 6 —	4 1 6 1 —	

Account: *Accounts Receivable* Account No. 110

Date		Item	Post. Ref.	Debit	Credit	Balance Debit	Balance Credit
19XX							
Aug.	31		CJ1	1 3 1 —		1 3 1 —	
	31		CJ1		9 7 —	3 4 —	

(continued)

Account: *Medical Supplies*						Account No. *112*	
		Post.				Balance	
Date	Item	Ref.	Debit	Credit		Debit	Credit
19XX							
Aug. 6		CJ1	2 1 5 —			2 1 5 —	
19		CJ1	3 2 1 —			5 3 6 —	

Account: *Accounts Payable*						Account No. *201*	
		Post.				Balance	
Date	Item	Ref.	Debit	Credit		Debit	Credit
19XX							
Aug. 31		CJ1		2 1 5 —			2 1 5 —
31		CJ1	2 1 5 —				— 0 —

Account: *Donna Mathews, Capital*						Account No. *301*	
		Post.				Balance	
Date	Item	Ref.	Debit	Credit		Debit	Credit
19XX							
Aug. 1		CJ1		5 0 0 0 —			5 0 0 0 —

Account: *Donna Mathews, Drawing*						Account No. *302*	
		Post.				Balance	
Date	Item	Ref.	Debit	Credit		Debit	Credit
19XX							
Aug. 31		CJ1	1 0 0 —			1 0 0 —	

(continued)

(continued)

Account: *Medical Fees*								Account No. *401*	
		Post.					Balance		
Date	Item	Ref.	Debit	Credit		Debit		Credit	
19XX									
Aug. 31		CJ1		2 3 1 —				2 3 1 —	

Account: *Wages Expense*								Account No. *501*	
		Post.					Balance		
Date	Item	Ref.	Debit	Credit		Debit		Credit	
19XX									
Aug. 15		CJ1	4 0 0 —			4 0 0 —			

A trial balance is then prepared as follows:

Donna Mathews, Medical Doctor
Trial Balance
August 31, 19XX

Accounts	Debit	Credit
Cash	4 1 6 1 —	
Accounts Receivable	3 4 —	
Medical Supplies	5 3 6 —	
Donna Mathews, Capital		5 0 0 0 —
Donna Mathews, Drawing	1 0 0 —	
Medical Fees		2 3 1 —
Wages Expense	4 0 0 —	
Totals	5 2 3 1 —	5 2 3 1 —

PROBLEMS

C-1   Joe Molina, Attorney at Law, had the following transactions for the month of July 19XX:

July 1   The owner, Joe Molina, started his law practice and deposited $7,510 in a bank account. Cash is account number 102, and Joe Molina, Capital, is number 301.

July 3   Mr. Molina completed a will and received $312 cash for Legal Fees, account number 401.

July 8   Bought $333 of Office Supplies, account number 115, on account. Accounts Payable is account number 201.

July 11   Billed a client $893 for a court hearing. Accounts Receivable is account number 109.

July 15   Paid Wages Expense, account number 501, $392, for a legal aide, Susan Smith. Check number 1 is issued.

July 19   Bought $654 of Office Supplies for cash, check number 2.

July 25   Billed a client $299 for Legal Fees.

July 27   Paid $333, check number 3, to pay for the July 8 purchase of Office Supplies.

July 28   Received $893 from a client to apply to the July 11 court hearing.

July 31   The owner, Joe Molina, withdrew $286 for personal use, check number 4. Joe Molina, Drawing, is account number 302.

REQUIRED

1. Record the transactions in a combined journal, page 1. Use Legal Fees as the revenue account.
2. Post to the general ledger.
3. Prepare a trial balance on July 31, 19XX.

C-2   Eva Shen, Certified Public Accountant, had the following transactions for the month of June 19XX:

June 2   The owner, Eva Shen, started her CPA practice and deposited $8,912 in a bank account. Cash is account number 101, and Eva Shen, Capital, is number 310.

June 5   Evan Shen completed a tax return and received $910 cash for CPA Fees, account number 401.

June 7   Bought $909 of Office Supplies, account number 119, on account. Accounts Payable is account number 201.

June 12   Billed a client $386 for a tax return (CPA Fees). Accounts Receivable is account number 110.

June 15   Paid Wages Expense, account number 521, $405, for a secretary, Mike Collins. Check number 1 is issued.

June 18   Bought $713 of Office Supplies for cash, check number 2.

June 21   Billed a client $218 for preparation of financial statements (CPA Fees).

June 25   Paid $400, check number 3, to apply to the June 7 purchase of Office Supplies.

June 27   Received $386 from a client to apply to the June 12 tax return.

June 29   The owner, Eva Shen, withdrew $120 for personal use, check number 4. Eva Shen, Drawing, is account number 311.

REQUIRED
1. Record the transactions in a combined journal, page 1. Use CPA Fees as the revenue account.
2. Post to the general ledger.
3. Prepare a trial balance on June 30, 19XX.

APPENDIX D
The Voucher System

Many firms use a voucher system to strengthen their control over cash. Under the voucher system, every expenditure must be recorded as soon as it is incurred. A voucher is prepared for each expenditure, and payment is made only when the voucher is approved. An approved voucher would verify the following:

1. The initial expenditure was authorized.
2. The goods or services were received.
3. The invoice presented for payment is correct.
4. Discounts, if any, are taken.
5. Payment of the expenditure will be made by check.

Thus, the voucher system is a method of verifying the accuracy of creditor invoices and the authorization of the payment.

The Voucher

The voucher is a prenumbered form prepared from an invoice sent by a supplier, creditor, and so on. The voucher is the basis for the accounting entry in a voucher system. The invoice, along with the supporting documentation, is the evidence for the voucher. Each time a voucher is prepared a liability for payment exists. The account, Vouchers Payable, is used to establish the liability, rather than Accounts Payable.

Petersen Company received the invoice shown in Exhibit D-1 on June 9, 19XX.

Petersen Company then prepares a voucher so the expenditure can be entered in the accounting system (as illustrated in Exhibit D-2).

The Voucher Register

Once the vouchers are properly approved, they are entered in the voucher register, which is a book of original entry, like the general journal and special journals. A voucher register is used for any type of expenditure, such as merchandise, expenses, payment of a note, purchase of office supplies, and so on. A voucher register is illustrated in Exhibit D-3. The listed columns for Purchases, Freight In, Wages Expense, and Vouchers

EXHIBIT D-1
Invoice

Invoice For Payment

Sold by: Lyons Steel Company
P.O. Box 11000
New York, NY 10015

Sold to: Petersen Company
1208 K Avenue
Chicago, IL 60520

Invoice Number: X947
Date: June 9, 19XX

Shipped to: Same

Terms	Order No.	Shipped Via	Date Due
2/10, n30	0968412A	Rail	ASAP

Quantity

Ordered	Shipped	Description	Unit Price	Amount
100	100	R94C8 Steel Rolls	$20	$2,000

EXHIBIT D-2
Voucher

Voucher

Petersen Company

Payee: Lyons Steel Company
Address: P.O. Box 11000
New York, NY 10015

Voucher No.: 913
Date Due: June 18, 19XX
Date Paid: June 18, 19XX
Check No.: 409

Terms: 2/10, n30

Date	Invoice No.	Description	Amount
June 9, 19XX	X947	R94C8 Steel Rolls	$2,000

Account Numbers	Account Name	Amount
Debit: 511	Purchases	2,000
Credit: 205	Vouchers Payable	2,000

Merchandise Inspected by: _Thomas J. Cook_

Prices Checked by: _Ralph Espinosa_

Approved for Payment by: _Elizabeth A. Carter_

EXHIBIT D-3
Voucher Register

VOUCHER REGISTER   Page ___1___

Date	Vouch. No.	Payee	Payment Date	Check Number	Credit Vouchers Payable	Other Accounts	Post. Ref.	Amount	Pur-chases	Freight In	Wages Expense
19XX											
6/5	912	AA Realty	6/7	405	600.00	Rent Expense	611	600.00			
6/9	913	Lyons Steel	6/18	409	2,000.00				2,000.00		
6/11	914	City Bank	6/12	406	3,700.00	Notes Payable	215	3,500.00			
						Interest					
						Expense	651	200.00			
6/14	915	By Supply	6/17	408	900.00				900.00		
6/15	916	J. Morgan	6/15	407	500.00						500.00
6/25	917	Lem									
		Freight			70.00					70.00	
6/26	918	Gib									
		Supply			610.00				610.00		
6/30	919	J. Morgan	6/30	410	500.00						500.00
					8,880.00			4,300.00	3,510.00	70.00	1,000.00
					(205)			(✓)	(511)	(512)	(601)

Payable are posted in total at the end of the accounting period to the general ledger. Entries in the Other Accounts column are posted daily or as they occur to the general ledger.

The Check Register

In a voucher system, a **check register** is used in place of the cash payments journal. As illustrated in Exhibit D-4, as a voucher is paid, it is debited to Vouchers Payable and credited to Cash and Purchases Discounts, if applicable. The checks are listed in consecutive order in the check register, whereas the vouchers are listed in consecutive order in the voucher register. Remember that vouchers are first recorded in the voucher register. When a voucher is paid, it is listed in the check register (see Exhibit D-4) by check number. The date of payment and the check number are then recorded in the voucher register. In Exhibit D-3, showing the voucher

EXHIBIT D-4
Check Register

CHECK REGISTER   Page ____1____

Check Number	Date	Payee	Voucher Number	Debit Vouchers Payable	Credits Purchases Discounts	Cash
405	6/7	AA Realty	912	600.00		600.00
406	6/12	City Bank	914	3,700.00		3,700.00
407	6/15	J. Morgan	916	500.00		500.00
408	6/17	By Supply	915	900.00	18.00	882.00
409	6/18	Lyons Steel	913	2,000.00	40.00	1,960.00
410	6/30	J. Morgan	919	500.00		500.00
				8,200.00	58.00	8,142.00
				(205)	(512)	(101)

register, two vouchers have not been paid—number 917, Lem Freight, and number 918, Gib Supply. When these are paid, the date and check number will be entered from the check register.

Any vouchers not paid at the end of the accounting period are listed in a schedule of unpaid vouchers.

The Schedule of Unpaid Vouchers

The schedule of unpaid vouchers (as shown in Exhibit D-5) lists all the vouchers that have not been paid at the end of the accounting period.

The sum of the unpaid vouchers, $680, must equal the credit balance of the Vouchers Payable account in the general ledger, which is shown on page 509.

PROBLEMS

D-1   Hartman Company uses a voucher system. The following transactions occurred during April 19XX:

April   1   Received an invoice from Alvin Realty for $655 for Rent Expense, voucher number 411.

EXHIBIT D-5
Schedule of Unpaid Vouchers

Petersen Company

Schedule of Unpaid Vouchers

June 30, 19XX

Payee	Voucher Number	Date	Amount
Lem Freight	*917*	*6/25*	*$ 70.00*
Gib Supply	*918*	*6/26*	*610.00*
			$680.00

GENERAL LEDGER ACCOUNT

Account: *Vouchers Payable*   Account No.   205

Date	Item	Post. Ref.	Debit	Credit	Balance Debit	Balance Credit
19XX						
June 30		VR1		8 8 8 0 —		8 8 8 0 —
30		CR1	8 2 0 0 —			6 8 0 —

April 4	An invoice was received from Synch Company for Purchases for $480. The terms were 5/30, n60, and voucher number 412 was assigned.
April 8	Paid voucher number 411, check number 1094.
April 13	Telephone, Inc. sent an invoice for $135 for Telephone Expense, voucher number 413.
April 15	An invoice was received from Columbus Supply for $900 for Purchases. Voucher number 414 was assigned, and terms were 2/10, n30.
April 18	An invoice was received from Fast Freight for $125 for Freight In, voucher number 415.
April 22	Paid voucher number 414, check number 1095.

April 23   Received an invoice from Hiller, Inc. for Office Supplies, $915. Voucher number 416 was assigned.

April 26   Lark Company sent an invoice for $246 for Freight In, voucher number 417.

April 28   Paid voucher number 416, check number 1096.

April 30   Paid voucher number 412, check number 1097.

REQUIRED

1. Record all invoices to be paid in the voucher register, page 5.
2. Record all payments in the check register (page 5) and then record the payment in the voucher register (1) above.
3. Post to the Vouchers Payable account (number 201) in the general ledger.
4. Prepare a schedule of unpaid vouchers and compare the balance to the Vouchers Payable account in the general ledger.

D-2   Padilla Company uses a voucher system. The following transactions occurred during March 19XX:

March 2   Received an invoice from Lynch Realty for $718 for Rent Expense, voucher number V816.

March 5   An invoice was received from Coper Company for Purchases for $800. The terms were 8/30, n60, and voucher number V817 was assigned.

March 9   Paid voucher number V817, check number 0049.

March 15   Gary Lines sent an invoice for $336 for Telephone Expense, voucher number V818.

March 18   An invoice was received from Servi Supply for $200 for Purchases. Voucher number V819 was assigned, and terms were 3/10, n30.

March 19   An invoice was received from Lucky Freight for $216 for Freight In, voucher number V820.

March 24   Paid voucher number V819, check number 0050.

March 25   Received an invoice from Credit, Inc. for Store Supplies, $329. Voucher number V821 was assigned.

March 27   Lucas Company sent an invoice for $388 for Freight In, voucher number V822.

March 29   Paid voucher number V821, check number 0051.

March 31   Paid voucher number V816, check number 0052.

REQUIRED

1. Record all invoices to be paid in the voucher register, page 7.
2. Record all payments in the check register (page 7) and then record the payment in the voucher register (1) above.
3. Post to the Vouchers Payable (number 202) account in the general ledger.
4. Prepare a schedule of unpaid vouchers and compare the balance to the Vouchers Payable account in the general ledger.

APPENDIX E

Calculating Interest and Discounting a Note

A note is a promise to pay a sum of money at a future date. The note is classified as a Current Asset or Liability if it is due within one year or accounting cycle. If the note is due after a year or accounting cycle, it is classified as a Long-term Asset or Liability.

There are normally two parties or signers of a note. The maker signs the note and promises to pay a sum of money at a future date to the payee, to whom the payment is to be made. For example, if a note is due within a year or accounting cycle, the *maker* records the note as a Notes Payable in the Current Liability section of his or her balance sheet. The *payee* would record the same note as a Notes Receivable in the Current Assets section of his or her balance sheet.

SIMPLE INTEREST

Interest is the cost of borrowing money. It is commonly called the "time value of money." There are two common forms of interest, *simple interest* and *compound interest*. We will discuss simple interest in this appendix. Compound interest will be examined in a more advanced accounting course. To calculate simple interest you will need to know three factors: (1) *principal*, which is the loan amount; (2) *rate of interest*; and (3) *length or time of the note*. The formula for finding simple interest is as follows:

$$\text{Simple Interest} = \text{Principal} \times \text{Rate} \times \text{Time}$$

Interest is stated as a percentage on an annual basis. We will use an annual basis of 360 days to simplify calculations. To calculate simple interest, let's assume that Jacobson Sales and Service has a $2,000 note at 6 percent for 90 days. The calculation to find simple interest is as follows:

$$\text{Simple Interest} = \$2,000 \times .06 \times \frac{90}{360} = \$30$$

Maturity Value

The maturity value of a note is the principal plus the interest. For the Jacobson Sales and Services note, the maturity value would be calculated as follows:

$$\text{Maturity Value} = \text{Principal} + \text{Interest} = \$2,000 + \$30 = \$2,030$$

DISCOUNTING A NOTE

Discount

Notes are commonly sold or discounted before they reach maturity (due date). Whenever a note is discounted, interest is taken out in advance. A note is usually discounted at a bank or finance company. To discount a note you will need to know three factors: (1) *maturity value;* (2) *discount rate of interest;* and (3) *time remaining before maturity.* The formula is as follows:

$$\text{Discount} = \text{Maturity Value} \times \text{Discount Rate}$$
$$\times \text{ Time Remaining Before Maturity}$$

Using our previous example of Jacobson Sales and Service, let's assume that the $2,000 note was discounted at a bank at 9 percent after thirty days. Thus, there are sixty days remaining. In other words, the bank will take out 9 percent of interest for sixty days on the maturity value amount. The discount would be as follows:

$$\text{Discount} = \$2,030 \times .09 \times \frac{60}{360} = 30.45$$

This $30.45 is the fee that the bank charges for buying this note from the payee.

Proceeds

After the note is discounted, the payee will receive the proceeds. To find the proceeds you must know two amounts: *maturity value,* and *the discount.* The formula for finding proceeds is as follows:

$$\text{Proceeds} = \text{Maturity Value} - \text{Discount}$$

In our example of Jacobson Sales and Service the proceeds would be calculated as follows:

$$\text{Proceeds} = \$2,030.00 - \$30.45 = \$1,999.55$$

PROBLEMS

E-1   Chan Company is the payee of a $3,000 note at 8 percent for 120 days. The note is discounted at Brasher State Bank at 12 percent after 45 days (75 days remaining).

REQUIRED
1. Find the amount of simple interest of the original note.
2. Find the maturity value of the original note.
3. Find the amount of the discount.
4. Find the proceeds after the note is discounted.

E-2   Barbara Gilbert, CPA, is the payee of a $6,000 note at 12 percent for 240 days. The note is discounted at Herrera State Bank at 15 percent after 65 days (175 days remaining).

REQUIRED
1. Find the amount of simple interest of the original note.
2. Find the maturity value of the original note.
3. Find the amount of the discount.
4. Find the proceeds after the note is discounted.

APPENDIX F

Methods for Valuing Inventory and Cost of Goods Sold

Inventory is a major cost for many firms. Since Ending Inventory is subtracted from Cost of Goods Available for Sale to arrive at Cost of Goods Sold, it is extremely important to assign an accurate cost. This appendix will illustrate four methods for assigning costs to Ending Inventory and Cost of Goods Sold: (1) **specific identification**; (2) **average cost**; (3) **FIFO**; and (4) **LIFO**.

Assume that at the end of July 19XX, Jordan Sales and Service had the following units in inventory (unsold and on hand):

	Units Purchased	Cost per Unit	Total Cost
July 1: Beginning Inventory	80	$15.10	$1,208.00
10: Purchase	40	17.50	700.00
19: Purchase	20	17.65	353.00
26: Purchase	70	17.50	1,225.00
Cost of Goods Available for Sale	210	**Total Cost**	$3,486.00
Less: Units Sold in July	110		
Units in Ending Inventory	100		

Specific Identification Method (1)

This method can be used whenever specific items in inventory can be counted or identified as sold or unsold. It is based on a *flow of goods,* not on a flow of costs. An automobile sales dealership, for example, could use this method since inventory (automobiles) are easy to count and then identified as sold or unsold.

Assume:
Twenty units unsold from July 1 beginning inventory.
Twenty-five units unsold from July 10 purchase.
Fifteen units unsold from July 19 purchase.
Forty units unsold from July 26 purchase.

The Cost of Goods Sold section of the income statement would appear as follows for July 31, 19XX:

Cost of Goods Sold
    Merchandise Inventory, July 1 $1,208.00
    Add: Purchases   2,278.00

    Cost of Goods Available for Sale $3,486.00
    Less: Merchandise Inventory, July 31*   1,704.25
        Cost of Goods Sold   1,781.75

*Twenty Units at $15.10 (July 1)	$ 302.00
Twenty-five Units at $17.50 (July 10)	437.50
Fifteen Units at $17.65 (July 19)	264.75
Forty Units at $17.50 (July 26)	700.00
Merchandise Inventory, July 31	$1,704.25

The remaining three methods of inventory valuation are based on a *flow of costs,* rather than a flow of goods. These three methods would probably be used by firms that manufacture and/or sell similar homogeneous products such as aspirins, nails, pencils, paper, and so on. For example, it would be too time-consuming and costly to count each aspirin or nail manufactured or sold.

Average Cost Method (2)

The **average cost method** assigns an equal cost to each unit in inventory by dividing the total dollar amount of Cost of Goods Available for Sale by the number of goods available to be sold, which for Jordan Sales and Service is as follows:

$$\text{Average Cost Per Unit} = \frac{\$3,486}{210 \text{ Units}} = \$16.60 \text{ per Unit}$$

The Cost of Goods Sold section of the income statement would appear as follows for July 31, 19XX:

Cost of Goods Sold
    Merchandise Inventory, July 1 $1,208.00
    Add: Purchases   2,278.00

    Cost of Goods Available for Sale $3,486.00
    Less: Merchandise Inventory, July 31*   1,660.00
        Cost of Goods Sold   1,826.00

*$16.60 per Unit × 100 Units = $1,660.00.

FIFO Method (3)

FIFO means *first in, first out*. The oldest units in inventory are assumed to be sold first, whether they actually are or not. Ending Inventory is valued at the most current purchases. The Cost of Goods Sold section of the income statement for the FIFO method would appear as follows:

Cost of Goods Sold		
Merchandise Inventory, July 1	$1,208.00	
Add: Purchases	2,278.00	
Cost of Goods Available for Sale	$3,486.00	
Less: Merchandise Inventory, July 31*	1,753.00	
Cost of Goods Sold		1,733.00

*Ten Units at $17.50 (July 10)	$ 175.00	
Twenty Units at $17.65 (July 19)	353.00	
Seventy Units at $17.50 (July 26)	1,225.00	
Merchandise Inventory, July 31	$1,753.00	

Of the 110 units sold, 80 units are taken from beginning inventory and the remaining 30 units from the next oldest purchase, July 10. Ten units of the July 10 purchase remain and are considered unsold and part of Ending Inventory. The remaining units (20 and 70) complete Ending Inventory.

LIFO Method (4)

LIFO stands for *last in, first out*. Ending inventory is valued at the oldest purchases. The most recent (newest) units are assumed to be sold first, regardless of the actual sales. The Cost of Goods Sold section of the income statement using the LIFO method would appear as follows for Jordan Sales and Service for July 31, 19XX:

Cost of Goods Sold		
Merchandise Inventory, July 1	$1,208.00	
Add: Purchases	2,278.00	
Cost of Goods Available for Sale	$3,486.00	
Less: Merchandise Inventory, July 31*	1,558.00	
Cost of Goods Sold		1,928.00

Of the 110 units sold, 70 units are taken from the July 26 purchase. Forty units are then remaining to be allocated, of which 20 are taken

*Eighty Units at $15.10 (July 1)	$1,208.00
Twenty Units at $17.50 (July 10)	350.00
Merchandise Inventory, July 31	$1,558.00

from the next newest purchase, July 19. So far, 90 units have been allocated. Twenty units remain, which are taken from the July 10 purchase. The remaining units are considered to be unsold and Ending Inventory.

PROBLEMS

F-1 Logan Paint Supply had the following Beginning Inventory, purchases, and sales for the month of October 19XX:

	Units Purchased	Cost per Unit	Total Cost
October 1: Beginning inventory	100	$12.00	$1,200.00
15: Purchase	200	15.00	3,000.00
28: Purchase	100	18.00	1,800.00
Cost of Goods Available for Sale	400	**Total Cost**	$6,000.00
Less: Units Sold in October	250		
Units in Ending Inventory	150		

Of the 250 units sold, 75 units were from Beginning Inventory; 110 units were from the October 15 purchase; and 65 units from the October 28 purchase.

REQUIRED

Compute Ending Inventory and Cost of Goods Sold under the (1) specific identification, (2) average cost, (3) FIFO, and (4) LIFO methods.

F-2 Shoulders Company had the following Beginning Inventory, Purchases, and Sales for the month of May 19XX:

	Units Purchased	Cost per Unit	Total Cost
May 1: Beginning inventory	100	$14.53	$ 1,453.00
13: Purchase	120	16.10	1,932.00
24: Purchase	180	14.60	2,628.00
28: Purchase	140	14.30	2,002.00
31: Purchase	160	14.00	2,240.00
Cost of Goods Available for Sale	700	**Total Cost**	$10,255.00
Less: Units Sold in May	540		
Units in Ending Inventory	160		

Of the 540 units sold, 100 units were from Beginning Inventory; 90 units were from the May 13 purchase; 165 were from the May 24 purchase; 110 from the May 28 purchase; and 75 from the May 31 purchase.

REQUIRED

Compute Ending Inventory and Cost of Goods Sold under the (1) specific identification, (2) average cost, (3) FIFO, and (4) LIFO methods.

APPENDIX G
Methods for Computing Depreciation

This appendix continues the discussion of depreciation which was introduced in Chapter 4. Five methods of computing depreciation will be examined: (1) straight-line; (2) units-of-production; (3) sum-of-the-years'-digits; (4) double-declining-balance; and (5) Modified and Accelerated Cost Recovery System (MACRS and ACRS).

To illustrate the five methods, assume that Western Consultants purchased an automobile on April 1, 19XX. The automobile cost $15,000 and will have a salvage value of $1,000. The useful life is four years, and the firm estimates that the automobile can be driven 70,000 miles before trade-in or disposal (useful life).

Straight-line Method of Depreciation (1)

a. Formula:

$$\frac{\text{Cost} - \text{Salvage Value}}{\text{No. of Periods of Useful Life}} = \text{Depreciation Expense Each Period}$$

b. Calculation (years 1 to 4):

$$\frac{\$15,000 - \$1,000}{4 \text{ Years}} = \$3,500 \text{ Each Year}$$

c. Result: Allocation of an equal amount of depreciation in each accounting period.

Units-of-Production Method of Depreciation (2)

a. Formula:

$$\frac{\text{Cost} - \text{Salvage Value}}{\text{Total Units, Miles, and so on}} = \text{Depreciation per Unit, Mile, and so on}$$

b. Calculation:

$$\frac{\$15,000 - \$1,000}{70,000 \text{ Miles}} = \$.20 \text{ Depreciation Expense per Mile}$$

c. Result

Year 1: The automobile was driven 19,000 miles. The depreciation expense is $3,800 ($.20 × 19,000 miles).

Year 2: The automobile was driven 18,000 miles. The depreciation expense is $3,600 ($.20 × 18,000 miles).

Year 3: The automobile was driven 18,000 miles. The depreciation expense is $3,600 ($.20 × 18,000 miles).

Year 4: The remaining 15,000 miles were driven in the fourth year. The depreciation expense is $3,000 ($.20 × 15,000 miles).

Sum-of-the-Years'-Digits Method of Depreciation (3)

a. Formula:

$$Cost - Salvage\ Value = Depreciable\ Cost$$

$$Depreciable\ Cost \times \frac{No.\ of\ Years\ Remaining}{S}$$

$$= Depreciation\ Expense\ each\ Period\ where,\ S = \frac{N(N + 1)}{2}$$

N is the number of years of estimated useful life.

b. Calculation:

$$S = \frac{N(N + 1)}{2} = \frac{4(4 + 1)}{2} = \frac{4(5)}{2} = \frac{20}{2} = 10$$

c. Result

Year 1: $14,000 \times \dfrac{4}{10} = \$5,600$ Depreciation Expense

Year 2: $14,000 \times \dfrac{3}{10} = \$4,200$ Depreciation Expense

Year 3: $14,000 \times \dfrac{2}{10} = \$2,800$ Depreciation Expense

Year 4: $14,000 \times \dfrac{1}{10} = \$1,400$ Depreciation Expense

Double-Declining-Balance Method of Depreciation (4)

a. Double-Declining-Balance Rate:

$$\frac{100\%}{Periods\ of\ useful\ life} \times 2$$

b. Formula: Beginning Carrying Value (or book value)
$\times$ Double-Declining-Balance Rate
$=$ Depreciation Expense

c. The salvage value is NOT subtracted from the cost.

d. The asset cannot be depreciated below salvage value; therefore, an adjustment must be made in the final depreciable year.

e. Calculation and result:

$$\text{Rate} = \frac{100\%}{4} \times 2 = 50\%$$

Year 1: $15,000 $\times$ 50% = $7,500 Depreciation Expense

Year 2:   ($15,000 − $7,500) $\times$ 50% = $3,750 Depreciation Expense

Year 3:   [$15,000 − ($7,500 + $3,750)] $\times$ 50% = $1,875 Depreciation Expense

Year 4:   An adjustment is made in the final useful year to reduce the book value (cost − accumulated depreciation) to the salvage value. The cost of $15,000 less accumulated depreciation of $13,125 ($7,500 + $3,750 + $1,875) equals $1,875. The salvage value is $1,000, so the depreciation in the fourth year is $875 ($1,875 − $1,000 salvage value).

Modified and Accelerated Cost Recovery System— MACRS and ACRS (5)

For tax reporting of depreciation, the accelerated cost recovery system (ACRS) is mandatory for most tangible assets placed in service from 1981 through 1986. The ACRS procedures are modified (and referred to as MACRS) for assets acquired after 1986.

Each item of property (tangible assets) depreciated under ACRS and MACRS is assigned to a property class with prescribed write-off periods. The class to which property is assigned is determined by its class life. The class life of an item of property determines its recovery period and the method of depreciation used. MACRS establishes eight property classes with prescribed write-off periods ranging from three years to 31.5 years.

For additional information on MACRS and ACRS, request Publication 534 on Depreciation, Department of the Treasury, Internal Revenue Service.

PROBLEMS

G-1   Avery Book Supply bought an automobile for $25,000 with an estimated useful life of five years. The company believes the automobile can be sold for $2,500 (salvage value) at the end of the fifth year and can be driven 90,000 miles. In the first year the automobile is driven 19,000 miles; the second year 17,700 miles; the third year, 18,500 miles; the fourth year, 18,000 miles; and 16,800 miles in the fifth year.

REQUIRED

Determine the Depreciation Expense for each of the five years using the following methods: (1) straight-line; (2) units-of-production; (3) sum-of-the-years'- digits; and (4) the double-declining-balance.

G-2   Littleton Company bought a machine for $1,250,000 that will produce 500,000 units of product V67. The machine will have a salvage value of $150,000 after a useful life of four years. The firm will produce 150,000 units in the first year, 125,000 the second, 175,000 the third, and 50,000 the last year.

REQUIRED

Determine the Depreciation Expense for each of the four years using the following methods: (1) straight-line; (2) units-of-production; (3) sum-of-the-years'-digits; and (4) the double-declining-balance.

MICROSTUDY+® OPERATING INSTRUCTIONS

These brief operating instructions will help you start using Micro-Study+, the software study aid. After you study a chapter in the textbook, use MicroStudy+ to reinforce your understanding. The program is as flexible and comprehensive as possible to speed the learning process. More complete operating instructions are available within the program itself.

HARDWARE AND SOFTWARE REQUIREMENTS

MicroStudy+ is available on both 5¼-inch and 3½-inch disks for use with most DOS-based microcomputers, such as the IBM PC® or PS/2®. Use PC DOS or MS DOS version 2.1 or higher.

Your instructor will tell you how to get or make a copy of the Micro-Study+ software. Typically the publisher gives each school a master disk for these purposes. You may run the software from an individual floppy disk or you can copy it onto a hard disk drive.

GETTING STARTED

These instructions assume that you know how to start your computer and obtain a DOS prompt, such as:

A>

The instructions also assume you will be running the software from the A drive.

1. At the **A>** prompt, type:

STUDY

(in either upper or lower case), and then press the **<RETURN>** key.

2. Next, you will see one or more introductory screens. Typically a screen will display for several seconds and then the next screen will replace it automatically, until the Main Menu appears.

3. At the Main Menu, take a minute to review your menu choices.

   1. Select Chapter in Textbook for Review
   2. Study Chapter Preview Questions
   3. List Key Terms in the Chapter
   4. Vocabulary Building with Matching Exercises
   5. True/False Statement Drill
   6. Multiple Choice Question Drill
   7. Review Instructions for Using MICROSTUDY+
   8. Set or Change the Operating Environment
                  <Esc> to Exit

For more detailed operating instructions, choose menu option 7 by obtaining the Main Menu and then pressing the <7> key.

BRIEF INSTRUCTIONS FOR USING SPREADSHEET TEMPLATES

These brief instructions are to be used as a reminder for users already familiar with computers and Lotus® 1-2-3 or other spreadsheet programs. They are not a substitute for the Lotus 1-2-3 User's Manual. The Study Guide *to accompany this book has more detailed instructions.*

An electronic spreadsheet is a computerized version of the worksheet. It is laid out just as a manual worksheet but performs all the mathematical calculations that are normally done by hand. Spreadsheet templates to complete certain problems in this book are available to each campus in the form of a copyable master disk. The templates are incomplete; you will have to enter data in some cells and formulas in others.

BEFORE YOU BEGIN

To use this free software ancillary, you will need the following:

1. *These brief instructions (or the more detailed instructions in the* Study Guide*).*

2. *A copy of the templates disk.* Your instructor will tell you how and where the disk is available for copying onto your own diskette.

3. *Access to Lotus 1-2-3, Release 2.0 or above (and preferably the Lotus tutorial).* Some campuses will be able to provide this spreadsheet software for your use. (You may use another spreadsheet program, such as *Quattro*, in place of Lotus 1-2-3.)

4. *Access to a DOS-based microcomputer, such as the IBM PC or PS/2.* Again, some campuses may have microcomputers available for your use.

GETTING STARTED

For simplicity, let's assume that you will run the Lotus software from the C drive of a microcomputer, and that the HBJ templates will be read from the A drive.

1. Obtain the **C>** prompt, as:

C>

2. Insert the templates disk in disk drive A and then close the disk drive door.

3. Type

LOTUS

(using either uppercase or lowercase), and press **<Return>**.

4. At the Lotus main menu, use the arrow keys to highlight

1-2-3

and press **<Return>**.

5. After Lotus 1-2-3 loads, the worksheet grid appears on-screen.

6. Press the / (slash) key to bring up the 1-2-3 menu along the top of the screen.

7. Then press the **F** key (or highlight the word *File* and press **<Return>**).

8. Next press the **D** key (or highlight the word *Directory* and press **<Return>**).

9. Now type **A:** to designate the drive/directory where files are located, and press **<Return>**.

10. Next press the **R** key (or highlight the word *Retrieve* and press **<Return>**). The file names of available templates will appear on a line near the top of the screen.

11. Assuming you want to load the template from Chapter 13, use the arrow keys to highlight

PAY.WK1

and press **<Return>**.

12. The template will load onto the screen. Use the arrow or cursor keys to move through the template.

WORKING WITH THE TEMPLATE (PAY.WK1)

1. From the information given in the textbook problem (P13-1A), enter the amounts and rates. The input cells will display a higher intensity (or a different color if you have a color monitor).

2. Enter cell formulas as necessary. (*Hint:* For PAY.WK1, cell formulas are necessary at cells B11, D7, D11, B19, D19, B27, B29, B37, D33, D37, B45, D45, B52, D41, and B59.

3. Enter your name as the preparer in the appropriate cell (A62).

4. Save your work by pressing */FS* **<Return>** and *R*. This will replace the old file with your newly completed file.

5. You can also print your electronic spreadsheet by selecting */PP* and *OOAQ*. Then select the range option *R*. Point to the range desired (remember to enter a period to anchor the first cell). Press **<Return>** and select *AG* to print.

6. Select the Quit option (*Q*) to return to the READY mode.

AVAILABLE TEMPLATES

The problems and template files available for your use are:

Problem	File
P 13-1A	PAY
P 14-4A	WORK

INDEX

(continued from front endpapers)

P 9-1A   (1) Cash, $44,770
P 9-2A   (1) Cash, $37,811
P 9-3A   (3) Cash, $15,704
P 9-4A   (3) Cash, $33,917
P 9-1B   (1) Cash, $46,453
P 9-2B   (1) Cash, $45,468
P 9-3B   (3) Cash, $10,726
P 9-4B   (3) Cash, $30,482

Special Journals Review Problem   (2) Cash, $60,811

P 10-1A   No key figure
P 10-2A   (1) Adjusted Cash Balance, $26,970
P 10-3A   (3) Cash Short or Over, $1
P 10-4A   (1) Adjusted Cash Balance, $5,004
P 10-1B   No key figure
P 10-2B   (1) Adjusted Cash Balance, $42,930
P 10-3B   (3) Cash Short or Over, $2
P 10-4B   (1) Adjusted Cash Balance, $8,380

P 11-1A   Net Income, $3,900
P 11-2A   No key figure
P 11-3A   (2) Net Income, $840
P 11-4A   (1) Net Income, $2,871
P 11-1B   Net Income, $10,100
P 11-2B   No key figure
P 11-3B   (2) Net Income, $2,010
P 11-4B   (1) Net Income, $4,160

P 12-1A   Net Income, $1,800
P 12-2A   (2) Totals, 93,190
P 12-3A   (1) Net Income, $4,890
P 12-4A   (1) Net Income, $6,823
P 12-1B   Net Income, $1,300
P 12-2B   (2) Totals, 159,940
P 12-3B   (1) Net Income, $2,930
P 12-4B   (1) Net Income, $6,495